FOR REFERENCE

Do Not Take From This Room

D1604760

All the World's a Stage

The reconstructed Globe Theatre on the south bank of the Thames, London, near the site of the original Globe, where Shakespeare's company began performing in 1599. © *iStock/LanceB*

All the World's a Stage

A Guide to Shakespearean Sites

JOSEPH ROSENBLUM

ROWMAN & LITTLEFIELD
Lanham • Boulder • New York • London

Published by Rowman & Littlefield
An imprint of The Rowman & Littlefield Publishing Group, Inc.
4501 Forbes Boulevard, Suite 200, Lanham, Maryland 20706
www.rowman.com

6 Tinworth Street, London, SE11 5AL, United Kingdom

British Library Cataloguing in Publication Information Available

Library of Congress Cataloging-in-Publication Data

Names: Rosenblum, Joseph, author.
Title: All the world's a stage : a guide to Shakespearean sites / Joseph Rosenblum.
Description: Lanham : Rowman & Littlefield, 2019. | Includes bibliographical references and index.
Identifiers: LCCN 2019017704 (print) | LCCN 2019019076 (ebook) | ISBN 9781538113813
    (Electronic) | ISBN 9781538113806 (cloth : alk. paper)
Subjects: LCSH: Shakespeare, William, 1564–1616—Knowledge—Geography. | Shakespeare,
    William, 1564–1616—Settings. | Setting (Literature)
Classification: LCC PR3014 (ebook) | LCC PR3014 .R65 2019 (print) | DDC 822.3/3—dc23
LC record available at https://lccn.loc.gov/2019017704

For Ida

Contents

Acknowledgments

I want to thank Stephen Ryan and Deni Remsberg for all their help and encouragement with this book. Without their many forms of assistance, this book would not be possible.

Introduction

And talking of the Alps and Apennines
The Pyrenean and the river Po
It draws toward supper in conversation so.

—*King John*, 1.1.202–4

This work serves as an introduction to Shakespeare's world in a variety of ways. Most obviously it discusses all the locations used for Shakespeare's scenes in his plays and in the poems when these can be localized. As far as can be determined, Shakespeare spent his entire life in the hundred miles between London and Stratford-upon-Avon. His writings, however, range from the "still-vex'd Bermoothes" (*The Tempest*, 1.2.229; i.e., Bermuda) to Arabia, from Denmark to North Africa. Shakespeare's theater was aptly named the Globe. Jeremy Black shows in *Mapping Shakespeare's World* (2018) that Shakespeare's audiences might well recognize geographical references because they were living in a great age of exploration and cartography. When Othello compares his thoughts to the Pontic Sea, which "Ne'er keeps retiring ebb" (3.3.452), the message would be clear even to those not familiar with Pliny the Elder's claim that the Black Sea does not ebb back, but many would also have some idea of the location of that body of water. Similarly, when in *The Merchant of Venice* Shylock says Antonio "hath an argosy bound to Tripolis [Tripoli], another to the Indies, . . . he hath a third at Mexico, a fourth for England" (1.3.17–20), at least some audience members would be able to visualize the location of those foreign places. At the same time, Shakespeare's plays often feel English wherever they are ostensibly set. In scene 3.5 of *The Two Noble Kinsmen*, set in prehistoric Athens, Shakespeare introduces English morris dancers, and in *A Midsummer Night's Dream*, with the same setting, Titania in 2.1.81–117 describes the wet English summer of 1594, still fresh in the memories of audiences seeing the play the next year. The woods outside Athens in *A Midsummer Night's Dream* are filled with English fairies, and the rude mechanicals who go there to rehearse their play have English names and seem to belong to Elizabethan London or Stratford rather than ancient Greece. Olivia's house in Illyria in *Twelfth Night* feels like an English country estate, and her uncle has the decidedly English name Sir Toby Belch. The Forest of Arden in *As You Like It*, located in France, according to the play's source, feels and sounds like the forest in Warwickshire, with the same name as Shakespeare's mother, Mary Arden.

Shakespeare's stage was bare, with no indication of where the action was unfolding, and the locations were more places of the imagination rather than of reality. Stage directions in the early quartos and the Folios, the first published versions of the plays, do not localize the action either. Sometimes the text itself will note where the action is unfolding. Petruchio in 1.2.1–2 of *The Taming of the Shrew* says he has left Verona to visit his friends in Padua. The prologue to *Romeo and Juliet* announces, "In fair Verona, where we lay our scene" (l. 2). In *As You Like It*, 1.1.112–13, Charles the wrestler reports the deposed Duke Senior is living in the Forest of Arden, and in 2.4.15–16 of that play, Touchstone declares, "Ay, now am I in Arden, the more fool I." More often, particularly in the history plays, in which what transpires on stage is based on actual events, audiences must rely on their knowledge of where the action occurred. Thus, the opening scene of *Richard II* is set at Windsor Castle. Henry V's funeral, which begins *1 Henry VI*, was held at Westminster Abbey. According to legend, King's Lear's capital was at Leicester and Cymbeline's at Colchester, but the plays themselves do not provide this information.

In some instances, even when the plays are based on historical events, scenes can be difficult or impossible to localize because the events they describe never happened. Scene 1.1 of *King John* and the Roman invasion of Britain during the reign of Cymbeline are fictional. Though placed among the tragedies in the First Folio, *King Lear* was based in part of Holinshed's *Chronicles of England, Scotland, and Ireland* (1587), just as Shakespeare's other English history plays were. Yet events are difficult to place. Albany refers to Scotland, but where in Scotland was the Duke of Albany's palace? Was the Earl of Gloucester's castle in Gloucester? The only location specified in the play is Dover, and the play does not arrive here until the fourth act. Even when the general setting can be determined, such as Padua in *The Taming of the Shrew*, the houses where the action unfolds are, of course, imaginary. As noted previously, the Forest of Arden and the woods outside Athens should be in France and Greece, respectively, but both seem English. The residents of the former have English names, like Audrey, William, and Phebe. The vicar here is Sir Oliver Mar-text, named for the pseudonymous English Puritan writer Martin Marprelate. Hence, wherever possible this book relies on modern editions, which specify locations; on history; and on Shakespeare's sources. *As You Like It* is based on Thomas Lodge's *Rosalynde: Euphues' Golden Legacie* (1590).

Here the scenes not set in the Forest of Ardennes unfold near Bordeaux. The fictional Portia lives in a fictional Belmont, but the Villa Foscari-Malcontenta on the Brenta River, ten miles from Venice and two miles from the monastery Ca' delle Monache (in 3.4.31 Portia says, "There is a monast'ry two miles off" from her house), is cited as a possible actual model. The imaginary Prospero now has a real cave named for him in Bermuda, and Othello now has a tower named for him in Famagusta, Cyprus. These places, too, are noted in this book.

The body of the work is arranged by work—there is an appendix listing the works by location as well—and for each play and poem discussed, the locations are listed alphabetically. Thus, the scenes are arranged by where they occur, not in the order they appear in the play. For each entry the reader will find location, a brief history, and a summary of the action set here. Wherever possible the book also notes when events are occurring. Shakespeare tended to conflate and even alter history for dramatic purposes; the discussion of the scenes presents the actual chronology and clarifies what actually happened. While the book contains much plot summary, the discussion offers some analysis of the choice of location, as well. Thus, the book notes the distinction in the comedies between the world of the city and court, where problems arise, and the green world, such as the woods outside Athens in *A Midsummer Night's Dream* and the Forest of Arden in *As You Like It*, where these problems are resolved. In *Othello* civilized Venice represents the rule of reason. The duke and his council logically determine the objective of the Turkish fleet is Cyprus rather than Rhodes. By way of contrast, in Cyprus passion predominates, resulting in error, as Othello decides Desdemona is unfaithful and so kills her. Recognizing that, in *The Merchant of Venice*, Shylock's house is located in the Jewish ghetto reinforces the sense of his isolation and alienation from the gentile world of Venice. Directors will find the information here useful in designing sets. Students of Shakespeare at any level will find the book helpful in giving "to airy nothings a local habitation and a name" (*A Midsummer Night's Dream*, 5.1.17).

This book also serves as a guide to Shakespeare's world by linking events, references, and locations to life in Shakespeare's England and to Shakespeare's biography. When Hamlet in scene 2.2 of his play asks why the acting company has come to Elsinore when they could make more money playing in the capital, the question seems out of place for Denmark because they are playing at the court. Rosencrantz and Guildenstern, whose names, the book notes, derive from two Danish noblemen who visited England in the 1590s, explain the players have left the capital because child acting companies are all the rage, drawing audiences away from the adult players. Shakespeare is describing the situation in London when *Hamlet* was first produced, circa 1600. *The Tempest* draws on Virgil's *Aeneid* and Ovid's *Metamorphoses*, but its plot was inspired by a 1609 shipwreck of an English vessel going to Jamestown,

Virginia. The ship that splits at the beginning of the play and is yare at its end recalls both Aeneas's and Sir George Somers's. This book points out such connections between art and life.

Shakespeare, like every other writer, drew on his own experiences in his work. In scene 3.5 of *The Two Noble Kinsmen*, Cicely has failed to appear for a performance by a group of countrymen who hoped to dance for Theseus. Without her they cannot proceed. Fortuitously, the jailer's daughter appears and agrees to take Cicely's part, allowing the dancers to entertain the duke. How Shakespeare came to act and write in London is unclear, but one theory is that he took the part of a murdered actor. As noted in the discussion of this scene, on June 13, 1587, while the Queen's Men were at Thame, the actors John Towne and William Knell fell out, and Towne killed Knell. The company went on to perform at Stratford but lacked a player. In *Shakespeare, the Globe and the World* (1979, p. 43), Samuel Schoenbaum suggests that this is how Shakespeare got his start in the theater. In his last play, Shakespeare may be reflecting on his theatrical beginnings. This scene is attributed to Fletcher, but Shakespeare might have introduced some autobiographical elements.

Another explanation of what brought Shakespeare to London involves a run-in with the justice of the peace Sir Thomas Lucy of Charlecote, near Stratford. As described in the discussion of this location (see "Charlecote, Warwickshire" in appendix A), according to the Reverend Richard Davies, the young Shakespeare was

> much given to all unluckiness in stealing venison and rabbits, particularly from Sir [Thomas] Lucy, who had him oft whipped and sometimes imprisoned and at last made him fly his native country to his great advancement; but his revenge was so great that he is his Justice Clodpole and calls him a great man and in allusion to his name bore three louses rampant for his arms.

Davies is referring to Justice Robert Shallow in *2 Henry IV* and *The Merry Wives of Windsor*. In scene 1.1 of the latter play, Shallow's nephew Slender describes his uncle's coat of arms as containing the "dozen white luces" (l. 15), which the Welsh parson Sir Hugh Evans calls louses (l. 17). A luce is a pike (fish). Sir Hugh may be modeled on Shakespeare's Welsh teacher at Stratford's grammar school, Thomas Jenkins. Also, *Notes and Queries* (G. E. P. A., "Sir Hugh Evans") describes a schoolmaster named Sir Hugh Evans in Gloucestershire, the county next to Shakespeare's Warwickshire and an area Shakespeare shows he knew well. In *2 Henry IV*, Falstaff recruits soldiers there. In scene 4.1 of *The Merry Wives*, Sir Hugh encounters young William Page in the street and tests his Latin. Was William Shakespeare recalling an experience he had had as a boy in Stratford?

Shakespeare's plays repeatedly warn against premarital sex. This attitude was conventional at the time, though as much honored in the breach as in the observance: 50 percent of brides in Shakespeare's day had sex before marriage, and 30 percent were pregnant. That statistic includes Anne Hathaway, three months pregnant when Shakespeare married her. In scene 4.1 of *The Tempest*, Prospero utters a particularly dire warning of what will happen if Ferdinand has sex with Miranda before they wed:

> No sweet aspersions shall the heavens let fall
> To make this contract grow, but barren hate,
> Sour-eyed disdain, and discord shall bestrew
> The union of your bed with weeds so loathly
> That you shall hate it both. (4.1.18–22)

Is he writing from experience? Shakespeare and Anne had no children after February 1585, and he spent most of his later life in London, even when the theaters were closed because of plague (e.g., 1592–1594). In his will he left Anne only their second-best bed. This bequest has been variously interpreted, but he left most of his estate to his older daughter, Susanna.

Shakespeare was not as politically involved as Christopher Marlowe, who worked for Her Majesty's Secret Service, or Ben Jonson, twice imprisoned for his political satires. Still, as discussed in the entry for Southampton House, under "London" in appendix A, Shakespeare was linked to the Southampton-Essex circle, and his plays occasionally carry political messages. He sometimes chose locations to convey these. The Scottish play (*Macbeth*) was designed as a compliment to King James I of England, who was also James VI of Scotland. In *King Lear* Shakespeare made Goneril's husband Duke of Albany (Scotland) rather than Cumbria (Wales), as his source play (*King Leir*) states, again a compliment to James and an endorsement of that king's policy to effect a political union between Scotland and England. This book also notes other political references. Hermione's trial in *The Winter's Tale* would have recalled to Shakespeare's audiences that of Catherine of Aragon, which Shakespeare also presented in *Henry VIII*, staged at the Globe but also at the indoor Blackfriars Theatre in the very room where Catherine's trial had been held. Both plays sympathize with the wife. Shakespeare's religious beliefs are a matter of conjecture. The seventeenth-century Reverend Richard Davies claimed Shakespeare "dyed a papist." In *Romeo and Juliet*, he muted his source's attack on "superstitious friars (the naturally fit instruments of unchastity)," as Arthur Brooke writes in his 1562 *The Tragicall History of Romeus and Juliet*. His *King John*, however, retains much of the anti-Catholic sentiment found in *The Troublesome Raigne of John King of England* (1591), on which Shakespeare drew for his play. The book's discussions of possible political implications seek to offer further insights into Shakespeare's world.

While the focus of the contents is on Shakespeare's plays and poems, it also discusses locations associated with Shakespeare that do not appear in his works. Anyone interested in a Shakespearean tour of England will find material here for designing such a trip. Some of the places included are more definitely linked to the bard than others, but even if Shakespeare never visited Hoghton, for example, the story of his serving there as a tutor is fascinating.

HISTORIES

1 Henry VI

ENGLAND

London

According to Geoffrey of Monmouth's *Historia Regum Britanniae* (c. 1136), London was founded by Brutus, great-grandson of Aeneas, about 1100 BCE. His settlement was called Caer Troia ("fortress or citadel of Troy") or Troia Nova. One of London's early legendary kings was Lud, who allegedly renamed the town Caer Ludein, the supposed origin of the city's name. Cymbeline refers to London as "Lud's Town" (*Cymbeline*, 5.5.181). When Julius Caesar's army arrived at what is now Southwark, they found no settlement here (55–54 BCE), but by the time of the second Roman invasion in 43 CE, a small port and commercial center had risen on the site. The Romans built a bridge across the Thames and established an administrative center on the north bank, calling it Londinium (50 CE). Boudica destroyed the Roman city in about 60 CE, but it was quickly rebuilt. In the second century CE, Londinium replaced Colchester as the administrative center of Roman Britain. Between 180 and 225 CE, the Romans built a wall around London; remains of this wall can still be seen. It encircled what is now essentially the City, London's financial district.

The Romans abandoned England in 410 CE and were replaced by the Middle Saxons, hence the county name of Middlesex. They named the settlement Lundenwic, the *-wic* denoting a trading center. Vikings sacked the city in 842 and 851, and the Danes held the city from 871 to 886 and again early in the eleventh century until 1042. Under the Normans London replaced Winchester as England's capital, and it has grown and prospered over the centuries. In Shakespeare's time it held about 200,000 people (c. 1600) and was, as it still is, the cultural as well as the political and commercial center of the country.

Eltham Palace, Greenwich
[Train stations: Mottingham, Eltham]

Given to Edward II by Anthony Bek, Bishop of Durham, in 1305, Eltham Palace served as a royal residence from the fourteenth through the sixteenth centuries. In the seventeenth century, the palace fell into ruin. The current building on the site was created by Stephen and Virginia Courtauld in the 1930s. It incorporates the Great Hall (built by Edward IV), with its massive hammer-beam ceiling, and the bridge over the moat dates from the fifteenth century. The property belongs to English Heritage and is open to the public.

Scene 1.1: At the funeral of Henry V, Humphrey, Duke of Gloucester (Lord Protector), announces he is going to Eltham Palace, where Henry VI is staying, to proclaim him king.

Middle Temple
Middle Temple Lane [Underground stop: Temple]

Originally constructed in about 1320, the present building dates from 1523. The order of the Knights Templar, established to guard pilgrims to the Holy Land, was based here. The thirteenth-century Temple Church contains effigies of Knights Templar. Middle Temple is one of the four Inns of Court, where lawyers were trained. On February 2, 1602, Shakespeare's *Twelfth Night* was staged here. John Manningham, a student at the Middle Temple, recorded in his diary,

> At our feast wee had a play called Twelue night or what you will much like the commedy of errores, or Menechmi in Plautus [the basis of *The Comedy of Errors*], but most like and neere to that in Italian called Inganni a good practice in it to make the steward beleeue his lady widdowe was in loue with him, by counterfayting a letter, as from his lady in generall termes, telling him what shee liked best in him, and prescribing his gesture in smilinge his apparraile, &c., and then when he came to practise making him beleeue they tooke him to be mad.

Scene 2.4: In the Middle Temple Gardens, according to a scene invented by Shakespeare, supporters of the Beaufort faction pluck red roses, while backers of Richard, Duke of York, chose white ones at the start of the Wars of the Roses.

Palace of Westminster
North Bank of the Thames [Underground stop: Westminster]

Originally built for Edward the Confessor, the Palace of Westminster served as a royal residence until Henry VIII made Whitehall Palace his chief residence in 1512 after the Palace of Westminster was damaged by fire. It has also been the meeting place of Parliament since the thirteenth century. In 1834 a fire destroyed most of the building. Only St. Mary Undercroft (the crypt under St. Stephen's Chapel), Westminster Hall (dating from 1097), the Cloisters, and the Jewel Tower (1365) survived. The current Gothic building was designed by Sir Charles Barry and Augustus Pugin. Construction began in 1837. Most of the restoration was completed by 1860, though work continued until 1870. The House of Commons was destroyed in the Blitz of 1940–1941; it was restored by Sir Giles Gilbert Scott after World War II during the period 1945–1950.

Scene 3.1: The supporters of the Cardinal of Winchester and the Duke of Gloucester argue. Henry VI restores Richard Plantagenet's dukedom, forfeited because of his father's (Richard of Conisburgh, Third Earl of Cambridge) involvement in the Southampton Plot against Henry V in 1415. In fact, after Richard's uncle Edward, Duke of York, died at Agincourt in 1415, Henry V recognized Richard as heir to the title. By having Henry VI return the dukedom to Richard, Shakespeare shows Henry VI as generous but naïve because Richard will seek to depose the king. As the scene ends, Thomas Beaufort, Duke of Exeter and great-uncle of Henry VI, foresees that these dissentions will result in civil war in England and the loss of France.

Scene 5.5: Henry VI, persuaded by the Duke of Suffolk, agrees to marry Margaret of Anjou. The Yorkists opposed the marriage, which brought no dowry to the king, who moreover had to pay for the wedding. The marriage exacerbated the rift between the supporters of Richard, Duke of York, and the Beauforts.

Tower of London
Tower Hill [Underground stop: Tower Hill]

The White Tower, the oldest part of the twelve-acre complex on the north bank of the Thames, was built by William the Conqueror as a fortress, though later legend claimed Julius Caesar constructed it (see *Richard III*, 3.1.69–70). The outer wall was completed by Edward I. Over the centuries the Tower of London has served as a fortress, a palace, a prison, a zoo, an armory, a place of execution (though only seven executions officially took place here), the site of the Royal Mint, a public records office, and a treasure house. It now houses the Crown Jewels. It is a World Heritage Site under the care of the Historic Royal Palaces charity.

Scene 1.3: Humphrey, Duke of Gloucester, who is the uncle of Henry VI and the Lord Protector, comes to inspect the tower, but Henry Beaufort, Cardinal of Winchester and the king's great-uncle, has ordered the gates be shut against him (October 1425). Their supporters skirmish before the Lord Mayor orders everyone to disperse. This scene presages the Wars of the Roses.

Scene 2.5: Edmund Mortimer, Earl of March, tells Richard Plantagenet, his nephew, that Richard has a stronger claim to the throne than has Henry VI. Contrary to the play, the Earl of March was never imprisoned in the Tower of London, where the scene claims Henry IV confined him. Henry IV did keep him in custody from 1405 until the king's death but not in the tower. Henry V freed him. Mortimer remained loyal to Henry V and was part of the Council of Regency after Henry V's death. Shakespeare has Mortimer dying in the tower. He died in Ireland on January 18, 1425.

Westminster Abbey

Broad Sanctuary [Underground stops: St. James Park, Westminster]

Edward the Confessor began a new Benedictine abbey on Thorney Island in 1050. The church was consecrated on December 28, 1065; Edward died eight days later. On Christmas Day 1066, William the Conqueror was crowned king of England here, and all subsequent English monarchs have been crowned here, as well (except Edward V and Edward VIII, neither of whom had a coronation ceremony).

A new church was begun by Henry III in 1245. Nothing remains aboveground of Edward the Confessor's cruciform church. The new church, with the tallest nave in England (103 feet high), is modeled on the cathedrals of Rheims and Amiens and on the Sainte-Chapelle in Paris. It is the most French of any English church, though it has English features, such as the single aisle in the nave. In 1269 Edward the Confessor's body was placed in a new shrine in the abbey. It was a popular pilgrimage site until the Reformation. The towers at the west end date from the eighteenth century.

Oliver Cromwell used the church as barracks for his soldiers. Over the past several centuries, the abbey has become Britain's pantheon. Among those buried in Poets' Corner are Shakespeare's contemporaries Ben Jonson, Michael Drayton, and Francis Beaumont. William Davenant, another playwright who claimed to be Shakespeare's son, is also interred here. While there is a life-size white marble statue of Shakespeare here dating from 1740, he is buried in Holy Trinity Church, Stratford-upon-Avon (see "Holy Trinity Church" under "Stratford-upon-Avon, Warwickshire" in appendix A).

Scene 1.1: The play opens with the funeral of Henry V in Westminster Abbey on November 7, 1422. Henry died of dysentery at the Château de Vincennes, France, on August 31, 1422, at the age of thirty-six. Messengers arrive from France announcing English setbacks. Two of the cities mentioned as lost to the French, Poitiers and Orléans, never were held by the English; the others were retaken by the French years later. Shakespeare violates historical accuracy to create the sense of failure of the reign of Henry VI at the very opening of the work.

FRANCE

Angiers

Capital of Anjou in western France. Henry II of England inherited the dukedom of Anjou; King John lost it in 1204. Part of Roman Gaul, Angiers was called Juliomagus

Andecavorum. The latter part of the name became Angiers in the twelfth century and later Angers. During the period depicted in the play, Anjou was ruled by King René.

Scene 5.2: French forces led by Joan of Arc prepare to fight the English.

Scene 5.3: The French and English fight. Joan of Arc is captured by the English. In fact, Joan of Arc was captured on May 23, 1430, by the Burgundians in a skirmish outside Compiègne. Shakespeare depicts a fight between Richard, Duke of York, and the Duke of Burgundy. In 1430 they were allies. Shakespeare also shows the capture of Margaret of Anjou by William de la Pole, Fourth Earl and First Duke of Suffolk, in this battle. Margaret was born in 1430. Shakespeare imagines an affair between Suffolk and Margaret, for which there is no historical evidence, though it makes for good drama. Suffolk arranged the marriage between Margaret and Henry VI in 1444.

Scene 5.4: Trial and condemnation of Joan of Arc. The trial actually occurred at Rouen after the Burgundians surrendered Joan to the English for 10,000 livres. The trial began on February 21, 1431, and continued through May 24. She was executed on May 30 at what is now the Place de la Pucelle. Immediately after Joan is condemned, in this scene Charles VII concludes a truce with the English. This was the Treaty of Tours, signed May 22, 1444, in which Charles VII consented to the marriage of his niece Margaret of Anjou to Henry VI and agreed to a twenty-one-month truce.

Auvergne

Region in south-central France.

Scene 2.3: Marie I, Countess of Auvergne (1376–1437), lures the English commander Lord Talbot to her castle and tries unsuccessfully to capture him. This scene has no historical basis.

Bordeaux

Located in southwest France on the Garonne River, Bordeaux is the capital of the Nouvelle-Aquitaine region. A Celtic tribe, the Bituriges Vivisci, settled here by about 300 BCE and named the town Burdigala. The city fell to the Romans circa 60 BCE, and it became the capital of Roman Aquitaine. In the late Middle Ages, the city flourished because of its wine trade. The marriage of Eleanor of Aquitaine to Henry II brought Bordeaux under English rule in 1152, and it remained so until 1453, when it became part of France. Edward the Black Prince had a court here, and Richard II was born at Bordeaux (April 3, 1365). Bordeaux is now the sixth-largest municipality in the country.

Scene 4.2: Although this scene immediately follows the 1431 coronation of Henry VI in Paris (scene 4.1), it actually depicts the prelude to the Battle of Castillon, fought on July 17, 1453, in which the French defeated the English outside Bordeaux.

Castillon-le-Bataille

Located in the Gironde Department in southwestern France on the Dordogne River. The town was known as Castillon-sur-Dordogne until 1953. (There is also a Castillon in southeastern France in the Alpes-Maritimes.)

Scenes 4.5–4.7: The Battle of Castillon (July 17, 1453), the final battle in the Hundred Years' War. John Talbot and his son, John Talbot, Viscount Lisle, are killed as the English are defeated by the French.

Gascony

An area of southwest France near Bordeaux.

Scenes 4.3–4.4: Sir William Lucy urges Richard, Duke of York, to help the beleaguered John Talbot outside Bordeaux. York refuses, blaming the Duke of Somerset for not sending him cavalry. Somerset initially also refuses to aid Talbot. By the time Somerset changes his mind, it is too late to save Talbot.

Orléans

North-central France, on the Loire River, sixty-nine miles southwest of Paris. It served as the capital of Merovingian France from 498 to 613. The university here was founded in 1305.

Scene 1.2: The French, besieged at Orléans, try unsuccessfully to drive away the English forces under Thomas Montagu, Fourth Earl of Salisbury. Joan of Arc joins the French forces in the city (May 8, 1429). Joan is known as "la pucelle d'Orléans" (the maid of Orléans).

Scene 1.4: Salisbury is wounded during the siege (October 27, 1428). Shakespeare here, as elsewhere, plays fast and loose with chronology because Joan would not join the French forces in the city for another half-year. Salisbury died on November 3, 1428, from his wounds.

Scenes 1.5–2.2: Fighting between the English and French continues outside and within the city. Orléans never fell to the English, though in scene 2.1 Shakespeare has the English forces take the city. This recapturing of Orléans derives from the retaking of Le Mans. According to one of Shakespeare's chief sources for his histories, Edward Hall's *The Union of the Two Noble and Illustre Famelies of Lancastre and Yorke* (1548), when the English retook Le Mans, "Some [of the French] rose out of their beddes in their shertes, and lepte over the walls." The stage direction at 2.1.37 of Shakespeare's play reads, "The French leap o'er the walls in their shirts."

Paris

In the third century BCE, the Parisii established a settlement on the Île de la Cité and along the banks of the Seine. Under Titus Labienus a Roman army defeated the Parisii and created a garrison town here, which the Romans named Lutetia (52 BCE). After the collapse of the Roman Empire, Clovis I, King of the Franks, made Paris his capital (508 CE). During the Middle Ages, Paris became Europe's largest city and emerged as a commercial and cultural center. Gothic architecture originated here, and the University of Paris was among Europe's first such institutions. The English occupied Paris from 1420 to 1436, as indicated in this play. In Shakespeare's time the city, like the rest of France, was riven by religious strife, but in the seventeenth century and after, it continued to grow and flourish.

The Louvre
Rue de Rivoli [Paris metro stop: Louvre]

Originally a fortress built by Philip II in the twelfth century, in the fourteenth century, Charles V converted it into a residence. Under Louis XIV, who lived at Versailles, the Louvre became a home for artists. On August 10, 1793, the one-year anniversary of the execution of Louis XVI, it opened as a public museum, and so it remains.

Scene 3.4: In December 1431 Henry VI came to Paris to be crowned king of France (crowned December 16, 1431). At the Louvre Henry meets Lord John Talbot, leader of the English forces, and makes him Earl of Shrewsbury. In fact, in 1431 Talbot was a French prisoner. He was ransomed only in 1433, and he became Earl of Shrewsbury while he was in England in 1442.

Notre Dame
6 Parvis Notre-Dame, Place Jean-Paul II [Paris metro stops: Cité, St.-Michel–Notre Dame]

Begun in 1163 during the reign of Louis VII, the cathedral was not completed until 1345. Henry VI was crowned here in 1431. Joan of Arc was canonized here in 1909.

Scene 4.1: Henry VI is crowned king of France by his great-uncle Cardinal-Bishop of Winchester. French kings were traditionally crowned at Rheims Cathedral, but that venue was not available to Henry VI, being controlled by the French. John Talbot strips Sir John Falstaff of the Order of the Garter for cowardice at the Battle of Patay (1429), where Talbot was captured by the French and not ransomed until 1433. Historically, Talbot accused Sir John Fastolf of cowardice at Patay, but Fastolf was vindicated. According to Edward Hall's *The Union of the Two Noble and Illustre Famelies of Lancastre and Yorke* (1548), an important source for Shakespeare's English history plays, John, Duke of Bedford, did indeed strip Sir John Fastolf of his garter after the battle of Patay but later restored it to him. Shakespeare transferred Fastolf's supposed cowardice to Sir John Falsatff in his *Henry IV* plays.

Gloucester receives a letter from the Duke of Burgundy, who had supported the English against the French, stating that Burgundy has switched sides. Shakespeare

Shakespeare's Britain. *Ngs Art Dept/National Geographic Creative*

credits Joan of Arc with effecting this change of allegiance, but in fact Burgundy did not switch sides until September 1435, four years after Joan was executed. Gloucester was in England when Henry VI was crowned at Paris.

After the Duke of York and John Beaufort, Duke of Somerset, quarrel, Henry VI puts on a red rose, the emblem of the Beaufort faction, while denying he is partial to either side. Henry names Richard, Duke of York, regent of France as successor to the deceased Duke of Bedford. Actually, the Duke of Bedford did not die until 1435.

Rouen

Capital of Normandy in northern France, located on the River Seine; it was the Ratumacos of the Gauls and Rotomagus of the Romans. Henry V captured the city in 1419, and it served as the seat of English power in France until Charles VII took Rouen in 1449.

Scene 3.2: Shakespeare invents a scene in which the French, led by Joan of Arc, briefly retake Rouen, only to lose it again to the English.

2 Henry VI

Bury St. Edmunds, Suffolk

The Villa Faustina of the Romans and the Saxon Beodericsworth, it assumed its current name in 925. *Bury* derives from *burg*, a castle or fortress. It is named for the last king of East Anglia (killed by the Vikings in 869). Its annual December fair dates from 1235. The abbey, now a ruin in a garden, dates from the eleventh century; it was founded by King Canute in 1020. Entrance is through the abbey gateway, built in 1327 and rebuilt after a 1347 fire. The Abbey Gardens are owned by St. Edmundsbury Borough Council and managed in conjunction with English Heritage. The seventeenth-century Abbey Bridge crosses the Lark River.

In *Past and Present* (1843), Thomas Carlyle described Bury St. Edmunds as a "prosperous brisk town beautifully diversifying, with its clear brick houses and ancient clean streets . . . the general grassy face of Suffolk; looking out right pleasantly, from its hill slope, towards the rising sun: and on the eastern edge of it, still runs, long, black and massive, a range of monastic ruins."

Scene 3.1: Parliament meets at the abbey (1447). Cardinal Beaufort wanted Parliament to meet here rather than in London because the Duke of Gloucester had more supporters in the capital. The Duke of Gloucester is arrested for treason (February 20, 1447). The queen, the Cardinal-Bishop of Winchester, and the Duke of Suffolk plot his death. A messenger arrives to announce a rebellion in Ireland; the Duke of York is placed in charge of the forces sent to suppress the uprising.

Scene 3.2: Two murderers discuss the death of the Duke of Gloucester (February 23, 1447). The Duke of Suffolk is banished from England for his part in the murder. Actually, after the murder Suffolk's power increased, but he was arrested and imprisoned in the Tower of London in 1450 after the loss of nearly all the English territory in France. He was then banished for five years (March 17, 1450).

Cade Street, East Sussex

A village that takes its name from the rebel Jack Cade.

Scene 4.10: On July 12, 1450, Alexander Iden, later to become High Sheriff of Kent, killed Jack Cade in Iden's garden. Shakespeare places the garden in Kent.

Iden actually mortally wounded Cade, who died on his way to London.

Dover, Kent

The closest English port to France (twenty-five miles away), Dover, one of the cinque ports on the English Channel and famous for its white chalk cliffs, has been inhabited since the Stone Age, and by the Bronze Age it was used for shipping. The Romans called it Portus Dubris and used it as a base for their navy. The Pharos (lighthouse) at Dover Castle dates from circa 50 CE and may be the oldest structure in England. The city takes its name from the Dour River, which empties here into the English Channel. It remains an important port: The crossing from Dover to Calais is the busiest shipping channel in the world. One of the white cliffs is called Shakespeare's Cliff because it is supposedly where Gloucester in *King Lear*, 4.6, tries to kill himself by leaping from it.

Dover Castle dates from the eleventh century. In scene 5.1 of *King John*, the Bastard announces that Kent has yielded to the invading French, but Dover Castle (under Hubert de Burgh) continued to resist. It held out for ten months. After his army was defeated at Lincoln and his navy destroyed near Dover, Louis of France abandoned his attempt to rule England. In World War II, the castle served as a command post; Admiral Sir Bertram Ramsey directed the Dunkirk evacuation from here. The castle is maintained by English Heritage and is open to the public.

Scene 4.1: The Duke of Suffolk is captured and executed by pirates. Having been exiled for five years in 1450, Suffolk sailed for Calais but was captured by the pirate ship *Nicholas of the Tower* and was executed (May 2, 1450). His body washed up on the sands near Dover.

Kenilworth Castle, Warwickshire

Occupied by the Romans, in the 1086 Domesday Book, the area is called Chinewrde (the farm of a woman named Cynehild).

Kenilworth Castle was begun in the 1120s by Geoffrey de Clinton. Among its owners was John of Gaunt, father of Henry IV, who added the Strong Tower, Banqueting Hall, and southern rooms. From 1399 to 1563, it served as a royal residence. In 1563 Queen Elizabeth gave the castle to Robert Dudley, Earl of Leicester, who enlarged the castle. He entertained her here in 1565, 1568, 1572, and 1575. The festivities for this last royal visit were the most elaborate. Sir Walter Scott described them in his novel *Waverley* (1814). Among the displays was a water pageant, with Arion riding on a dolphin's back, which Shakespeare mentions in *A Midsummer Night's Dream* (2.1.148–54) and again in *Twelfth Night* (1.2.15). The story of Arion charming a dolphin with his music is recounted in Ovid's *Fasti*, 3.83–118, from which Shakespeare could have drawn his allusion. Still, it is pleasant to imagine that in July 1575 the eleven-year-old Shakespeare went to Kenilworth, about eleven miles from Stratford-upon-Avon, and saw Dudley's aquatic entertainment. Because Shakespeare's father was a prominent Stratford citizen, he may even have been invited to the festivities. In *A Midsummer Night's Dream*, Shakespeare also mentions Cupid aiming his arrow "At a fair vestal thronèd by the west," but "the imperial vot'ress passed on, / In maiden meditation, fancy free" (2.1.158, 163–64), perhaps a reference to Dudley's unsuccessful attempt to win Elizabeth's hand at this 1575 celebration.

In 1611 the castle again became a royal possession. Charles II gave the castle to Edward Hyde, Earl of Clarendon, whose descendants owned the property until 1937. The extensive ruins of the castle and its Elizabethan garden are maintained by English Heritage, and the site is open to the public.

Scene 4.9: Henry VI and Margaret flee here to escape Jack Cade's rebellion. The Duke of Buckingham and Lord Clifford arrive to announce the end of the uprising. This good news is countered by the arrival of another messenger saying that the Duke of York has returned from fighting in Ireland. York has an army and wants to capture the Duke of Somerset. Somerset agrees to be imprisoned in the Tower of London.

London

Blackheath
An open heath south of Greenwich Park [Train station: Blackheath]

The name may be a corruption of Bleak Heath. In 1166 it was called Blachehed-feld (dark heath). Both Wat Tyler, leader of the Peasants' Revolt (1381), and Jack Cade (1450) led their followers here on their way to London. In the seventeenth and eighteenth centuries, it was haunted by robbers. The area is now surrounded by fine Georgian and Victorian houses.

Scenes 4.2–4.3: Jack Cade and his followers assemble at Blackheath. Sir Humphrey Stafford and his brother Sir William Stafford confront them and are killed (June 18, 1450). According to Shakespeare, the Duke of York is responsible for Cade's uprising, though in fact York was not. In *2 Henry VI*, 3.1.356–59, York declares before heading off to the Irish war, "I have seduced a headstrong Kentishman, / John Cade of Ashford, / To make commotion, as full well he can, / Under the title John Mortimer."

Cannon Street
[Underground stop: Cannon Street]

Originally Candlewrithe, then Candlewick, then Canwick Street, for the candle-makers who lived here. London Stone (a piece of limestone) was at one time embedded in St. Swithin's Church, having been moved from its original location some thirty-five feet away on the south side of the street in 1742. The stone is now located in the wall of the Oversea-Chinese Banking Corporation, 111 Cannon Street. The stone is mentioned as early as 1198.

Scene 4.6: Jack Cade strikes his sword on London Stone and declares, "Now is Mortimer Lord of the City." Cade denied his lowly origins and claimed to be a descendant of the aristocratic Mortimers. Richard II named Edmund Mortimer, Fifth Earl of March, his successor, but when Henry IV seized the throne in 1399, Mortimer lost his claim to the crown. This claim was revived by his nephew, Richard, Third Duke of York, in the Wars of the Roses to justify his own attempt to become king.

Duke of Gloucester's House
Greenwich Park [Train stations: Greenwich, Mars Hill]

Humphrey, Duke of Gloucester, began his palace in 1428 and completed construction in 1443. Henry VI and Queen Margaret honeymooned here in 1445. The duke assembled an extensive library, which he bequeathed to Oxford University. The palace was named Bella Court; later Queen Margaret, who seized the property after the duke's arrest and death in 1447, called it Palace of Placentia or Palace of Pleasaunce. Henry VII rebuilt the palace between 1498 and 1504, and it remained a royal residence for the next two hundred years. Henry VIII, Queen Mary, and Queen Elizabeth were all born here. It was Henry VIII's favorite residence, and Queen Elizabeth liked to summer here. During the visit of James I's brother-in-law Christian IV of Denmark in the summer of 1606, the King's Men performed for him here twice, and in June 1613 Shakespeare and John Fletcher's lost play *Cardenio* was staged here for the ambassador of the Duke of Savoy. Charles II sought to rebuild the palace after it had fallen into disrepair during the English Civil War, and he completed King Charles Court. Most of the palace was demolished to make room for Greenwich Hospital. The two hundred acres enclosed by the duke became Greenwich Park.

Scene 1.2: Gloucester recounts a dream in which his staff, emblem of his being Lord Protector of England, is broken and the heads of the Dukes of Somerset and Suffolk are placed on the pieces. His dream portends his loss of his office and the deaths of the dukes. His wife, Eleanor, dismisses his vision and recounts her dreams of being queen. Gloucester chides her for presumption. After Gloucester is summoned to St. Albans and departs, Eleanor meets with the priest John Hume (her chaplain), who promises her his confederates will conjure up a spirit to answer her questions about her royal future. Eleanor in fact consulted with the astrologers Thomas Southwell, a canon of St. Stephen's Chapel, Westminster, and the scholar, astronomer, and cleric Roger Bolingbroke and with Margery Jourdemayne, the so-called Witch of Eye. Shakespeare calls her Margery Jourdain. The astrologers predicted Henry VI would die in 1441, in which case Gloucester would become king and she queen.

Scene 1.4: In the garden Eleanor, Margery Jourdain, the priests Hum and Southwell, and the conjuror Roger Bolingbroke raise a spirit to foretell the fates of the king, the Duke of Suffolk, and the Duke of Somerset. The Dukes of York and Buckingham discover the conjuring and arrest the participants.

Duke of York's Gardens
Scene 2.2: The Duke of York explains to the Earl of Salisbury and to Salisbury's son Richard Neville, Earl of Warwick ("the Kingmaker"), York's claim to the English throne. They hail him as king of England.

Palace of Westminster
North bank of the Thames [Underground stop: Westminster]
Originally built for Edward the Confessor, the Palace of Westminster served as a royal residence until Henry VIII made Whitehall Palace his chief residence in 1512 after the Palace of Westminster was damaged by fire. It has also been the meeting place of Parliament since the thirteenth century. In 1834 a fire destroyed most of the building. Only St. Mary Undercroft (the crypt under St. Stephen's Chapel), Westminster Hall (dating from 1097), the Cloisters, and the Jewel Tower (1365) survived. The current Gothic building was designed by Sir Charles Barry and Augustus Pugin. Construction began in 1837. Most of the restoration was completed by 1860, though work continued until 1870. The House of Commons was destroyed in the Blitz of 1940–1941; it was restored by Sir Giles Gilbert Scott after World War II during the period 1945–1950.

Scene 1.1: Henry VI welcomes Margaret of Anjou (1445). By the terms of the marriage contract, England ceded Anjou and Maine to the French.

Scene 1.3: The Duke of Suffolk and Queen Margaret dismiss a group of petitioners, showing the duke and queen to be callous.

Scene 4.4: Margaret enters with the head of Suffolk. Henry reads Jack Cade's petition. A messenger informs the court that the rebels have reached Southwark, and Henry withdraws from London. A second messenger states Cade has taken London Bridge.

Smithfield
[Underground stops: Barbican, Farrington]
Originally a grassy field north of London's Roman walls, it was the site of a weekly horse market and the annual Bartholomew Fair (August 24), as well as jousting tournaments. Smithfield was also a place of execution. In *2 Henry VI*, 2.3.7, the king declares, "The witch [Margery Jourdain] in Smithfield shall be burnt to ashes." During the reign of Queen Mary, more than two hundred Protestants were burned here.

It became a cattle market in 1638 and remained so until 1855, but in *2 Henry IV*, 1.2.50–51, Falstaff's page says Bardolph has gone to Smithfield to buy Falstaff a horse, so by the 1590s, it was already famous for such transactions. Many other plays of the period also refer to buying horses here. Friday seems to have the day for such transactions. In *Annales* (1631) Edmund Howes wrote that Smithfield "was for many years called Ruffians Hall by reason it was the usual place of frays and common fighting during the time that swords and bucklers were in use." In *Oliver Twist* (1838) Charles Dickens described the area: "The ground was covered, nearly ankle-deep, with filth and mire; a thick steam perpetually rising from the reeking bodies of the cattle." It is now a large meat market.

Wat Tyler met King Richard II here in 1381, and Tyler was stabbed to death (June 15).

Scene 4.7: Jack Cade orders his followers to destroy the Savoy Palace and the Inns of Court. The Savoy Palace on the Strand had belonged to John of Gaunt. Much of the palace had already been destroyed in the Peasants' Revolt of 1381. In 1505 Henry VII turned the property into a hospital. The area was cleared in 1816–1820.

The Inns of Court were the training places of lawyers since the fourteenth century. In scene 4.2 of *2 Henry VI*, Dick, one of Cade's lieutenants, declares, "The first thing we do, let's kill all the lawyers."

Cade orders the execution of James Fiennes, First Baron Saye and Sele, who was Lord High Treasurer, and Saye's son-in-law Sir James Cromer. Cade says he will carry their heads through London's streets instead of a mace as a symbol of his authority (July 4, 1450).

Southwark

[Underground stops: London Bridge, Lambeth, Southwark, Waterloo]

A London borough south of the Thames. The Saxon Suthriganaweorc or Suthringa geweorche ("fort of the men of Surrey"), in the Domesday Book of 1086, it is listed as Sudweca (southern defensive works). During the Roman occupation, it was the southern terminus of a wooden London Bridge. In Shakespeare's day it was a popular entertainment site, with theaters, bearbaiting, and brothels. Shakespeare lived in Southwark, in the Liberty of the Clink (see "Liberty of the Clink" under "London" in appendix A), from 1599 to circa 1603.

Scene 4.8: Jack Cade orders his followers, "Up Fish Street! Down Saint Magnus Corner! Kill and knock down! Throw them into Thames!" Here Thomas Clifford, Eighth Baron de Clifford, and Humphrey Stafford, First Duke of Buckingham, Sixth Earl of Stafford, confront the rebels. Deserted by his followers, Cade flees.

Named for its fishmongers, Fish Street was, until the nineteenth century, the main route to London Bridge from the north. St. Magnus Corner at the foot of London

Bridge north of the Thames was an important medieval meeting place. The Church of St. Magnus the Martyr takes its name from the Norwegian Earl of the Orkneys, who was killed circa 1116. There has been a church on this site at least since the early twelfth century. The current church here was designed by Sir Christopher Wren and built 1671–1676.

Shakespeare omits the battle on July 8–9, 1450, between Cade's forces and London citizens on and near London Bridge.

A Street

Scene 2.4: Gloucester and his wife part. She is to be taken to the Isle of Man. In this scene Eleanor appears barefoot, in a white sheet, and holding a candle. Her sentence required her to undertake such penance three times, the first of these on November 13, 1441. Edwin Austen Abbey painted this scene (1900).

St. Stephen's Chapel, Westminster

Completed circa 1297 as the royal chapel, between 1547 and 1834, when it was destroyed in the fire that engulfed Parliament, it served as the chamber for the House of Commons. St. Stephen's Hall in the new Parliament is built on the floorplan of the former chapel.

Scene 2.3: Eleanor, Duchess of Gloucester, is exiled to the Isle of Man (1441). Eleanor was examined here on July 24–24, 1441, and again on October 19 and 23 of that year. She was convicted of sorcery and witchcraft.

Henry VI orders Gloucester to surrender his staff, the mark of his being Lord Protector. Horner, an armorer, and his man Peter enter. Peter has accused Horner of treason. They fight, and Peter kills Horner. The latter confesses his treason as he is dying.

The Isle of Man sits midway between England and Ireland in the Irish Sea. It is thirty-three miles long and twelve miles wide. England has ruled the island since 1333. In 1406 Henry IV gave the island to the Stanleys, Earls of Derby. It was purchased by Parliament in 1825. The island has its own legislature and executive, the Court of Tynwald. Laws passed by the island's legislature require royal approval. Parliamentary laws do not apply to the island unless the laws explicitly state they should.

In 1442 Eleanor was imprisoned at Chester Castle, then in 1443 was moved to Kenilworth Castle. In July 1446 she was moved to the Isle of Man and in March 1449 to Beaumaris Castle in Anglesey, where she died on July 7, 1452.

Tower of London
Tower Hill [Underground stop: Tower Hill]

The White Tower, the oldest part of the twelve-acre complex on the north bank of the Thames, was built by William the Conqueror as a fortress, though later legend claimed Julius Caesar constructed it (see *Richard III*, 3.1.69–70). The outer wall was completed by Edward I. Over the centuries the Tower of London has served as a fortress, a palace, a prison, a zoo, an armory, a place of execution (though only seven executions officially took place here), the site of the Royal Mint, a public records office, and a treasure house. It now houses the Crown Jewels. It is a World Heritage Site under the care of the Historic Royal Palaces charity.

Scene 4.5: Lord Thomas de Scales defends the Tower of London against Jack Cade's rebels.

St. Albans, Hertfordshire

Nineteen miles northwest of London.

The Roman Verulam, located on the Ver River. The town is named for England's first martyr-saint, Alban, executed by the Romans in 297 for protecting Christian converts. Offa, King of Mercia, founded a Benedictine Abbey here circa 793. The abbey church has the longest nave ever built (284 feet).

The First Battle of St. Albans was fought here on May 22, 1455, near Holywell Hill. In this Yorkist victory, Henry VI was wounded. The Second Battle of St. Albans occurred on February 17, 1461. The Lancastrians won and retrieved Henry VI, who had been held by the Yorkists since his capture at the Battle of Northampton (July 10, 1460).

Scene 1.2: A messenger instructs the Duke of Gloucester to join Henry VI and Queen Margaret at St. Albans, where the king and queen have gone to hunt with hawks.

Scene 2.1: The king and queen and their entourage have gone to St. Albans for hawking. The supporters of the Duke of Gloucester and Cardinal Beaufort quarrel. The impostor Saunder Simpcox falsely claims St. Alban's shrine has cured him of his blindness. Gloucester exposes his hoax.

Scene 5.1: This scene unfolds outside the Castle Inn, which stood at the north corner of St. Peter's Street and Victoria Street. When he learns Somerset has gone to the Tower of London, the Duke of York agrees to dismiss his army. Henry VI arrives, followed by Alexander Iden with Jack Cade's head. Henry knights Iden and gives him 1,000 marks (£666 pounds), the promised reward for Cade's killer. Somerset and the queen enter. York's sons now bring up an army, and the Cliffords do the same to oppose them. The Earls of Warwick and Salisbury come to aid York.

Scenes 5.2–5.3: At the First Battle of St. Albans, Richard Plantagenet, Duke of York, kills the elder Lord Clifford and the Duke of Somerset. The Yorkist forces triumph.

Wakefield, West Yorkshire

The site of a major battle in the Wars of the Roses fought on December 30, 1460. The Lancastrians won a decisive (though short-lived) victory. Richard, Duke of York, the

Yorkist claimant to the English throne, and his son Edmund were among those killed in the battle. Pomfret (Pontefract) Castle, built around 1070, is located in the town of Pontefract. It belonged to John of Gaunt and was inherited by his son Henry Boling-broke, who deposed Richard II and became Henry IV. Richard II died here. Only ruins of the castle remain; the site is open to the public free of charge. Wakefield was noted for its cloth trade.

Scene 2.2: Richard Plantagenet, Duke of York, mentions the murder of Richard II at Pomfret Castle.

Winchester, Hampshire

The pre-Roman Caer Gwent, the Roman Venta Belgarum, and the Saxon Wente-ceastre, it served as the capital of Wessex (519). In 827 Egbert was crowned king of all England here. Alfred the Great and King Canute used the city as their capital. Edward the Confessor was crowned king here in 1043; William the Conqueror was crowned here, as well as in London, and erected two castles here. The city has an impressive cathedral. Winchester is one of the places identified as Camelot, and the castle contains a round table, supposedly Arthur's. The medieval oak table, about eighteen feet in diameter, dates from about 1290. Henry VIII had the table painted with a Tudor rose in the center and himself as King Arthur. The city was an important center of wool and cloth trade in the thirteenth and fourteenth centuries, with four annual fairs.

Wolvesey Castle
College Street

The Bishop's Palace near the cathedral is now in ruins. It dates from the twelfth century. The palace was built by Bishop Henry of Blois, brother of King Stephen. The ruins are managed by English Heritage.

Scene 3.3: Henry Beaufort, Cardinal-Bishop of Winchester, dies here (April 11, 1447). Shakespeare has him confess to arranging the poisoning of Humphrey, Duke of Gloucester. The bishop was buried at Winchester Cathedral.

3 Henry VI

ENGLAND

Barnet, Hertfordshire

Fifty miles north of London.

Scenes 5.2–5.3: Forces under Edward IV defeat the Lancastrians here on Easter Sunday, April 14, 1471. The Earl of Warwick and his brother John, Marquess of Montague, are killed.

Clitheroe, Lancashire

Thirty-four miles northwest of Manchester. The town's name derives from the Anglo-Saxon for "rocky hill."

Scene 3.1: Henry VI is captured here (July 1465).

Coventry, Warwickshire

Ninety-five miles northwest of London.

In the Middle Ages, Coventry was an important center of the cloth trade and one of England's largest cities. It produced a thread of a color known as Coventry blue. The city was famous for its Corpus Christi Day mystery plays, which Shakespeare may have seen as a child; Coventry is twenty miles from Stratford. It was heavily damaged by German bombs in World War II (November 14, 1940), and its cathedral was destroyed. Coventry is the site of Lady Godiva's legendary ride. Supposedly, she had repeatedly asked her husband, Leofric, Earl of Mercia, to remit his taxes on Coventry. He finally agreed if she would ride naked through the city. The story of her ride was extant by 1235; that of Peeping Tom, the only townsperson to watch her ride naked through the streets, dates from the eighteenth century. Historians reject the story of the ride. To "send someone to Coventry" means to ignore or ostracize that person. The origin of this phrase is uncertain.

Scene 5.1: Warwick awaits reinforcements, as Edward IV's army appears before the walls of the city. John de Vere, Thirteenth Earl of Oxford; John Neville, First Marquess of Montague (brother of Richard Neville, Sixteenth Earl of Warwick); and Edmund Beaufort, Fourth Duke of Somerset, enter the city. When George, Duke of Clarence, arrives with his forces and is about to join his father-in-law (Warwick) inside the city, he changes sides and declares his loyalty to Edward IV. Clarence actually had abandoned the Lancastrians during his brother's march south.

Daventry, Northamptonshire

Seventy-five miles northwest of London.

Borough Hill, overlooking the town, contains the remains of an Iron-Age fort and a Roman villa. The town takes its name from *dwy-afon-tre,* "town of two rivers," it being situated between the Rivers Leam and Nene. Shakespeare refers to the town as Daintree/Daintry for an oak tree that Danish settlers supposedly planted on Borough Hill to mark the center of England. The town's seal shows a Viking or Saxon axman and an oak tree. Before the coming of the railroad, Daventry was an important coaching town with many inns. In *1 Henry IV,* 4.2.47, Shakespeare mentions the "red-nose innkeeper at Daventry." In the 1914 Arden edition of *1 Henry IV,* Richard Cowl writes, "Shakespeare must frequently have passed through . . . Daventry on his journey to and from Stratford, and the red-nosed innkeeper was probably described from life."

Scene 5.1: A messenger reports to Warwick that his ally the Marquess of Montague and his forces have reached Daventry (called Daintry in this scene) on their way to Coventry (see "Coventry, Warwickshire" under "England" in this chapter).

London

Fulham Palace

Bishops Avenue [Underground stop: Putney Bridge]

Formerly the residence of the Bishops of London starting in the eighth century. The current building was constructed by Richard FitzJames in the early sixteenth century. Still the property of the Church of England, it is managed by the Fulham Palace Trust.

Scene 4.8: Learning of Edward IV's return to England, the Lancastrians plan to marshal forces to oppose him. Edward's forces surprise the king and send him back to the Tower of London (April 11, 1471); then, in the play, they head north to Coventry (actually Barnet). In fact, Edward had skirted Coventry on his march south, while Warwick remained behind that city's walls waiting for reinforcements (as shown in scene 5.1).

Palace of Westminster

North bank of the Thames [Underground stop: Westminster]

Originally built for Edward the Confessor, the Palace of Westminster served as a royal residence until Henry VIII made Whitehall Palace his chief residence in 1512 after the Palace of Westminster was damaged by fire. It has also been the meeting place of Parliament since the thirteenth century. In 1834 a fire destroyed most of the building. Only St. Mary Undercroft (the crypt under St. Stephen's Chapel), Westminster Hall (dating from 1097), the Cloisters, and the Jewel Tower (1365) survived. The current Gothic building was designed by Sir Charles Barry and Augustus Pugin. Construction began in 1837. Most of the restoration was completed by 1860, though work continued until 1870. The House of Commons was destroyed in the Blitz of 1940–1941; it was restored by Sir Giles Gilbert Scott after World War II during the period 1945–1950.

Scene 1.1: Flushed with victory at the First Battle of St. Albans (1455, shown in act 5 of *2 Henry VI*), Richard, Duke of York, ascends the throne. He agrees to let Henry reign if the king makes York and his descendants his heirs to the crown. Henry agrees, but Margaret and her son Prince Edward reject this arrangement.

Scene 3.2: Elizabeth Woodville, Lady Grey, appeals to King Edward for the restoration of her husband's property after Lord John Grey (called Richard in this scene) was killed at St. Albans in 1461. Lord Grey fought against Edward, but in this scene, Shakespeare makes him a Yorkist rather than a Lancastrian. Edward agrees to restore her lands—if she'll have sex with him. She refuses, but he is so taken with her he decides to marry her (May 1, 1464).

Scene 4.1: Edward's brothers are unhappy about his marriage to Elizabeth Woodville, Lady Grey. George, Duke of Clarence, leaves to join Warwick and says he'll marry Warwick's younger daughter; he married Warwick's older daughter, Isabel, on July 11, 1469, at Calais. Richard remains with Edward, though, as he says, "I / Stay not for the love of Edward, but the crown," which he is already plotting to seize (ll. 125–26).

Scene 4.4: Queen Elizabeth and her relatives learn of Edward's capture at Olney after his defeat at Edgecote Moor on July 26, 1469. They resolve to flee Warwick's advancing army.

Scene 5.7: Edward IV sits on the English throne.

Tower of London

Tower Hill [Underground stop: Tower Hill]

The White Tower, the oldest part of the twelve-acre complex on the north bank of the Thames, was built by William the Conqueror as a fortress, though later legend claimed Julius Caesar constructed it (see *Richard III*, 3.1.69–70). The outer wall was completed by Edward I. Over the centuries the Tower of London has served as a fortress, a palace, a prison, a zoo, an armory, a place of execution (though only seven executions officially took place here), the site of the Royal Mint, a public records office, and a treasure house. It now houses the Crown Jewels. It is a World Heritage Site under the care of the Historic Royal Palaces charity.

Scene 4.6: Henry VI is set free and again becomes king (the Readeption of Henry VI, October 3, 1470). He names George, Duke of Clarence, and the Earl of Warwick Protectors of England. Henry VI predicts Henry, Earl of Richmond (the future Henry VII), will rule England. A messenger announces Edward IV's flight to Flanders.

Henry was too feeble-minded to reign unaided. Warwick was the power behind the throne.

Scene 5.6: On May 21, 1471, Henry VI was killed in the tower. Shakespeare has Richard, Duke of Gloucester, kill the last Lancastrian king the same evening as the Battle of Tewkesbury (May 14, 1471).

Middleham Castle, Yorkshire

Castle Hill, Middleham, Wensleydale.

Middleham Castle in Wensleydale, in the county of North Yorkshire, England, was built by Robert FitzRandolph, Third Lord of Middleham and Spennithorne, beginning in 1190 on the site of an earlier fortress. In 1270 the castle came into the Neville family. Richard III spent part of his youth here. After Richard, Duke of Gloucester, married Anne Neville in 1474, the castle became his, and it was his favorite residence. The castle remained a royal property until James I sold it. It fell into disrepair, and only ruins remain. These are overseen by English Heritage.

Scene 4.5: Edward IV escapes his imprisonment at Middleham Castle. Edward flees to Flanders, which was ruled by his brother-in-law the Duke of Burgundy. Edward in fact had been released from Middleham Castle on September 10, 1469. He fled to Flanders on October 2, 1470.

Mortimer's Cross, Hertfordshire

Two miles from Leominster.

Scene 2.1: On February 2 or 3, 1461, the Yorkists defeated Queen Margaret's forces. Shakespeare does not show this battle, but he does show Edward, Earl of March, Richard Plantagenet's oldest son, observing parhelion, the appearance of three suns. Edward regarded this vision as a good omen and adopted the three suns as his emblem.

A messenger announces the death of the Duke of York. Warwick reports the Lancastrian victory at the Second Battle of St. Albans (February 17, 1461) and the Lancastrian recovery of Henry VI, who had been imprisoned by the Yorkists. The Second Battle of St. Albans occurred two weeks after the Battle of Mortimer's Cross.

Tewkesbury, Gloucestershire

The town is named for Theoc, a Saxon who founded an abbey here in the seventh century. The Norman abbey church, consecrated in 1125, survived the dissolution of the monasteries because the townspeople bought the building to use as their place of worship. It has one of the tallest remaining Norman towers. The city was famous for its mustard; Falstaff refers to it in *2 Henry IV*, 2.4.246. William Camden describes Tewkesbury as a "great and fair town, having three bridges to pass over, standing upon three rivers, famous for making woolen cloth, and the best mustard, which for the quick heat it hath, biteth most and pierceth deepest." Fynes Moryson notes its "excellent mustard" in his 1617 *An Itinerary: Containing His Ten Years Travel through the Twelve Dominions of Germany, Bohemia, Switzerland, Netherland, Denmark, Poland, Italy, Turkey, France, England, Scotland and Ireland.*

Scenes 5.4–5.5: On May 4, 1471, Yorkists defeat the Lancastrians. Prince Edward, son of Henry VI, is killed along with the Duke of Somerset. Shakespeare has the Earl of Oxford captured, but he was not at this battle and not imprisoned until 1474.

Towton, Yorkshire

A village located twenty-six miles from York, the site of a climactic battle in the Wars of the Roses and perhaps the bloodiest fight on English soil, fought on Palm Sunday, March 29, 1461, during a snowstorm; 30,000 combatants died here.

Scenes 2.3–2.6: Battle of Towton. John Clifford, Ninth Baron Clifford, is among those killed. Henry VI, Margaret, and their son flee to Scotland. In fact, Clifford was killed the previous day in a skirmish with Yorkist forces. Traditionally, Clifford was killed at Dittingdale. Shakespeare has Clifford killed with an arrow through his throat, which accords with accounts of his death. Though Shakespeare includes them in these scenes, neither Richard, Duke of Gloucester, nor George, Duke of Clarence, was present at this battle, having been sent to Philip of Burgundy for safety following the Lancastrian victory at the Second Battle of St. Albans. At 2.6.88–89 Warwick says he will go to France to ask for the hand of Lady Bona for Edward. This proposal came in 1464, three years after the battle described here.

Wakefield, West Yorkshire

The site of a major battle in the Wars of the Roses fought on December 30, 1460. The Lancastrians won a decisive (though short-lived) victory. Richard, Duke of York, the Yorkist claimant to the English throne, and his son Edmund were among those killed in the battle. Pomfret (Pontefract) Castle, built around 1070, is located in the town of Pontefract. It belonged to John of Gaunt and was inherited by his son Henry Bolingbroke, who deposed Richard II and became Henry IV. Richard II died here. Only ruins of the castle remain. Wakefield was noted for its cloth trade.

Scenes 1.3–1.4: The Battle of Wakefield (December 30, 1460). Young Clifford kills Edmund, Earl of Rutland, the Duke of York's youngest son, in revenge for the death of Clifford's father at the First Battle of St. Albans. York is captured and executed. In scene 2.1 the Earl of Warwick mentions the Battle of Wakefield in his account of recent Yorkist reversals.

Sandal Castle

Located about two miles south of Wakefield. The castle was built by William de Warenne, Second Earl of Surrey, in the twelfth century. The castle was dismantled by Parliament in 1646, and little remains.

Scene 1.2: Richard Plantagenet resolves to break his promise to Henry VI and seize the throne. A messenger announces Queen Margaret is approaching with 20,000 soldiers. Though outnumbered, the Duke of York sets forth with his army to confront her.

Warwickshire

A county in England's west midlands that includes Stratford-upon-Avon, Shakespeare's birthplace.

Scene 4.2: The Earls of Warwick and Oxford and the Dukes of Somerset and Clarence gather with French soldiers intent on restoring Henry VI to the English throne (September 1470).

Scene 4.3: Warwick captures Edward IV. Actually, Edward surrendered to Warwick at Olney.

York, Yorkshire

On the banks of the Ouse and Foss Rivers. The British Caer-Ebroc or Eorauc and the Roman Eboracum (founded 71 CE), capital of the province of Britain. The emperor Hadrian held court here in 120 CE, and Constantine was declared emperor here. When the Danes ruled this area, they called the city Jorvik. The first English Parliament was held here in 1175. York Minster sits on the site of a church dating from at least 627; it is the largest Gothic church in northern Europe. The city retains its medieval walls, which date mainly from the reign of Edward III (1327–1377).

Scene 1.4: Margaret orders that, following the Battle of Wakefield, York's head be placed on Micklegate, one of the four gates in York's walls.

Scene 2.2: Lancastrian forces assemble in front of the walls of York, and the Yorkist forces arrive to confront them.

Scene 4.7: Edward IV, having returned to England with a small army, seeks admission to York (March 1471). At first the mayor refuses. Edward then says he has come only to reclaim his dukedom, a ploy Henry Bolingbroke (later Henry IV) had used in 1399. The mayor opens the city's gates. Once inside, Edward has himself proclaimed king.

Warwick Castle, home of the Earl of Warwick, the "kingmaker." *Private Collection © Look and Learn/Bridgeman Images*

FRANCE

Paris

The Louvre

Rue de Rivoli [Paris metro stop: Louvre]

Originally a fortress built by Philip II in the twelfth century, in the fourteenth century, Charles V converted it into a residence. Under Louis XIV, who lived at Versailles, the Louvre became a home for artists. On August 10, 1793, the one-year anniversary of the execution of Louis XVI, it opened as a public museum, and so it remains.

Scene 3.3: In 1464 Queen Margaret comes to ask Louis XI for help against King Edward. The Earl of Warwick comes to ask for the hand of the French king's sister-in-law Lady Bona for Edward IV. Louis agrees to this union, scuttling Margaret's chances for aid. Then, a messenger arrives to say Edward has already married Lady Grey. Warwick now switches sides. He agrees to help Margaret and offers his second daughter, Anne, to Prince Edward, Margaret's son. Shakespeare says Warwick offered the prince his oldest daughter, though Holinshed states George married Isabel, the eldest daughter, on July 11, 1469. Shakespeare conflates Warwick's 1464 visit to Louis XI and his turning against Edward IV. Warwick remained loyal to Edward until 1469. In that year he fled to France, and Louis XI arranged for the reconciliation of Queen Margaret and Warwick and the betrothal of Anne Neville to Prince Edward.

Richard III

ENGLAND

Bosworth Field, Leicestershire

Two miles south of Market Bosworth.

The site of the climactic battle of the Wars of the Roses. On August 22, 1485, the Tudor Earl of Richmond defeated the Yorkist Richard III, who was killed. The spot where Stanley put the crown on Richmond's head is called Crown Hill. According to John Speed in *The Theatre of the Empire of Great Britain* (1611), Richard III's army lost 4,400 men to Richmond's 10. Speed wrote that after the battle the

> corps of ye dead king [Richard III] being tugged and despitefully torne, was layd all naked upon an horse, and trussed like a hogge [Richard's emblem] behind a pursuivant of Armes and as homely buryed in the Graye Fr[iars] within Leicester, which being ruinated [because of Henry VIII's dissolution of the monasteries] his grave rests as obscure, overgrown with nettles and weedes.

As noted under "Leicester, Leicestershire" in this chapter, Richard's remains were discovered under a car park in 2012.

Scenes 5.3–5.5: These scenes describe the battle.

Chertsey, Surrey

Site of an ancient monastery on the south side of the Thames, twenty-eight miles southeast of London. This Benedictine monastery was founded in 666 AD by Saint Erkenwald. Very little remains.

Scene 1.2: Henry VI is to be buried at Chertsey Abbey. His body was later transferred to St. George's Chapel, Windsor, its present location.

Leicester, Leicestershire

Leicester sits on the bank of the River Soar. The city was the Roman Ratae Coriel-tauvorum, or Ratiscorion, the Anglo-Saxon Ligora-caestra (*Ligora* being the name of the river and *caestra* from the Latin *castrum*, "fortified military camp"). The 1086 Domesday Book calls it Ledecestre. Romans found an Iron-Age settlement here. In the Middle Ages, the city was part of the kingdom of Mercia and then part of the Danelaw, ruled by Vikings. The castle, originally built by Hugh de Grandmesnil (1032–1098), served as a royal residence under the Lancastrians, and three parliaments met here. Part of the hall and two of the gateways remain. Thomas Cook in 1841 arranged his first railway excursion from Leicester to Loughborough and back. In 2012 Richard III's remains were discovered under the ruins of Greyfriars Abbey (under what is now a parking lot) near Leicester, and in 2015 these remains were buried in Leicester Cathedral. Cardinal Thomas Wolsey died in Leicester in 1530 and is buried in the Abbey Park. Leicester is also the traditional home of King Lear and his daughters, though Shakespeare's play about them does not mention the city. Geoffrey of Monmouth's twelfth-century *Historia Regum Britanniae* (*History of the Kings of Britain*) called Leicester by its old Welsh name, Kaerleir, "Lear's city." Leir derives from the Brittonic name for the River Soar: Leir, Liger, or Ligora.

Scene 5.2: Richmond announces that Richard III and his army are close to Leicester. Richard III slept in Leicester the night before the Battle of Bosworth Field (see "Bosworth Field, Leicestershire" in this chapter).

London

Baynard's Castle

135 Queen Victoria Street [Underground stops: Blackfriars, St. Paul's]

Located on the north bank of the Thames between Paul's Wharf and Blackfriars, the castle was built by Ralph Bairnardus, or Baynard, who came to England with William the Conqueror, on a site that had previously been a fort. In 1111 it was forfeited to the crown and given to Robert FitzWalter. During the reign of King John, the contemporary Robert FitzWalter sided with the barons against the king, who ordered the castle demolished in 1213. When Robert reconciled with the king, he was allowed to rebuild the castle. After a fire destroyed it in 1428, Humphrey, Duke of Gloucester, rebuilt it. In 1447 it became the property of Henry VI, then of Richard, Duke of Gloucester. Edward IV was proclaimed king here. Henry VII refashioned the castle in 1487; Henry VIII used it for lavish banquets. Catherine of Aragon, Anne Boleyn, and Anne of Cleves lived here. In 1553 both Lady Jane Grey and Mary Tudor were proclaimed queen at Baynard's Castle. Blackfriars Theatre was located just behind the castle. The 1666 Great Fire of London destroyed all but a turret, which survived until 1720. The site is now occupied by Baynard House, an office block that houses the BT Group.

Scene 3.7: When the Lord Mayor and citizens of London arrive at the invitation of the Duke of Buckingham, Richard appears between two churchmen. He feigns reluctance to accept the crown Buckingham offers but eventually yields.

Crosby House (or Crosby Place)
Danvers Street, Chelsea [Underground stop: Sloane Square]
The London home of Richard, Duke of Gloucester, Crosby House originally stood in Bishopsgate. The house was built for a rich grocer, Sir John Crosby, in 1466. It was the tallest house in London. Richard, Duke of Gloucester, was living here in 1483; he acquired the house after Crosby died in 1475. Later, Sir Thomas More owned the house and lived here from 1516 to 1523. Sir Walter Raleigh lived here in 1594–1595, and later the Countess of Pembroke stayed here. It served as the headquarters of the East India Company (1621–1638). In 1906 the Banqueting Hall was serving as a restaurant. The Great Hall was moved to Sir Thomas More's garden in Chelsea and in 1926–1927 was incorporated into the International Hostel of the British Federation of University Women. Crosby Hall was bought in 1989 by Christopher Moran, who has included it in a new Tudor Palace on Cheyne Walk, Chelsea.
    Scene 1.2: Richard tells Anne Neville to meet him at Crosby House.

Lord Hastings's House
Scene 3.2: A messenger arrives from Sir William Stanley urging William Hastings, First Baron Hastings, to flee Richard. Hastings refuses. William Catesby arrives and suggests crowning Richard, Duke of Gloucester, king. Hastings rejects this idea. Catesby also says Hastings's enemies Lord Grey and Earl Rivers are to be executed at Pomfret. Henry Stafford, Second Duke of Buckingham, enters; he and Hastings go to attend a council meeting at the Tower of London.

Palace of Westminster
North bank of the Thames [Underground stop: Westminster]
Originally built for Edward the Confessor, the Palace of Westminster served as a royal residence until 1512, when the Palace of Westminster was damaged by fire and Henry VIII made Whitehall Palace his chief residence. It has also been the meeting place of Parliament since the thirteenth century. In 1834 a fire destroyed most of the building. Only St. Mary Undercroft (the crypt under St. Stephen's Chapel), Westminster Hall (dating from 1097), the Cloisters, and the Jewel Tower (1365) survived. The current Gothic building was designed by Sir Charles Barry and Augustus Pugin. Construction began in 1837. Most of the restoration was completed by 1860, though work continued until 1870. The House of Commons was destroyed in the Blitz of 1940–1941; it was restored by Sir Giles Gilbert Scott after World War II during the period 1945–1950.

The Great Hall of Crosby Hall, the only surviving part of the house, was moved to Chelsea in 1910 and has been incorporated into a private residence there. *Private Collection © Look and Learn/Elgar Collection/Bridgeman Images*

Scene 1.3: Queen Elizabeth and Richard, Duke of Gloucester, quarrel. The former Queen Margaret enters and argues with everyone present. Queen Margaret was imprisoned in the Tower of London from 1471 to 1475 and lived in France from 1476 until her death in 1482, so her presence in this play is historically inaccurate because this scene probably would have occurred in early 1478. As noted later, George, Duke of Clarence, was killed on February 18, 1478, and in this scene, after everyone else leaves, Richard arranges with two murderers for the death of his brother George.

Scene 2.1: Edward IV believes he has reconciled the factions in his court. Richard informs the court of the death of George, Duke of Clarence, and blames Edward for it.

Scene 2.2: Elizabeth reports the death of Edward IV (April 9, 1483). Richard and the Duke of Buckingham intend to join the group bringing the young Edward V to London.

Scene 2.4: A messenger reports that Sir Thomas Vaughn; Anthony Woodville, Lord Rivers, the queen's brother; and her son Lord Grey have been sent by Richard to Pomfret Castle as prisoners. Queen Elizabeth flees with her younger son, Richard, to the Sanctuary of Westminster within the precincts of Westminster Abbey, later the site of Westminster Hospital.

Scene 4.2: Richard, now king, tells the Duke of Buckingham he wants Edward IV's children killed. Buckingham balks at this proposal and leaves. Richard asks his page whether he knows anyone who will undertake the killing of the princes. The page recommends Sir James Tyrrel, whom Richard engages to commit the crime. When Buckingham returns to claim the earldom of Herford Richard had once promised him, the king replies, "I am not in the giving vein to-day" (l. 115). Buckingham resolves to flee the court to Brecknock Castle in Wales (1483).

Lord Stanley enters to report the flight of the Marquis of Dorset. Richard tells Stanley to spread the news Queen Anne is ill. Anne died on March 16, 1485 (probably of tuberculosis), and was buried in Westminster Abbey. Richard was rumored to have poisoned her. To secure his claim to the throne, Richard wants to marry Elizabeth IV's daughter (Richard's niece), also named Elizabeth, so Anne must be eliminated. Richard also wants to marry Margaret Plantagenet to "some mean poor gentleman" (l. 52) to distance her children from royal pretensions. Shakespeare confuses Margaret, who was only ten in 1483, with her sister Cecily, who first married Ralph Scrope of Upsall, an ally of Richard. After Henry Tudor came to the throne, this marriage was annulled. She then married John Welles, First Viscount Welles. After his death she married Thomas Kyme. Margaret married Sir Richard Pole in 1487, after Richard III's death.

Scene 4.3: Tyrrel reports the murder of the princes in the Tower of London (1483). Richard says he has imprisoned the Duke of Clarence's son Edward Plantagenet, Seventeenth Earl of Warwick, and married the duke's daughter, Margaret, "meanly" (l. 37). Also, his wife, Anne, is dead. (As noted in 4.2, she would not die until 1485.) Sir

Richard Ratcliffe arrives with news John Morton, Bishop of Ely, has fled to the Earl of Richmond, and Buckingham has raised a Welsh army to unseat Richard. This scene covers the period July–September 1483.

Scene 4.4: Before the palace, Queen Elizabeth, Queen Margaret, and the Duchess of York meet. Margaret taunts Elizabeth; Elizabeth and the duchess lament. After Margaret leaves, Richard arrives with his soldiers, ready to battle the Duke of Buckingham. Elizabeth and the duchess curse him. Richard says he wants to marry Elizabeth's daughter, and after some arguing she seems to agree. Sir Richard Ratcliffe and Lord Stanley announce the Earl of Richmond's imminent invasion of England. Richard sends Stanley to muster troops, but because Richmond is the son of Stanley's wife by a previous marriage, Richard intends to keep Stanley's son George as hostage to ensure Stanley's loyalty. A messenger reports Richmond has returned to Brittany. William Catesby arrives with news of the capture of the Duke of Buckingham and the landing of Richmond at Milford Haven.

Shakespeare here compresses history. In October 1483 Buckingham raised a rebellion against Richard. Richmond attempted to join him, but his small force was forced by winds back to Brittany. Richmond landed at Plymouth but, learning of Buckingham's capture, returned to Brittany. Buckingham was captured and executed in November 1483. Richmond landed at Milford Haven on August 7, 1485.

Sir William Stanley's House

Scene 4.5: Stanley sends Sir Christopher Urswick, a chaplain, to convey his good wishes to the Earl of Richmond and to tell the earl that Queen Elizabeth wants her daughter to marry Richmond. Sir Christopher reports various forces are converging on London to depose Richard.

St. Paul's Cathedral

Ludgate Hill [Underground stops: St. Paul's, Mansion House]

Bishop Mellitus built the first church here in 604. A new church was begun in 1087 by Maurice, Bishop of London. A fire destroyed it in 1136, and the Gothic church Shakespeare knew was not completed until 1283. Built of Caen stone, it was one of the largest buildings in England, at 596 feet long and 104 feet wide, and was topped by the tallest spire ever built. The tower at the crossing was 285 feet tall, with a spire on top that was another 208 feet high, about 100 feet taller than the current dome. In 1561 this steeple collapsed after it was struck by lightning and was not rebuilt.

In the sixteenth century, the building served as a meeting place and market, as well as a church, and publishers and booksellers worked within its precincts. Booksellers offered their wares in Paul's churchyard; among these were Shakespeare's plays. The 1594 quarto of *Titus Andronicus* was "sold by Edward White and Thomas Millington, at the little North doore of Paules at the sign of the Crosse." The 1597 quarto of *Rich-ard III* was printed "for Andrew Wise, dwelling in Paules Church-yard, at the Signe of the Angell." The 1600 *Merchant of Venice* could be purchased from Thomas Heyes "in Paules Church-yard, at the signe of the Greene Dragon," and the 1608 *King Lear* was available from Nathaniel Butter "at his shop in Paule Church-yard at the signe of the Pide Bull."

Oliver Cromwell used the church as a barracks for cavalry. Even before the Great Fire of London in 1666 destroyed the building, Christopher Wren had been asked to advise on renovating the structure. He recommended demolishing it and erecting an-other. After the fire in 1666, Wren began the new cathedral in 1675. The first service was held here in 1697; construction was completed in 1710. Wren's dome stands 360 feet high; the only church dome higher is that of St. Peter's in Rome. Among those buried here are Sir Christopher Wren, John Donne, and Admiral Lord Nelson. The ca-thedral survived the Blitz but suffered damage to the north transept, and the Victorian high altar was destroyed. The Jesus Chapel, damaged by German bombs, was restored as the American Memorial Chapel, dedicated to the 28,000 American citizens based in Britain who died during World War II.

Scene 1.2: Near St. Paul's, Henry VI's corpse is being taken from that church fol-lowing his funeral to be buried at Chertsey (see "Chertsey, Surrey" in this chapter). Richard, Duke of Gloucester, who according to Shakespeare killed Henry (though he may have been killed on the order of Edward IV), orders the casket set down. Richard woos Anne Neville, even though he has killed her husband, Edward, Prince of Wales, son of Henry VI, as well as her father-in-law. (Anne married Prince Edward on De-cember 13, 1470.) Richard III is so charismatic that she agrees to marry him. Anne was not, in fact, present at the funeral of Henry VI.

Henry VI's funeral occurred in 1471, and Richard's marriage to Anne Neville in 1472.

A Street

Scene 2.3: Three citizens discuss the death of Edward IV and the matter of succession.

Scene 3.6: A scrivener notes the illegality of Richard's posthumous indictment of Lord Hastings.

Tower of London

Tower Hill [Underground stop: Tower Hill]

The White Tower, the oldest part of the twelve-acre complex on the north bank of the Thames, was built by William the Conqueror as a fortress, though later legend claimed Julius Caesar constructed it (see *Richard III*, 3.1.69–70). The outer wall was completed by Edward I. Over the centuries the Tower of London has served as a fortress, a palace, a prison, a zoo, an armory, a place of execution (though only seven executions officially took place here), the site of the Royal Mint, a public records office, and a treasure house. It now houses the Crown Jewels. It is a World Heritage Site under the care of the Historic Royal Palaces charity.

Scene 1.1: Before the Tower of London, George, Duke of Clarence, is being led to imprisonment. Although his brother Richard, Duke of Gloucester, is responsible for his arrest, they blame the queen. Richard promises to help Clarence gain his freedom, though in fact Richard is plotting against him. Lord Hastings is released from the tower as Clarence is taken there. Hastings was not, in fact, imprisoned; Shakespeare added this detail. While Shakespeare blames Richard for Clarence's arrest, King Edward IV was the one who accused him of treason. Clarence was imprisoned in 1477, yet the next scene, showing the burial of Henry VI, dates from 1471, and Richard III's opening speech, "Now is the winter of our discontent / Made glorious summer by this sun of York" (1.1.1–2), seems to refer to the recent Yorkist triumph at the Battle of Tewkesbury (May 14, 1471; see *3 Henry VI*, 5.6).

Scene 1.4: George, Duke of Clarence, is murdered in the Bowyer Tower (February 18, 1478). Bowyer Tower was built by Henry III (1238–1241). Only the ground floor is original. The rest of the Bowyer Tower was rebuilt in the nineteenth century after a fire destroyed the upper part (October 30, 1841). The tower takes its name from the bowmakers who once worked here.

Scene 3.1: Richard, Duke of Gloucester, sends Edward, Prince of Wales, son of Edward IV, to the tower to await his coronation. (According to Edward Hall's *The Union of the Two Noble and Illustre Famelies of Lancastre and Yorke*, when Edward V first came to London, he lodged with the Bishop of London.) After the prince and attendants depart, the Duke of Buckingham sends Catesby to determine whether Lord Hastings will agree to the crowning of Richard instead of Edward.

Scene 3.4: Richard has convened a council to discuss the coronation of Edward V. Richard accuses Lord Hastings of treason and orders his immediate beheading (June 13, 1483).

Scene 3.5: Richard and the Duke of Buckingham, clad in "rotten armor," appear on the tower walls as if in imminent danger. Catesby has brought London's Lord Mayor to see this charade. Francis Lovell, First Viscount Lovell, and Sir Richard Ratcliffe enter with Hastings's head. Buckingham claims Hastings planned to kill him and Richard. After the Lord Mayor departs, Richard sends Buckingham to defame Edward IV and claim Edward's sons are illegitimate. Buckingham is to bring the Lord Mayor and London citizens to Baynard's Castle (see "Baynard's Castle" under "London" in this chapter).

Scene 4.1: Queen Elizabeth; the Duchess of York; Thomas Grey (the Marquis of Dorset and son of Queen Elizabeth); Anne, Duchess of Gloucester; and Margaret

Plantagenet (daughter of George, Duke of Clarence) meet in front of the Tower of London. They have come to visit the princes, but Sir Robert Brakenbury, lieutenant of the tower, says the king has forbidden them to enter. By calling Richard king, he reveals Richard's intention to seize the throne. Confirming this plan, Lord Stanley arrives to take Anne to be crowned queen at Westminster (July 6, 1483). Elizabeth urges Dorset to flee to Henry, Earl of Richmond, in Brittany. Brankenbury did not become constable of the tower until March 1484. The Marquis of Dorset held this post in 1483 when this scene unfolds.

Salisbury, Wiltshire

A cathedral city located on the north bank of the River Avon, eight miles from Stonehenge; Anthony Trollope's Barchester and Thomas Hardy's Melchester. Roman Celtic Sorviodunum (*dunon* means "fortress") and later New Sarum (established 1220). Its imposing cathedral, with the tallest spire in England (404 feet high), was begun in 1220. The city wall around the Close dates to the fourteenth century. The English Parliament met in Salisbury in 1324, 1328, and 1384. The Duke of Buckingham was executed here near the Bull's Head Inn after the failure of his revolt against Richard III.

Scene 5.1: The Duke of Buckingham is about to be executed (November 2, 1483).

Tamworth, Staffordshire

Named for the River Tame, the town served as the capital of Mercia. It is the site of an eleventh-century Norman castle.

Scene 5.2: The Earl of Richmond's forces camp here before the Battle of Bosworth Field. Historically, Richmond proceeded slowly through Staffordshire to gather recruits.

Wakefield, West Yorkshire

Pomfret Castle

Pontefract, or Pomfret, Castle, once known as the Key to the North, is located in the town of Pontefract within the city of Wakefield. It was begun as a wooden fortress about 1070 by Ilbert de Lacy and later rebuilt in stone. In 1310 it passed into the possession of the House of Lancaster. The castle was slighted during the English Civil War. The ruins that remain are open to the public.

Scene 3.3: Anthony Woodville (Second Earl Rivers), Lord Richard Grey, and Sir Thomas Vaughan are executed at Pomfret Castle (June 25, 1483).

King John

Bury St. Edmunds, Suffolk

The Villa Faustina of the Romans and the Saxon Beodericsworth, it assumed its current name in 925. *Bury* derives from *burg*, a "castle or fortress." It is named for the last king of East Anglia (killed by the Vikings in 869). Its annual December fair dates from 1235. The abbey, now a ruin in a garden, dates from the eleventh century; it was founded by King Canute in 1020. Entrance is through the abbey gateway, built in 1327 and rebuilt after a 1347 fire. The Abbey Gardens are owned by St. Edmundsbury Borough Council and managed in conjunction with English Heritage. The seventeenth-century Abbey Bridge crosses the Lark River.

In *Past and Present* (1843), Thomas Carlyle described Bury St. Edmunds as a "prosperous brisk town beautifully diversifying, with its clear brick houses and ancient clean streets . . . the general grassy face of Suffolk; looking out right pleasantly, from its hill slope, towards the rising sun: and on the eastern edge of it, still runs, long, black and massive, a range of monastic ruins."

Scene 5.2: At the camp of the dauphin, the Earls of Salisbury and Pembroke join the French. In 1214 English nobles met at Bury St. Edmunds and agreed to oppose King John. The French invasion occurred in 1216. Pandulph arrives to report John has "reconcil'd / Himself to Rome" (ll. 69–70), so Louis should not fight him. Louis still wants the English throne. Philip the Bastard enters and declares the English are ready for battle.

Lincoln, Lincolnshire

Occupied since the Iron Age, the Romans called Lincoln Lindum Colonia, perhaps from the Celtic *Lindon* ("pool"). The River Witham forms a pool (Brayford Pool) at the foot of a hill here. Edmund Spenser wrote that Lincoln and London were founded by Brute, grandson (or great-grandson) of Aeneas and Britain's first king. In the early Norman period, Lincoln prospered. In the thirteenth century, it was England's third-largest city.

Scenes 5.3–5.5: On May 17, 1217, the English under William Marshall, Earl of Pembroke, defeated the French. King John was dead by the time the battle occurred (died October 19, 1216). Shakespeare has Pembroke and Salisbury siding with the French. Melure tells them Louis plans to kill them if he wins the battle. These scenes derive from *The Troublesome Raigne of King John,* which is responsible for many of the historical inaccuracies in Shakespeare's play.

London

Palace of Westminster
North Bank of the Thames [Underground stop: Westminster]

Originally built for Edward the Confessor, the Palace of Westminster served as a royal residence until Henry VIII made Whitehall Palace his chief residence in 1512 after the Palace of Westminster was damaged by fire. It has also been the meeting place of Parliament since the thirteenth century. In 1834 a fire destroyed most of the building. Only St. Mary Undercroft (the crypt under St. Stephen's Chapel), Westminster Hall (dating from 1097), the Cloisters, and the Jewel Tower (1365) survived. The current Gothic building was designed by Sir Charles Barry and Augustus Pugin. Construction began in 1837. Most of the restoration was completed by 1860, though work continued until 1870. The House of Commons was destroyed in the Blitz of 1940–1941; it was restored by Sir Giles Gilbert Scott after World War II during the period 1945–1950.

Two other London sites connected with King John's residence are (1) the Stone House, Lombard Street (Underground stops: Cannon Street, Bank, or Monument), which has been called King John's House; and (2) King John's Gate, Stepney (Underground stop: Stepney Green) is also associated with this monarch.

Scene 1.1: Because this opening scene is not localized and has no basis in fact, it is impossible to know where Shakespeare imagined it occurring. He took this scene from the anonymous *The Troublesome Raigne of King John.* Some commentators place scene 1.1 in King John's palace in Clipstone, northwest Nottinghamshire, now a ruin.

Chatillon, ambassador from King Philip II of France, tells King John to yield the throne to John's nephew, Arthur Plantagenet (son of John's dead older brother, Geoffrey) or face war. John refuses to surrender the crown and promises to invade France.

The brothers Robert Faulconbridge and Philip the Bastard enter. Philip is older and so should inherit his father's estate according to the law of primogeniture, but their father left his property to Robert, claiming Philip is illegitimate. John and his mother, Eleanor, note Philip's resemblance to King Richard I. Eleanor suggests Philip give up his claim to his father's estate and join her in the invasion of France. Philip agrees.

John knights him Sir Richard Plantagenet. At the end of this scene, Philip's mother confirms Philip's royal parentage.

Scene 4.2: Back in England King John has been crowned for the second or third time (October 8, 1200, or March 25, 1201). William Marshal, First Earl of Pembroke, asks John to free Arthur (not yet captured historically). Hubert arrives to report (falsely) the death of Arthur. A messenger reports a French invasion led by Louis (May 21, 1216). He adds that the king's mother died on April 1, 1204 (true), and Arthur's mother, three days before (actually, three years earlier, c. September 5, 1201). Philip the Bastard enters with Peter of Pomfret, who in 1212 foretold King John's downfall. John imprisons Peter. Peter was hanged in June 1213. Hubert reports five moons were seen at night. (This phenomenon was observed in December 1200.) When John berates Hubert for obeying the order to kill Arthur, Hubert replies that Arthur still lives.

Scene 5.1: John surrenders his crown to Pandulph, who gives it back to him as from the pope (Innocent III), making John the pope's liege (May 16, 1213). Shakespeare does not mention that King John agreed to pay the pope one thousand marks a year to hold the crown as the pope's liege. Pandulph promises to pacify the French, who have taken Kent. Philip the Bastard wants to fight them; John allows him to prepare for war.

Swinstead (i.e., Swineshead) Abbey, Lincolnshire

The Abbey of St. Mary was founded in 1134 by Robert de Gresley. In King John's time, it was a Cistercian monastery. The abbey was dissolved in 1536. A few remains have been incorporated into a farmhouse.

Scenes 5.6–5.7: King John dies. He actually died of dysentery in Newark Castle, Nottinghamshire. The castle has an ecclesiastical connection, having been built by the Bishop of Lincoln. Hubert claims King John was poisoned by a monk. While Shakespeare's play is less anti-Catholic than *The Troublesome Raigne of King John*, it remains anti-Catholic, and its treatment of John is ambivalent. His attempt to break with the pope foreshadows Henry VIII's Reformation and hence was viewed favorably in Protestant England, but his claim to the throne is questionable, and his reign is presented as vexed. John is to be buried in Worcester Cathedral. His tomb there has the oldest royal effigy in England, dating from 1232. His brief will usually is on display at the cathedral. It includes the request that he "be buried in the church of St. Mary and St. Wulfstan of Worcester." Prince Arthur, older brother of Henry VIII, is also buried here. Raphael Holinshed's *Chronicles of England, Scotland, and Ireland* (1587) gives the correct information about King John's death. While Shakespeare relied heavily on Holinshed for his English history plays, he took the details here from *The Troublesome Raigne of King John*, John Bale's *King Johan* (1538–1560), and John Foxe's *Actes and Monuments of Martyrs* (first edition, 1563). All these Protestant, anti-Catholic works place John's death at Swineshead Abbey and blame a monk for his death. John stayed at Swineshead Abbey but did not die there.

FRANCE

Angiers

Capital of Anjou in western France. Henry II of England inherited the dukedom of Anjou; King John lost it in 1204. Part of Roman Gaul, Angiers was called Juliomagus Andecavorum. The latter part of the name became Angiers in the twelfth century and later Angers. During the period depicted in the play, Anjou was ruled by King René.

Scene 2.1: Philip II of France, the dauphin (the future Louis VIII), Constance, her son Arthur, with an army, along with the Archduke of Austria and his forces, meet. They plan to put Arthur on the English throne, and they will begin by capturing Angiers, then held by England as part of the Angevin Empire, which is resisting them. Chatillon announces the arrival of the English forces led by King John, his mother, his niece (Lady Blanche of Castile), and Philip the Bastard. Each side asks the citizens of Angiers which side it supports: Arthur or John. Hubert of Angiers replies ambiguously that the city supports the English king but refuses to open its gates to either side. After an indecisive skirmish between the armies, each again seeks admittance to the city, and each is again refused. The Bastard urges Philip and John to join in sacking Angiers and then return to fighting each other. The two kings agree. Hubert suggests instead that Lady Blanche marry the dauphin, thus uniting the two sides; the marriage was arranged in 1200. John agrees and offers five English provinces in France as Blanche's dowry. Philip abandons his support for Arthur. John consents to making Arthur Duke of Brittany and Earl of Richmond and to giving him Angiers.

According to the Treaty of Le Goulet, concluded in May 1200 between John and Philip II, Philip recognized John as king of England. John agreed that he held lands in France as a vassal of Philip. On May 22, 1200, King John and Philip II signed a treaty of marriage between Blanche and Louis. John gave the fiefs of Issoudon and Graçay, together with those that André de Chauvign, Lord of Châteauroux, held in Berry as a grant from the English Crown, as Blanche's dowry.

Scene 3.1: Arthur's mother, Constance, criticizes Philip for not keeping his promise to put Arthur on the English throne. Pandulph, a papal legate, arrives to upbraid John for keeping Stephen Langton, the pope's choice for Archbishop of Canterbury, from his see. Shakespeare has Pandulph call himself Cardinal of Milan. Pandulph was actually archdeacon, but Shakespeare is following his chief source for this play, the anonymous *The Troublesome Raigne of King John* (1590–1591). John rejects the pope's authority. Despite Philip's objections, John remains adamant. Pandulph excommunicates John and deposes him. Pandulph orders Philip to declare war on John if John does not recant. Philip is reluctant to fight, but Pandulph threatens him with excommunication if he does not. Philip yields.

Though Shakespeare has this scene immediately follow the previous one, Pandulph's excommunication occurred in 1212, twelve years after the events shown there.

Scene 3.2: France and England fight. The Bastard enters with the head of the Archduke of Austria. John puts the captured Arthur in the custody of Hubert. Arthur was indeed placed by John in the custody of Hubert de Burgh in 1202 at the Château de Falaise in Normandy. Again, Shakespeare is playing fast and loose with history; Arthur's capture occurred a decade before John's excommunication shown in 3.1.

Scene 3.3: John sends Philip the Bastard to England to raise funds for the war. John tells Hubert to kill Arthur.

Scene 3.4: King Philip laments the defeat of the French fleet, which was preparing to invade Flanders, by William Longespée, Third Earl of Salisbury, King John's half-brother, on May 30–31, 1213, in the Battle of Damme. In this engagement the English captured three hundred ships laden with arms and provisions and sank more than a hundred more. Still others were scuttled by the crew. The harbor of Damme was so cluttered with wreckage that Philip burned what remained of his fleet. Philip says Arthur has been captured. As already noted (scene 3.2), Arthur was captured in 1202. He was dead a decade before the Battle of Damme. Pandulph warns King John that, if he kills Arthur, the English will revolt and choose Louis as their monarch.

Falaise, Normandy

Falaise, meaning "cliff," is the birthplace of William the Conqueror. The town, which lies on the Ante River, grew up around the twelfth-to-thirteenth-century château named William the Conqueror's Castle, though most of the castle postdates him. Much of the city was destroyed by Allied bombing in World War II but has been rebuilt.

Scene 4.1: Although Shakespeare places this scene and 4.3 in an unnamed castle, Arthur was imprisoned first in the Château de Falaise (see scene 3.2) and then in Rouen, where he died. In this scene executioners are about to blind Arthur, thus rendering him unable to reign. Arthur pleads for mercy, which Hubert de Burgh grants.

Rouen

Capital of Normandy in northern France, located on the River Seine; it was the Ratumacos of the Gauls and Rotomagus of the Romans. Henry V captured the city in 1419, and it served as the seat of English power in France until Charles VII took Rouen in 1449.

Scene 4.3: Attempting to escape imprisonment, Arthur leaps from the castle wall and dies. Arthur's fate is obscure. King John may have had him killed. He disappeared in 1203. Shakespeare situates Arthur's death in England, where in this scene Philip the Bastard tries unsuccessfully to reconcile William Marshal, First Earl of Pembroke; William Longespée, Third Earl of Salisbury; and Roger Bigot (Bigod), Earl of Norfolk, with King John. They intend to join the dauphin's invasion of England (which actually occurred more than a decade later).

Richard II

ENGLAND

Berkeley Castle, Gloucestershire

The first Berkeley Castle dates from about 1067, built by William FitzOsbern. It was a motte-and-bailey fortification. Much of the present castle was built in the fourteenth century for Thomas de Berkeley, Third Baron Berkeley. It is (in)famous for the murder here of Edward II (September 21, 1327). The castle remains the property of the Berkeley family but is open to the public.

Scene 2.3: Near the castle Henry Percy joins his father, the First Earl of Northumberland (also named Henry Percy), and Henry Bolingbroke. Thomas de Berkeley, Fifth Lord Berkeley, and the Duke of York, confront Bolingbroke, who claims he has returned to England despite his banishment only to reclaim his property seized unlawfully by Richard. York admits he lacks sufficient soldiers to arrest Bolingbroke, who intends to go to Bristol Castle.

Bristol Castle, Bristol

Originally a timber motte-and-bailey fortification built by Geoffrey of Coutances by 1088, it was rebuilt in stone circa 1135 by Robert, Earl of Gloucester. After William, Earl of Gloucester, supported the abortive rebellion by Henry III's sons Richard and Geoffrey, Henry III seized the castle, and it remained royal property. It suffered from neglect, and in 1656 Oliver Cromwell ordered its demolition. Part of the banqueting hall survives (Castle Vaults).

Scene 3.1: Bolingbroke orders the execution of William le Scrope, First Earl of Wiltshire; Bushy (Sir John Bussy); and Sir Henry Green (July 29, 1399).

Coventry, Warwickshire

Ninety-five miles northwest of London.

In the Middle Ages, Coventry was an important center of the cloth trade and one of England's largest cities. It produced a thread of a color known as Coventry blue. The city was famous for its Corpus Christi Day mystery plays, which Shakespeare may have seen as a child; Coventry is twenty miles from Stratford. It was heavily damaged by German bombs in World War II (November 14, 1940), and its cathedral was destroyed. Coventry is the site of Lady Godiva's legendary ride. Supposedly, she had repeatedly asked her husband, Leofric, Earl of Mercia, to remit his taxes on Coventry. He finally agreed if she would ride naked through the city. The story of her ride was extant by 1235; that of Peeping Tom, the only townsperson to watch her ride naked through the streets, dates from the eighteenth century. Historians reject the story of the ride. To "send someone to Coventry" means to ignore or ostracize that person. The origin of this phrase is uncertain.

Scene 1.3: Henry Bolingbroke and Thomas Mowbray prepare to fight to determine which one is a traitor. Before they can come to blows, Richard stops this trial by combat (September 16, 1398). He banishes Mowbray for life and Bolingbroke for ten years, which, as a favor to his uncle John of Gaunt, Richard shortens to six. Mowbray left England on October 19, 1398, and died in Venice on September 22, 1399.

Kings Langley Castle, Hertfordshire

The manor of Chiltern Langley became a royal possession in 1276. King Edward I and Queen Eleanor lived here. Edmund of Langley, First Duke of York (1341–1402), was born and died here. Nothing of the palace remains. The site is occupied by Rudolf Steiner School.

Scene 3.4: Queen Isabella overhears gardeners discussing her husband's capture and impending loss of his crown. The gardeners note Richard was not a good gardener of his realm. The queen prepares to go to London to join Richard.

Scene 5.2: Learning of a plot in which his son Aumerle is involved to kill Bolingbroke (now King Henry IV) at a joust in Oxford, the Duke of York sets off to warn the new king, despite York's wife's pleas to spare their son, who will be executed for taking part in the conspiracy. The duchess urges her son to rush to the king to confess before York arrives, and she sets off to beg Henry IV for her son's life. The plot, known as the Epiphany Rising, was to seize Henry IV at a tournament to be held at Windsor at Epiphany (January 6, 1400), kill him, and restore Richard II to the throne.

London

Ely Palace

Ely Place [Underground stops: Farringdon, Chancery Lane]

The London townhouse of the Bishops of Ely, Cambridgeshire, from 1290 to 1772. John of Gaunt lived here from 1382 until his death in 1399 after his Savoy Palace was severely damaged in the 1381 Peasants' Revolt. The estate was sold to the Crown in 1772, and the palace demolished, though the chapel, St. Etheldreda's, that was part of the palace has survived. The rows of townhouses now on the site have their own gatehouse and beadles, legacies of the old palace.

Scene 1.2: John of Gaunt and his sister-in-law discuss the murder of Thomas of Woodstock, Duke of Gloucester, John of Gaunt's brother. The anonymous play *Thomas of Woodstock* is a source for Shakespeare's *Richard II*. Woodstock was killed at Calais on September 8 or 9, 1397, probably under orders from Richard II, Gloucester's nephew. The duchess wants her brother-in-law to avenge her husband's death, but Gaunt refuses to act against God's anointed king.

Scene 2.1: February 3, 1399. The dying John of Gaunt delivers his famous panegyric about England: "This royal throne of kings, this sceptered isle, / This earth of majesty, this seat of Mars, / This other Eden, demi-paradise" (ll. 40–42). King Richard enters with his queen, Isabella of Valois, and their followers. Gaunt tells the king he is ruling badly, but Richard rejects his uncle's warning. After Gaunt dies offstage, Richard seizes his property (March 18, 1399). Edmund of Langley (Duke of York), the king's uncle, urges Richard not to do so, but again, the king ignores good advice. After Richard and his entourage depart, Henry Percy, First Earl of Northumberland; Lord Ross (William de Ros), Sixth Baron Ros; and Lord Willoughby (William Willoughby), Fifth Baron Willoughby de Eresby, criticize Richard's rule. Northumberland informs them that Henry Bolingbroke, despite his recent banishment, is returning to England with three thousand soldiers provided by the Duke of Brittany.

Palace of Westminster

North Bank of the Thames [Underground stop: Westminster]

Originally built for Edward the Confessor, the Palace of Westminster served as a royal residence until Henry VIII made Whitehall Palace his chief residence in 1512 after the Palace of Westminster was damaged by fire. It has also been the meeting place of Parliament since the thirteenth century. In 1834 a fire destroyed most of the building. Only St. Mary Undercroft (the crypt under St. Stephen's Chapel), Westminster Hall (dating from 1097), the Cloisters, and the Jewel Tower (1365) survived. The current Gothic building was designed by Sir Charles Barry and Augustus Pugin. Construction began in 1837. Most of the restoration was completed by 1860, though work continued until 1870. The House of Commons was destroyed in the Blitz of

1940–1941; it was restored by Sir Giles Gilbert Scott after World War II during the period 1945–1950.

Scene 1.4: The Duke of Aumerle (Edward of Norwich), John Bagot, and Sir Henry Green discuss Bolingbroke's departure from England and a rebellion in Ireland. Sir John Bushy arrives with news that John of Gaunt is dying. Richard plans to seize Gaunt's property to pay for his Irish war.

Scene 4.1: Several people accuse the Duke of Aumerle of complicity in the death of the Duke of Gloucester and of opposing Henry Bolingbroke's return to England. Aumerle denies the charges. This episode echoes 1.1. The Duke of York arrives to report Richard II is ready to abdicate. Richard abdicated on September 29, 1399. According to Holinshed, the abdication occurred at the Tower of London. Shakespeare moved it to the Palace of Westminster, perhaps for irony because Richard had reroofed the hall and decorated it with his symbol of the white hart. Oliver Cromwell chose to execute Charles I just outside the Banqueting Hall of Whitehall because it, too, reflected the glories of his reign, with its Rubens ceiling and the great art collection Charles I had assembled, which Cromwell would sell off.

When the Bishop of Carlisle protests Bolingbroke's seizing the throne, the Earl of Northumberland arrests him for treason. Richard enters and after some demurral surrenders his crown to Bolingbroke, but he refuses to read the list of indictments against him. Richard is sent to the Tower of London. After everyone else leaves, the Abbot of Westminster (William de Colchester), the Bishop of Carlisle (Thomas Merke), and the Duke of Aumerle remain behind to plot against Bolingbroke. The conspirators met on December 17, 1399, at the abbey house in Westminster.

This scene was cut from the first three printings of the play (Q1 in 1597; Q2 and Q3 in 1598) as being too controversial, though it seems to have been staged. As noted in the "Southampton House" entry in appendix A, the Second Earl of Essex had Shakespeare's company perform this play on February 7, 1601, the day before his abortive coup against Queen Elizabeth, who was identified with Richard II. On August 4, 1601, Elizabeth told the Kent antiquary, mapmaker, and Justice of the Peace William Lambarde (1536–1601), "I am Richard II. Know ye not that?" At least as early as 1599, Essex had thoughts of playing Bolingbroke/Henry IV to Elizabeth's Richard II. In that year Sir John Hayward published *The First Part of the Life and Raigne of King Henrie IV*, which he dedicated to Essex. Elizabeth instructed Francis Bacon to examine the work for treasonous comments that could be used against Essex. Bacon did not find any, but Hayward was imprisoned until 1602, and the book was cited against Essex at his 1601 trial. On February 18, 1601, Augustine Phillips of the Lord Chamberlain's Company was questioned about the staging of *Richard II* on the eve of Essex's rebellion. Phillips claimed that, on February 5 or 6, Essex's supporters Sir Charles Percy, Sir Jocelyn Percy, and Lord Monteagle (who would warn King James of the Gunpowder

Plot in 1605) had asked that the play be staged on February 7. Phillips said the company did not want to put on *Richard II*, declaring it was an old play no one wanted to see, but the men promised to pay forty shillings (two pounds) above the house earnings that day. It was just about the money, Phillips was saying, not politics. On February 24, 1601, the eve of Essex's execution, Elizabeth had the Lord Chamberlain's Men perform for her, just as they had performed for Essex's supporters on the eve of what might have been her death. The play they presented is not recorded. If Elizabeth's sense of irony was keen enough, she might have requested *Richard II*. See Evelyn May Albright, "Shakespeare's *Richard II* and the Essex Conspiracy," *PMLA* 42, no. 3 (September 1927): 686–720.

Tower of London
Tower Hill [Underground stop: Tower Hill]
The White Tower, the oldest part of the twelve-acre complex on the north bank of the Thames, was built by William the Conqueror as a fortress, though later legend claimed Julius Caesar constructed it (see *Richard III*, 3.1.69–70). The outer wall was completed by Edward I. Over the centuries the Tower of London has served as a fortress, a palace, a prison, a zoo, an armory, a place of execution (though only seven executions officially took place here), the site of the Royal Mint, a public records office, and a treasure house. It now houses the Crown Jewels. It is a World Heritage Site under the care of the Historic Royal Palaces charity.

Scene 5.1: As Richard is being led to the Tower of London, he and his queen, Isabella, have a tearful final meeting. Northumberland separates them and sends Richard to Pomfret Castle.

Wakefield, Yorkshire

Pomfret Castle
Pontefract, or Pomfret, Castle, once known as the Key to the North, is located in the town of Pontefract within the city of Wakefield. It was begun as a wooden fortress about 1070 by Ilbert de Lacy and later rebuilt in stone. In 1310 it passed into the possession of the House of Lancaster. The castle was slighted during the English Civil War. The ruins that remain are open to the public.

Scene 5.5: Sir Pierce Exton kills Richard. The manner and exact date of Richard's death are uncertain, but he was dead by mid-February 1400.

Windsor, Berkshire

Windsor Castle
In 1070 William the Conqueror built a timber motte-and-bailey castle here. Henry II, Henry III, and Edward III added to the castle in stone, and George IV extensively

remodeled the castle, which has been a royal residence since the eleventh century. St. George's Chapel, dedicated to the patron saint of the Order of the Garter (founded by Edward III) was rebuilt circa 1478 by Henry Janyns for Edward IV and continued by William Vertue (1501–1511). Vertue's portrait appears in the great west window (c. 1500). The chapel is the site of celebrations of the investiture of the Order of the Garter. *The Merry Wives of Windsor* was written for such an occasion, probably in 1597. The Gothic chapel was an important pilgrimage site, with the tomb of Henry VI and a piece of True Cross, until the Reformation. The ten monarchs buried here include Henry VI, Edward IV, Henry VIII (with Jane Seymour, his third wife), Charles I, George III, George IV, William IV, Edward VII and Queen Alexandra, George V and Queen Mary, and George VI. In 1922 Windsor became a royal borough. Prince Charles married Camilla Parker Bowles at Windsor on April 8, 2005, and his son Prince Harry married Meghan Markle here on May 19, 2018. It is the longest continuously occupied castle in Europe. A fire on November 20, 1992, destroyed nine state rooms and damaged a hundred others. Repairs, completed in 1997, cost £37 million.

Scene 1.1: John of Gaunt's son, Henry Bolingbroke, Duke of Herford, and Thomas Mowbray, Duke of Norfolk, accuse each other of treason (1398). Their quarrel resulted from the murder of Thomas of Woodstock, uncle of Richard II and Henry Bolingbroke. Mowbray probably was responsible for Woodstock's death, which was likely ordered by Richard II. Thomas of Woodstock was a political opponent of the king. When Richard II's efforts to reconcile Mowbray and Bolingbroke fail, the king appoints St. Lombard's Day for a trial by combat to be held between the antagonists at Gosford Green near Mowbray's Caludon Castle in Coventry. The date of St. Lombard's Day is debated. It falls sometime in August or September.

Scene 2.2: Sir John Bushy tries to cheer up the queen. Sir Henry Green enters to report Bolingbroke's return to England (June 1399) and the support he is receiving from powerful nobles. The regent, the Duke of York, prepares to confront Bolingbroke. Bushy and Green flee for safety to Bristol Castle, while John Bagot heads to Ireland to join Richard.

Scene 5.3: The king asks about his wayward son Prince Hal, thus preparing audiences for Hal's exploits in the *Henry IV* plays. Aumerle arrives and requests a private audience with the king. Before Aumerle can confess his role in the plot to kill Henry, the Duke of York arrives to denounce his son. Although Aumerle repents, the duke urges Henry to punish the would-be traitor. The duchess enters to plead for Aumerle. Henry pardons him but pledges to kill all the other conspirators, as indeed he did.

Scene 5.4: Sir Pierce Exton plans to kill Richard.

Scene 5.6: The Earl of Northumberland and Lord FitzWater (Walter FitzWater, Fourth Baron FitzWater) report the deaths of those who had plotted against Henry IV. (The leaders of the Epiphany Rising were quickly captured and killed by mid-January

1400.) The Bishop of Carlisle is ordered to a religious house of his choice. (The bishop was imprisoned in the Tower of London in 1400. Though released in 1401 and conditionally pardoned, he was not restored to his bishopric. He served as Acting Bishop of Winchester and died in 1409.)

Exton arrives with Richard II's coffin. Henry banishes Exton and promises to atone for Richard's death by undertaking a pilgrimage to the Holy Land.

WALES

Flint, Flintshire

Flint Castle
Begun in 1277 under Edward I, it was the first castle of his "Iron Ring" of fortifications to control the Welsh. Oliver Cromwell slighted it after it fell to parliamentary forces in the English Civil War (1647). Substantial ruins remain. The site is maintained by Cadw, the Welsh agency charged with preserving historic buildings, and is open to the public free of charge.

Scene 3.3: Richard II here surrenders to Henry Bolingbroke (August 19, 1399). According to Shakespeare, Richard sought refuge here. In fact, Richard had been captured by Henry Percy, First Earl of Northumberland, and compelled to go here as a prisoner.

Merionethshire

Harlech Castle
Located in Harlech, Gwynedd, Wales, it was built by Edward I between 1282 and 1289 as part of his "Iron Ring" of fortresses to control the Welsh. It was the last stronghold to surrender to parliamentary forces during the English Civil War. The castle is maintained by Cadw, the Welsh government's historic environment preservation service.

Scene 3.2: July 24, 1399. Richard II returns from Ireland to learn of the dispersal of his Welsh supporters, the execution of William le Scrope, First Earl of Wiltshire; Bushy (Sir John Bussy), and Sir Henry Green by Bolingbroke at Bristol Castle and the defection of the Duke of York to Bolingbroke. Richard dismisses his remaining soldiers. Shakespeare places this scene at the nonexistent Barkloughly Castle. Shakespeare took this name from Holinshed's *Chronicles*, which refers to Berklowlie Castle, a confusion with Berkeley Castle or a misspelling of Hertlowlie (i.e., Harlech).

Milford Haven, Pembrokeshire

On the west coast of Pembrokeshire in southwest Wales. The town of Milford itself dates from 1793. William Camden wrote of Milford Haven,

> From here runneth the shore along not many miles continuate, but at length the land shrinketh back on both sides giving place unto the sea, which encroaching upon it a great

way, maketh the Haven which Englishmen call *Milford Haven*, than which there is not another in all Europe more noble or safer, such variety it hath of nouked Bayes, and so many coves and creekes, for harbour of ships, wherewith the bankes are on every side indented, and that I may use the Poets words:

> Hic exarmatum terris cingentibus aquor,
> Clauditur & placidem discit servare quietem.
> The sea disarmed here of windes, within high banke and hill,
> Enclosed is and learnes thereby to be both calme and still.

Neither is this haven famous for the secure safeness thereof more, than for the arrival therein of King Henrie the Seventh a Prince of most happy memory, who from hence gave forth unto England then hopeless the first signall to hope well, and raise it selfe up, when as now it had long languished in civill miseries and domesticall calamities, within it selfe.

Richard II landed here upon his return from Ireland.

Scene 2.4: John Montagu, Third Earl of Salisbury, fails to prevent the Welsh soldiers loyal to Richard II from dispersing.

1 Henry IV

Coventry, Warwickshire

Ninety-five miles northwest of London.

In the Middle Ages, Coventry was an important center of the cloth trade and one of England's largest cities. It produced a thread of a color known as Coventry blue. The city was famous for its Corpus Christi Day mystery plays, which Shakespeare may have seen as a child; Coventry is twenty miles from Stratford. It was heavily damaged by German bombs in World War II (November 14, 1940), and its cathedral was destroyed. Coventry is the site of Lady Godiva's legendary ride. Supposedly, she had repeatedly asked her husband, Leofric, Earl of Mercia, to remit his taxes on Coventry. He finally agreed if she would ride naked through the city. The story of her ride was extant by 1235; that of Peeping Tom, the only townsperson to watch her ride naked through the streets, dates from the eighteenth century. Historians reject the story of the ride. To "send someone to Coventry" means to ignore or ostracize that person. The origin of this phrase is uncertain.

Scene 4.3: As Falstaff's ragtag army marches toward Shrewsbury, Prince Hal and the Earl of Westmerland arrive. They criticize the soldiers' poor appearance. Falstaff has taken bribes from all the able-bodied men to avoid fighting, so his company consists of those too poor to pay him off. Both here and in *2 Henry IV* 3.2, Shakespeare exposes abuses in military recruiting. Barnaby Riche's *Allarme for England* (1579) and Dudley Digges's *Four Paradoxes, or Politique Discourses* (1604) complained of the practices Shakespeare depicts.

Gadshill, Kent

A manuscript in the hand of Sir Roger Manwood, Chief Baron of the Exchequer, dated July 3, 1590, records, "In the course of Mychaelmas Terme, I being at London, manye robberyes weare done in the hye wayes at Gadshill on the west part of Rochester . . . by horse theeves . . . and no man durst trauell that waye without greate companye." The area was notorious for robberies. Shakespeare even names one of the thieves in this play Gadshill.

Scene 2.2: Falstaff and his cohorts rob rich travelers. Then Hal and Poins rob Falstaff and his crew, just as Poins had planned in scene 1.2.

London

Boar's Head Tavern, Eastcheap
Cannon Street [Underground stops: Monument, Cannon Street]

This most famous tavern in literature is never named in Shakespeare's plays, though Shakespeare puns on the name in *2 Henry IV*, scene 2.2: "Doth the old boar feed at the old frank [sty]?" (ll. 145–46). There were six taverns named the Boar's Head but none in Eastcheap during the reign of Henry IV. There was an Elizabethan tavern of that name near Blackfriars' Theatre. On the south side of Great Eastcheap, in St. Michaels, was a Boar's Head Tavern that, by the mid-seventeenth century, was associated with Falstaff, Prince Hal, and their comrades. John Stow, in his *Survey of London* (1603), wrote that Eastcheap was "always famous for its convivial doings." Another Boar's Head Tavern stood in Southwark, near the Globe. It was located in what is now the Borough High Street. The property on which it was located belonged to Sir John Fastolf, whose name may have suggested "Falstaff" to Shakespeare (see *1 Henry VI*), though there is a minor character of that name in *The Famous Victories of Henry the Fifth*. The Elizabethan Boar's Head in Eastcheap served as a sometime theater. It was destroyed in the Great Fire of London (1666) but was quickly rebuilt in stone (1668). A figure of Falstaff was carved on either side of the door. The sign of this tavern resides in the new Globe Theatre.

James Boswell referred to this rebuilt tavern as the "very tavern where Falstaff and his companions met." A club met here in the eighteenth century; its members assumed the identities of Shakespearean characters. Samuel Johnson warned Boswell not to join: "Now that you have a name, you must be careful to avoid many things, not bad in themselves, but which will lessen your character" (*A Journal of a Tour of the Hebrides*, September 23, 1773). Though Boswell disagreed with Johnson about the club, he apparently never joined.

Washington Irving visited the site in 1817, by which time the tavern no longer existed, and wrote an essay about it in *The Sketchbook of Geoffrey Crayon* (1819). By 1831, when it was demolished, the tavern had been converted into shops. In 1868 Robert Louis Roumieu designed a neo-Gothic building near the old Boar's Head. Its decorations pay homage to the tavern, with carvings of a boar's head and portraits of Henry IV and Henry V.

Scene 2.4: Prince Hal and Poins tease the tapster Francis. When Falstaff and his crew arrive, Falstaff recounts how they stole a thousand pounds but were in turn robbed by a band of a hundred men. Hal reveals the truth. The hostess, Mistress Nel Quickly, tells the prince a nobleman sent by the king wants to speak with him. Hal sends Falstaff to dismiss the messenger. Knowing Hal will "be horribly chid to-morrow when thou comest to thy father," Falstaff urges him to "practice his answer" (ll. 375–77). Falstaff assumes the role of the king, but soon the two men exchange roles. As they are acting their parts, Bardolph rushes in to say the sheriff and a band of constables are at the door because of the recent robbery. Falstaff and his friends hide, and Hal assures the sheriff Falstaff is not at the tavern. Finding Falstaff asleep, the prince picks his pocket. As the scene ends, Hal tells Peto the stolen money will be repaid, and they "must all to the wars" (l. 549) to fight against Hotspur.

Scene 3.3: Falstaff complains of having his pocket picked. He claims his grandfather's signet ring worth forty marks (twenty-six pounds, thirteen shillings, sixpence) was stolen. When Prince Hal arrives, Falstaff repeats his claim and adds the loss of "three of four bonds of forty pounds apiece." Hal reveals he was the pickpocket and found only bills and "one poor pennyworth of sugar-candy." Hal informs Falstaff he has repaid the money stolen at Gadshill and has secured for Falstaff the command of a company of infantry. The fat Falstaff will thus have to march.

Palace of Westminster
North bank of the Thames [Underground stop: Westminster]

Originally built for Edward the Confessor, the Palace of Westminster served as a royal residence until Henry VIII made Whitehall Palace his chief residence in 1512 after the Palace of Westminster was damaged by fire. It has also been the meeting place of Parliament since the thirteenth century. In 1834 a fire destroyed most of the building. Only St. Mary Undercroft (the crypt under St. Stephen's Chapel), Westminster Hall (dating from 1097), the Cloisters, and the Jewel Tower (1365) survived. The current Gothic building was designed by Sir Charles Barry and Augustus Pugin. Construction began in 1837. Most of the restoration was completed by 1860, though work continued until 1870. The House of Commons was destroyed in the Blitz of 1940–1941; it was restored by Sir Giles Gilbert Scott after World War II during the period 1945–1950.

Scene 1.1: Henry IV is forced to defer his pilgrimage to the Holy Land (pledged in *Richard II*, scene 5.6) because of domestic unrest (June 1402). Ralph Neville, First Earl of Westmerland, informs Henry that Owen Glendower, fighting for Welsh independence, has defeated an English force under Sir Edmund Mortimer, whom Glendower has taken prisoner (Battle of Bryn Glas, June 22, 1402). Shakespeare confuses this Sir Edmund Mortimer with his nephew Edmund Mortimer, Fifth Earl of March, whom

Richard had named his heir to the English throne. The historians Raphael Holinshed and Edward Hall, key sources for Shakespeare's history plays, make the same mistake. As Shakespeare notes, Sir Edmund Mortimer married one of Owen Glendower's daughters. Glendower had offered to release Mortimer for ransom, which Henry, as Shakespeare shows, refused to pay. Westmerland adds that Henry Hotspur has defeated the Scot Archibald Douglas (Battle of Homildon Hill, September 14, 1402) but refuses to surrender his prisoners to the king despite Henry's demand for them.

Scene 1.2: The location of this scene is questionable. It may unfold in another part of the palace. The nineteenth-century Shakespeare scholar James Orchard Halliwell-Phillips places it in the Painted Tavern in the Vintry (or the Three Cranes Tavern in Painted Tavern Lane). Cold Harbour, Upper Thames Street, has also been suggested, but Henry IV did not give this property to Prince Hal until 1410. Many productions place the scene at the Boar's Head Tavern.

Prince Hal banters with Sir John Falstaff. Falstaff tries to enlist the prince in a robbery planned at Gadshill. Hal initially refuses to join, but Poins convinces him to take part in order to rob Falstaff after he robs the travelers.

Scene 1.3: Henry IV quarrels with Henry Percy, First Earl of Northumberland; his son Henry Hotspur (Percy); and his brother Thomas Percy, Earl of Worcester. Holinshed's *Chronicles* places this event at Windsor. All three had supported Henry against Richard II. Now they plot to overthrow him, as Richard had predicted. In *Richard II*, 5.1.57–65, Richard had told Northumberland,

> The time shall not be many hours of age
> More than it is, ere foul sin, gathering head,
> Shall break into corruption. Thou shalt think,
> Though he divide the realm and give thee half,
> It is too little, helping him to all;
> He shall think that thou which knowest the way
> To plant unrightful kings, wilt know again,
> Being ne'er so little urged another way,
> To pluck him headlong from the usurped throne.

Scene 3.2: As Falstaff had predicted in scene 2.4, Prince Hal is "horribly chid." He promises to reform.

Rochester, Kent

The Roman Durobrivae (to which *castra* was added; *castra* means "military camp") and the Saxon Hroffecaster, the city twenty-nine miles south of London, is located on the River Medway. Augustine founded a cathedral here in 604. The Danes destroyed it, and another was constructed early in the twelfth century. Because of its location near the meeting of the Thames and Medway Rivers, it had strategic importance. The royal dockyards were located in nearby Chatham. Charles Dickens spent much time here and used it as a setting for some of his fiction.

Scene 2.1: At the Crown Inn, Bridge Lane, a chamberlain informs the robber Gadshill of a rich landowner traveling with three hundred marks (two hundred pounds).

Shrewsbury, Shropshire

Located on the River Severn, it is the ancient British Pengwern (alder hill) and the Angles's Scrobbesburh (Scrobb's fort). In the eighth century, it was part of the kingdom of Mercia. In the late Middle Ages, it prospered as a center of the wool trade. Because it was hardly bombed in World War II, many fifteenth- and sixteenth-century buildings survive. It is pronounced "Shrosbury," with a long *o*.

Scene 4.1: At the rebel camp near Shrewsbury, Hotspur learns his father will not be joining him for the upcoming encounter with the king's forces. Sir Richard Vernon reports that the army is approaching. Vernon praises Prince Hal and adds that the Earl of Worcester and his soldiers will not be present at the impending battle.

Scene 4.3: The rebels debate launching a night attack. Sir Walter Blunt brings an offer from the king promising pardon and redress. Hotspur agrees to negotiate.

Scene 5.1: At the king's camp, Sir Richard Vernon and the Earl of Worcester (representing Hotspur) go off to negotiate a possible settlement to avoid a battle. Alone onstage, Falstaff delivers his catechism on honor.

Scene 5.2: At the rebel camp, the Earl of Worcester, returned from negotiation, persuades Sir Richard Vernon not to tell Hotspur about the king's offer of reconciliation. The rebels prepare for battle.

Scenes 5.3–5.4: The Battle of Shrewsbury (July 21, 1403). Henry IV wins; Prince Hal kills Hotspur in hand-to-hand combat. Shakespeare invented this encounter. Hotspur was actually killed by an arrow. According to John Speed's 1611 map of Shropshire, 6,600 men died in the battle.

Scene 5.5: After the battle Henry IV orders the execution of the Earl of Worcester (Thomas Percy) and Sir Richard Vernon. Sir Richard Venables and Sir Henry Boynton were also executed. Prince Hal secures a pardon for Archibald, Fourth Earl of Douglas. In fact, Douglas had to provide hostages to guarantee his return to captivity after attending to his affairs in Scotland and promising allegiance to the king. Douglas did not return. The hostages were not ransomed until 1413.

As *1 Henry IV* ends, Henry sends his son Prince John of Lancaster and the Earl of Westmerland to York to confront the rebels there, while he and Prince Hal will go to Wales to confront Owen Glendower. Skirmishing continued between the English and Glendower until 1412.

Warkworth Castle, Northumberland

Built in the twelfth century, this castle was granted by Henry II to Robert FitzRichard circa 1164. In 1345 Henry de Percy, Second Baron Percy, became the owner. The castle remained the property of the earls and then dukes of Northumberland until 1922, when Alan Percy, Eighth Duke of Northumberland, gave it to the Office of Works. In *2 Henry IV*, Rumor refers to the castle as "this worm-eaten hole of ragged stone" (Induction, 35). Since 1984 the extensive ruins have been managed by English Heritage.

Scene 2.3: Henry Hotspur reads a letter warning him against rebellion. His wife enters and asks, "What is it carries you away?" He replies, "Why, my horse, my love, my horse" (ll. 77–78). He refuses to tell her his plans but promises she will soon join him.

York, Yorkshire

On the banks of the Ouse and Foss Rivers. The British Caer-Ebroc, or Eorauc, and the Roman Eboracum (founded 71 CE), capital of the province of Britain. The emperor Hadrian held court here in 120 CE, and Constantine was declared emperor here. When the Danes ruled this area, they called the city Jorvik. The first English Parliament was held here in 1175. York Minster sits on the site of a church dating from at least 627; it is the largest Gothic church in northern Europe. The city retains its medieval walls, which date mainly from the reign of Edward III (1327–1377).

Bishopthorpe Palace
Palace Flats, Bishopthorpe

Built by Archbishop Walter de Grey, the palace has served as the home of the Archbishop of York since 1241. The palace was expanded between 1480 and 1500, when Archbishop Thomas Rotherham built the north wing, and in the 1760s, under Archbishop Robert Hay Drummond, a stable block, gatehouse, entrance hall, and drawing room were added.

Scene 4.4: The Archbishop of York (Richard Scrope) sends Sir Michael with letters to various rebels to prepare to confront Henry IV's army if Hotspur loses the Battle of Shrewsbury. The Archbishop of York did not openly rebel until 1405; he was beheaded on June 8, 1405, outside the walls of York.

WALES

Merionethshire

Harlech Castle

Located in Harlech, Gwynedd, Wales, it was built by Edward I between 1282 and 1289 as part of his "Iron Ring" of fortresses to control the Welsh. It was the last stronghold to surrender to parliamentary forces during the English Civil War. The castle is maintained by Cadw, the Welsh government's historic environment preservation service.

In 1404 Harlech Castle fell to Owen Glendower. Holinshed's *Chronicles* places the meeting in this scene at Bangor, Wales, in the house of the archdeacon. Since the archdeacon is absent from this scene, the *Riverside Shakespeare* (Blackmore 1997) places it at Glendower's castle.

Scene 3.1: Henry Hotpsur, the Earl of Worcester; Sir Edmund Mortimer; and Owen Glendower meet to divide Britain. This meeting to create the Tripartite Indenture actually occurred in February 1405, by which time Henry Hotspur's spur was cold; he was killed at the Battle of Shrewsbury on July 21, 1403. His father, the Earl of Northumberland, was present at this meeting, not Hotspur. Holinshed, however, places this division of the kingdom before the Battle of Shrewsbury.

2 Henry IV

ENGLAND

Gaultree Forest, Yorkshire

Located north of the city of York, Gaultree Forest extended for 100,000 acres. It remained a royal forest until 1670.

Scenes 4.1–4.3: On May 29, 1405, the rebel forces led by the Archbishop of York confront the king's army under the command of Prince John of Lancaster. Raphael Holinshed's *Chronicles* places this event at Shipton Moor within the forest. The Archbishop of York gives Ralph Neville, Earl of Westmerland, a list of the rebels' grievances. Westmerland leaves and then returns with Prince John, who promises redress. The rebel leaders dismiss their troops; Westmerland then arrests the archbishop. As the king's army pursues the scattering rebels, Sir John Falstaff captures Sir Richard Coleville of the Dale, whom Prince John orders sent to York for execution. As scene 4.3 ends, Falstaff plans to return to Gloucestershire to get money from Robert Shallow.

Gloucestershire

The county southwest of Shakespeare's native Warwickshire.

Scene 3.2: At Justice Robert Shallow's house, Silence and Shallow reminisce about their student days at Clement's Inn, an inn of chancery in London. (The inns of chancery were preparatory schools for the inns of court, where barristers were trained; Clement's Inn was linked with the Inner Temple. Clement's Inn, located near the church of St. Clement Dane on the Strand, closed in 1903.)

Sir John Falstaff, a former classmate of Robert Shallow, arrives to recruit soldiers to fight against the rebels. As he had done in *1 Henry IV*, scene 4.3, Falstaff takes bribes to exempt those who can pay and drafts those who cannot.

Scene 5.1: Robert Shallow entertains Falstaff.

Scene 5.3: As Shallow, Silence, Falstaff, and Bardolph are relaxing, Pistol arrives to report the death of Henry IV. Now that Prince Hal is king, Falstaff believes the "laws of England are at my commandment" (ll. 140–41).

London

Boar's Head Tavern, Eastcheap

Cannon Street [Underground stops: Monument, Cannon Street]

This most famous tavern in literature is never named in Shakespeare's plays, though Shakespeare puns on the name in *2 Henry IV*, scene 2.2: "Doth the old boar feed at the old frank [sty]?" (ll. 145–46). There were six taverns named the Boar's Head but none in Eastcheap during the reign of Henry IV. There was an Elizabethan tavern of that name near Blackfriars' Theatre. On the south side of Great Eastcheap, in St. Michaels, was a Boar's Head Tavern that, by the mid-seventeenth century was associated with Falstaff, Prince Hal, and their comrades. John Stow, in his *Survey of London* (1603), wrote that Eastcheap was "always famous for its convivial doings." Another Boar's Head Tavern stood in Southwark, near the Globe. It was located in what is now the Borough High Street. The property on which it was located belonged to Sir John Fastolf, whose name may have suggested "Falstaff" to Shakespeare (see *1 Henry VI*), though there is a minor character of that name in *The Famous Victories of Henry the Fifth*. The Elizabethan Boar's Head in Eastcheap served as a sometime theater. It was destroyed in the Great Fire of London (1666) but quickly was rebuilt in stone (1668). A figure of Falstaff was carved on either side of the door. The sign of this tavern resides in the new Globe Theatre.

James Boswell referred to this rebuilt tavern as the "very tavern where Falstaff and his companions met." A club met here in the eighteenth century; its members assumed the identities of Shakespearean characters. Samuel Johnson warned Boswell not to join: "Now that you have a name, you must be careful to avoid many things, not bad in themselves, but which will lessen your character" (*A Journal of a Tour of the Hebrides*, September 23, 1773). Though Boswell disagreed with Johnson about the club, he apparently never joined.

Washington Irving visited the site in 1817, by which time the tavern no longer existed, and wrote an essay about it in *The Sketchbook of Geoffrey Crayon* (1819). By 1831, when it was demolished, the tavern had been converted into shops. In 1868 Robert Louis Roumieu designed a neo-Gothic building near the old Boar's Head. Its decorations pay homage to the tavern, with carvings of a boar's head and portraits of Henry IV and Henry V.

Scene 2.4: Falstaff and Doll Tearsheet argue. When Pistol enters, Doll Tearsheet quarrels with him, as well. Falstaff drives Pistol out of the room. While Prince Hal and Poins spy unseen, Falstaff mocks them. Hal and Poins reveal themselves. Falstaff explains he defames the prince to prevent the wicked from falling in love with him. Peto interrupts their conversation to say Falstaff is wanted at court. After Hal and Poins leave, Bardolph enters to repeat the summons. As Falstaff leaves, Doll Tearsheet and Mistress Quickly lament his departure.

Scene 5.4: In front of the tavern, Mistress Quickly and Doll Tearsheet are arrested.

Palace of Westminster
North bank of the Thames [Underground stop: Westminster]

Originally built for Edward the Confessor, the Palace of Westminster served as a royal residence until Henry VIII made Whitehall Palace his chief residence in 1512 after the Palace of Westminster was damaged by fire. It has also been the meeting place of Parliament since the thirteenth century. In 1834 a fire destroyed most of the building. Only St. Mary Undercroft (the crypt under St. Stephen's Chapel), Westminster Hall (dating from 1097), the Cloisters, and the Jewel Tower (1365) survived. The current Gothic building was designed by Sir Charles Barry and Augustus Pugin. Construction began in 1837. Most of the restoration was completed by 1860, though work continued until 1870. The House of Commons was destroyed in the Blitz of 1940–1941; it was restored by Sir Giles Gilbert Scott after World War II during the period 1945–1950.

Scene 3.1: Henry IV delivers a soliloquy on sleep. He then confers with the Earls of Warwick (Richard de Beauchamp, Thirteenth Earl of Warwick) and Surrey (Thomas FitzAlan, Sixth Earl of Arundel and Tenth Earl of Surrey) about the rebellion led by Archbishop Scrope. Shakespeare dates this rebellion to 1407, two years after it occurred. Warwick assures the king he will triumph and adds that Owen Glendower is dead. Raphael Holinshed's *Chronicles* (1577; second edition, 1587), a key source for Shakespeare's English history plays, states Glendower died in 1409, though in fact he outlived Henry IV, dying circa 1416. Edward Hall's *The Union of the Two Noble and Illustre Famelies of Lancastre and Yorke* (1548) claimed Glendower died shortly after the Battle of Shrewsbury (1403). The scene concludes with Henry IV again planning a pilgrimage to the Holy Land, as he had in *Richard II*, 5.6.

Scene 5.2: The Lord Chief Justice, the Earl of Warwick, and Henry IV's younger sons worry about how Hal, now Henry V, will treat them. The new king reassures them, "This is the English, not the Turkish court" (l. 47). Sultan Mehmed II the Conqueror's Law of Governance states that when "Any of my sons ascend the throne, it is acceptable for him to kill his brothers for the common benefit of the people (nizam-i alem). The majority of the ulama (Muslim scholars) have approved this; let action be taken accordingly." Selim I (ruled 1512–1520) killed his brothers when he came to power in 1512. When Murad III became sultan in 1574, he had his five brothers strangled. His son Mehmed III (reigned 1595–1603, contemporary with the composition of *Henry V*) similarly had his half-brothers strangled.

A Street

Scene 1.2: On a street the Lord Chief Justice (Sir William Gascoigne) urges Falstaff to mend his ways. Falstaff has no intention of changing.

Scene 2.1: In another street scene, Mistress Nell Quickly urges the aptly named sergeants Fang and Snare to arrest Falstaff for a debt of one hundred marks (sixty-six pounds, thirteen shillings, sixpence). When Falstaff appears, he resists arrest. The Lord Chief Justice and his men arrive to keep the peace. Falstaff protests his innocence and persuades Mistress Quickly to withdraw her suit against him.

Scene 2.2: In an unspecified location, Prince Hal discusses his seemingly dissolute life and his father's illness. Falstaff's companion Bardolph delivers a letter to Hal from Sir John. Prince Hal and Poins plan to spy on Falstaff at dinner at the Boar's Head Tavern in Eastcheap.

Westminster Abbey

Broad Sanctuary [Underground stops: St. James Park, Westminster]

Edward the Confessor began a new Benedictine abbey on Thorney Island in 1050. The church was consecrated on December 28, 1065; Edward died eight days later. On Christmas Day 1066, William the Conqueror was crowned king of England here, and all subsequent English monarchs have been crowned here, as well (except Edward V and Edward VIII, neither of whom had a coronation ceremony).

A new church was begun by Henry III in 1245. Nothing remains aboveground of Edward the Confessor's cruciform church. The new church, with the tallest nave in England (103 feet high), is modeled on the cathedrals of Rheims and Amiens and on the Sainte-Chapelle in Paris. It is the most French of any English church, though it has English features, such as the single aisle in the nave. In 1269 Edward the Confessor's body was placed in a new shrine in the abbey. It was a popular pilgrimage site until the Reformation. The towers at the west end date from the eighteenth century.

Oliver Cromwell used the church as barracks for his soldiers. Over the past several centuries, the abbey has become Britain's pantheon. Among those buried in Poets' Corner are Shakespeare's contemporaries Ben Jonson, Michael Drayton, and Francis Beaumont. William Davenant, another playwright who claimed to be Shakespeare's son, is also interred here. While there is a life-size white marble statue of Shakespeare here dating from 1740, he is buried in Holy Trinity Church, Stratford-upon-Avon (see "Holy Trinity Church" under "Stratford-upon-Avon" in appendix A).

Scenes 4.4–4.5: In the Jerusalem Chamber, built by Nicholas Litlyngton (Abbot of Westminster 1362–1386) at the west end of the abbey in what was the abbot's house, Henry IV expresses his fears for England under the reign of Prince Hal. The Earl of Warwick tries to reassure the king. Westmerland enters and announces the defeat of the rebels and the execution of their leaders. Henry IV in fact oversaw the execution of the Archbishop of York and his co-conspirators at York. Harcourt reports the defeat of the Earl of Northumberland. Henry's forces defeated the earl at the Battle of Branham Moor (February 19, 1408). The sheriff of York told Henry about the victory as Henry was leading troops through Nottingham to confront the earl. Henry suddenly feels ill and is carried to a bed near the Jerusalem Chamber, where he will die (March 20, 1413). Scene 4.4 condenses events that occurred over the space of eight years.

As the king sleeps, Prince Hal enters. Thinking his father is dead, Hal takes away the crown. Henry wakes and asks for it. In a final conversation between Hal and his father, the two are reconciled. Henry IV asks to be carried back to the Jerusalem Chamber to fulfill the prophecy that he should die in Jerusalem.

Scene 5.5: Falstaff, Shallow, Pistol, Bardolph, and Falstaff's page wait outside the abbey for Hal to pass after his coronation (April 9, 1413). Pistol tells Falstaff of the arrest of Mistress Nell Quickly and Doll Tearsheet (shown in scene 5.4). Falstaff promises to free them. When the new king and his entourage arrive, Falstaff and Pistol greet him familiarly. Hal, now Henry V, replies, "I know thee not, old man" (l. 47), and banishes Falstaff and his comrades. After the royal procession passes, Falstaff reassures Shallow, "I shall be sent for in private" (l. 78), but he will not be. The Chief Justice arrests Falstaff and his companions. As the play ends, Prince John says he expects war with France before the end of the year.

Warkworth Castle, Northumberland

Built in the twelfth century, this castle was granted by Henry II to Robert FitzRichard circa 1164. In 1345 Henry de Percy, Second Baron Percy, became the owner. The castle remained the property of the earls and then dukes of Northumberland until 1922, when Alan Percy, Eighth Duke of Northumberland, gave it to the Office of Works. In *2 Henry IV*, Rumor refers to the castle as "this worm-eaten hole of ragged stone" (Induction, 35). Since 1984 the extensive ruins have been managed by English Heritage.

Scene 1.1: Morton tells Henry Percy, First Earl of Northumberland, that the earl's son, Henry Hotspur, has been killed at the Battle of Shrewsbury and Henry IV's forces under Prince John of Lancaster and the Earl of Westmerland (Ralph Neville) are approaching. Northumberland prepares to confront them.

This scene seems to follow immediately after act 5 of *1 Henry IV*, but the earl and Henry IV were reconciled. The earl did not rebel until 1405, when he considered joining the uprising led by Richard Scrope, Archbishop of York. Just as he failed to aid his son at Shrewsbury, so in this event, the earl fled to Scotland (see scene 2.3).

Scene 2.3: The Earl of Northumberland's wife and daughter persuade him to flee to Scotland rather than join Richard Scrope's uprising (1405).

York, Yorkshire

On the banks of the Ouse and Foss Rivers. The British Caer-Ebroc, or Eorauc, and the Roman Eboracum (founded 71 CE), capital of the province of Britain. The emperor Hadrian held court here in 120 CE, and Constantine was declared emperor here. When the Danes ruled this area, they called the city Jorvik. The first English Parliament was held here in 1175. York Minster sits on the site of a church dating from at least 627; it is the largest Gothic church in northern Europe. The city retains its medieval walls, which date mainly from the reign of Edward III (1327–1377).

Bishopthorpe Palace
Palace Flats, Bishopthorpe

Built by Archbishop Walter de Grey, the palace has served as the home of the Archbishop of York since 1241. The palace was expanded between 1480 and 1500, when Archbishop Thomas Rotherham built the north wing, and in the 1760s, under Archbishop Robert Hay Drummond, a stable block, gatehouse, entrance hall, and drawing room were added.

Scene 1.3: The Archbishop of York holds a council of war (1405). Thomas Mowbray, Earl of Norfolk, and Lord Bardolph (Thomas Bardolph, Baron Bardolph, no relation to Falstaff's companion, plain Bardolph) urge caution. The latter warns of the unreliability of the Earl of Northumberland. William, Lord Hastings, and the archbishop are more optimistic and resolve to proceed with their rebellion.

Henry V

London

Boar's Head Tavern, Eastcheap
Cannon Street [Underground stops: Monument, Cannon Street]

This most famous tavern in literature is never named in Shakespeare's plays, though Shakespeare puns on the name in *2 Henry IV*, scene 2.2: "Doth the old boar feed at the old frank [sty]?" (ll. 145–46). There were six taverns named the Boar's Head but none in Eastcheap during the reign of Henry IV. There was an Elizabethan tavern of that name near Blackfriars' Theatre. On the south side of Great Eastcheap, in St. Michaels, was a Boar's Head Tavern that, by the mid-seventeenth century, was associated with Falstaff, Prince Hal, and their comrades. John Stow, in his *Survey of London* (1603), wrote that Eastcheap was "always famous for its convivial doings." Another Boar's Head Tavern stood in Southwark, near the Globe. It was located in what is now the Borough High Street. The property on which it was located belonged to Sir John Fastolf, whose name may have suggested "Falstaff" to Shakespeare (see *1 Henry VI*), though there is a minor character of that name in *The Famous Victories of Henry the Fifth*. The Elizabethan Boar's Head in Eastcheap served as a sometime theater. It was destroyed in the Great Fire of London (1666) but quickly was rebuilt in stone (1668). A figure of Falstaff was carved on either side of the door. The sign of this tavern resides in the new Globe Theatre.

James Boswell referred to this rebuilt tavern as the "very tavern where Falstaff and his companions met." A club met here in the eighteenth century; its members assumed the identities of Shakespearean characters. Samuel Johnson warned Boswell not to join: "Now that you have a name, you must be careful to avoid many things, not bad in themselves, but which will lessen your character" (*A Journal of a Tour of the Hebrides*, September 23, 1773). Though Boswell disagreed with Johnson about the club, he apparently never joined.

Washington Irving visited the site in 1817, by which time the tavern no longer existed, and wrote an essay about it in *The Sketchbook of Geoffrey Crayon* (1819). By 1831, when it was demolished, the tavern had been converted into shops. In 1868 Robert Louis Roumieu designed a neo-Gothic building near the old Boar's Head. Its decorations pay homage to the tavern, with carvings of a boar's head and portraits of Henry IV and Henry V.

Scene 2.1: Outside the tavern Pistol and Nym quarrel because Pistol has married Mistress Quickly, hostess of the tavern, even though she had been betrothed to Nym. Falstaff's page enters to say that Falstaff is sick. Bardolph reconciles Nym and Pistol, and they all leave to visit Falstaff.

Scene 2.3: Mistress Quickly describes Falstaff's death. Her malapropisms make her reconstruction comic, but it echoes Plato's description of the death of Socrates in the *Phaedo*. Pistol, Nym, Bardolph, and Falstaff's page set off for the French war, in which they hope to enrich themselves.

Palace of Westminster
North bank of the Thames [Underground stop: Westminster]

Originally built for Edward the Confessor, the Palace of Westminster served as a royal residence until Henry VIII made Whitehall Palace his chief residence in 1512 after the Palace of Westminster was damaged by fire. It has also been the meeting place of Parliament since the thirteenth century. In 1834 a fire destroyed most of the building. Only St. Mary Undercroft (the crypt under St. Stephen's Chapel), Westminster Hall (dating from 1097), the Cloisters, and the Jewel Tower (1365) survived. The current Gothic building was designed by Sir Charles Barry and Augustus Pugin. Construction began in 1837. Most of the restoration was completed by 1860, though work continued until 1870. The House of Commons was destroyed in the Blitz of 1940–1941; it was restored by Sir Giles Gilbert Scott after World War II during the period 1945–1950.

Scene 1.1: To sway Henry V against a bill in Parliament that would seize much church property, Henry Chichele, Archbishop of Canterbury, tells the Bishop of Ely, John Fordham, he has promised a large sum of money to help finance the king's French war.

Scene 1.2: Henry V asks the Archbishop of Canterbury whether he may legitimately claim the throne of France through his great-great-grandmother Isabel, daughter of King Philip IV of France and wife of Edward II. This is the same basis on which Edward III staked his claim to France. The French maintain that the Salic Law, drafted by King Clovis circa 500 CE and named for the Salian Franks, bars matrilineal succession to the French throne. In a rambling, recondite speech, the archbishop assures the king that the Salic Law does not apply to French territory. As scene 1.1 shows, the archbishop has an ulterior motive for urging Henry V to go to war. Scene 1.1 is sometimes cut in production, but it casts a shadow on Henry's claim to France and on the Catholic clergy's support for that claim.

The Bishop of Ely; the First Earl of Westmerland, Ralph Neville; and the Duke of Exeter, Thomas Beaufort, Henry's uncle, urge him to pursue his claim. Resolved to do so, Henry summons the French ambassador from the dauphin, who is responding to Henry's claim to various French dukedoms inherited through Edward III. The ambassador says the dauphin rejects Henry's claim and instead offers a barrel filled with tennis balls. Shakespeare reproduces this episode from *The Famous Victories of Henry the Fifth* (1598). Raphael Holinshed's *Chronicles*, an important source for Shakespeare's English history plays, also records this incident, which Holinshed places at Kenilworth Castle rather than in London. Henry responds forcefully with a speech that repeatedly puns on terms from the game of tennis as it was then played. Henry dismisses the ambassador, warning him, "I am coming on" (l. 291).

Southampton, Hampshire

Located seventy-five miles southwest of London, Southampton is an important port. It was a Roman settlement (Clausentum). Abandoned by the Romans in 410 CE, it became the Saxon Hamwic, then Hamtun (Hampton), which gives Hampshire its name. After the Norman Conquest, it served as a major transit point between the capital at Winchester (a role it shared with London for a time even after the Norman Conquest; William the Conqueror had himself crowned at both Winchester and London) and Normandy and a commercial port for the trade of French wine for English wool and cloth. It was also the entry point into England for the Black Death (1348).

Scene 2.2: Henry V's forces have gathered at Southampton. The king enters with Richard, Earl of Cambridge; Henry, Lord Scroop (Third Baron Scrope) of Masham; and Sir Thomas Grey of Northumberland. These three men were involved in the Southampton Plot (1415) to kill Henry and put Edmund Mortimer, Fifth Earl of March, on the throne. Mortimer alerted Henry about the plot (July 31, 1415). The Earl of Cambridge was Mortimer's brother-in-law, and Grey was Cambridge's son-in-law. Mortimer, descended from the second son of Edward III (Lionel, Duke of Clarence), had a stronger claim to the throne than Henry, who descended from John of Gaunt, Edward III's third son. This plot foreshadows the Wars of the Roses, in which Henry VI's claim to throne would be disputed by Richard, Duke of York, son of the Earl of Cambridge and Anne Mortimer, daughter of the Fourth Earl of March (uncle of the fifth earl).

Henry reveals his knowledge of the plot. When the three conspirators are arrested, they repent. Henry orders their execution. The three were beheaded at Southampton on August 5, 1415.

FRANCE

Agincourt, Artois

Located south of Calais, the town takes its name from the battle fought near the castle of Agincourt on October 25, 1415.

Scene 3.7: In the French camp, the French nobles argue on the eve of battle. Shakespeare places the dauphin at Agincourt, though actually the dauphin was not present at the battle. Shakespeare seems to have known the dauphin was not present because in 3.5 the French king says, "Prince Dauphin, you shall stay with us in Rouen" (l. 64). The foolish dauphin serves as a dramatic foil to Henry V, as this scene contrasts the dauphin's behavior with that of the English king in 4.1.

Scene 4.1: In the English camp on the eve of battle, Henry disguises himself and moves among the soldiers. Pistol praises the king but promises to beat the Welsh captain Fluellen. Henry joins three soldiers: John Bates, Alexander Court, and Michael Williams. Bates says he wishes the king were alone at Agincourt. Henry claims the war with France is justified, but Williams says, "That's more than we know" (l. 129). Bates says soldiers should obey the king, but Williams adds that, if the king's cause is not just, the king is guilty of the soldiers' deaths. Williams also does not believe the king will refuse to ransom himself. The disguised Henry and Williams agree to fight after the battle if they survive. They exchange gloves to be sure they will recognize each other. After the soldiers depart, Henry bemoans the kingly lot and prays that God will not punish him for his father's usurping the Crown. Gloucester summons Henry.

Henry's disguising himself and mingling with the troops is based on Tacitus's description of Germanicus doing the same. *The Annals of Cornelius Tacitus: The Description of Germanie*, translated by R. Greenway (1598), book 2, chapter 3, describes this episode: "As soon as it was night, going out at the Augural gate, accompanied with one alone, in secret and unknown places to the watch, casting a savage beast's skin on his back, he went from one place to another, stood listening at the tents, and joyeth in the praise of himself."

Scene 4.2: Back in the French camp, the overconfident French prepare for battle.

Scene 4.3: In the English camp, Henry delivers his famous "Band of Brothers" speech, after which the French are doomed. Shakespeare developed this brilliant speech from hints in Holinshed's *Chronicles*. Historians credit the English victory at Agincourt to the longbow, but Shakespeare ascribes it to language. Although Shakespeare showed battle scenes in other plays, in this play (contrary to the movies based on it), he does not. The siege of Harfleur and the Battle of Agincourt are won through speech. Shakespeare has Henry V marshal the English language and send it into battle, as Winston Churchill would do in World War II. Mountjoy the herald comes again for ransom and is rebuffed. Mountjoy says Henry will not hear a herald again, thinking Henry will soon be dead.

Scene 4.4: Pistol captures the French soldier Master Fer, who promises two hundred crowns for his ransom.

Scene 4.5: The French lament their defeat.

Scene 4.6: Exeter reports the death of Edward, Second Duke of York, and Michael de la Pole, Third Earl of Suffolk, in the fighting. When the French reinforce their positions, Henry orders the killing of all the French prisoners, so Pistol will not get the ransom he had expected. Henry feared the French prisoners would attack the small English army from the rear, where the captives were being held.

Scene 4.7: Fluellen condemns the French attack on the luggage train and the killing of the boys, including Robin, Falstaff's page, who were guarding it. Fluellen says it was this attack that prompted the king to order the killing of the French prisoners. Contemporary accounts say nothing about the killing of those guarding the baggage train. The first mention of the killing occurs in Polydore Vergil's 1513 *Anglica Historia,* which speaks of those guarding the baggage but not the boys. Shakespeare's account makes the French appear more villainous, makes Henry's killing of his prisoners seem perhaps more justified, and highlights the horrors of war.

The French remain in the field. Henry orders his herald to tell them to withdraw or fight. Otherwise, he will kill his prisoners. Shakespeare thus presents three versions of the fate of the French who were captured: killed because Henry feared a counterattack (4.6), killed because Henry is angry about the killing of the boys guarding the luggage (4.7), or not killed (4.7). Historically, the French who could be held for ransom were taken back to England after the battle, but Henry, in fact, killed most of his prisoners because he feared a renewed French attack.

Despite his promise that Henry would never hear from a herald again, Mountjoy reappears to ask permission for the French to bury their dead.

Scene 4.8: The king resolves his dispute with Williams. A herald reports on the French casualties (10,000) and those of the English (about 25). Actual figures are impossible to determine, but the French lost at least 1,500, perhaps as many as 11,000; the English, about 100 men. Henry prepares to return to England.

Scene 5.1: Although the Chorus before act 5 reports on Henry's return to England (November 16, 1415) and "back return again to France" in 1417 (l. 41) and scene 5.2 occurs in 1420, this scene seems to be set still in the English camp shortly after the battle. Pistol insults the Welsh Fluellen, who beats him and forces him to eat a leek, a Welsh symbol. As the scene ends, Pistol reports the death of his wife. He plans to return to England to resume his life of crime. Elizabeth made no provision for veterans returning from her wars in Ireland and the Continent, many of whom would have turned to crime like Pistol.

Harfleur, Normandy

Harfleur was the principal seaport in northwestern France until the sixteenth century, when Le Havre was built three miles away. The Romans used the site as a harbor, which they named Caracotinum. After the Battle of Agincourt, Henry V built a Gothic church here as a thanksgiving offering. Edward the Black Prince captured the town in 1346, as did Henry V in 1415.

Scenes 3.1–3.3: The English besiege Harfleur (August 18–Septeber 22, 1415), which surrenders after fierce fighting. In the play Henry urges his uncle Exeter to treat the inhabitants kindly. Holinshed reports the town was sacked. Historically, Henry allowed those who swore allegiance to him to remain. Those who refused were forced to leave the town. Henry lost between a quarter and a third of his men to dysentery during the siege, the same disease that would kill him in 1422. Henry left Harfleur on October 8, 1415, for Calais.

Paris

The Louvre

Rue de Rivoli [Paris metro stop: Louvre]

Originally a fortress built by Philip II in the twelfth century, in the fourteenth century, Charles V converted it into a residence. Under Louis XIV, who lived at Versailles, the Louvre became a home for artists. On August 10, 1793, the one-year anniversary of the execution of Louis XVI, it opened as a public museum, and so it remains.

Scene 2.4: Charles VI, king of France, prepares for the English invasion. Charles, in fact, was mad; Louis, the dauphin, organized the French defense. The Duke of Exeter arrives to demand Charles surrender his throne or face war. Exeter conveys Henry's contempt for the dauphin.

Picardy

Located in northwest France, the region includes the port of Calais, which Henry was trying to reach with his army after the siege of Harfleur ended. Louis XI added Picardy to France in 1477 after defeating Charles of Burgundy at Nancy; the dukes of Burgundy had ruled Picardy since the early fifteenth century.

Scene 3.6: The English defeat a French force trying to destroy a bridge over the Ternoise near Blangy to block the English march to Calais (October 24, 1415). Bardolph, a former companion of Henry V during his tavern days, has stolen a pyx (a box containing holy wafers) or a pax (a piece of metal with the image of the crucifix stamped on it) from a church despite the king's order not to loot. Pistol pleads with the Welsh captain Fluellen to intercede for Bardolph with the Duke of Exeter, but Fluellen refuses to help, thus prompting Pistol's later argument with the Welshman. When Henry V arrives, Fluellen tells him Bardolph is about to be executed, but Henry does not save his old friend. Fluellen may be based on the Welsh soldier Sir Roger Williams, who served under the Earl of Essex and wrote a treatise on warfare, *A Briefe Discourse of Warre* (1590).

The French herald Mountjoy appears and demands ransom. Henry tells him he would prefer to proceed to Calais peacefully, but if the French try to prevent him, he will fight. Henry refuses to pay any ransom.

Rouen

Capital of Normandy in northern France, located on the River Seine; it was the Ratumacos of the Gauls and Rotomagus of the Romans. Henry V captured the city in 1419, and it served as the seat of English power in France until Charles VII took Rouen in 1449.

Rouen Castle

Built by Philip II between 1204 and 1210, it served as the administrative center for Normandy during the Middle Ages. Joan of Arc was imprisoned there. The Tour Jeanne d'Arc (the keep) remains. The rest of the castle was destroyed in 1591.

Scene 3.4: Katherine of Valois, daughter of Charles VI, asks her maid, Alice, to teach her English because Alice has spent time in England. The lesson is confined to parts of the body and provides comic relief through Katherine's sometimes-bawdy mispronunciations. This scene, placed at the center of the play, shows the triumph of the English over the French language and presages the English victory that will require Katherine, as Henry's queen, to learn his language.

Scene 3.5: Charles VI orders his nobles to attack Henry V and dispatches the herald Mountjoy to demand ransom from the English king.

Troyes

The Roman Augustobona Tricassium, Troyes is located on the River Seine, ninety-three miles southeast of Paris in the Champagne region of France. It served as the capital of the province of Champagne from the end of the ninth century until the French Revolution. It was an important medieval trading center, giving its name to troy weight. There are twelve ounces to a troy pound; precious metals and gems are measured in troy weight. At the time of the Treaty of Troyes (May 21, 1420), Troyes was held by the Burgundians, who were allied to England. The treaty betrothed Henry V to Katherine, daughter of Charles VI (they married at Troyes Cathedral on June 2, 1420), and made Henry V heir to the throne of France.

Scene 5.2: The Treaty of Troyes is concluded, ending the play. Shakespeare omits the fighting between France and England in the five years between the Battle of Agincourt and the conclusion of the treaty. Also, Shakespeare has Henry V meet Katherine for the first time at Troyes. In fact, he first saw her at the Conference of Melun (May 29–30, 1419). An epilogue notes that, after Henry V's death in 1422, his son Henry VI would lose all of Henry V's French gains, and England would suffer civil war, as depicted in Shakespeare's first tetralogy (*1*, *2*, and *3 Henry VI* and *Richard III*). The epilogue thus suggests all the fighting and killing in the play was pointless.

Henry VIII

ENGLAND

Kimbolton Castle, Huntingdonshire

Originally a medieval castle, it was rebuilt as a Tudor manor house by the Wingfield family. In April 1534 Queen Katherine was sent here, and she died at the castle on January 7, 1536. Sir Henry Montagu bought the castle in 1615; it remained in his family until 1950. They made extensive renovations to the building. In 1950 it was bought by Kimbolton School, which still owns it. During school holidays and weekends, there is limited public access to the building.

Scene 4.2: Griffin recounts the death of Cardinal Wolsey (November 29, 1530) at Leicester. As Katherine sleeps she has a vision of six white-robed figures wearing garlands of bay leaves and golden masks. They carry branches of bay or palms in their hands. They dance. Two by two they hold a garland over Katherine's head. Eustace Chapuys, ambassador of Emperor Charles V, arrives with greetings from Henry. She gives him a letter asking the king to care for their daughter, Mary, and her ladies-in-waiting and to pay the wages of the men who attended her. She dies.

London

Blackfriars

[Underground stop: Blackfriars]

The theater takes its name from the Dominican priory, founded in 1276, that occupied this location until the dissolution of the monasteries under Henry VIII. The Dominicans wore black robes that gave them their nickname. In 1529 a court met here to hear Henry VIII's divorce case against Catherine of Aragon (the king's "great matter"), and in November of that year, Parliament met here to bring a Bill of Attainder against Cardinal Thomas Wolsey (who had failed to get Henry the divorce he wanted).

In 1538 the monastery was dissolved. Most of the buildings were demolished, but in 1556–1584 and again in 1597–1642, the refectory was used as a theater. The Children of the Chapel performed here (1577–1584 and 1600–1608). In 1596 James Burbage bought this location for six hundred pounds to serve as an indoor venue for the Lord Chamberlain's Men (Shakespeare's company), since the Theatre (see "The Theatre" under "London" in appendix A) was open to the air. Hence, the Theatre was cold in the winter and relied on natural lighting. Local residents objected to an adult acting company using this space—theaters attracted prostitutes and pickpockets, as well as crowds blocking the streets. Their petition stated, "A common playhouse . . . will grow to be a very great annoyance and trouble, not only to all noblemen and gentlemen near thereabout inhabiting, but also a general inconvenience to all the inhabitants of the same precinct, by reason of the gathering together of all manner of lewd and vagrant persons." They also objected to the noise. Among those who signed the petition was George Carey, Second Lord Hunsdon, who would soon become Lord Chamberlain, the licenser of plays and patron of Shakespeare's company. Richard Field, Shakespeare's friend from Stratford who published *Venus and Adonis* and printed *The Rape of Lucrece*, also signed. The Children of the Chapel, a boys' acting company, were allowed to use the Blackfriars Theatre from 1600 to 1608, when the King's Men (formerly Lord Chamberlain's Men) were given permission to perform here. The boys' company had offended the French ambassador with their production of George Chapman's *The Conspiracy and Tragedy of Charles, Duke of Byron* (1608). As a result, the boys' company was suppressed. The King's Men continued to perform here until the Puritans closed the theaters in 1642.

This theater was sixty-six feet long and forty-six feet wide, with two or three galleries. The seating capacity was six hundred to one thousand. Prices began at sixpence, six times the cost of a place to stand in the pit of an open-air theater like the Globe. According to one account, the King's Men "got, and yet doth, more in one winter in the said great hall by a thousand pounds than they were used to get on the Bankside" (i.e., at the Globe). Neighbors still objected to the crowds the theater drew, complaining, "Inhabitants cannot come to their houses, nor bring in their necessary provisions of beer, wood, coal or hay, nor the tradesmen or shopkeepers utter their wares, nor the passengers go to the common water stairs without danger of their lives and limbs."

Because the stage used artificial lighting, actors could achieve more special effects, and because the higher ticket prices attracted a more educated audience, plays performed here could be more sophisticated. Because the candles had to be trimmed, music was played between acts. The five-act structure of plays may have resulted from this need to trim candles periodically during performances. The new Globe Theatre (see "The Globe Theatre" under "London" in appendix A) now includes an indoor acting space (Sam Wanamaker Theatre) that replicates the experience of seeing a play at the Blackfriars. The Sam Wanamaker Theatre is smaller than the Blackfriars and, unlike the Globe, does not try to reconstruct the earlier acting space. But productions are lit exclusively with candles, and audiences sit on backless benches.

On March 10, 1613, Shakespeare bought Blackfriars' Gatehouse in Ireland Yard for 140 pounds. Henry Walker had bought the gatehouse from Matthew Bacon in 1604, and Walker sold it to Shakespeare. The gatehouse had connections to Catholic missionaries and to Catholic members of the Gunpowder Plot, who sought refuge here after the plot failed. (See *The Times* [London], April 23, 1928, p. 15) Shakespeare rented the gatehouse to John Robinson, who lived here until 1639. Robinson's brother Edward studied at the Catholic seminary of the English College in Rome. The refectory was torn down on August 6, 1655, and the Great Fire of London (1666) destroyed the remains of the monastery, except for part of a wall that survives in Ireland Yard. Playhouse Yard stands at the site of the former theater.

Scene 2.4: Katherine's divorce hearing was held on June 18, 1529. When *Henry VIII* was staged at Blackfriars Theatre, the scene was played exactly where the hearing had occurred. Katherine pleads eloquently. She rejects Wolsey as a judge, blaming him for the rift between her and Henry, and appeals to the pope for judgment. The king praises Katherine and exonerates Wolsey. Henry explains that his scruples about the validity of his marriage to Katherine first arose when he was negotiating a marriage contract between their daughter Mary, when she was two years old, and the dauphin (later Henry II), son of Francis I of France (1518). The French ambassador, the Bishop of Bayonne, questioned Mary's legitimacy because Katherine had been married to Henry's brother, Arthur, before she married Henry. Henry claims that, if the hearing determines his marriage to Katherine is lawful, then he will remain with her. Cardinal Campeius says, because Katherine has left the court, the hearing must adjourn.

Church of the Observant Friars, Greenwich

The church was located near the Palace of Placentia. Nothing of the church remains.

Scene 5.4: At her christening, Cranmer predicts greatness for Queen Elizabeth and her successor, James I, who was reigning when the play was written and first performed.

Palace of Placentia, Greenwich
Greenwich Park [Train stations: Greenwich, Mars Hill]

Humphrey, Duke of Gloucester, began his palace in 1428 and completed construction in 1443. Henry VI and Queen Margaret honeymooned here in 1445. The duke assembled an extensive library, which he bequeathed to Oxford University. The palace was named Bella Court; later Queen Margaret, who seized the property after the duke's arrest and death in 1447, called it Palace of Placentia or Palace of Pleasaunce.

Henry VII rebuilt the palace between 1498 and 1504, and it remained a royal residence for the next two hundred years. Henry VIII, Queen Mary, and Queen Elizabeth were all born here. It was Henry VIII's favorite residence, and Queen Elizabeth liked to summer here. During the visit of James I's brother-in-law Christian IV of Denmark in the summer of 1606, the King's Men performed for him here twice, and in June 1613 Shakespeare and John Fletcher's lost play *Cardenio* was staged here for the ambassador of the Duke of Savoy. Charles II sought to rebuild the palace after it had fallen into disrepair during the English Civil War, and he completed King Charles Court. Most of the palace was demolished to make room for Greenwich Hospital. The two hundred acres enclosed by the duke became Greenwich Park.

Scene 1.1: In an antechamber of the palace, Edward Stafford, Third Duke of Buckingham; Thomas Howard, Third Duke of Norfolk; and Lord Aburgavenny (George Neville, Third Baron Bergavenny) discuss the meeting between Henry VIII and Francis I of France at the Field of the Cloth of Gold in June 1520. They then talk about the pride and power of Cardinal Thomas Wolsey. Buckingham intends to denounce Wolsey to the king, but before he can do so, Brandon (not to be confused with Charles Brandon, First Duke of Suffolk, also in this play) and a sergeant-at-arms arrest Buckingham (April 1521), acting under Wolsey's orders. According to Raphael Holinshed's *Chronicles*, the arresting officer was Henry Marney, First Baron Marney, captain of the king's guard. He was acting under the king's order.

Elise Lathrop, in *Where Shakespeare Set His Stage* (1906), suggests the palace scenes in acts 1–3 occur at Bridewell Palace, London, which was one of Henry's chief London residences in the period 1515–1523. Henry built the palace on the site of St. Bride's Inn near St. Bride's Church in what is now Bridewell Court. The papal delegates who came to London in 1528 to consider Henry's divorce met here. The French ambassador lived here in 1531–1539; it is the setting for Holbein's painting *The Ambassadors* (1533). Edward VI gave the palace to the city of London to house homeless children and also for a facility to "correct" wayward women. Much of the building was destroyed in the 1666 Great Fire of London. It was rebuilt to serve as a prison, which closed in 1855. In William Hogarth's *A Harlot's Progress* (painted 1731, engraved 1732), the prostitute Moll Hackabout ends up in Bridewell Prison. The buildings were demolished in 1863–1864.

Scene 1.2: Henry VIII enters the Council Chamber leaning on Cardinal Wolsey's shoulder, an image showing the king's dependence on the cardinal, who is also Lord Chancellor of England. The king thanks Wolsey for uncovering Buckingham's plot against him. Historically, the king himself investigated Buckingham. Thomas More claimed the charge of treason against Buckingham was based on evidence extracted under torture.

Queen Katherine enters to petition the king to remit taxes Wolsey has levied to finance the king's war against France (1525). This was the Amicable Grant, a forced loan, levied by Wolsey without parliamentary approval. Henry is unaware of these taxes in the play, though resistance was so widespread that he must have known of them after they were levied, if not before. Popular resistance, not Katherine's intervention (which Holinshed does not mention), led to the canceling of this grant. The scene shows Katherine as compassionate and Wolsey as unsympathetic. Wolsey first denies his role in the levying of these taxes and then defends them. When the king orders them revoked, Wolsey tells his secretary to claim he is the one responsible for their cancellation.

Though scene 1.2 occurs four years after Buckingham's execution in May 1521, the duke's surveyor Charles Knevet, whom Buckingham had dismissed, enters and repeats his denunciation of his former employer. The duke is not convicted until scene 2.1.

Scene 1.3: The Lord Chamberlain (William FitzAlan, Eighteenth Earl of Arundel and Eighth Baron Maltravers), Lord William Sands (who was actually still Sir William Sands), and Sir Thomas Lovell discuss the banning of French fashions and Cardinal Wolsey's upcoming banquet, which occurred on January 3, 1527.

Scene 2.2: The Lord Chamberlain and the Dukes of Norfolk and Suffolk criticize Cardinal Wolsey. Norfolk blames Wolsey for Henry's decision to divorce Katherine, but Suffolk recognizes Henry wants to marry Anne Boleyn. Wolsey and Cardinal Campeius, the papal legate sent to adjudicate Henry's request for a divorce, visit the king, who decides to hold the divorce hearing at Blackfriars.

Scene 2.3: In the queen's apartments, an old lady and Anne Boleyn, who was one of Katherine's ladies-in-waiting, lament Katherine's fate. When Anne says she does not want to be queen, the old lady says she herself does. She says she would venture her virginity for a crown and adds Anne would, too. The Lord Chamberlain enters to say the king has named Anne Marchioness of Pembroke and given her one hundred pounds a year. According to Holinshed, Henry gave her the title at Windsor on September 1, 1532.

Scene 3.1: Cardinals Wolsey and Campeius visit Katherine in her apartments and ask her to let the king decide her case. She refuses.

Scene 3.2: The Dukes of Norfolk and Suffolk, the Earl of Surrey, and the Lord Chamberlain discuss Wolsey. Suffolk says the king discovered letters from Wolsey to the pope opposing the divorce. Wolsey, in fact, never wrote such letters. The Lord Chamberlain claims Henry has already married Anne Boleyn. The wedding occurred about January 25, 1533. Shakespeare places this marriage before Wolsey's fall in 1529 and before Henry divorced Katherine. James I, king of England when this play was produced, had no reason to love Elizabeth (Anne Boleyn's daughter), who was responsible, however reluctantly, for the execution of his mother, Mary, Queen of Scots. The play treats Katherine sympathetically, Anne Boleyn less so, and Henry's marriage to Anne as perhaps bigamous and hence illegal.

Supposedly, among state papers Wolsey sent Henry is an inventory of the cardinal's great wealth. The king hands Wolsey this list, as well as his letter to the pope opposing the king's divorce, and then departs with his nobles. The Dukes of Norfolk and Suffolk, the Earl of Surrey, and the Lord Chamberlain return, and Norfolk demands Wolsey's Great Seal, which he kept as Lord Chancellor. He also commands Wolsey to move to Asher House near Hampton Court. Wolsey demands to see their commission in writing, which Norfolk does not have. Suffolk accuses Wolsey of the judicial murder of his father-in-law Buckingham, a charge Wolsey denies.

Surrey and Suffolk present a list of charges against Wolsey and demand he surrender all his goods and properties. Thomas Cromwell enters and informs Wolsey that Sir Thomas More has been named Lord Chancellor (October 1529), Thomas Cranmer has been made Archbishop of Canterbury (October 1, 1532), and Anne Boleyn is to be crowned queen (May 29, 1533). Wolsey tells Cromwell to leave him and serve Henry. Cromwell would serve as Henry's principal secretary and chief minister from 1534 to 1540.

Scene 5.1: Stephen Gardiner denounces Thomas Cromwell, Thomas Cranmer, and Anne Boleyn. After Gardiner leaves, the king enters with the Duke of Suffolk. Sir Anthony Denny brings Cranmer to the king. Henry warns Cranmer of powerful enemies and gives him a ring to show his accusers at the upcoming council meeting. Henry tells Cranmer to appeal to the king for judgment. An old lady enters to announce the birth of Anne and Henry's daughter, Elizabeth (born at the Palace of Placentia, Greenwich, September 7, 1533).

Scene 5.2: As Henry and his physician, Dr. William Butts, unseen, watch a council meeting, Stephen Gardiner denounces Cranmer as a schismatic and orders him to the tower (c. 1544). When Thomas Cromwell defends Cranmer, Gardiner denounces him as religiously unsound, as well. (Cromwell was executed in 1540.) As guards arrive to take Cranmer to the tower, Cranmer shows the king's ring and appeals to the king for judgment. The king enters and defends Cranmer and then asks him to be Elizabeth's godfather.

Scene 5.3: A crowd gathers in the palace yard for Elizabeth's christening (September 10, 1533).

Palace of Westminster
North bank of the Thames [Underground stop: Westminster]

Originally built for Edward the Confessor, the Palace of Westminster served as a royal residence until Henry VIII made Whitehall Palace his chief residence in 1512 after the Palace of Westminster was damaged by fire. It has also been the meeting place of Parliament since the thirteenth century. In 1834 a fire destroyed most of the building. Only St. Mary Undercroft (the crypt under St. Stephen's Chapel), Westminster Hall (dating from 1097), the Cloisters, and the Jewel Tower (1365) survived. The current Gothic building was designed by Sir Charles Barry and Augustus Pugin. Construction began in 1837. Most of the restoration was completed by 1860, though work continued until 1870. The House of Commons was destroyed in the Blitz of 1940–1941; it was restored by Sir Giles Gilbert Scott after World War II during the period 1945–1950.

Scene 2.1: Outside Westminster Hall two gentlemen discuss the trial of the Duke of Buckingham (April 1521). In the midst of their conversation, Buckingham enters, accompanied by Sir Thomas Lovell, Sir Nicholas Vaux, Sir Walter Sands, bailiffs, and commoners. The duke protests his innocence. After he departs the gentlemen discuss Henry's desire for a divorce from Katherine. The second gentleman blames Wolsey and tells the first that Cardinal Lorenzo Campeius has come from Rome about this matter (October 1528). The first gentleman says Wolsey promoted the divorce to be revenged on Katherine's nephew, the Holy Roman emperor and king of Spain, for not making him Archbishop of Toledo. This scene includes events that occurred seven years apart.

Palace of Whitehall (Former York Palace)
Whitehall [Underground stops: Charing Cross, Embankment, Westminster]

Hubert de Burgh had a palace here during the reign of Henry II. He gave it to the Blackfriars in 1240, who sold it to Walter de Grey, Archbishop of York. Walter de Grey gave this house to the See of York to serve as the official London residence of the Archbishop of York. Between 1514 and 1529, Cardinal Thomas Wolsey enlarged the building, creating a Great Hall in 1528. After Wolsey's fall in 1529, Henry took over the house and renamed it Whitehall, as Shakespeare writes in *Henry VIII*, 4.1.95–97:

> You must no more call it York Place; that's past.
> For since the cardinal fell, that title's lost;
> 'Tis now the king's, and called Whitehall.

Henry preferred this house to the Palace of Westminster. (Hampton Court was another Wolsey house Henry seized when the cardinal fell, and Cardinal College, Oxford, was renamed Henry VIII's College. It is now Christ Church College.) Henry continued the rebuilding process, adding Whitehall Gate (1531–1532) and steps leading to the river, along with gardens and orchards, a tilting yard, a bowling green, and an indoor tennis court. He married Anne Boleyn here in 1533 and Jane Seymour here in 1536. Henry died at the Palace of Whitehall in 1547. For a time it was the largest palace in Europe, with 1,500 rooms. The 1591 Ralph Agas map of London shows Whitehall linked by two arches over King's Street to St. James's Park.

During Elizabeth's and James I's reigns, the Great Hall was used for theatrical performances. Shakespeare would have acted here in some of his own plays. On November 1, 1604, *Othello* was staged here, and during this season so were *The Merry Wives
of Windsor* and *Measure for Measure*. *King Lear* was performed here on December 26,
1606. In February 1613, to celebrate the wedding of James's daughter Princess Elizabeth to Prince Frederick, Elector of the Palatine, the King's Men staged fourteen plays
here, including the lost *Cardenio*. Some of Ben Jonson's masques were also staged at
Whitehall. While the Banqueting Hall was the usual place of performance, James I
also used the Cockpit, which Charles I in 1632 converted into a little theater designed
by Inigo Jones.

James I planned further renovations, but only the Banqueting House was built.
Completed in 1622, it was designed by Inigo Jones and was the first Palladian building in London. Charles I commissioned Peter Paul Rubens to paint the ceiling, which
Rubens never saw, though he painted the canvases, installed in 1636, depicting the
union of the Crowns of England and Scotland, the peaceful reign of James I, and James
I's apotheosis. The ceiling was one of the last things Charles I saw as he was led to his
execution outside the Banqueting Hall on January 30, 1649.

Charles II occupied Whitehall after his restoration, along with his mistresses Bar-
bara Castlemain and the Duchess of Portsmouth (Louise Renée de Penancoët de Kér-
ouaille), as well as his wife, Queen Catherine of Braganza. Charles died here in 1685.
William and Mary were offered the joint monarchy of Britain at the Banqueting Hall
on February 13, 1689. William found the palace's proximity to the Thames bad for his
asthma. The palace was damaged by fire on April 10,1691, an event perhaps recalled
in book 1 of Jonathan Swift's *Gulliver's Travels* when the Palace at Lilliput catches fire
(chapter 5; the reference might be to the 1698 fire). Christopher Wren added a terrace, but on January 4, 1698, the palace again burned; the Banqueting House survived,
along with a few other buildings, later incorporated into government offices, as well
as the Holbein Gate (demolished 1769). Wren converted the Banqueting Hall into
the Chapel Royal, which in 1809 became the Chapel of the Horse Guards. From 1829
to 1890, it reverted to be the Chapel Royal before becoming a museum for the Royal
United Services Institute. Since 1963 it has been open to the public.

Scene 1.4: At Cardinal Wolsey's banquet (January 3, 1527), Henry VIII and his
companions enter dressed as foreign shepherds who do not speak English. Henry
liked to disguise himself and then unmask to surprise guests, as he does here. Henry
dances and falls in love with Anne Boleyn. Lady Antonia Fraser in *The Wives of Henry
VIII* (1992) suggests Henry fell in love with Anne during Shrovetide 1526. Some years
earlier Henry had had an affair with Anne's sister, Mary Boleyn. Mary then married
William Carey, a gentleman of Henry's Privy Council. Their son Henry Carey became

Lord Hunsdon under his cousin Queen Elizabeth and her Lord Chamberlain; he was the patron of Shakespeare's acting company.

As noted under "The Globe Theatre" under "London" in appendix A, the firing of cannon preceding Henry VIII's entrance in this scene caused the fire that burned down the first Globe in 1613.

Westminster Abbey
Broad Sanctuary [Underground stops: St. James Park, Westminster]
Edward the Confessor began a new Benedictine abbey on Thorney Island in 1050. The church was consecrated on December 28, 1065; Edward died eight days later. On Christmas Day 1066, William the Conqueror was crowned king of England here, and all subsequent English monarchs have been crowned here, as well (except Edward V and Edward VIII, neither of whom had a coronation ceremony).

A new church was begun by Henry III in 1245. Nothing remains aboveground of Edward the Confessor's cruciform church. The new church, with the tallest nave in England (103 feet high), is modeled on the cathedrals of Rheims and Amiens and on the Sainte-Chapelle in Paris. It is the most French of any English church, though it has English features, such as the single aisle in the nave. In 1269 Edward the Confessor's body was placed in a new shrine in the abbey. It was a popular pilgrimage site until the Reformation. The towers at the west end date from the eighteenth century.

Oliver Cromwell used the church as barracks for his soldiers. Over the past several centuries, the abbey has become Britain's pantheon. Among those buried in Poets' Corner are Shakespeare's contemporaries Ben Jonson, Michael Drayton, and Francis Beaumont. William Davenant, another playwright who claimed to be Shakespeare's son, is also interred here. While there is a life-size white marble statue of Shakespeare here dating from 1740, he is buried in Holy Trinity Church, Stratford-upon-Avon (see "Holy Trinity Church" under "Stratford-upon-Avon" in appendix A).

Scene 4.1: Outside Westminster Abbey two gentlemen wait for Anne Boleyn to return from her coronation. The second gentleman notes that Archbishop Cranmer has voided Henry's marriage to Katherine (May 23, 1533), who has been sent to Kimbolton Castle in Huntingdonshire. As noted previously, Katherine was sent to Kimbolton Castle in April 1534; in May 1533 she was living at Ampthill Castle, Bedfordshire. Queen Anne and her attendants appear with great pageantry. A third gentleman, who has attended the coronation, describes the event. All three gentlemen discuss the rivalry between Thomas Cranmer and Stephen Gardiner, Bishop of Winchester.

Edward III

London

Palace of Westminster
North bank of the Thames [Underground stop: Westminster]

Originally built for Edward the Confessor, the Palace of Westminster served as a royal residence until Henry VIII made Whitehall Palace his chief residence in 1512 after the Palace of Westminster was damaged by fire. It has also been the meeting place of Parliament since the thirteenth century. In 1834 a fire destroyed most of the building. Only St. Mary Undercroft (the crypt under St. Stephen's Chapel), Westminster Hall (dating from 1097), the Cloisters, and the Jewel Tower (1365) survived. The current Gothic building was designed by Sir Charles Barry and Augustus Pugin. Construction began in 1837. Most of the restoration was completed by 1860, though work continued until 1870. The House of Commons was destroyed in the Blitz of 1940–1941; it was restored by Sir Giles Gilbert Scott after World War II during the period 1945–1950.

Scene 1.1: Edward III, son of Isabella, the daughter of Philip IV of France, claims the throne of France through his mother because Philip's son Charles IV died without issue. But John (actually Philip VI of Valois) has been made king because the Salic Law of France does not allow inheritance of the crown through the female line. This same argument is used later against Henry V (*Henry V*, 1.2). The Duke of Lorraine arrives to demand homage from Edward III for holding the dukedom of Guyenne. In fact, Philip sent the Abbot of Fécamp, Pierre Roger, to demand Edward III of England pay homage for the dukedoms of Aquitaine and Gascony. Historically, Edward III agreed, but in the play Edward responds by claiming the throne of France. Lorraine and Edward defy each other. After Lorraine leaves, Sir William Montague enters to say the Scots have taken Berwick and Newcastle and are besieging Roxburghe Castle, where Catherine Grandison, Countess of Salisbury, is living. She was actually living at Wark Castle in Northumberland. Shakespeare makes her the daughter of the Tenth Earl of Warwick (Guy de Beauchamp), though her father was William de Grandison, First Baron Grandison. Edward sends his son Prince Edward, together with Audley, to raise troops for the war with France, while he will go with his current force to repel the Scots.

FRANCE

Brittany

In northwest coastal France. The Roman Armorica, the province took its name from settlers from Britain circa 419 CE. When Henry II's son Geoffrey married Constance, daughter of a claimant to the duchy, Brittany became a Plantagenet possession. Brittany did not become part of France until 1532. During the Hundred Years' War, it was an independent duchy with a shifting foreign policy.

Scene 4.1: The Earl of Salisbury promises his prisoner Villiers freedom if Villiers will secure him a promise of safe passage from the Duke of Normandy.

Calais

A major French port on the English Channel. Edward III besieged Calais from September 4, 1346, to August 3, 1347, when the city surrendered. It remained under English control until 1558. It was called the "brightest jewel in the English crown." When it fell to France, Queen Mary of England declared, "When I am dead and opened, you shall find 'Philip' [Philip of Spain, her husband] and 'Calais' lying in my heart."

Scene 4.2: As Edward III prepares to besiege Calais, Lord Percy arrives with news that Queen Philippa's forces have captured King David II of Scotland. David II was captured by Sir John de Coupland at the Battle of Neville's Cross on October 17, 1346. Calais surrenders. Because the city resisted, Edward offers clemency only if six burghers will come to him in their shirts, with halters around their necks, and prostrate themselves before him. Auguste Rodin created a sculpture commemorating this event (1884–1889).

Scene 5.1: Six burghers of Calais appear in their shirts, with halters around their necks. King Edward intends to assault the city, but the burghers plead for mercy. The king agrees to spare the city but wants to hang the burghers. Queen Philippa pleads for them, and Edward yields to her entreaties. This episode indeed occurred as Shakespeare describes it, though it happened a decade before the Battle of Poitiers already depicted in scenes 4.6–9. John Copeland (Sir John de Coupland) arrives with King David, having refused to surrender the Scottish king to Queen Philippa. The queen is angry with Copeland, but Edward asks her to pardon him. While this incident makes a nice parallel with the queen's intercession for the burghers, it never actually happened. David remained a prisoner in England. Edward knights John (who was already a knight) and promises him and his heirs 550 marks (roughly 330 pounds) a year.

Salisbury arrives to report what he thinks is the French victory at Poitiers, but a herald enters with the news of the English success. Prince Edward comes with King John and Prince Philip. As the play ends, Edward III plans to return to England with his royal prisoners.

Crécy

Crécy-en-Ponthieu, Hauts-de France, in northern France, south of Calais.

Scene 3.2: French civilians flee the English army.

Scene 3.3: Prince Edward joins his father and reports the capture or destruction of various French cities. He says the French army has withdrawn to Crécy. King John tries to bribe Edward to leave France. Edward in turn asks him to surrender his crown. As each side prepares for battle, Edward places his son at the head of his army.

Scene 3.4: The English defeat the French at the Battle of Crécy (August 26, 1346).

Scene 3.5: Artois, Derby, and Audley urge Edward to rescue his son, who is beset by French soldiers. The king refuses. The prince returns safely with the body of the king of Bohemia. The English under Prince Edward prepare to move to Poitiers, while King Edward will besiege Calais. The Battle of Poitiers occurred a decade after Crécy, but Shakespeare telescopes time for dramatic effect.

Flanders

Scene 3.1: The king of France, his sons Charles and Philip, and the Duke of Lorraine watch a naval engagement between English and French ships. The French expect to win, but they lose. This is probably the naval Battle of Sluys (June 24, 1340), in which the French fleet was almost completely destroyed.

The king of Bohemia, Danish soldiers, and a Polish captain come to reinforce the French army.

Poitiers

Located on the Clain River, Poitiers is the capital of the Vienne *département* in west-central France. It was a major Roman settlement, with a large amphitheater and at least three aqueducts. Here Clovis defeated Alaric in 507, Charles Martel defeated the Saracens in 732, and Edward the Black Prince defeated Jean II of France in 1356. When English forces occupied Paris during the Hundred Years' War, the French royal parliament met at Poitiers (1418–1436). Joan of Arc was examined here by the French for three weeks in March and April 1429 in the chapel attached to the palace of the

Counts of Poitou under the direction of the Archbishop of Reims before she was allowed to try to save the country.

Scene 4.3: After some hesitation, Charles, Duke of Normandy, gives Villiers a passport for the Earl of Salisbury. Villiers departs. King John II of France claims he has trapped Prince Edward.

Scene 4.4: A French herald asks for a hundred English prisoners and the Prince of Wales to be held for ransom to avoid a battle. Though outnumbered (6,000 to about 11,000), Edward refuses the herald's demand. Another herald urges Prince Edward to flee. Prince Edward again refuses. A third herald brings Prince Edward a prayer book from Prince Philip of France for Edward to meditate on because his death is at hand. Edward returns the book, saying Philip may need it. This episode with the heralds resembles the French herald's repeated visits in *Henry V.*

Historically, the English and French negotiated before the battle. The English offered to restore all the booty they had taken during their raids in France and to agree to a seven-year truce. Confident of victory, King John II, who came to the throne in 1350, unwisely rejected these terms.

Scene 4.5: The French capture the Earl of Salisbury. King John wants to hang him despite the safe-conduct pass issued by the king's son. Charles protests, and John agrees to let Salisbury go to Calais to report to Edward III what John expects to be a French victory.

Scenes 4.6–4.9: The Battle of Poitiers. On September 19, 1356, at Nouaillé, the French and English armies clash. King John, his son Charles, and Prince Philip are captured.

SCOTLAND

Roxburghshire

Roxburghe Castle

Located in the Border region between England and Scotland at the junction of the Tweed and Teviot Rivers in what is now southeastern Scotland, the castle was built by King David I of Scotland before about 1128. It was surrendered to the English in 1174. The Scots tried repeatedly to retake the castle. Sir James Douglas captured it in 1314, and the Scots began demolishing it. In 1334 it served as Edward III's base in his war against the Scots. In 1460 the Scots again captured it, though James II was killed in the process. His queen, Mary of Guelders, had the castle destroyed. The ruins (mainly a mound, with a little stonework) sit on the grounds of Floors Castle, seat of the Duke of Roxburghe.

Scene 1.2: King David II of Scotland promises Lorraine to help France in its war with England. After Lorraine leaves, a Scot announces Edward III and his army are approaching. The Scots decamp. Edward arrives, sees the Countess of Salisbury, and falls in love with her. He wants to pursue the Scots, but when she urges him to stay at the castle, he agrees.

Scene 2.1: Lodowick notes the king's love for the countess. Edward asks him to write a love poem praising the lady and expressing the king's love. When Lodowick reads what he has written, the king objects. The countess enters, and Edward tells her he loves her. She rejects him. Edward now asks her father (Warwick in the play) to command her to become the king's lover. Warwick pleads with her for the king, but she still refuses him, and Warwick commends her for doing so.

Scene 2.2: Audley arrives with soldiers he has raised for the French war. Derby reports the emperor of Germany has agreed to support Edward. But the king can think only of love. When Prince Edward arrives, the king sees in him the image of his wife, Philippa of Hainault. He resolves to abandon his pursuit of the countess and to conquer France. When Lodowick announces the countess's approach, Edward's infatuation returns. She says she'll be his lover if he kills his queen and her husband. Edward agrees to the murders. The countess says she will kill herself if he does not give up his suit, and Edward yields.

COMEDIES

The Comedy of Errors

TURKEY

Ephesus

Ephesus, in present-day Turkey, was settled by Greek colonists in the tenth century BCE on the site of the former capital of Arzawa. It was an important port on the Aegean Sea until the harbor silted up. Today the old harbor is three miles inland. It came under Roman rule in 129 BCE. The Temple of Artemis (Diana) here was one of the seven wonders of the ancient world, and it figures in the final act of this play. The temple was rebuilt three times before an earthquake destroyed the last structure on the site in 401 CE. Augustus made Ephesus the capital of proconsular Asia. Strabo described Ephesus as second only to Rome in size and importance.

Ephesus became an important center of early Christianity. Paul lived here in 52–54 CE and later wrote his Epistles of the Ephesians while imprisoned in Rome (62 CE). The Gospel of John may have been written here (c. 90–100 CE), and it is one the seven cities addressed in the Book of Revelation. A legend claims Jesus's mother spent her last years here. The aged Emilia's living in the Temple of Diana in the play may draw on this account.

Shakespeare's play is based on Plautus's *Menaechmi*, which is set in Epidamnus (modern Durrës in Albania), a Greek city founded in 627 BCE. References to this city remain in Shakespeare's play, where it is called Epidamnum. Egeus and his family are shipwrecked a "league from Epidamnum" (1.1.65). A merchant warns Antipholus of Syracuse to say he is from Epidamnum (1.2.1). Dromio of Syracuse secures passage for his master and himself on a ship "of Epidamnum" (4.1.85), and Aemilia, Antipholus of Ephesus, and Dromio of Ephesus were rescued by men of that city (5.1.350).

Shakespeare probably moved the location of his play because of biblical references to Ephesus that he uses. Acts, chapter 19, refers to exorcists in the city (verse 13), and those who use "curious artes" (verse 19). Antipholus of Syracuse observes, "They say this town is full of cozenage: / As nimble jugglers that deceive the eye, / Dark-working sorcerers that change the mind, / Soul-killing witches that deform the body, / Disguised cheaters, prating mountebanks, / And many suchlike liberties of sin" (1.2.97–102). Later he remarks, "There's none but witches do inhabit here" (3.2.157). In that same chapter of Acts, "The man in whome ye euil spirit was, ran on them [seven sons of Sceua], & ouercame them, & preuailed against them, so that they fled out of that house, naked, and wounded" (verse 16). Adriana thinks her husband is possessed and has him bound, along with his servant. Then Antipholus of Syracuse and his servant rush in and chase everyone away (scene 4.4). In scene 5.1 a messenger announces that Antipholus of Ephesus, who was bound because he was thought mad, has broken loose. These incidents may echo the biblical passage.

The play also draws thematically on Paul's Epistle to the Ephesians. Marital relationships are vexed here. Adriana criticizes her husband, who in Plautus's original is unfaithful and in Shakespeare's rewriting is at least flirting with a courtesan. In chapter 5 of Paul's Epistle to the Ephesians, he tells wives to obey their husbands (verse 22) and husbands to love their wives (verses 25, 28). Both Antipholuses beat their servants, who are not always submissive. In chapter 6 of his epistle, Paul urges servants to be obedient (verse 5) and writes that masters should "put away threatening" (verse 9).

House of Antipholus of Ephesus (E)

Scene 2.1: Adriana, wife of Antipholus (E), objects to men's having greater freedom than women. Her sister Luciana urges patience. Dromio (E) enters to report Antipholus (E) is insane. Adriana sends him back to fetch her husband. After he leaves, Adriana criticizes her mate.

Scene 3.1: When Antipholus (E), accompanied by his servant Dromio (E), tries to enter his house with his guests, the goldsmith Angelo and the merchant Balthasar, Dromio of Syracuse (S) and then Adriana refuse to admit them. Antipholus (E) initially thinks of forcing his way in, but Balthasar urges him to leave peacefully and dine at the Tiger Inn. Antipholus (E) instead decides to go to the house of a courtesan he knows. He instructs Angelo to bring him the chain he had ordered for Adriana but now will give to the courtesan.

Scene 3.2: Inside the house of Antipholus (E), Antipholus (S) woos Luciana, who, mistaking him for his twin, replies he should be faithful to his wife, her sister. Dromio (S) enters to say the cook claims he is engaged to her. Antipholus (S) resolves to flee Ephesus immediately. As he is leaving the house, Angelo gives him the gold chain his twin had ordered.

Scene 4.2: Luciana tells Adriana of Antipholus (S)'s wooing her, though they both think it is Antipholus (E) who is pursuing Adriana. Dromio (S) reports the arrest of Antipholus (E) and asks for money for bail, which Adriana gives him.

The Marketplace

Scene 1.2: Unbeknownst to Egeon, his son Antipholus of Syracuse, on a five-year quest to find his lost twin brother, has arrived at Ephesus with his servant, Dromio of Syracuse. A merchant warns him not to reveal his Syracusan connection because of hostilities between Ephesus and Syracuse. The twin brothers have twin servants; both sets of twins not only look alike but also have the same names. Shakespeare's source has one set of twins. Shakespeare, himself the father of twins, doubles the twinning to heighten the comedy deriving from the ensuing confusion. Antipholus of Syracuse gives Dromio (S) money and tells him to wait for him at their inn, the Centaur. No such inn existed in Shakespeare's London, but critics have linked the inn's name to the story of the centaurs interrupting the wedding of Pirithous and Hippodamia, as Antipholus of Syracuse threatens the already-rocky marriage of his twin and Adriana. (Othello stays at the Sagittary in Venice [1.1.155]; Sagittarius is a centaur.)

Shortly after Dromio (S) leaves, Dromio (E) arrives to invite Antipholus (S) to dinner. When Antipholus (S) asks about the money he just gave Dromio (S), Dromio (E) denies knowing anything about it. Antipholus (S) beats him. After Dromio (E) leaves, Antipholus departs for his inn.

Scene 2.2: Meeting Dromio (S), Antipholus (S) confronts him with his recent odd behavior (in fact, that of his twin). When Dromio (S) denies these actions, Antipholus (S) beats him. Adriana and Luciana arrive to summon Antipholus (S) to dinner. Though confused, he and Dromio (S) go with them.

Scene 4.1: A merchant demands that Angelo repay a debt. Angelo says Antipholus (E) owes him exactly the sum he owes the merchant. When Antipholus (E) and Dromio (E) enter, Angelo asks for payment for the chain he just delivered to Antipholus (S). When Antipholus (E) denies having received the chain, Angelo demands the officer arrest Antipholus (E) for debt. Dromio (S) arrives to report he has secured passage on a ship. Antipholus (E) denies sending him to book passage and tells him to go to Adriana for money so he can post bail.

Scene 4.3: Dromio (S) gives Antipholus (S) the money Antipholus (E) sent him to collect. The courtesan enters. Seeing Antipholus (S) with the chain Antipholus (E) promised her, she asks for it. Antipholus (S) refuses to give it to her. She then demands back the ring she thinks he took from her, though she is mistaking him for his twin. Antipholus (S) and Dromio (S) flee.

Scene 4.4: Dromio (E) enters with a rope his master asked him to get to beat Adriana for locking him out of his house. Antipholus (E) asks for the money he sent him to fetch. Dromio (E) says Antipholus (E) did not ask for money. Adriana, Luciana, the courtesan, and the doctor/schoolmaster Pinch appear. Concluding Antipholus (E) is mad, they have him and Dromio (E) bound and taken away. Dromio (S) and Antipholus (S) enter, the latter with his sword drawn. All flee from them. Antipholus (S) again resolves to leave Ephesus immediately.

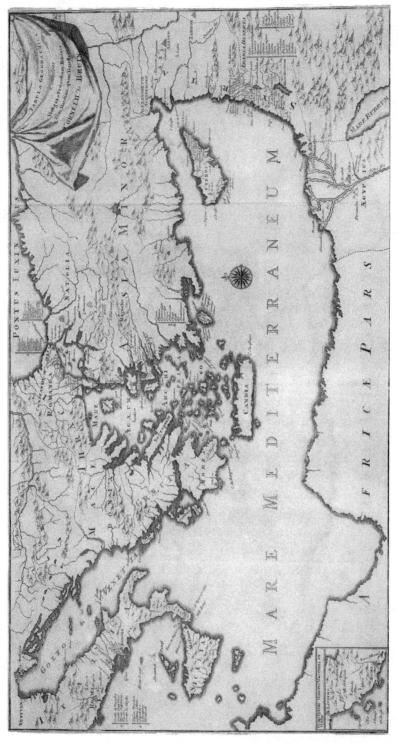

The Mediterranean world, site of many of Shakespeare's plays. DS7.B9 Cage Fo., Bruyn, Cornelis de, 1652–1726 or 1727. Used by permission of the Folger Shakespeare Library

A Priory/Temple of Artemis
See headnote to the play.

Scene 5.1: In front of the priory, as Angelo and a merchant converse, Antipholus (S) and Dromio (S) enter. Antipholus (S) is wearing the chain Angelo made for Antipholus (E). When Angelo confronts him about denying receiving the chain, Antipholus (S) says he never denied receiving it, but the merchant confirms Angelo's accusation. The merchant and Antipholus (S) draw their swords. Adriana, Luciana, the courtesan, and others arrive. Adriana insists her husband is insane and urges the merchant not to hurt him. Antipholus (S) and Dromio (S) flee into the priory.

Emilia, the abbess, emerges to urge calm. Adriana says she wants her husband, who has lost his wits. The abbess proves Adriana drove him mad. The abbess refuses to surrender Antipholus (S) but promises to try to cure him.

The duke arrives with Egeon. Adriana appeals to the duke to take her husband from the priory. A messenger arrives to warn Adriana that Antipholus (E) and Dromio (E) have broken loose, and both men appear. Antipholus (E) complains to the duke that his wife barred him from his house, a charge she denies. Antipholus (E) also says Angelo wrongly reported giving him a chain and then had him arrested for nonpayment. Then his wife, Pinch, and others bound him and placed him in a dark room.

Angelo agrees Antipholus (E) was locked out of his house but says he gave him the chain, and the merchant agrees. The merchant tells of his quarrel with Antipholus (S) and Antipholus (S)'s flight into the priory, both of which Antipholus (E) denies. Dromio (E) and the courtesan agree Antipholus (E) did not dine at home.

To sort out the confusion, the duke summons Emilia. Egeon claims to recognize Antipholus (E) and Dromio (E), mistaking them for their twins. They deny knowing him, and the duke says they have been living in Ephesus for at least twenty years.

The abbess enters with Antipholus (S) and Dromio (S). She recognizes Egeon as her long-lost husband. After some further confusion, the mistakes of the day are cleared up. The duke pardons Egeon. All go off to celebrate with Antipholus (E).

A Public Square
Scene 1.1: Ephesus and Syracuse have embargoed trade with each other, and anyone from one city caught in the other is condemned to death and his goods forfeit unless he can pay a thousand marks. Egeon of Syracuse, who has come to Ephesus in search of his long-lost son, has been arrested. The Duke of Ephesus, Solinus, gives him until the end of the day to raise the money to avoid execution. In a long expository speech, Egeon tells how he lost his wife and children and the children's servants.

The Taming of the Shrew

Wincot, Warwickshire (Formerly Gloucestershire)

Four miles south of Stratford. Almost nothing of the village remains. Because of the vagaries of British pronunciation, Wilnecote, about thirty miles north of Stratford near the Warwickshire border with Staffordshire and famous for its ale, and Wilmcote, where Shakespeare's mother was born (see "Wilmcote, Warwickshire" in appendix A), have also been suggested as the "Wincot" of the Induction. Shakespeare's main source for the play, the anonymous *The Taming of the Shrew* (1594) does not localize the action of the induction. Shakespeare chose a location that would have been familiar to him.

Induction, scenes 1–3: The drunken Christopher Sly and the Hostess (perhaps "Marian Hacket, the fat alewife of Wincot" Sly mentions in Induction, 2.21–22) argue. On November 21, 1591, Sara, daughter of Robert Hacket, was baptized at Quinton Church, so the Hackets lived here. Perhaps Shakespeare knew the family. Wincot was part of the parish of Quinton. Sly himself lives at Barton-on-the Heath (the "Burton-heath" of induction 2.18). A Stephen Sly, whose name appears later in this scene, was living in Stratford in 1615 (see "Barton-on-the Heath, Warwickshire" in appendix A).

Sly falls asleep. A lord and his attendants arrive, and the lord decides to play a trick on Sly. Sly is taken to the lord's house and treated as if it were Sly's. A group of actors appear to perform a play for Sly; that play is *The Taming of the Shrew*. When Sly awakes, everyone treats him as a lord who for fifteen years has been insane. At the end of the induction, all prepare to watch the play.

In *The Taming of the Shrew*, Sly comments on the action four times in the course of the play, and in the final scene (19), Sly is returned to the tavern where the lord found him. When he awakes he at first still thinks he is a lord and then decides he dreamed his experience (like Bottom in *A Midsummer Night's Dream*, who also cannot tell whether events of the previous night occurred or were only a dream). The tapster warns Sly his wife will be angry with him for staying out all night, but Sly responds he now knows how to tame her thanks to the play he has seen (or dreamed). The tapster follows Sly to hear about his dream.

ITALY

Padua

Located in the Veneto on the Bacchiglione and Brenta Rivers, the city takes its name from the Roman Patavium. The city claims to have been founded circa 1183 BCE by Antenor, a Trojan refugee. It became a Roman city in the 40s BCE and prospered, becoming the second-richest city in Italy. The city was sacked by Attila the Hun in 450 CE and later by the Lombards and the Magyars, the latter in 899 CE. In the later Middle Ages, the city again flourished. The University of Padua was founded in 1222. Its medical school was popular with the English. William Harvey, who discovered the circulation of the blood, graduated from the University of Padua in 1602. Its law school was also famous. Portia's lawyer-cousin Bellario in *The Merchant of Venice* lives in Padua. Bellarmina in Christopher Marlowe's *The Jew of Malta* says, "From Padua / Were wont to come rare-witted gentlemen, / Scholars, I mean, learned and liberal."

In 1405 the city came under Venetian rule, and it remained so until the fall of the Venetian Republic in 1797. After Napoleon's defeat in 1815, the city was ruled by Austria until 1866, when it joined the kingdom of Italy.

The main action in *The Taming of the Shrew* occurs in Athens. Shakespeare relocated it to Padua, perhaps because Italy was a popular setting for plays in Shakespeare's day and because Padua's university would be a logical place for Lucentio to attend. In George Gascoinge's *Supposes* (1566, published 1575), another source for Shakespeare's play, Cleander (who becomes Hortensio in *The Taming of the Shrew*) says he came to Ferrara, the setting of Gascoigne's work, from Padua. This reference may also have influenced Shakespeare's choice of locale for his play.

Baptista Minola's House

Scene 1.1: In front of Baptista Minola's house, Lucentio Bentivoli appears with his servant Tranio, newly arrived from Pisa. Lucentio has come to study philosophy at the University of Padua. Though it was founded as a law school, in Shakespeare's day it was also renowned for medicine, astronomy, and philosophy. Baptista Minola enters with his two daughters, Katherina (the older) and Bianca, and two suitors for the latter, Gremio and Hortensio. Baptista declares he will not let Bianca marry until the shrewish Katherina has found a husband. He asks Bianca's suitors to find tutors for his daughters. Lucentio, having fallen in love with Bianca at first sight, resolves to exchange roles with Tranio. Tranio will act as Lucentio, while the real Lucentio will pretend to be a teacher who will tutor Bianca so he can woo and win her.

Scene 2.1: Bianca and Katherina quarrel until Baptista stops them. Petruchio arrives to woo Katherina and to offer Hortensio, disguised as Litio, as Bianca's music teacher. Gremio presents Lucentio as Cambio to tutor Bianca, as well. The name *Cambio* is well chosen because in Italian it means "change," and Lucentio is changing his identity to woo Bianca. The name suggests metamorphosis, and in Ovid's *Metamorphoses*, Shakespeare's favorite classical work, characters repeatedly change because of love. It also means "switch," and Lucentio is switching identities with Tranio. Tranio as Lucentio says he, too, wishes to marry Bianca and gives her a lute and books.

Alone with Baptista, Petruchio repeats his desire to marry Katherina. As they talk, Hortensio emerges; Katherina has broken the lute over his head. After Baptista leaves with Hortensio, Petruchio and Katherina spar verbally and physically. Upon Baptista's return, Petruchio declares Katherina has agreed to marry him. She protests she has not, but Petruchio insists she has and says he will return on Sunday for the wedding. With Katherina now engaged, Gremio and Tranio seek Bianca's hand. Baptista says he will marry her to whoever offers the larger dowry. Tranio outbids Gremio, but Baptista requires Tranio's father to guarantee the marriage settlement.

Scene 3.1: Lucentio as Cambio and Hortensio as Litio vie for Bianca's affection until Bianca is called away to help with Katherina's wedding preparations.

Scene 3.2: Everyone is waiting for Petruchio to arrive. At last Biondello announces he is coming with his servant but in strange attire. When Baptista objects to Petruchio's appearance, he replies Katherina is marrying him, not his clothes. All but Tranio and Lucentio leave for the wedding; these two discuss how Lucentio is to marry Bianca. Gremio returns to report on the chaotic marriage ceremony. After the wedding Petruchio insists he and Katherina leave at once, skipping the marriage feast. Katherina objects but is forced away.

Scene 4.2: Seeing Bianca's love for her schoolmaster, Cambio/Lucentio, Tranio (as Lucentio) and Hortensio agree to abandon their pursuit of her. Hortensio plans to marry a rich widow who has long been in love with him. Tranio/Lucentio recruits a pedant to serve as his father to guarantee Bianca's dowry.

Scene 4.4: In front of Baptista's house, the pedant whom Tranio as Lucentio has recruited to be his father (Vincentio) guarantees Bianca's dowry. While Tranio, Baptista, and the pedant go off to draw up the marriage contract, Lucentio and Biondello plan for Lucentio to marry Bianca.

Hortensio's House
Scene 1.2: Petruchio and his servant Grumio have just arrived from Verona to visit Hortensio and to seek a rich wife. Hortensio suggests Petruchio marry Katherina. Hortensio asks Petruchio to present him in disguise as Litio, a music teacher, so he can woo Bianca. Gremio comes with Lucentio, who is disguised as Cambio the schoolmas-

ter. Lucentio promises Gremio to woo Bianca for him, though he intends to court her for himself. Gremio, Hortensio, and Tranio as Lucentio agree to reward Petruchio if he can win Katherina's hand.

Lucentio's House

Scene 5.1: Lucentio departs to marry Bianca. Petruchio, Katherina, Vincentio, Grumio, and attendants arrive. The pedant pretending to be Vincentio tries to send away the real Vincentio. When Biondello returns from Lucentio's wedding, he pretends he does not know Vincentio, who concludes Tranio and Biondello have killed the real Lucentio. Lucentio and Bianca return from church and clarify the confusion. All go inside for a wedding feast.

Scene 5.2: Petruchio bets Lucentio and Hortensio a hundred crowns that his wife is more obedient than theirs. They eagerly accept the challenge. Neither Bianca nor Hortensio's widow will come when summoned, but Katherina does. Petruchio sends her back to fetch the disobedient wives, and when she returns she delivers a speech on wifely obedience. Baptista is so impressed he gives Petruchio another dowry "for another daughter / For she is changed" (ll. 114–15). Petruchio and Katherina depart, leaving behind an amazed Hortensio and Lucentio.

Road to Padua

Scene 4.5: As Katherina and Petruchio set off for Padua, Katherina shows she has learned to humor Petruchio. When he calls the sun the moon, she initially disputes with him, but when he says they will not return to Padua until she agrees with him, she yields, "And be it moon or sun or what you please, / And if you please to call it a rush-candle, / Henceforth I vow it shall be so for me" (ll. 13–15). They encounter Vincentio, the real father of Lucentio. Kate plays along when Petruchio at first greets the old man as a young woman and then admits her mistake after Petruchio corrects her. She has discovered she can have more fun playing along with Petruchio than arguing with him.

Shakespeare's audiences would not have been bothered by a woman's becoming obedient to her husband. For modern audiences the play works better not as a triumph of patriarchy but of play, as Kate uses her wits to join with and even surpass Petruchio in his whimsical behavior. John Fletcher's *The Woman's Prize, or the Tamer Tamed* (early seventeenth century) responds to Shakespeare's play, as Petruchio's second wife, Maria (Katherina has died), tames him. Once he reforms, she declares, "I have tam'd ye, / And now am vowd your servant" (ll. 3339–40). Thus, Fletcher's play becomes more conventional than Shakespeare's. Maria submits to Petruchio, whereas Shakespeare's Katherina becomes an equal partner with him.

Petruchio tells Vincentio that Lucentio has married Bianca, though the wedding has not yet occurred.

Verona
Located on the Adige River in the Veneto, seventy miles from Venice, Verona became a Roman colony in 89 BCE. It takes its name perhaps from its location on the road to Rome from the Alps ("versus Romae," "toward Rome") or from the Adige River, on which the city sits; the Adige was formerly called Vera, and *-ona* is a common Goth suffix. It fell to the Goths in 489 CE, and Theodoric built one of his palaces here. In 569 it became part of the Lombard kingdom. The Della Scala family ruled Verona from 1260 to 1387, when the Visconti of Milan annexed it, but in 1405 it fell under the control of Venice. In *Othello*, 2.1, a gentleman refers to a "noble ship of Venice" as a "Veronesa" (ll. 22, 26; i.e., a ship Verona provided to Venice). The city prospered in the Middle Ages. From 1814 to 1866, it was ruled by Austria, before becoming part of a united Italy.

Petruchio says, "Verona, for a while I take my leave / To see my friends in Padua" (1.2.1–2), indicating he is a resident of Verona. Verona is about sixty miles from Padua.

Petruchio's House
Scene 4.1: Grumio and Curtis prepare for the arrival of Petruchio and Katherina. Grumio relates the misadventures of their journey. As soon as Petruchio arrives, he complains of his servants' negligence. When they bring supper, Petruchio finds fault with the food and so prevents Katherina from eating. In the bedroom he delivers a sermon and keeps Katherina awake all night as part of his effort to tame her.

Scene 4.3: Katherina fails to get food from Grumio. Petruchio brings her some and allows her to eat after she has thanked him. A haberdasher brings Katherina a cap she likes, but Petruchio finds fault with it and will not let her have it. He similarly criticizes and sends away a gown she wants. Petruchio proposes returning to Padua. When Katherina says it's too late to set off, Petruchio says they will not go until she agrees "It shall be what o'clock I say it is" (l. 195).

The Two Gentlemen of Verona

ITALY

Mantua

Located in Lombardy, Mantua has been occupied since about 2000 BCE. By the sixth century BCE, it was inhabited by Etruscans. The name may derive from the Etruscan deity Mantus or the mythical daughter of Tiresias, Manto. Virgil was born in a village (Virgilio) close enough to the city for Mantua to claim him. After the fall of the Roman Empire, Mantua was ruled by Ostrogoths, Lombards, and Franks, like so many other Italian cities. After being part of the Holy Roman Empire and being ruled by Tuscany, it achieved independence in the twelfth century. The three artificial lakes that surround the city were constructed in this period for defense. A fourth lake created at the same time was filled in during the eighteenth century. The Gonzaga family controlled the city from 1329 to 1708, when Mantua fell under Austrian rule and remained so, except during the Napoleonic period, until 1866, when it became part of the kingdom of Italy.

Forest of Mantua

Between Milan and Mantua

Scene 4.1: Valentine agrees to become the leader of a band of outlawed gentlemen.

Scene 5.3: Silvia has been captured by the outlaws, who are taking her to their leader, Valentine.

Scene 5.4: Proteus has rescued Silvia, but she still rejects him and urges him to be faithful to Julia, who is present in the disguise of Sebastian, and to Valentine. Proteus then tries to rape Silvia, but Valentine intervenes. Proteus begs forgiveness, which Valentine grants, and offers Silvia to him, illustrating (or highlighting the absurdity of) the classical/Renaissance belief that friendship is stronger than love. Julia reveals herself, and Proteus chooses her over Silvia. The outlaws enter with the duke and

Thurio as captives. Thurio claims Silvia, but Valentine threatens to kill him if he persists in his demand. A coward, Thurio now finds Silvia less enticing and yields her to Valentine. The duke, impressed by Valentine's valor, accepts him as his son-in-law. Valentine asks the duke to pardon the outlaws, which he does. (The ending of *The Pirates of Penzance* comes to mind.) Proteus and Julia and Valentine and Silvia are to marry on the same day.

Milan

Settled by the Celt Insubres about 400 BCE, the city was captured by the Romans in 222 BCE, who renamed it Mediolanum. When Diocletian divided the empire (285 CE), Maximian, who ruled the western part of the empire, lived here. In 313 the Emperors Constantine and Licinius issued the Edict of Milan, which ended the persecution of Christians in the empire. Huns, Ostrogoths, and Lombards ruled the city in the early Middle Ages before it became part of Charlemagne's empire in 774. For a few centuries, it was governed by German emperors. The Peace of Constance (1183) secured independence for Lombard cities. During the Renaissance it was an important cultural center; it is home to Leonardo da Vinci's *Last Supper*. The Visconti held power from 1277 to 1450, when they were replaced by the Sforza family, who retained the dukedom until 1535. When Shakespeare wrote *Two Gentlemen*, the city was part of the Spanish Hapsburg Empire, though Shakespeare gives it a duke. Austria took control of Milan in 1714 and, except for the Napoleonic era, held it until Milan became part of the kingdom of Sardinia in 1859 and part of the kingdom of Italy in 1861. Milan, a fashion center, has long been famous for its haberdashery, hence the word *milliner*, an "inhabitant of Milan." Shakespeare gives Milan a seacoast its geography did not provide: Valentine in *The Two Gentlemen of Verona* sails there (1.1.71–72), and Prospero in *The Tempest* is set adrift with his infant daughter from the city.

The Duke's Palace

Begun by Francesco Sforza in 1452 on the site of a fourteenth-century castle, Sforza Castle now houses museums and art collections. When Milan came under French and then Spanish rule, this palace served mainly for fortifications, and a royal palace next to the cathedral became the seat of government. It is not clear which location, if either, Shakespeare has in mind. This may be a palace of the mind. Having given Milan a duke, Shakespeare would need to give him a palace.

Scene 2.1: Valentine has fallen in love with Silvia, daughter of the duke, and she loves him. She has asked him to write a love letter for her, which she then gives to him. Valentine is confused until Speed, his servant, explains she is wooing him with his own letter.

Scene 2.4: Valentine and Thurio (also in love with Silvia) quarrel. The duke arrives to inform Valentine of Proteus's arrival in Milan. When the two friends are alone, Valentine tells Proteus of his love for Silvia. He also says the duke wants Silvia to marry Thurio because Thurio is rich, but Silvia and Valentine have agreed to marry secretly. After Valentine leaves, Proteus declares he, too, loves Silvia.

Scene 2.6: In a soliloquy Proteus decides to abandon Julia for Silvia and to reveal to the duke Valentine's plan to elope with her.

Scene 3.1: Proteus tells the duke of Valentine's plan to elope with Silvia. The duke then banishes Valentine. Proteus pretends to pity his friend and promises to deliver his letters to Silvia. Launce and Speed discuss Launce's love for a milkmaid before Speed goes off to join his master.

Scene 3.2: Proteus agrees to help Thurio win Silvia.

Scene 4.2: Outside the ducal palace, Julia, disguised as Sebastian, listens to Thurio present a love song to Silvia and then hears Proteus woo Silvia for himself.

Scene 4.3: Outside the palace, Sir Eglamore agrees to aid Silvia in escaping from Milan to join Valentine.

Scene 4.4: Beneath Silvia's window Proteus hires Sebastian (Julia in disguise) and sends her to give to Silvia the ring Julia gave him. Silvia rejects the gift and says she pities the absent Julia. But she gives Sebastian her picture to present to Proteus as she had promised.

Scene 5.2: The duke learns of Silvia's flight. The duke, Proteus, Thurio, and Sebastian pursue her.

Friar Patrick's Cell
Scene 5.1: Sir Eglamore and Silvia meet here and flee to the forest.

A Street
Scene 2.5: Launce and Speed meet.

Verona
Located on the Adige River in the Veneto, seventy miles from Venice, Verona became a Roman colony in 89 BCE. It takes its name perhaps from its location on the road to Rome from the Alps (*versus Romae,* "toward Rome") or from the Adige River, on which the city sits; the Adige was formerly called Vera, and *-ona* is a common Goth suffix. It fell to the Goths in 489 CE, and Theodoric built one of his palaces here. In 569 it became part of the Lombard kingdom. The Della Scala family ruled Verona from 1260 to 1387, when the Visconti of Milan annexed it, but in 1405 it fell under the control of Venice. In *Othello,* 2.1, a gentleman refers to a "noble ship of Venice" as a "Veronesa" (ll. 22, 26; i.e., a ship Verona provided to Venice). The city prospered

in the Middle Ages. From 1814 to 1866, it was ruled by Austria, before becoming part of a united Italy.

Antonio's House

Scene 1.3: Panthio, servant of Antonio (Proteus's father), says Antonio's brother thinks Proteus should travel, and Panthio recommends Milan, where Valentine has gone. Proteus protests; he does not want to leave Julia. But Antonio tells him he must depart the next day.

Julia's House

Scene 1.2: In the garden Julia and her waiting woman Lucetta discuss love. Lucetta tries to give Julia a letter from Proteus, which Julia rejects even though she wants it. Lucetta drops the letter, and Julia tells her to leave it. Julia takes it; tears it; and then, after Lucetta leaves, reads it.

Scene 2.2: Proteus takes his leave of Julia. They exchange rings.

Scene 2.7: Julia resolves to disguise herself as a man and travel to Milan in pursuit of Proteus.

A Street

Scene 1.1: Valentine prepares to leave his friend Proteus and set off for Milan. After some bantering between Valentine's servant Speed and Proteus, Speed goes off to join Valentine.

Scene 2.3: Launce, Proteus's servant, describes his sad leave-taking of his family and then sets off to accompany his master.

Love's Labor's Lost

Navarre

Once covering parts of Spain and France on either side of the Pyrenees Mountains, the area was settled by Proto-Basque-speaking Vascones and related tribes. By 74 BCE the region had come under Roman control. In the eighth century CE, it became part of the Córboda Emirate. In the tenth century it became an independent kingdom, but in 1512 the southwestern part came under Spanish rule. The rest of the kingdom, north of the Pyrenees, joined France in 1589 when Henry IV, who was king of Navarre (as Henry III) from 1572, assumed the throne of France in 1589.

All the action of the play occurs in the park of the court of the king of Navarre.

Scene 1.1: Ferdinand, king of Navarre, has resolved to turn his court into an academy. Berowne, Dumaine, and Longaville have agreed to join him for three years of celibate study. Berowne is willing to study, but he does not like the ascetic terms the king is imposing, including the banning of conversation with women. Reluctantly he agrees to the conditions, but he then reminds the king they must be abandoned because the daughter of the king of France is coming to discuss the surrender of Aquitaine. In 1578 Marguerite de Valois with her ladies-in-waiting visited her estranged husband, Henry of Navarre, to negotiate about this province.

The aptly named Constable Dull arrives with Costard, who was apprehended consorting with Jaquenetta despite the king's edict against entertaining women at court. The king sentences Costard to a week's fasting on bran and water, the sentence to be overseen by Don Adriano de Armado, perhaps modeled on John Florio, Italian tutor to the Third Earl of Southampton (to whom Shakespeare dedicated *Venus and Adonis* and *The Rape of Lucrece*) and translator of Montaigne's essays, from which Shakespeare drew Gonzalo's description of his ideal commonwealth in *The Tempest*, 2.1.

Scene 1.2: Don Armado tells his page Moth of his love for Jaquenetta. Dull surrenders Costard to Don Armado, and Moth leads Costard away to prison. Alone, Don Armado again confesses his love, even though he, too, has subscribed to the king's strict rules for abstemious study.

Scene 2.1: The princess of France; her ladies-in-waiting (Rosaline, Maria, and Katharine); and three lords, including Boyet and Mercade, arrive at the court of the king of Navarre. Ferdinand greets them but refuses to admit them to his court because of his oath. While the king and princess converse, Berowne and Rosaline engage in a battle of wits. The king tells the princess France owes him 100,000 crowns; until the sum is paid, he will keep part of Aquitaine. The princess replies that France has repaid the money. Navarre asks for proof; Boyet says the proof has not yet arrived. The king and his attendants leave, and Berowne and Rosaline resume their verbal dueling. After Berowne departs, Dumaine asks Boyet the name of one of the ladies (Katharine), Longaville asks the name of Maria, and Berowne returns to ask Rosaline's name. Alone with the princess, Boyet assures her Ferdinand is so in love with her that he will yield Aquitaine for a kiss.

Scene 3.1: Don Armado sends Moth to free Costard from prison so he can take a letter to Jaquenetta. After Armado and Moth leave, Berowne gives Costard a sonnet for Rosaline, with whom Berowne has fallen in love.

Scene 4.1: Costard mistakenly delivers Armado's love letter to the princess, who reads it to her entourage. They then go off to hunt.

Scene 4.2: Dull, the pedant Holofernes, and the curate Nathaniel discuss the recent hunt. Jaquenetta arrives with Costard, who has given her the sonnet Berowne intended for Rosaline. She asks Nathaniel to read it to her. Holofernes tells Jaquenetta and Costard to take the poem to the king, and he invites Dull and Nathaniel to dine with him at the house of a pupil's father.

Scene 4.3: Berowne overhears the king reading a sonnet the king has written to the princess. The king hides as Longaville enters reading a sonnet he has penned for Maria. Then he, too, hides when Dumaine appears, reading his sonnet to Katharine. The men criticize each other for breaking their oath to shun women for three years, and Berowne chides them all—until Costard and Jaquenetta deliver his sonnet written for Rosaline. Berowne tries to conceal his love by tearing the sonnet, but Dumaine reassembles it and exposes him. The others criticize Rosaline for her dark complexion, suggesting the Dark Lady in the sonnets Shakespeare was writing circa 1594 as he was working on this play. The sonnets of Berowne, Longaville, and Dumaine were published in 1599 in *The Passionate Pilgrim*, along with two sonnets (138 and 144) addressed to the Dark Lady. Berowne defends Rosaline's beauty (as Shakespeare does in his Dark Lady sonnets). The king asks Berowne to use his wit to prove they have not broken their oath to study and avoid women. Berowne replies women's eyes are the true source of knowledge, and the men resolve to pursue their loves.

Scene 5.1: When Holofernes, Nathaniel, and Dull return from lunch, Armado asks them to devise an entertainment for the French ladies. Holofernes proposes a pageant of the Nine Worthies.

Scene 5.2: The princess shows her ladies a jewel she has received from Ferdinand, along with a set of verses. The other women have also received gifts and poems. Boyet informs them that the king, Berowne, Dumaine, and Longaville are about to visit them in the disguise of Russians. England's Muscovy Company was chartered in 1555, and Czar Ivan IV sought Queen Elizabeth's hand in marriage in 1567. The princess thinks the men want to mock them, so she has the women don masks of their own and exchange the gifts they have received so the men will woo the wrong women. The king goes off with Rosaline, Berowne with the princess, Dumaine with Maria, and Longaville with Katharine. After the men leave and return without their disguises, the princess tells them of a visit by Russians. The men admit they were in disguise, and the women reveal the trick they played.

Costard announces the pageant of the Nine Worthies. Berowne, Boyet, Dumaine, and Longaville mock the performance, but the princess pities and encourages them. Shakespeare would repeat this situation in act 5 of *A Midsummer Night's Dream*. In the middle of Armado's speech as Hector, Costard informs everyone Armado has gotten Jaquenetta pregnant.

Mercade arrives with the news the king of France has died. The princess declares she and her ladies must depart at once. Navarre asks her and her ladies to grant the men their loves, but the princess replies the time is too short for making a lifelong commitment. She tells the king to spend the next year in a hermitage, as he has proposed to do at the beginning of the play. If he still wants to marry her after a year, she will agree. Rosaline instructs Berowne to spend a year entertaining the sick, and Maria and Katharine also ask their lovers to propose again in a year. The play ends with a song of the owl and the cuckoo.

A Midsummer Night's Dream

GREECE

Athens

An important Mycenean center, the city-state in the eighth century BCE was aristocratic. In 508 BCE Cleisthenes created a form of democracy in Athens, though broader democracy did not arrive until the 460s. Women and foreign residents still were not allowed to vote. Of a population of some 100,000, probably only about 10,000 could. Sacked by a Persian army in 480 BCE shortly before the Athenian navy defeated Persia at the Battle of Salamis (September 480 BCE), in 478 BCE Athens became an imperial city-state when it assumed leadership of the Delian League. Throughout the fifth century BCE, Athens and Sparta battled for hegemony in the First Peloponnesian War (461–446 BCE), followed by the Second Peloponnesian War (431–404 BCE), which ended in the defeat of Athens. The city quickly recovered, resumed its democracy in 403 BCE, and established a second Athenian Confederacy in 378 BCE. Following Philip of Macedon's victory at the Battle of Chaeronea (338 BCE), Greece came under Macedonian rule. In the Hellenistic period, Athens became a cultural center of the Mediterranean world under the rule of Alexander the Great's successors, the Antigonids, and remained so into the sixth century CE. After 146 BCE Greece was ruled by Rome. Later, Greece became part of the Ottoman Empire. When Greece gained independence in the nineteenth century, Athens became its capital. Shakespeare's Athens is, like its ruler, Theseus, mythical rather than historical. Shakespeare would have found accounts of Theseus and Hippolyta in Thomas North's translation of Plutarch's *Lives*, first published in 1579, and in Chaucer's "The Knight's Tale," a source for this play, as well as for *The Two Noble Kinsmen*. Though born in Troezen, Theseus, son of Aegeus, king of Athens, came to Athens as an adult and succeeded his father as ruler of that city, which celebrated him in the Theseia each October.

Palace of Theseus

Scene 1.1: Theseus, Duke of Athens, and Hippolyta, queen of the Amazons, discuss their upcoming wedding, to take place, they say, in four days. In the play they marry on day 3. *Romeo and Juliet*, which immediately preceded *A Midsummer Night's Dream*, unfolds over four days, and Shakespeare may have intended this play, a comic riposte to *Romeo and Juliet*, with its fickle, quarreling lovers and its fifth act that mocks the earlier work, to cover four days, as well. But *A Midsummer Night's Dream* is filled with contradictions. For example, the roles Peter Quince assigns his actors in 1.2 are not the roles they assume in 5.1. The few lines Bottom as Pyramus rehearses in 3.1 are not lines he speaks in 5.1. Snug, worried about learning his lines as the lion, is told in 1.2 his part consists of nothing but roaring, yet in the actual performance, he speaks eight lines (5.1.218–25). In 1.1 Theseus says he cannot overrule Egeus's decision about whom Hermia must marry, but in 4.2.180, the duke declares, "Egeus, I will overbear your will." When Oberon asks for Titania's changeling boy in 2.1, Titania replies, "The fairy land buys not the child of me" (l. 22), yet in 4.1 Oberon reports she has meekly surrendered the boy. The play thus has an oneiric quality suiting its title.

In Greek mythology Theseus is the son of Aegeus (the father of Hermia in the play) and Aethra. He kills the Minotaur of Crete with the help of Ariadne, daughter of Minos, the Cretan king. Theseus and Ariadne flee Crete together, but he abandons her on the island of Naxos (see 2.1.80). He had told his father his ships would display white sails if he survived his encounter with the Minotaur, black sails if he had died. Absentmindedly, he forgets to change his sails from black to white. Aegeus, thinking his son is dead, kills himself. Theseus's absentmindedness is alluded to in 1.1.113–14: "But, being overfull of self-affairs, / My mind did lose it." In an expedition against the Amazons, Theseus won Antiope, or Hippolyta. Shakespeare treats these two names as belonging to two different people (2.1.80), either a misunderstanding on his part or a conscious decision. Theseus kidnapped Helen of Troy, who gives her name to Helena in the play. Whereas Helen of Troy was much sought after, Helena here is abandoned by her lover, whom she pursues rather than being pursued.

As Theseus and Hippolyta talk about their wedding, Egeus enters with his daughter, Hermia, and her two suitors, Lysander and Demetrius. Egeus wants his daughter to marry the latter; Hermia wants to marry the former. Theseus tells Hermia she must obey her father or suffer death or become a virgin votaress of Diana. Hermia still rejects Demetrius. The Athenian lawgiver Solon (c. 638–558 BCE) gave parents the power of life and death over their children. Theseus gives her four days to decide her fate. Alone with Lysander, Hermia agrees to flee Athens with him so they can marry. They confide their plan to Helena, who loves Demetrius. With Hermia gone, Demetrius may return to Helena, whom he abandoned for Hermia. Yet Helena resolves to tell Demetrius of Hermia's flight.

The Temple of Theseus, Athens, dedicated to the mythical king. © *Stephen Coyne/Bridgeman Images*

Scene 5.1: Hippolyta and Theseus disagree about the veracity of the story the lovers tell about their night in the woods. The mechanicals stage *Pyramus and Thisbe*, to much laughter and ridicule. Then the mortals retire, and Oberon blesses them. Alone on stage, Puck concludes the play by telling the audience if they dislike the performance they can think it was just a dream.

Peter Quince's House
Scene 1.2: To celebrate the nuptials of Theseus and Hippolyta, Athenian workmen prepare to stage a play, "The most lamentable comedy, and most cruel death of Pyramus and Thisbe" (ll. 11–13), at the palace after the wedding. They agree to meet the following night in the woods outside Athens to rehearse. This play-within-the-play mocks the older acting style the Lord Chamberlain's Men rejected for what was viewed in the 1590s as a more natural method.

Scene 4.2: As the mechanicals lament Bottom's disappearance and their consequent inability to perform their play before the duke, Bottom appears. He tells them to prepare to put on their play. A similar situation occurs in act 3, scene 5, of *The Two Noble Kinsmen*. See the discussion there for a possible link to the beginning of Shakespeare's theatrical career.

The Woods outside Athens

Though the play's setting is ancient Greece, the woods are English, and its fairies and sprites are drawn from English folklore rather than Greek mythology. The weather Titania describes in 2.1.81–117 reflects the cold, excessively wet English summer of 1594, likely the year before Shakespeare wrote this play. In his *Annales or a Generale Chronicle of England*, John Stow described that summer:

> This year in the month of May, fell many great showers of rain, but in the months of June and July, much more; for it commonly rained every day, or night, until St. James's Day [July 25], and two days after together most extremely, all which, notwithstanding in the month of August there followed a fair harvest, but in the month of September fell great rains, which raised high waters, such as stayed the carriages, and bare down bridges, at Cambridge, Ware and elsewhere, in many places.

Scene 2.1: Puck (also known as Robin Goodfellow, an apotropaic name that contradicts his mischievous nature), who serves Oberon, king of the fairies, meets a fairy who attends on Titania, the fairy queen. Oberon and Titania enter with their attendants and quarrel over an orphan Indian boy left to Titania to raise. Oberon wants the boy as a page, but Titania refuses to surrender to him. After Titania departs, Oberon, resolved to have the boy, sends Puck to find the herb love-in-idleness (pansy). When the juice of this plant is placed in the eye, the person so anointed will fall in love with the first creature he or she sees. Oberon will anoint Titania's eyes so she will fall in love with some vile thing, and he will remove the spell only when she surrenders the boy.

Oberon hides when Demetrius and Helena enter, Demetrius in pursuit of Hermia, Helena in pursuit of Demetrius. Sympathizing with Helena, Oberon instructs Puck to use the juice of love-in-idleness to make Demetrius fall in love with Helena. Oberon's description of Demetrius is vague, though. Puck goes off to seek an Athenian man, while Oberon searches for Titania.

Scene 2.2: Titania's fairy attendants sing her to sleep. Oberon finds her and squeezes the love-in-idleness juice onto her eyes. He leaves as Lysander and Hermia appear. Lost in the woods, they decide to sleep until daylight. Lysander wants to sleep next to Hermia, but she makes him lie by himself. Finding them sleeping apart, Puck concludes Lysander is the scornful lover and so puts the magic juice in Lysander's eyes. After Puck departs, Helena and Demetrius enter. Demetrius quickly runs off. Helena awakens Lysander, who falls in love with her immediately and begins to woo her. Thinking he is mocking her, she flees, with Lysander in pursuit and Hermia abandoned.

Scene 3.1: The rude mechanicals gather to rehearse their play. Puck comes upon them and magically puts an ass's head on Bottom. Bottom's translation in part reflects his character. It also derives from Apuleius's *Golden Ass* (second century CE), in which Lucius is transformed into a donkey and eventually restored to human form. Seeing Bottom's metamorphosis, the other actors flee. Titania awakes, sees Bottom, and falls in love with him. She instructs her fairies to lead him to her bower.

Scene 3.2: Puck reports to Oberon about his recent activities. He believes he has discharged successfully the task Oberon set him, but then Demetrius and Hermia enter. Oberon recognizes Puck has enchanted the wrong man. Hermia flees Demetrius, who lies down to sleep. Oberon then anoints his eyelids, while Puck goes off to fetch Helena. As Puck recognizes, Oberon has enhanced the confusion of the night because now both Lysander and Demetrius will woo Helena. That is what happens when Helena arrives with Lysander. Hermia accuses Helena of stealing Lysander from her, and Helena accuses Hermia of joining with the men in mocking her because she does not believe the professions of love of either Demetrius or Lysander. Lysander and Demetrius go off to fight for Helena (a mock Trojan War), who runs away from the enraged Hermia. Having witnessed the lovers' dissension, Oberon instructs Puck on how to sort out the confusion. Oberon goes to ask Titania again for her Indian boy and to undo the spell that made her love Bottom. One by one the Athenians arrive and fall asleep. Puck undoes the charm on Lysander, who will now love Hermia, but Demetrius will still love Helena.

Scene 4.1: At Titania's bower, Titania and Bottom sleep. Oberon, having secured the Indian boy from the fairy queen, undoes his charm. Titania awakes and loathes Bottom. Puck removes the ass's head from the sleeping Bottom. After Titania leaves with Oberon and Puck, Theseus, Hippolyta, Egeus, and attendants come to hunt in the woods and find the two couples lying together asleep. Theseus awakens them. Egeus still wants Hermia to marry Demetrius, but Demetrius now loves Helena. Theseus overrules Egeus and declares the Athenian lovers will marry when he weds Hippolyta that day.

Bottom awakes and says he will ask Peter Quince to write a ballad about the strange dream he has had about being turned into an ass.

The Merchant of Venice

ITALY

Belmont

Shakespeare's Belmont, located on the Italian mainland close to Venice, is a fictional place. However, the Foscari family lived at Villa Foscari-Malcontenta on the Brenta River, ten miles from Venice and two miles from the monastery Ca' delle Monache; in 3.4.31 Portia says, "There is a monast'ry two miles off" from her house. The villa is now part of the University of Venice. Shakespeare may have known of this location and given it to Portia. Whereas Venice is a city of commerce and strife, Belmont, like the woods outside Athens in *A Midsummer Night's Dream* or the Forest of Arden in *As You Like It*, is a retreat where romance and magic prevail.

Scene 1.2: Portia and her maid, Nerissa, mock Portia's suitors and praise Bassanio, who had visited Belmont with the Marquis of Montferrat when Portia's father was alive. (Montferrat is in the Piedmont region of Italy. It became a duchy in 1574.) They discuss (and thus reveal to the audience) the test Portia's dead father had devised to determine whom she will wed: The successful suitor must guess which one of three caskets (gold, silver, or lead) contains her picture. If he chooses correctly, he will wed Portia (and she must marry him). If he chooses incorrectly, he must leave Belmont at once and never marry.

Scene 2.1: The Prince of Morocco accepts the challenge of the caskets.

Scene 2.7: The Prince of Morocco, hoping to win Portia's hand in marriage, chooses the gold casket, which, he discovers, contains the picture of a death's head, not Portia's image. After he departs, Portia's comment about him reveals she is a racist.

Scene 2.9: The Prince of Aragon chooses the silver casket and finds within a picture of a fool's head. After he leaves, a messenger announces the arrival of a Venetian. Nerissa hopes it is Bassanio.

Scene 3.2: Portia, in love with Bassanio and eager to enjoy his company longer, urges him to delay choosing among the caskets, but he insists on doing so immediately. As he ponders the caskets, he hears a song, the last word of its first three lines rhyming with *lead*, which is the casket he picks. Portia knows which casket holds her picture, and she tells Bassanio, "I could teach you / How to choose right, but then I am forsworn. / So I will never be" (3.2.10–12). Yet, the song she has sung as Bassanio ponders the caskets is at least a subliminal hint. Inside the lead casket, he finds Portia's picture. Gratiano asks to marry Nerissa, and Bassanio agrees to a double wedding.

Lorenzo, Jessica, and Salerio arrive. Salerio gives Bassanio a letter from Antonio reporting the loss of all his ships, so he will be unable to repay Shylock. Portia offers to pay the debt. She instructs Bassanio to marry her and then go to Venice with money to discharge Antonio's loan.

Scene 3.4: Portia entrusts her house to Lorenzo and Jessica while she and Nerissa supposedly go to a nearby monastery to pray and contemplate until their husbands return. Once the women leave, Portia sends her servant Balthasar to Padua to consult her cousin Doctor Bellario about Antonio's case. As noted in the section on *The Taming of the Shrew*, the University of Padua was noted for legal studies in Shakespeare's day. Portia and Nerissa will go to Venice in disguise to attend Antonio's trial.

Scene 3.5: In Portia's garden Launcelot Gobbo, Lorenzo, and Jessica banter as they prepare to dine.

Scene 5.1: On the grounds of Portia's house, Lorenzo and Jessica enjoy the night. A messenger announces the immediate return of Portia and Jessica, and Launcelot Gobbo declares Bassanio is coming, as well. While musicians play, Jessica and Lorenzo speak the words Ralph Vaughn Williams used in his "Serenade to Music" (1938). Portia and Nerissa arrive, followed by Bassanio, Antonio, Gratiano, and attendants. Gratiano and Nerissa and Bassanio and Portia quarrel over the missing rings the men gave away. Then the women reveal they have the rings and explain how they got them. Portia instructs Antonio to return her ring to Bassanio, thus letting Antonio know she is Bassanio's true love, which he cannot alienate. Portia also informs Antonio his ships have come safely to harbor. Nerissa tells Lorenzo and Jessica they are Shylock's heirs. Portia invites everyone to go inside to discuss further the recent events, and Gratiano ends the play with a bawdy pun about keeping Nerissa's "ring" safe.

Some productions end with Antonio and Jessica left behind. Antonio has lost his beloved Bassanio, and Jessica may suspect that as a Jew she remains an outsider and Lorenzo married her only for her money. The play's final stage direction, however, indicates everyone goes off together to show the restoration of harmony and a happy ending for all.

Venice

Venice consists of many islands linked by bridges. The city takes its name from the Veneti, who settled in the area in the tenth century BCE. The First Doge (Duke) of Venice, Paolo Lucio Anafesto, was elected in 697 CE. Beginning in the ninth century CE, Venice became an important commercial city-state, as well as a powerful naval power; by the end of the thirteenth century, it was the most prosperous city in Europe and ruled many islands in the Mediterranean, including Crete and Cyprus. In Shakespeare's day the city's power was waning, but it still was an important commercial center.

On March 29, 1516, Venice established a Jewish ghetto, which took its name from *geti*, "foundries," that had been located on the site. Residents were confined here from dusk until daylight the next day. The ghetto was located on a northern island on the outskirts of the city, with only two bridges, which were closed each evening. The island, seven acres in size, allowed Jews to own property in the city for the first time. Previously, Jews could work in Venice but could not maintain a permanent residence here. Shylock's house in this play would have been in the ghetto. Occupations open to Jews were limited—they were allowed to be doctors, traders in secondhand clothes, and money lenders because Christians were not supposed to charge interest. Jews also had to wear an identifying piece of clothing, such as a yellow badge or yellow hat. Jews were permitted to build synagogues and practice their religion in the ghetto. In 1608 Thomas Coryat wrote that six thousand Jews lived in the ghetto. While Jews were living in England in the sixteenth century, they were legally not supposed to be. England had expelled its Jews in 1290 and would not legally readmit them until 1656. Despite its legal restrictions on Jews, Venice was therefore viewed in Shakespeare's time as tolerant toward them. Venice was the center of Hebrew printing from the sixteenth into the eighteenth centuries. Napoleon abolished the ghetto in 1797 after capturing Venice.

Venice's relatively tolerant policy toward Jews (from a sixteenth-century perspective) and its large Jewish population were well known in Shakespeare's time and may explain his placing the play in this city. An Elizabethan ballad "The Crueltie of Gernulus a Jew" is set here. In his *Schoole of Abuse* (1578), Stephen Gosson refers to a now-lost play, *The Jew*, that may be a source for *The Merchant of Venice*. Ser Giovanni Fiorentino's fourteenth-century *Il Pecorone* (published 1558) includes the story about a bond for a pound of flesh. It, too, is set in Venice. Shakespeare's two plays set partly in Venice both focus on outsiders, a Jew and an African, a liminal location for works about liminal characters.

Court of Justice

The Quaranties, three rooms used as courts and so named because there were forty judges, was located in the Palace of the Doges. Located at 1 Piazza San Marco, the current Gothic palace was begun about 1340. A 1574 fire destroyed the Council Chamber, which was subsequently decorated by Andrea Palladio, Tintoretto, and Veronese, whose ceiling mural depicts good government.

Scene 4.1: At Antonio's trial Bassanio offers Shylock six thousand ducats, twice the sum owed, but Shylock insists on his pound of flesh. Nerissa, disguised as a lawyer's clerk, enters with a letter from Doctor Bellario (not a medical doctor but holding a doctorate in law), commending a "young and learned doctor" (l. 144) i.e., Portia disguised as Balthasar, to represent Antonio. Portia delivers her "quality of mercy speech" (ll. 183–201), but Shylock insists on law, not mercy. Bassanio again offers Shylock twice, even ten times, the amount of the loan, but Shylock is adamant. Portia agrees Shylock is entitled to his pound of flesh but offers him nine thousand ducats, which he refuses. Portia again says he may take his pound of flesh, and Shylock praises "Balthasar's" judgment. Then Portia declares his bond does not allow him any blood. If Shylock spills any, his lands and goods will be forfeit to the state. Bassanio yet again wants to give Shylock money, but Portia insists Shylock shall have nothing but his bond. Admitting defeat, Shylock prepares to leave the courtroom, but Portia says because of his attempt on the life of Antonio, half of Shylock's goods are forfeit to his intended victim and the other half to the state, and his own life "lies in the mercy / Of the Duke only" (ll. 355–56).

The duke grants Shylock his life but declares half of Shylock's wealth will go immediately to Antonio. The other half that should go to the state may be reduced to a fine. Antonio asks that his half be given to Lorenzo and Jessica after Shylock dies; also, Shylock must convert to Christianity and make Lorenzo and Jessica his heirs. The duke orders Shylock to agree on pain of death if he refuse. Shylock consents and leaves the courtroom. Shylock's decision not to kill Antonio, even at the cost of his own life, allows the play to be a comedy.

Bassanio offers the disguised Portia three thousand ducats, but Portia asks only for the ring he is wearing, which was given to him by her and which he had promised never to remove. He refuses to surrender the ring, but after Portia leaves Antonio persuades him to send the lawyer the ring. Antonio and Portia are vying for Bassanio's love, and Antonio wins—for the moment.

Shylock's House

As noted previously, Shylock's house would perforce have been located in the ghetto.

Scene 2.3: Launcelot Gobbo bids farewell to Shylock's daughter, Jessica.

Scene 2.5: Shylock, about to go to dine with Bassanio, tells Jessica to lock up the house.

Scene 2.6: In front of Shylock's house, Jessica, disguised as a boy, elopes with Lorenzo, taking with her money and jewels belonging to her father.

A Street

Scene 1.1: Bassanio asks Antonio for a loan to woo Portia, a rich heiress. Antonio's money is tied up in various shipping ventures, but he agrees to borrow the money Bassanio needs.

Scene 1.3: Bassanio asks Shylock for a loan of three thousand ducats for three months; Antonio will guarantee repayment. In an aside Shylock reveals his hatred of Antonio for lending money without interest. Antonio is also an anti-Semite. Shylock agrees to lend the money without interest, but for a "merry sport" (l. 142), he proposes that, if the loan is not repaid on time, he can cut a pound of flesh from Antonio. Bassanio, horrified, urges Antonio not to agree, but Antonio assures him he will be able to repay the money within the time allotted.

Scene 2.2: Shylock's servant, Launcelot Gobbo, debates with himself whether he should leave his master. Old Gobbo, Launcelot's father, arrives with a present for Shylock. Old Gobbo, who is very nearsighted, does not recognize his son, who teases him before revealing his identity. When Bassanio appears, Launcelot asks to serve him, and Bassanio agrees. Gratiano enters to say he wants to accompany Bassanio to Belmont. Bassanio is hesitant because of Gratiano's sometimes wild behavior, but Gratiano promises to "put on a sober habit" (l. 190).

Scene 2.4: Lorenzo prepares to elope with Shylock's daughter, Jessica.

Scene 2.8: Salerio and Solanio discuss Bassanio's departure for Belmont, Jessica's flight with Lorenzo, and Antonio's shipping losses.

Scene 3.1: Solanio and Salerio discuss a report that Antonio has lost another ship. When Shylock appears, they mock him. He delivers his "Hath not a Jew eyes" speech (ll. 59–73), concluding he intends to revenge himself on Antonio. A messenger comes to summon Salerio and Solanio to Antonio's house. As they depart, Tubal enters. Shylock had sent him to Genoa for news about Jessica. Tubal has not found her but reports on her extravagance. Shylock laments her lavish spending but rejoices that "Antonio is certainly undone" (l. 124).

Scene 3.3: Shylock has Antonio arrested for debt.

Scene 4.2: Gratiano overtakes Portia and gives her Bassanio's ring. Nerissa says she will get her ring from Gratiano, even though he, like Bassanio, had promised never to remove it.

The Merry Wives of Windsor

ENGLAND

Windsor, Berkshire

Windsor is located twenty-one miles west of London on the south bank of the Thames; Eton sits on the north bank across from the town. Windsor was the Anglo-Saxon Windlesora ("winch/windlass by the riverside"). For the castle, see *Richard II*.

The entire play unfolds in and near Windsor. This is Shakespeare's only play set in contemporary England, though many of the characters appear in the *Henry IV* plays set almost two hundred years earlier. Falstaff died in *Henry V* in 1415, but he is so full of life, he revives in Elizabethan Windsor. Slender and Shallow appear in *2 Henry IV*, and Shallow is an old man in that play, so they would be over two hundred years old by now. Robin, Falstaff's page, is killed in *Henry V* at the Battle of Agincourt (1415) but again serves Falstaff in this play.

As noted later (scene 4.3), *The Merry Wives* may well have been composed as a Garter play, particularly to celebrate the investiture of Lord Hunsdon, the Lord Chamberlain, into the order. Because St. George's Chapel in Windsor Castle is the seat of the Order of the Garter, the choice of Windsor for the setting would be ideal. The Thames runs through Windsor and so provides a good location for the ducking of Falstaff in Datchet Meadow about a half-mile from the town, and the forest, with its legend of Herne the Hunter, serves well for the last act.

Dr. Caius's House

Scene 1.4: Mistress Quickly promises Simple she will help Slender win Anne Page. As Dr. Caius approaches, Simple hides in a closet, but Caius finds him. Simple claims he came from the Welsh parson Sir Hugh Evans to ask Mistress Quickly, the doctor's housekeeper, to help Slender marry Anne Page. Because Dr. Caius is himself in love with Anne, he sends a challenge to the parson. Everyone leaves except Mistress

Quickly. Fenton, a gentleman in love with Anne, enters. Mistress Quickly assures him Anne loves him and promises to help him win her. Alone, Mistress Quickly says Anne does not love Fenton, though Anne does.

A Field outside Windsor
Scene 2.3: Dr. Caius awaits the arrival of Sir Hugh Evans for their duel. Page, Shallow, Slender, and the host of the Garter arrive. The host takes Caius to see Anne Page.

A(nother) Field outside Windsor, near Frogmore
Scene 3.1: Sir Hugh asks Simple about Dr. Caius. Page, Shallow, Slender, the host of the Garter, Dr. Caius, and Caius's servant John Rugby arrive. The host orders the doctor and parson disarmed and explains he did not want either man killed, so he sent them to different locations to avoid a duel. Left alone, the doctor and parson swear revenge on the host.

Ford's House
Scene 3.3: Mistress Page hides when Falstaff arrives to court Mistress Ford. As the women had planned, Robin enters to say Ford is at the door. Mistress Page warns he is coming with officers to search the house. Falstaff hides in a laundry basket, and the women cover him with dirty clothes. Mistress Ford then orders her servants to carry the basket to Datchet Meadow, along the Thames near Windsor Park, where they will dump Falstaff into a muddy ditch. Ford, Page, Dr. Caius, and Sir Hugh arrive at Ford's house, and Ford tells them to look for Falstaff. While the men go off to search, the two women agree to arrange another meeting between Falstaff and Mistress Ford to torment the knight again. When the men return from a fruitless search, they rebuke Ford for his unfounded suspicion.

  Scene 4.2: As soon as Falstaff begins to court Mistress Ford, Mistress Page announces that Ford and Page are coming to look for Falstaff. The women decide to disguise him as the Fat Woman of Brainford, the aunt of Mistress Ford's maid. Brentford (or Brainford) is a village near Windsor, where the "witch of Brentford" kept a tavern. Thomas Dekker and John Webster's *Westward Ho* (1607) refers to "that old hag, Gillian of Brainford" as a witch, and she is mentioned in other contemporary works as well. Brainford was presented as a place where women went to make merry. The 1602 quarto of *Merry Wives* calls the Fat Woman "Gillian of Brainford." Ford hates the woman. While Falstaff is disguising himself offstage, Ford, Page, Dr. Caius, Sir Hugh Evans, and Shallow enter the house. Ford searches the laundry basket but finds no one. The other men again reprimand him for his jealousy. When Falstaff appears as the Fat Woman, Ford beats "her," and "she" runs away. The other men go off to search the house.

Scene 4.4: Mistresses Page and Ford tell their husbands about their encounters with Falstaff. They agree to arrange yet another meeting, this time in Windsor Park at midnight at Herne's Oak. The tree was actually in Home Park, Windsor. Herne, a keeper of the forest, supposedly hanged himself from this tree, and his ghost haunted it at midnight. One candidate for being this tree fell in 1796. Another died in 1791 and blew down in a storm in 1863. Falstaff is to disguise himself as Herne the Hunter, with horns on his head, alluding to Actaeon, who was punished by being turned into a stag for seeing Diana naked. The horns on Falstaff's head also suggest the cuckold's horns he sought to put on the foreheads of Page and Ford. The women will dress children as fairies and give them candles. The children will pinch and singe Falstaff before the adults reveal themselves and mock the knight. Page intends to use this occasion for Anne to run off with Slender, and Mistress Page plans for Dr. Caius to elope with Anne.

Garter Inn
31 High Street

The Garter Inn stood opposite the present statue of Queen Victoria and was replaced by Ye Harte and Garter Hotel.

Scene 1.3: To save money Falstaff dismisses Bardolph, who goes to work for the host of the Garter Inn. When Falstaff asks Nym and Pistol to take love letters to Mistresses Page and Ford, the men refuse. Falstaff's page, Robin, takes the letters. Falstaff dismisses Nym and Pistol, who vow revenge.

Scene 2.2: Falstaff refuses to lend Pistol money. Mistress Quickly tells Falstaff that Ford will be away from home between ten and eleven o'clock, so Falstaff can meet with Mistress Ford then. Mistress Quickly adds that Mistress Page hopes to find a time she, too, can meet with the knight.

Bardolph tells Falstaff a Master Brooke wishes to see him. Brooke says he loves Ford's wife. He gives Falstaff money to seduce her because, he says, if she yields to Falstaff, then Brooke can get her to sleep with him as well. Falstaff tells Brooke he plans to meet Mistress Ford between ten and eleven.

Scene 3.5: Falstaff complains of being dumped in the river. Mistress Quickly tells him Mistress Ford regrets what happened and asks him to come to her house between eight and nine, when her husband will be out birding. Falstaff consents. Ford enters disguised as Brooke, and Falstaff reveals the misadventure with the laundry basket. Falstaff then says he has another rendezvous planned. Ford resolves to catch Falstaff this time.

Scene 4.3: Bardolph tells the host some German visitors want horses, and a German duke is about to arrive. In 1597 Frederick, Duke of Württemberg, was awarded the Order of the Garter, though he did not attend the investiture ceremony at Windsor that year. Lord Hunsdon, the patron of Shakespeare's theater company, was also inducted into the order that year; the play was likely written for this occasion. The story that the play was written because Queen Elizabeth wanted a play showing Falstaff in love is less likely.

Scene 4.5: Simple, having heard that the wise woman of Brentford has visited Falstaff, asks him whether Slender will marry Anne. Falstaff assures him Slender will. After Simple leaves, Bardolph tells the host the Germans stole the horses, but the host says they have merely gone to meet the duke. Evans and Dr. Caius say the Germans were thieves in disguise, thus reinforcing the play's theme of disguises and mistaken identity. Mistress Quickly brings Falstaff a letter setting up a midnight assignation.

Scene 4.6: Fenton promises to give the host one hundred pounds for his help in marrying Anne Page. The host agrees to secure a vicar to marry them.

Scene 5.1: Falstaff agrees to meet Mistress Ford at Herne's Oak at midnight. He tells Brooke of his recent escapade as the Fat Woman of Brainford.

Page's House

Scene 1.1: In front of George Page's house, Justice Robert Shallow complains to his cousin Abraham Slender and the Welsh parson Sir Hugh Evans about Sir John Falstaff. Shallow claims Falstaff has "beaten my men, kill'd my deer, and broke open my lodge" (ll. 111–12). See the entry for "Charlecote, Warwickshire" (appendix A) for possible autobiographical elements here. Sir Hugh Evans speaks of Mistress Anne Page, who has a nice dowry and, he says, would be a good wife for Slender.

Sir Hugh knocks on Page's door. When Page answers, Shallow again complains about Falstaff, who does not deny the charges against him when he appears with his comrades. Slender adds that Falstaff's associates Bardolph, Nym, and Pistol, also resurrected from the *Henry IV* and *Henry V* plays written at the same time as this work, got him drunk and picked his pocket. (In *1 Henry IV*, scene 2.4, Prince Hal picks Falstaff's pocket while the knight sleeps.) They deny Slender's accusation.

Anne Page, her mother, and Mistress Ford join the men. Anne quickly withdraws. Falstaff kisses Mistress Ford. After he and his colleagues go inside with Page and the women, Shallow, Slender, and the parson again discuss Slender's marrying Anne Page. Slender wishes he had his "Book of Songs and Sonnets" with him (l. 199), perhaps a reference to Thomas Watson's *Hecatompathia or, the Passionate Century of Love* (1582), the model for Shakespeare's Sonnet 145, probably his earliest extant poem, addressed to his Anne, Anne Hathaway. Anne Page emerges from her house to invite the men to dine. Shallow and Evans go inside, leaving Anne and Slender together with his servant, Simple. Slender at first declines Anne's invitation to join the others, but he yields when Page asks him.

Scene 1.2: In front of Page's house, Sir Hugh gives Simple a letter to deliver to Mistress Quickly asking her to help Slender win Anne Page. Mistress Quickly is another carryover from the *Henry IV* plays; she was married to Pistol in *Henry V* and died in that play, but she has been resurrected for this one.

Scene 2.1: In front of Page's house, Mistress Page reads Falstaff's letter. Mistress Alice Ford arrives and shows her the love letter she has received from Falstaff, which is identical to Mistress Page's. They go off to plot revenge. Ford and Page arrive with Pistol and Nym. Pistol says that Falstaff is in love with Ford's wife, and Nym tells Page that Falstaff is in love with his wife, as well. Their wives briefly return, then go off with Mistress Quickly when she appears. Shallow comes to invite Page and Ford to watch the duel between Dr. Caius and Sir Hugh, but because the host of the Garter Inn has told each combatant to meet at a different place, no duel will occur.

Jealous, Ford asks the host of the Garter to introduce him to Falstaff as Brooke to learn of Falstaff's plans. Brooke is a clever alias for Ford, but Shakespeare had a darker purpose in choosing that name. William Brooke, Tenth Baron Cobham, was Lord Chamberlain from August 8, 1596, to March 5, 1597 (when he died). Shakespeare had already offended the Brooke family by originally calling Falstaff Oldcastle in *1 Henry IV*; Oldcastle was a Protestant martyr ancestor of the Brookes. The Brooke family had objected to Oldcastle, and Shakespeare had changed the name. The Brookes were enemies of the Earl of Southampton (Shakespeare's patron) and the Earl of Essex, and William Brooke had supplanted George Carey, son of the former Lord Chamberlain who had patronized Shakespeare's company, in that office. Shakespeare may again have been mocking the Cobhams here. Either William Brooke or his son Henry (Eleventh Baron Cobham) protested, and Shakespeare changed Ford's alias in the play to Broome. In the 1602 quarto of the play, the original Brooke is used, but in the 1623 Folio version the name is Broome. In a letter to Robert Cecil in February 1598, Essex referred to Henry Brooke as Falstaff; the Countess of Southampton also called him Falstaff. Henry Brooke helped quash Essex's uprising on February 8, 1601.

Scene 3.4: In front of Page's house, Anne converses with Fenton. Shallow, Slender, and Mistress Quickly arrive. Quickly tells Anne that Slender wants to speak with her, though Shallow does most of the talking. Page and his wife join them. Page chides Fenton for continuing to pursue Anne. After Page, Shallow, and Slender leave, Fenton tells Mistress Page he loves Anne. Mistress Page promises to talk to Anne, though Mistress Page favors her marrying Dr. Caius. Alone, Mistress Quickly says she will help all three of Anne's suitors. Then she goes off to arrange another meeting between Falstaff and Mistress Ford.

A Street

Scene 3.2: Ford encounters Mistress Page going to see his wife. Page, Shallow, Slender, the host of the Garter, Sir Hugh Evans, Dr. Caius, and Rugby (Caius's servant) greet Ford. Slender and Shallow are going to dine with Anne Page. Page wants his daughter to marry Slender. When the host suggests Fenton as a match for Anne, Page rejects the idea. Ford asks some of the men to come with him to his house to see a monster, by which he means Falstaff, though he himself is a monster of jealousy.

Scene 4.1: Mistress Page is taking her son William to school. Hugh Evans meets them and quizzes the boy in Latin, perhaps recalling an experience the playwright had as a child in Stratford. The Welsh Thomas Jenkins (a possible model for Sir Hugh Evans) was headmaster at King Edward VI School there from 1575 to 1579. Also, *Notes and Queries* (ninth series, 3, May 20, 1899, 381–82) describes a schoolmaster named Sir Hugh Evans in Gloucestershire, the county next to Shakespeare's Warwickshire.

Windsor Park

Located south of the town of Windsor, the park now covers five thousand acres, though historically it was larger. It includes a deer park. Windsor Forest was a royal hunting preserve. Charles II laid out the Long Walk. William, Duke of Cumberland, began Virginia Water in 1746 when he was ranger of the park. The park is open to the public. As noted previously, the scenes set here should occur in Home Park, which, unlike the larger Windsor Park, is not open to the public. It lies east of the castle and is now divided from Windsor Park by the A308 road.

Windsor Castle, where some scenes in Shakespeare's history plays occur. The Order of the Garter investiture occurs at St. George's Chapel at the castle; *The Merry Wives of Windsor* may have been written for this event in the late 1590s. © *iStock/retosteffen*

Scene 5.2: Outside Windsor Park, Page, Shallow, and Slender prepare for Slender to marry Anne Page.

Scene 5.3: In another area outside the park, Mistress Page, Mistress Ford, and Dr. Caius prepare for the doctor to marry Anne Page.

Scene 5.4: Inside the park Sir Hugh Evans, dressed as a satyr, leads his troop of children disguised as fairies.

Scene 5.5: Falstaff arrives wearing a buck's head and meets Mistress Ford and Mistress Page. As he prepares to have sex with both of them, they hear a horn sound; the women flee. Sir Hugh arrives with Anne Page, boys dressed as fairies, Pistol as a hobgoblin, and Mistress Quickly as queen of the fairies. They surround Falstaff, burn his fingers, and pinch him. Dr. Caius joins them, takes a boy he thinks is Anne Page, and leaves. The Fords and Pages reveal the trick they have played on Falstaff. Page invites him to his house to celebrate Anne Page's marriage to Slender, but Slender appears to say the person he took to Eton to marry turned out to be a boy. Dr. Caius comes with the same news. Fenton and Anne arrive to announce their marriage, and the Pages accept the situation.

Much Ado about Nothing

ITALY

Messina, Sicily

Founded by Greek settlers in the eighth century BCE, Messina, located in northeast Sicily, was originally named Zancle, from the Greek word for "scythe," the shape of its natural harbor. Anaxilas of Rhegium renamed it Messene in the early fifth century BCE after a Greek mainland city. Before becoming part of Italy, it was ruled successively by Romans, Goths, the Byzantine Empire, Arabs, Normans, and the Spanish, under the last of which Messina prospered. Spain seized Sicily in 1282 after the islanders massacred their French rulers in the Sicilian Vespers. Don Pedro I of Aragon was offered the crown by the Sicilians. In 1571 Don John of Austria, illegitimate stepbrother of King Philip II of Spain, commanded the Christian fleet that defeated the Turks at the Battle of Lepanto. Through the names of his characters, Shakespeare alludes to historical events in Sicily. In Shakespeare's day Messina was one of the greatest cities in Europe. Prone to earthquakes, the city has been repeatedly destroyed. It is now the third-largest city on the island of Sicily.

A likely source for this play is Matteo Bandello's twenty-second *Novella* (1554), which tells of the love of Sir Timbreo di Cardona (Shakespeare's Claudio) for Fenicia (Hero in the play), daughter of Lionato de'Lionati of Messina. Shakespeare took his setting, as well as his plot, from this work.

A Church

Scene 4.1: Don Pedro, Don John, Leonato, Claudio, Hero, Benedict, Beatrice, Friar Francis, and attendants gather for Hero's wedding. Claudio accuses Hero of being unchaste. Don Pedro, Don John, and Claudio claim they saw Hero talking with a man at her bedroom window the previous night. Hero denies the accusation, then faints. Don Pedro, Don John, and Claudio leave. Leonato believes the allegation, but Beatrice and the friar do not. Hero recovers and again asserts her innocence. The friar advises Hero should be assumed dead. Claudio will then repent his rejecting her.

Left alone with Beatrice, Benedict confesses his love for her, and she admits she loves him. He says he will do anything for her, to which she replies, "Kill Claudio" (l. 288). At first Benedict refuses, but as the scene ends, he agrees to challenge his now former friend.

Scene 5.3: In the churchyard Claudio, Don Pedro, and attendants gather to hang an epitaph on Hero's tomb to proclaim her innocence. They then sing a dirge for her.

Leonato's House

Scene 1.1: In front of Leonato's house, Leonato (governor of Messina), his daughter, Hero, and his niece Beatrice receive a messenger telling them Don Pedro, Prince of Aragon, will arrive that night from a recent military victory. Beatrice mockingly asks about one of his attendant lords, Benedict of Padua. Don Pedro arrives with Claudio, a lord of Florence; Benedict; Balthasar, Don Pedro's attendant; and Don John, Don Pedro's bastard half-brother. Benedict and Beatrice engage in a battle of wits. Alone with Benedict, Claudio declares his love for Hero. When Don Pedro joins them, Benedict tells him of Claudio's feelings. Don Pedro sends Benedict to tell Leonato he is coming to dinner and promises to help Claudio win Hero.

Scene 1.2: Antonio, Leonato's brother, mistakenly tells Leonato that Don Pedro loves Hero. This scene introduces the theme of misprision that pervades the play.

Scene 1.3: Elsewhere in Leonato's house, Don John, who hates his half-brother and his associates, plots with Conrade and Borachio (whose name means "drunkard") to use Don Pedro's wooing of Hero for Claudio to make mischief.

Scene 2.1: Leonato, Antonio, Beatrice, Hero, Hero's two attendants (Ursula and Margaret), and another relative discuss marriage in general and Hero's in particular. A masked dance begins. Don Pedro takes Hero as his partner. Borachio chooses Margaret, Ursula dances with Antonio, and Beatrice with Benedict. Pretending not to recognize him, Beatrice insults him.

Don John and Borachio, pretending to mistake Claudio for Benedict, claim Don Pedro is wooing Hero for himself, and Benedict thinks the same thing. Claudio is angry, but Don Pedro clarifies matters, announcing he has won Hero for the young lord. As the scene ends, Don Pedro schemes with Claudio, Leonato, and Hero to make Benedict fall in love with Beatrice.

Scene 2.2: Borachio tells Don John, who delights in mischief, he knows how to prevent Claudio from marrying Hero. Don John is to tell Don Pedro and Claudio that Hero loves Borachio and they should watch Hero's window at night. While they watch, Borachio will go to Margaret's bedroom; at her window he'll call her Hero, and she will call him Claudio. They will thus deceive Don Pedro and Claudio. Don John promises Borachio a thousand ducats if he successfully executes this plot.

Scene 2.3: In Leonato's garden Benedict professes himself a confirmed bachelor. He hides when Don Pedro, Leonato, and Claudio appear. Balthasar plays and sings a song, then leaves. The others, pretending they do not know Benedict is eavesdropping, discuss how much Beatrice loves Benedict. Claudio says he thinks Beatrice will die but will not admit her passion because she knows Benedict will rebuff her. Left alone, Benedict resolves to reciprocate Beatrice's love. When she comes to call him to dinner, he thinks she is revealing her tender feelings for him.

Scene 3.1: Once more in Leonato's garden, Hero sends Margaret to lure Beatrice outside, where Margaret, Ursula, and Hero will discuss Benedict's supposed love for Beatrice to make Beatrice fall in love with him just as the men have tricked Benedict. As Beatrice listens from hiding, the women say Beatrice is too proud to respond to Benedict's affection. After the other women leave, Beatrice says she will love Benedict.

Scene 3.2: On the day before Hero's wedding, Don Pedro, Leonato, and Claudio mock Benedict for being in love. After Benedict leaves, Don John arrives to tell Don Pedro and Claudio that Hero is unchaste. To prove his claim, he urges them to watch her window that night. Don Pedro and Claudio agree, if they see anything untoward, they will shame Hero at her wedding the next day.

Scene 3.4: In her room, Hero prepares for her wedding. When Beatrice appears, Margaret mocks her for loving Benedict.

Scene 3.5: Dogberry and Verges try to tell Leonato about the watchmen's apprehending of Borachio and Verges, but they proceed so tediously and obliquely that Leonato, preoccupied with the imminent wedding, tells them to deal with the culprits themselves.

Scene 5.1: Near Leonato's house Leonato challenges Claudio to a duel for killing Hero, and Leonato's brother Antonio insults Claudio and Don Pedro. After the brothers leave, Benedict enters and challenges Claudio, then departs. Dogberry, Verges, and the watchmen produce Conrade and Borachio; the latter confesses his trick and exposes Don John's role in it. Informed by the sexton of this news, Leonato and Antonio return. Borachio admits to killing Hero through his actions, but Leonato says Don Pedro and Claudio are equally responsible. For recompense he instructs Claudio and Don Pedro to publish Hero's innocence that night, and the next day Claudio is to marry Leonato's heretofore unknown niece (not Beatrice).

Scene 5.2: In Leonato's orchard Benedict sends Margaret to summon Beatrice. When she appears, he tells her he has challenged Claudio. Ursula arrives with the news that Hero has been declared innocent and Don John is responsible for her false condemnation.

Scene 5.4: Leonato, Antonio, Benedict, Beatrice, Margaret, Ursula, Hero, and Friar Francis again prepare for Hero's wedding. The women withdraw with Antonio. Benedict asks the friar to marry him and Beatrice. Don Pedro and Claudio arrive with a few attendants, and Antonio emerges with the women, masked. Claudio wants to see his bride's face, but Leonato says he must marry her sight unseen, and he agrees. Hero then reveals herself. Beatrice and Benedict now try to deny their love for each other, but Claudio and Hero produce sonnets they wrote proclaiming their feelings. A messenger arrives to announce the capture of Don John. Benedict promises to devise proper punishment for him tomorrow, but for now he asks everyone to dance. The play ends with this symbol of harmony.

A Prison

Scene 4.2: Dogberry, Verges, the town clerk, and the watchmen assemble to examine Borachio and Conrade. Despite Dogberry's bumbling efforts, the interrogation reveals the villainy of Borachio, Conrade, and Don John. Borachio and Conrade are tied up and are to be taken to Leonato.

A Street

Scene 3.3: The constable Dogberry and the headborough (petty constable) Verges charge two watchmen to be vigilant. Shakespeare's father served as a borough constable in Stratford in 1558. Dogberry's charge is filled with malapropisms and faulty logic. After Dogberry and Verges leave, the two watchmen overhear Borachio brag to Conrade of wooing Margaret by the name of Hero to deceive Claudio and Don Pedro. The watchmen arrest Borachio and Conrade.

As You Like It

FRANCE

Bordeaux

Located in southwest France on the Garonne River, Bordeaux is the capital of the Nouvelle-Aquitaine region. A Celtic tribe, the Bituriges Vivisci, settled here by about 300 BCE and named the town Burdigala. The city fell to the Romans, circa 60 BCE, and it became the capital of Roman Aquitaine. In the late Middle Ages, the city flourished because of its wine trade. The marriage of Eleanor of Aquitaine to Henry II brought Bordeaux under English rule in 1152, and it remained so until 1453, when it became part of France. Edward the Black Prince had a court here, and Richard II was born at Bordeaux (April 3, 1365). Bordeaux is now the sixth-largest municipality in the country.

Shakespeare does not localize the action outside the forest, but his chief source, Thomas Lodge's *Rosalynde*, begins, "Adioyning the citie of Bourdeaux."

The Duke's Palace

Scene 1.2: On the lawn outside the ducal palace, Celia, daughter of Duke Frederick, and Rosalind, daughter of the banished Duke Senior, converse. Celia promises to restore the dukedom to Rosalind when she inherits it from her father. The Clown summons Celia to Duke Frederick. Le Beau, a courtier attending on the new duke, reports on the recent wrestling. Duke Frederick, Orlando, Charles, and attendants assemble to continue the wrestling. Celia and Rosalind urge Orlando not to fight, but he insists and defeats Charles. When Duke Frederick learns of Orlando's parentage, he is displeased.

The two women remain with Orlando after everyone else leaves. Rosalind, who has fallen in love with Orlando at first sight, takes a chain from her neck and gives it to him. The women then leave the tongue-tied Orlando, who has fallen in love with

Rosalind. Le Beau returns to warn Orlando to leave the court immediately because Duke Frederick is angry with the youth.

Scene 1.3: Rosalind confesses to Celia her love for Orlando. Duke Frederick enters and banishes Rosalind. Celia and Rosalind resolve to flee the court. Rosalind, the taller of the two, will disguise herself as a man and take the name Ganymede, while Celia will pretend to be her sister and will adopt the name Aliena. They will take the clown Touchstone with them.

Scene 2.2: Duke Frederick learns of the flight of Celia, Rosalind, and Touchstone. A lord suggests Orlando has fled with them. Duke Frederick sends for Oliver.

Scene 3.1: Duke Frederick orders Oliver to find Orlando within a year or suffer permanent banishment. Meanwhile, the duke will seize Oliver's lands and goods.

Oliver de Boys's House

Scene 1.1: Orlando, the youngest son of Sir Rowland de Boys, complains to the elderly servant Adam of the way Orlando's brother Oliver behaves toward him, denying him an education and treating him like a farm worker. When Oliver appears, Orlando insists he be treated as a gentleman or given his inheritance so he can seek his fortune elsewhere. Oliver promises Orlando a portion of his inheritance but does not want to part with the money.

After Orlando goes away, Charles, Duke Frederick's wrestler, enters. They discuss the situation at court because Duke Frederick has usurped his older brother's duchy. The theme of male sibling rivalry thus pervades both court and country and contrasts with the affection between the cousins Rosalind and Celia. Charles warns Oliver not to let Orlando fight with him the next day, but Oliver says Orlando is dangerous: If Charles only slightly injures Orlando, Orlando will try to kill him. Oliver thus hopes to rid himself of his brother by having Charles kill or at least seriously harm Orlando.

Scene 2.3: Adam warns Orlando to flee because Oliver plans to kill him. Adam offers Orlando his life's savings of five hundred crowns and says he will accompany the youth.

The Forest of Arden

Much of the action in Lodge's *Rosalynde* is set in the Forest of Ardennes, which stretches through France, Germany, Belgium, and Luxembourg and was the scene of heavy fighting in World Wars I and II. Despite the presence of a lion and a serpent, Shakespeare's forest has more in common with the English Forest of Arden, which once occupied the northwest section of Warwickshire near Stratford-upon-Avon and extended into Staffordshire. In *Poly-Olbion* (1612) Michael Drayton described the Forest of Arden as "Her one hand touching Trent, the other Severn's side." Little of the forest now survives. Many of Shakespeare's relatives lived in this area, and his mother's family's name derives from the forest. In Shakespeare's day the region was strongly Catholic. Shakespeare's forest also is linked to Sherwood Forest in Nottingham, home to the legendary Robin Hood. In scene 1.1 Charles tells Oliver that the banished duke has gone to the Forest of Arden, "and a many merry men with him; and there they live like the old Robin Hood of England" (1.1.113–14). Like the woods outside Athens and Portia's Belmont, this forest is ultimately mythic, a place removed from the strife at court. Here love can flourish and problems be resolved. See Northrup Frye's discussion of Shakespeare's green world in *Anatomy of Criticism* (1957). For another, darker view of the woods, see Anne Barton, *The Shakespearean Forest* (2017).

Scene 2.1: Duke Senior praises his sylvan life. He and a lord discuss the melancholic Jaques's moralizing about a wounded deer.

Scene 2.4: Rosalind, Celia, and Touchstone come upon the shepherds Corin and Silvius. Silvius tells Corin of his love for Phebe, a disdainful shepherdess. After the lovelorn Silvius departs, Rosalind asks Corin if she can buy food and lodging. Corin replies the flock he is tending and the cottage where he lives are not his, but they are for sale. Rosalind replies she will give Corin the money to buy the flock, pasture, and cottage from his master, and she will retain him as her shepherd.

Scene 2.5: In another part of the forest Amiens, Jaques, and others sing "Under the Greenwood Tree," a song Jaques then mocks. With the departure of Will Kemp as the Lord Chamberlain's Men's leading comic actor and his replacement by Robert Armin, the character of the Fool became more reflective, and Shakespeare's comedies became more musical because Armin had a good singing voice.

Scene 2.6: Adam is too tired to walk any farther. Orlando leaves him to seek help.

Scene 2.7: Jaques joins Duke Senior, Amiens, and other lords to report his meeting with Touchstone. Orlando enters with his sword drawn to demand food for Adam. Receiving a gentle reply from Duke Senior, Orlando goes off to bring Adam. In his absence Jaques delivers his "All the world's a stage" speech (ll. 138–65). The opening line echoes the Globe's motto, *Totus mundus agit histrionem* ("All the world plays the player"), which appeared on the theater's flag that flew on performance days. *As You Like It* may have been the first play staged at the new Globe in 1599. *Henry V* and *Julius Caesar* are other candidates for this distinction.

Orlando returns with Adam (who then vanishes from the play). As they eat, Amiens sings "Blow, blow, thou winter wind" (ll. 173–89). Duke Senior, learning Orlando is the son of Sir Rowland de Boys, welcomes him and his companion.

Scene 3.2: Orlando leaves love poems on trees and carves love verses in their trunks. As Corin and Touchstone converse, Rosalind enters holding one of Orlando's poems about her, which Touchstone mocks. Celia comes with another poem. She dismisses Corin and Touchstone and then tells Rosalind that Orlando is the author. Orlando and Jaques enter. Jaques tells Orlando to "mar no more trees with writing love songs in their bark" (ll. 260–61). Orlando does not recognize Rosalind disguised as Ganymede, who offers to cure him of his love. He is to woo Ganymede as Rosalind, who will be so changeable Orlando will stop loving her. Orlando agrees to the scheme, though he does not want to be cured.

Scene 3.3: Touchstone wants to marry the goatherd Audrey and asks Sir Oliver Mar-text to perform the ceremony. The priest's name recalls the Martin Marprelate controversy that began in 1588, in which a Puritan pamphleteer attacked the Anglican Church, and the English government paid writers, including John Lyly, Thomas Nashe, and Robert Greene, to respond. Jaques tells Touchstone to be married in a church by a proper priest, not in the field by an unsound one. Shakespeare probably was married at Temple Grafton by John Frith, who was described in 1586 as an "old priest & unsound in religion." Shakespeare repeatedly in his plays alludes to his marriage, as when in *Twelfth Night* Orsino says a woman should marry a man older than she is (2.4.29–31)—Anne Hathaway was eight years older than Shakespeare when they married—or in *The Tempest*, when Prospero warns Ferdinand and Perdita against premarital sex (4.1.14–23); Anne was three months pregnant when she and Shakespeare married. Shakespeare may be alluding to his marriage here as well. Touchstone would prefer a dubious marriage, in case he wants to be free of Audrey later, but he yields to Jaques's urging.

Scene 3.4: Rosalind laments Orlando's failure to keep his appointment with her. Corin offers to show her and Celia Phebe scorning her lover, Silvius.

Scene 3.5: Phebe spurns Silvius. When Rosalind as Ganymede intervenes on behalf of Silvius and chides Phebe, Phebe falls in love with her. After Rosalind, Celia, and Corin leave, Phebe asks Silvius to take a "very taunting letter" (l. 134) to Rosalind/Ganymede.

Scene 4.1: Orlando arrives while Rosalind is conversing with Jaques, who leaves. Rosalind rebukes him for his tardiness, then asks him to woo her. Orlando asks Celia to conduct a mock marriage, which she does. After some witty dialogue, Orlando departs, promising to return at two o'clock that afternoon.

Scene 4.2: Jaques and sundry lords sing a song as they carry a dead deer to the duke.

Scene 4.3: Orlando is again late for his rendezvous with Rosalind. Silvius gives Rosalind Phebe's letter, which is a love poem. Rosalind reads it aloud to Silvius. She then sends Silvius to Phebe with the message that Phebe should love Silvius if she hopes to gain Ganymede's affection.

Oliver de Boys arrives with a bloody napkin sent by Orlando. He relates how Orlando saved his life, confesses his former villainy, and professes himself reformed. Rosalind faints; when she recovers, she claims she was just pretending.

Scene 5.1: Touchstone dismisses his rustic rival for Audrey, William (perhaps played by William Shakespeare). Corin summons Touchstone and Audrey to join Rosalind and Celia.

Scene 5.2: When Oliver tells Orlando of his love for Celia, Orlando says he will arrange for their marriage the next day. He wishes he could marry Rosalind, who, as Ganymede, says she can make that happen. Phebe and Silvius arrive. Silvius is still in love with Phebe, who is in love with Ganymede. Rosalind says she will marry Phebe if ever she marries a woman and charges everyone to meet together the next day.

Scene 5.3: Two pages meet Touchstone and sing, "It was a lover and his lass" (l. 15).

Scene 5.4: Rosalind as Ganymede asks Duke Senior if he will agree to his daughter's marriage to Orlando if she appears. He consents, and Orlando agrees to marry her. Phebe is eager to marry Ganymede, but if she refuses "him," she will marry Silvius. Rosalind and Celia leave. Touchstone and Audrey join the group to be married.

Rosalind and Celia return undisguised with Hymen, god of marriage, who addresses each of the four couples. Because Ganymede is Rosalind, Phebe will marry Silvius. Jaques de Boys (not the melancholy Jaques) enters to report that Duke Frederick had mustered an army to kill Duke Senior but was converted by an old religious man he met at the edge of the forest. Frederick has relinquished his dukedom and restored all the lands he confiscated from Duke Senior's supporters. Duke Senior now intends to return to court, but the melancholy Jaques plans to join Frederick. The play ends with Rosalind's epilogue requesting the audience's approval of the play.

Twelfth Night

ILLYRIA

Originally an independent kingdom, Illyria became a Roman province (conquered 168 BCE) embracing what are now part of Albania, Herzegovina, Bosnia, and Croatia. The name derives from the mythical Illyrius, son of Cadmus, mythical king of the region, and Harmonia. In Shakespeare's time this area was ruled by Venice. Despite the foreign setting, Olivia's house resembles an English country home, and Sir Toby Belch and Sir Andrew Aguecheek are quintessentially English. Orsino's court may be in Zadar, Croatia.

The Coast

Scene 1.2: Saved from a shipwreck in which she believes her brother Sebastian drowned, Viola asks the captain who rescued her to disguise her as a eunuch and present her to the court so she can serve Orsino.

Scene 2.1: Sebastian, who believes his sister Viola drowned in the shipwreck that has stranded him in Illyria, prepares to leave his rescuer, Antonio. Antonio, who may harbor homoerotic feelings for Sebastian, asks to accompany him as his servant, but Sebastian declines the offer. After Sebastian leaves, Antonio resolves to follow him anyway.

The Duke's Palace

Scene 1.1: Valentine tells Duke Orsino that Olivia, whom the duke loves, intends to mourn for her dead brother for seven years and so will not listen to his professions of love.

Scene 1.4: Viola, disguised as Cesario, has grown close to Orsino, who sends "him" to Olivia to tell of his love for her. In an aside Viola expresses her love for Orsino.

Scene 2.4: The duke and Cesario talk of love. When Feste arrives, the duke has him sing "Come away, come away death" (ll. 51–66). Orsino again sends Cesario to plead with Olivia. Cesario tries to reason with him to give up his suit, but he persists.

Olivia's House

Scene 1.3: Maria, Olivia's gentlewoman, tells Sir Toby Belch, Olivia's uncle, he should drink less, and she criticizes his foolish friend Sir Andrew Aguecheek, who then enters. Sir Andrew has been trying without success to woo Olivia. Sir Andrew proposes leaving, but Sir Toby convinces him to stay.

Scene 1.5: Maria chides the clown Feste for his absence. As Maria departs Olivia arrives with her steward, Malvolio (whose name means "ill-wisher"). Olivia initially wants to dismiss Feste, but despite Malvolio's criticism of the clown, Feste persuades her to change her mind. Maria returns to announce Viola/Cesario seeks an audience. Olivia sends Maria and Malvolio to dismiss her visitor. Sir Toby, half-drunk, passes through to report Cesario's visit. Malvolio returns to say Cesario is obdurate and refuses to depart. Olivia reneges, but she tells Cesario she cannot love Orsino. Still, having fallen in love with Cesario at first sight, she tells the youth to return. After Cesario leaves, Olivia sends Malvolio after "him" with a ring the youth supposedly left with her.

Scene 2.2: Outside Olivia's house Malvolio gives Cesario Olivia's ring. Cesario recognizes Olivia has fallen in love with "him."

Scene 2.3: Sir Toby Belch, Sir Andrew Aguecheek, and Feste revel after midnight. Feste sings, "O mistress mine, where are you roaming?" (ll. 39–52). Maria enters to chide them, and Malvolio comes shortly afterward to say Sir Toby must behave better if he wishes to continue living with his niece. After Malvolio goes off, Maria devises a plot to revenge themselves on the steward: Maria will write a thinly veiled love letter to him that appears to be from Olivia, and she will place the letter where he will find it. The letter will ask him to behave in ways Olivia detests.

Scene 2.5: In Olivia's garden Sir Toby, Sir Andrew, and Fabian, another of Olivia's servants, watch as Malvolio finds Maria's letter and convinces himself Olivia loves him. The letter instructs him to wear yellow stockings (a color Olivia hates), cross-gartered (a fashion she detests), and to smile (which ill-suits with Olivia's mourning).

Scene 3.1: Still in the garden, Cesario banters with Feste and speaks briefly with Sir Toby and Sir Andrew. Olivia sees Cesario and sends everyone else away, then confesses her love. Cesario says "he" cannot love her, but Olivia still wants "him" to continue visiting.

Scene 3.2: Sir Andrew again plans to leave because he sees Olivia prefers Cesario to him. Sir Toby does not want Sir Andrew to leave because Sir Toby is living at Sir Andrew's expense, so he claims Olivia was hoping Sir Andrew would attack Cesario to display his ardor. He says Sir Andrew can still confront the youth to impress Olivia, and Sir Andrew goes off to write a challenge. Maria summons Sir Toby and Fabian to witness the effects of her letter on Malvolio.

Scene 3.4: Olivia sends Maria to summon Malvolio, who appears in yellow hose, cross-gartered, and smiling. Olivia is puzzled by the transformation in the usually solemn Malvolio. A servant reports Cesario's arrival. Olivia sends for Sir Toby to look after her steward and goes off with Maria. Maria soon returns with Sir Toby and Fabian, who mock Malvolio. The steward leaves, and Sir Andrew comes with a letter containing a foolish challenge for Cesario. Sir Toby sends Sir Andrew away to watch for the youth.

Seeing Olivia and Cesario approach, Sir Toby, Fabian, and Maria withdraw. Olivia again professes her love for Cesario and asks "him" to come the next day. After Olivia withdraws, Sir Toby and Fabian tell Cesario that Sir Andrew intends to challenge "him" to a duel. Though Sir Andrew is a coward of the first water, they claim he is a deadly fencer. Cesario asks Sir Toby to intercede for "him." Sir Toby then goes to Sir Andrew and tells him Cesario is a fierce opponent. Fabian and Sir Toby bring the two reluctant duelists together.

At that moment Antonio appears and draws his sword to protect the person he believes is Sebastian. Sir Toby draws, as well. Officers appear and arrest Antonio, who asks Cesario for his purse. Cesario denies any knowledge of a purse, though "he" offers to share what little money "he" has. Angered, Antonio relates saving the youth, whom he names Sebastian. Viola now hopes her brother lives. Fabian, Sir Andrew, and Sir Toby pursue Cesario as "he" leaves. Sir Andrew intends to beat Cesario.

Scene 4.1: In front of Olivia's house, Sir Andrew, Sir Toby, and Fabian encounter Sebastian, whom they mistake for Cesario. Sir Andrew strikes Sebastian, who strikes him back. Sir Toby tries unsuccessfully to restrain Sebastian. They draw their swords as Olivia appears and sends Sir Toby away. She invites Sebastian into her house, and he goes off with her.

Scene 4.2: At Maria's urging, Feste disguises himself as Sir Topas and visits Malvolio, who has been confined to a dark room and treated by Sir Toby, Feste, and Maria as mad. After tormenting Malvolio, Feste at length agrees to bring him light, paper, and ink so he can write to Olivia.

Scene 4.3: In Olivia's garden Sebastian is confused by Olivia's affectionate treatment of him but agrees to marry her.

Scene 5.1: Feste, Fabian, Orsino, Viola (as Cesario), Curio, and lords assemble in front of Olivia's house. Orsino sends Feste to summon Olivia. Antonio is brought in by officers. Viola tells Orsino that Antonio intervened to save her. Antonio accuses Cesario of ingratitude: After he saved Cesario from drowning, Cesario refused to acknowledge Antonio when Antonio was arrested. When Antonio says he and Cesario just arrived in town that day, Orsino replies that Cesario has been at court three months.

Olivia emerges and rebuffs Orsino's wooing. The duke knows Olivia loves Cesario and says he will kill the youth, much as he himself loves "him." Cesario replies "he" would willingly die by Orsino's hand and confesses to loving the duke. Olivia feels betrayed and reminds Cesario of their recent marriage, which Cesario denies but which the priest confirms. Sir Andrew, entering with a wounded head, accuses Cesario of hurting him. Cesario again denies the charge. Sir Toby, who also has been hurt, arrives with Feste. After Fabian, Feste, Sir Toby, and Sir Andrew leave, Sebastian comes to apologize for harming Olivia's kinsman. Not observing his twin at first, he notices he is receiving strange looks. He warmly greets Antonio, who asks, "How have you made division of yourself?" (l. 222). Sebastian now sees Cesario/Viola, who reveals her identity. Orsino proposes to her. Although Viola and Sebastian are fraternal twins, in the play they are also identical. Shakespeare had a set of twins and wrote two plays (twins?) about identical siblings. *The Comedy of Errors* has two (twin) pairs of twins. In this play a supposedly dead twin brother returns to life. In 1596 Hamnet/Hamlet, twin to Shakespeare's younger daughter, Judith, died. In the play Shakespeare brought him back to life. Just before beginning *The Brothers Karamazov*, Fyodor Dostoevsky, the Russian Shakespeare, lost his three-year-old son Alexei. In that novel, Fyodor Karamazov is killed, while his son Alexei lives. Through fiction, writers can attempt to repair the losses of life.

Feste brings Malvolio's letter, which he begins to read as if he were mad because he claims the author is. Olivia asks Fabian to read it properly; from the letter she understands Malvolio is sane. She sends Fabian to fetch him. When Malvolio arrives with the letter he thinks Olivia wrote to him, she recognizes Maria's handwriting. She says Malvolio will choose the punishment for those who wronged him. Fabian admits he and Sir Toby devised the plot, and Maria wrote the letter, for which Sir Toby has married her. Malvolio exits declaring, "I'll be revenged on the whole pack of you" (l. 378). Orsino urges Olivia to pursue and pacify the steward. The play ends with Feste's singing.

A Street

Scene 3.3: Antonio, having met Sebastian, gives him a purse in case he wants to buy something. Antonio is a wanted man in Illyria because he fought against Orsino, so he will retire to the Elephant Inn "[i]n the south suburbs" (l. 39). The Elephant and Elephant and Castle were common signs in Elizabethan London. The Elephant and Castle is still an area in Southwark, southeast London. (See "Paris Garden" under "London" in appendix A.)

Troilus and Cressida

TURKEY

The play occurs during the Trojan War in the twelfth century BCE.

The Greek Camp near Troy

Achilles's Tent

Scene 2.1: Near Achilles's tent, when Ajax asks Thersites about Agamemnon's proclamation concerning Hector's challenge, Thersites refuses to inform him and instead insults him, so Ajax beats him. Achilles and Patroclus enter and intervene. Thersites curses them, too. After Thersites leaves, Achilles tells Ajax the contents of the proclamation.

This play probably was produced during the "War of the Theatres" (1599–1602), in which rival playwrights satirized each other. Ajax may represent Ben Jonson; Thersites, Thomas Dekker. Another possible contemporary allusion is to the Earl of Essex. George Chapman dedicated his *Seaven Bookes of the Iliades of Homer* (1598) to Essex and called him "most true Achilles." Chapman's Homer served as a key source for Shakespeare's play. If the play predates Essex's execution in February 1601, it might have been an admonition to the earl, who had withdrawn from court following his failed Irish military expedition, to stop sulking. If the play postdates Essex's execution, it may have served as an elegy but also an acknowledgment of Essex's flaws.

Scene 2.3: In front of Achilles's tent, Thersites insults Achilles and Patroclus. Agamemnon, Ulysses, Nestor, Diomedes, Ajax, and the Trojan priest Calchas (who has defected to the Greeks) join them. Achilles and Thersites leave. Agamemnon sends Patroclus to bring Achilles back, but Patroclus returns alone. Agamemnon again sends Patroclus, now with Ulysses, to bring Achilles, but Ulysses returns to say Achilles refuses to fight. Agamemnon now wants to send Ajax to summon Achilles, but Ulysses objects, praising Ajax and saying the sending of Ajax would make Achilles even prouder than he already is. Even as the Greeks mock Ajax in asides, aloud they praise him. Ulysses urges Agamemnon to call a council of war, and everyone leaves. In book 9 of the *Iliad*, Agamemnon sends Odysseus, Ajax, and Phoinix together to try (unsuccessfully) to persuade Achilles to rejoin the fight against Troy.

Scene 3.3: Ulysses, Diomedes, Nestor, Agamemnon, Ajax, Menelaus, and Calchas gather near Achilles's tent. As his reward for abandoning Troy for the Greeks, Calchas wants the Greeks to exchange the Trojan prisoner Antenor for Calchas's daughter, Cressida. Agamemnon agrees. Achilles and Patroclus emerge from their tent. Ulysses advises the Greek leaders to ignore Achilles as they walk past. Ulysses will come last, and he expects Achilles will ask why he is being slighted. When Achilles does indeed ask, Ulysses praises Ajax and observes that to retain honor one must continue to act well. If Achilles refuses to fight, he will not be honored. Ulysses adds that the Greeks know of Achilles's love for Polyxena, a daughter of Priam. Polyxena does not appear in Homer but figures in Euripides's *The Trojan Women* and *Hecuba*.

After Ulysses leaves, Patroclus urges Achilles to return to the war. Achilles sends Thersites to Ajax to invite Hector to visit his tent the next day when Hector comes to fight Ajax and to ask Agamemnon for a safe-conduct pass for Hector to allow the visit. Thersites says Ajax is so self-absorbed he will pay no attention to the request. Thersites pretends to be Ajax, while Patroclus plays Thersites speaking to him and not being understood. Achilles decides to write a letter to Ajax for Thersites to take to him.

Scene 5.1: In front of Achilles's tent Thersites delivers a letter from Hecuba, wife of Priam and mother of Polyxena, along with a love token from Polyxena. Achilles says he will not fight against Troy, just as he had promised Hecuba. Achilles and Patroclus retire into their tent to prepare for Hector's arrival. In the *Iliad* Achilles withdraws from the fighting after Agamemnon dishonors him by taking Briseis, one of Achilles's war prizes, from him.

Achilles emerges from his tent to greet Agamemnon, Hector, Troilus, Ajax, Ulysses, Nestor, Menelaus, and Diomedes when they arrive. Agamemnon and Menelaus leave. Achilles asks the others to stay, but Diomedes, Ulysses, and Troilus also depart. Diomedes has an assignation planned with Cressida, and the other two follow him to spy on him. The rest enter Achilles's tent.

Agamemnon's Tent

Scene 1.3: In front of his tent, Agamemnon, leader of the Greek forces, addresses Nestor, Ulysses, Diomedes, Menelaus, and other Greeks. He notes that seven years of fighting have not yielded victory. (The *Iliad*, on which this play is based, is set in the tenth year of the Trojan War.) Ulysses replies that Troy still stands because the Greeks have failed to observe order and degree and have dissolved into factions. Aeneas arrives with a challenge from Hector to fight a Greek in single combat the next day. All leave except Nestor and Ulysses. They understand the challenge is meant for Achilles. Ulysses says the Greeks should arrange the lottery to choose Hector's opponent so that Ajax is selected instead. Ulysses hopes thereby to quell the pride of Achilles, who has withdrawn from the fighting and now mocks Agamemnon and old Nestor.

Scene 4.5: The Greek leaders assemble. Diomedes arrives with Cressida, whom Agamemnon, Nestor, Achilles, and Patroclus kiss in turn. Diomedes goes off with Cressida. The Trojan princes arrive to watch the battle between Ajax and Hector, but because the two men are cousins, Hector quickly stops the fighting. The Greeks welcome the Trojans, but Achilles and Hector talk of killing each other. After everyone but Troilus and Ulysses leave, Troilus asks Ulysses to take him to Calchas's tent after the reception at Agamemnon's.

Calchas's Tent

Scene 5.2: In front of Calchas's tent, Diomedes asks Calchas about Cressida, who appears. While Troilus, Ulysses, and Thersites watch unobserved, Cressida flirts with Diomedes. Ulysses urges Troilus to depart, but he refuses. He sees Cressida give Diomedes the sleeve he had given her as a love token. After more flirting, Cressida agrees to meet Diomedes the next night. Aeneas comes to summon Troilus back to Troy.

The Plain between the Greek Camp and Troy

Scene 5.4: Troilus and Diomedes fight. Hector encounters Thersites but spares him.

Scene 5.5: Diomedes sends his servant to Cressida with Troilus's horse. Agamemnon reports the death of Patroclus as the Trojans triumph. The death of Patroclus prompts Achilles to fight. Ajax, too, has lost a friend and returns to the fray.

Scene 5.6: Ajax and Diomedes encounter Troilus; they exit fighting. Achilles and Hector confront each other. After a brief struggle, Achilles leaves. Troilus appears, then goes off to rescue Aeneas, captured by Ajax. Hector pursues a Greek soldier.

Scene 5.7: Menelaus and Paris fight. Thersites refuses to combat the Trojan Margarelon.

Scene 5.8: Hector rests from battle. He removes his helmet and hangs up his shield. Achilles and his Myrmidons find Hector and kill him. This account of the death of Hector shows Achilles in a much less heroic light than the *Iliad*, book 22, as the play depicts the Trojan War more satirically and cynically than Homer does.

In John Lydgate's *The Hystorye, Sege and Dystruccyon of Troye* (1513), one of Shakespeare's sources for this play, Achilles and his Myrmidons kill Troilus and later Menon in this way, and Achilles ties Troilus to his horse's tail and drags him around the field as Shakespeare has Achilles do to Hector. In Homer, Achilles ties Hector's dead body to his chariot. William Caxton's *The Recuyell of the Hystoryes of Troye* (c.

1474), the first book printed in English and another source for the play, shows Achilles killing Hector when the latter is vulnerable, not in fair combat.

Scene 5.9: Greek soldiers announce Achilles has killed Hector.

Scene 5.10: Troilus informs Aeneas, Paris, and Antenor that Hector is dead, and Achilles has tied Hector's body behind his horse and is dragging it around the battlefield. When Pandarus appears, Troilus slaps him. All the Trojans withdraw, leaving Pandarus alone. He concludes the play by bequeathing his venereal diseases to the audience. Since brothels were located near the Globe, Pandarus's talk of such ailments is apt.

Troy

The modern Hissarlik (unoccupied) in Turkey, Asia Minor, about four miles from the Aegean coast and near the Hellespont. According to mythology, Troy was founded by Teucer, the walls built by Apollo and Poseidon for King Laomedon. When Laomedon did not pay the gods, Poseidon sent a sea monster to ravage the land. Hercules killed the monster, but again Laomedon refused to pay him, so Hercules killed him and all his children except Priam, who became king. In 1865 Frank Calvert identified Hissarlik as Troy, and three years later Heinrich Schliemann began excavating here. This location was inhabited between circa 3000 BCE and 1200 CE. There are nine layers of ruins. The lowest three date to the Early Bronze Age, layers 4 and 5 belong to the Middle Bronze Age, and layer 6 to the Late Bronze Age. Layer 7, which is believed to be Homer's Troy, also belongs to this period. The top two layers were Hellenistic, Roman, and Byzantine settlements.

Troy was originally situated on a bay, but that silted up in classical times. Even the earliest city was walled. Troy VI introduced larger buildings and had impressive walls. This city was violently destroyed circa 1270 BCE, as was Troy VIIa about 1190 BCE. Troy VIIb was rebuilt and occupied for about forty years. Greek colonists arrived about 700 BCE. Augustus founded Ilium here. The city's temple of Athena was an important religious site.

Calchas's House

Scene 3.2: In Calchas's garden Pandarus, true to his name, brings Cressida to Troilus. Cressida admits she has loved Troilus since she first saw him. Troilus promises to love Cressida so truly that his name will be a byword for faithful lovers. Cressida says, if she proves unfaithful, her name will be a byword for infidelity. Pandarus adds that, if Troilus and Cressida are not true to each other, go-betweens will be called pandars. Pandarus leads the lovers to a bedroom.

Scene 4.2: Troilus wants Cressida to come back to bed. Pandarus responds to knocking at the door as Troilus and Cressida withdraw. Aeneas enters and asks for

Troilus, who appears. Aeneas tells him of the exchange of Antenor for Cressida. Aeneas and Troilus depart. When Cressida returns, Pandarus tells her she must join her father in the Greek camp. She says she will not leave Troy.

Scene 4.3: Paris pities Troilus, who prepares to surrender Cressida to Diomedes.

Scene 4.4: Troilus and Cressida lament their separation and promise to be faithful to each other. He says he will bribe the Greek sentries so he can see her. Aeneas, Paris, Antenor, Deiphobus, and Diomedes arrive. Troilus gives Cressida to Diomedes and goes off with them. A trumpet sounds, and the others leave to watch the combat between Ajax and Hector.

Priam's Palace

Scene 2.2: The Trojans debate whether to return Helen to the Greeks and so end the Trojan War. Hector and Helenus favor returning her. Hector says, "She is not worth what she doth cost / the keeping" (ll. 51–52). Troilus and Paris want to keep her. Cassandra enters to prophesy the destruction of Troy if Helen remains in the city. Although Hector recognizes that Helen should be returned to her Greek husband, Menelaus, he finally concurs in keeping her.

Scene 3.1: Pandarus asks Paris to make an excuse for Troilus if Priam asks his sons to dinner. Paris understands Troilus plans to spend the night with Cressida. Helen keeps interrupting the conversation by asking Pandarus to sing, which he finally does before retiring. When Trojan soldiers return from battle, Paris and Helen go to greet them. Paris asks Helen to help unarm Hector.

Scene 5.3: In front of Priam's palace, Andromache, wife of Hector, and his sister Cassandra urge Hector not to fight. Hector rebuffs their pleas but asks Troilus not to fight. Troilus insists. Cassandra brings Hector's father, Priam, to plead with Hector, but Hector ignores him as well. Pandarus brings Troilus a letter from Cressida, which he reads and then tears, having seen her with Diomedes in the previous scene.

A Street

Scene 1.2: Alexander, Cressida's servant, tells her Queen Hecuba and Helen are going to watch the battle between the Greeks and Trojans. Pandarus joins his niece and her servant and praises Troilus. As they talk, the Trojans return from fighting. Pandarus commends each of the warriors, and when Troilus passes, Pandarus again lauds him. Troilus's boy summons Pandarus, who exits. Alone, Cressida admits she loves Troilus but is concealing her feelings because "Men prize the thing ungained more than it is" (l. 296).

Scene 4.1: Aeneas, Paris, Deiphobus, Antenor, Diomedes, and others meet. Paris informs Aeneas that Diomedes has brought Antenor to exchange for Cressida. Paris asks Diomedes whether he or Menelaus deserves Helen more. Diomedes replies that the cuckold Menelaus and the lecher Paris deserve her equally.

Troilus's House

Scene 1.1: Troilus tells Pandarus, uncle of Cressida, he will not fight against the Greeks because he is too much in love with Cressida. Pandarus advises patience and refuses to help Troilus. After Pandarus leaves, Aeneas enters to report Paris has been wounded by Menelaus. Aeneas and Troilus go off together.

All's Well That Ends Well

This play derives from Boccaccio's *Decameron* (1353), day 3, story 9, and William Painter's close retelling in *The Palace of Pleasure* (1575), novel 38. All the settings in the play appear in these works, except that on her return to Roussillon from Italy, Giletta (Shakespeare's Helen) stops at Montpellier rather than Marseilles.

FRANCE

Marseille, Provençal

The second-largest city in France, Marseille is located on the Mediterranean coast. The city was founded by Greeks (c. 600 BCE), who called the settlement Massalia. Julius Caesar captured the city in 49 BCE. It was conquered by Visigoths in the fifth century CE and destroyed by Charles Martel in 739. In the tenth century, it was part of the county of Provence. It became part of France in 1482. The French national anthem originated here in 1792, as citizens sang this song while marching from Marseille to Paris to support the revolutionary government; the song came to be known as "Le Marseillaise."

A Street

Scene 5.1: Helena, Diana, and the widow with two attendants have come in search of the king of France, but a lord informs them he left the previous night for Roussillon. Helena gives the lord a petition for the king. Then she and the rest of her party set off for Roussillon.

Paris

In the third century BCE, the Parisii established a settlement on the Île de la Cité and along the banks of the Seine. Under Titus Labienus a Roman army defeated the Parisii and created a garrison town here, which the Romans named Lutetia (52 BCE). After the collapse of the Roman Empire, Clovis I, king of the Franks, made Paris his capital (508 CE). During the Middle Ages, Paris became Europe's largest city and emerged as a commercial and cultural center. Gothic architecture originated here, and the University of Paris was among Europe's first such institutions. The English occupied Paris from 1420 to 1436, as indicated in this play. In Shakespeare's time the city, like the rest of France, was riven by religious strife, but in the seventeenth century and after it continued to grow and flourish.

The Louvre
Rue de Rivoli [Paris metro stop: Louvre]
Originally a fortress built by Philip II in the twelfth century, in the fourteenth century, Charles V converted it into a residence. Under Louis XIV, who lived at Versailles, the Louvre became a home for artists. On August 10, 1793, the one-year anniversary of the execution of Louis XVI, it opened as a public museum, and so it remains.

Scene 1.2: The French king welcomes Bertram.

Scene 2.1: The king bids farewell to lords going to fight in the war between Florence and Siena. Florence and Siena fought often in the thirteenth through fifteenth centuries. The most famous encounter occurred on September 4, 1260, at the Battle of Montaperti, noted in Dante's *Commedia*. Bocca degli Abati, though supposedly fighting for Florence's Guelphs, supported the Sienese Ghibellines. Late in the day, as the Sienese counterattacked, Abati cut off the hand of Florence's standard-bearer, causing confusion in the Florentine ranks and leading to a Sienese victory. Dante placed Abati in the ninth circle of the *Inferno*, the circle of betrayers ("compound fraud"). Farinata degli Uberti, leader of the Sienese forces that day, appears in canto 10 of the *Inferno* in the circle of heretics, where Farinata declares he alone among the Ghibelline leaders argued to spare Florence from being razed. It is not clear in the play which conflict Shakespeare had in mind.

Bertram, who has been forced to remain in France, accompanies Parolles to watch the lords leaving for Italy. Lafew, an old lord, informs the king of Helena's arrival. The king initially rejects Helena's offer to try to cure him of his fistula but relents. She says if she succeeds, she wants the king to give her as her husband any man she wants, barring those of royal blood.

Scene 2.3: Bertram, Lafew, and Parolles discuss the king's recovery. The king enters with Helena and attendants. Four lords appear as possible husbands for Helena, but she rejects them and asks Bertram to marry her. He refuses because of her low birth. The king orders Bertram to marry her, which he does, but he refuses to consummate the marriage. Instead he intends to go to the Tuscan War.

Scene 2.4: Parolles informs Helena of Bertram's decision to go to Italy and his wish that she leave the court.

Scene 2.5: Lafew tells Bertram that Parolles is a coward, but Bertram does not believe him. Lafew leaves, and Helena appears. Bertram tells her to go back to Roussillon and gives her a letter for his mother. After she leaves, Bertram says he will not go home as long as he can fight.

Scene 3.4: In December 1431 Henry VI came to Paris to be crowned king of France (crowned December 16, 1431). At the Louvre Henry meets Lord John Talbot, leader of the English forces, and makes him Earl of Shrewsbury. In fact, in 1431 Talbot was a French prisoner. He was ransomed only in 1433, and he became Earl of Shrewsbury while he was in England in 1442.

Roussillon

Located in southwest France. Ruscino was settled in the seventh century BCE. It became part of the Roman Empire in the second century BCE. It fell to the Visigoths in 462 CE, to the Arabs in about 720, and then to the Franks in the 750s. In the thirteenth century, Roussillon was part of the kingdom of Majorca. It was ruled by the king of Aragon until the 1640s; Spain ceded it to France in the Treaty of the Pyrenees in 1659.

The Count's Palace

Scene 1.1: Bertram, Count of Roussillon, whose father has recently died, prepares to leave his mother, the dowager countess, to join the king of France. Parolles goes with him. The king is gravely ill with a fistula. (Louis XIV had an anal fistula; his illness occurred in 1685, well after Shakespeare's death. It is a case of life imitating art.) The countess's ward, Helena, daughter of the recently deceased physician Gerard de Narbon, loves Bertram. She intends to follow him to court, where she will try to cure the king.

Scene 1.3: Helena confesses to the countess that she loves Bertram. The countess agrees to Helena's going to Paris to try to help the king.

Scene 2.2: The countess sends Lavatch to court to give Helena a letter and to greet Bertram and her other relatives there.

Scene 3.2: Lavatch says his love for Isbel has declined since he went to the French court. The countess reads a letter from her son saying he has married Helena but will not consummate the marriage, and he has fled to avoid his new wife. A French lord informs her Bertram has gone to serve the Duke of Florence. Bertram has written to Helena stating he will not be her husband until she gets his ring, which he never intends to remove from his finger, and gets a child by him. He also says he will not return to France as long as he is married to Helena. Helena resolves to leave France so Bertram can return and not endanger himself fighting for Florence.

Scene 4.5: Lavatch, the countess, and Lafew discuss Helena's supposed death. After Lavatch leaves to tend to the horses, Lafew reports that the king of France is coming to Roussillon from Marseille, as is Bertram. Lavatch returns to announce the arrival of Bertram with a dozen soldiers.

Scene 5.2: In front of the count's palace, Parolles gives Lavatch a letter for Lafew, who arrives as the two men are talking. Parolles asks Lafew to help him regain his position, and Lafew agrees.

Scene 5.3: The countess asks the king to forgive Bertram for abandoning Helena, now believed dead. The king consents. When Lafew offers his daughter Maudlin as Bertram's wife, Bertram and the king approve the match. Bertram gives Lafew a ring for Maudlin, which the king recognizes as the one he himself gave Helena. Bertram in vain denies it was hers. The king now accuses Bertram of killing his wife, and guards take him away.

An astringer (keeper of hawks) delivers to the king a petition from Diana saying Bertram had promised to marry her once Helena died, and she asks the king to make Bertram keep his promise. Bertram returns under guard; the widow and Diana enter. Bertram denies promising to marry Diana and calls her a whore. She shows the king Bertram's ring. Parolles is brought in to confirm Bertram's promise to marry Diana, who says she gave Bertram the ring the king had given Helena. When she refuses to explain how she got that ring, she is arrested. Diana says she can produce bail. Her mother leaves and returns with Helena. Bertram asks Helena's forgiveness. Because Helena has gotten his ring and is carrying his child, he agrees to be her husband "If she . . . can make me know this clearly" (l. 315). Shakespeare's women often marry men unworthy of them, and Bertram may be the most unworthy of the lot ("If," indeed!). Still, Helena wants him. The play ends with the king's promising to provide a dowry for Diana when she marries.

ITALY

Florence

The capital of Tuscany, Florence sits on the Arno River. A small Etruscan settlement existed at Fiesole by 200 BCE. The Etruscans gave their name to the Tuscan region. Florence was founded by Sulla in 59 BCE for his veteran soldiers. The city was called Fluentia because it was situated between two rivers (Mugnone and Arno), later changed to Florentia (flowing). After the collapse of the Western Roman Empire, the city was ruled by Ostrogoths, Lombards, and Franks. Florence flourished in the Middle Ages as a cultural, military, and commercial center, and it was the birthplace of the Italian Renaissance, fostered by the Medici family. In the eighteenth and nineteenth centuries, it was ruled by Austria, except during the Napoleonic era, when Tuscany was attached to France. Tuscany became part of the kingdom of Italy in 1861, and Florence served as the kingdom's capital from 1865 to 1871.

The Duke's Palace

The Palazzo Vecchio, overlooking the Piazza della Signora, is now a museum and Florence's town hall. Begun at the end of the thirteenth century, it became the home of Duke Cosimo I de' Medici in 1540. In 1549 he acquired the Renaissance Pitti Palace (named for Lucca Pitti, the Florentine banker who built the palace in 1458) on the south side of the Arno River and made it the ducal residence. It is now a museum. Before moving to the Palazzo Vecchio, the Medici lived in the Palazzo Medici (built 1444–1484), which now serves as a museum and houses government offices. Which of these palaces Shakespeare envisioned or whether he envisioned just a generic ducal palace is unclear.

Scene 3.1: The Duke of Florence tells two French lords he wonders why the French king will not support him in his war against Siena but welcomes those Frenchmen who have come to help. In the play the French king is neutral. In the fifteenth century, France supported Siena against Florence.

Scene 3.3: In front of the ducal palace, the duke appoints Bertram general of his cavalry.

Outside Florence

Scene 3.5: A Florentine widow, her daughter (Diana), Violetta, Mariana (the widow's neighbor), and other citizens have gathered to see the army. The widow reports that Bertram has captured the greatest Sienese commander and killed the Sienese duke's brother. Parolles has propositioned Diana for Bertram.

Helena arrives disguised as a pilgrim to the shrine of St. Jaques. She is taking a curious route to this shrine in Spain, but the play requires her to be in Florence. In the play's source, the Helena character is on pilgrimage but to no specified destination. Helena will lodge with the widow, who tells her of Bertram's lust for Diana. Bertram, Parolles, and the Florentine army pass by. Helena leaves with the other women.

Scene 3.6: In the camp of the Florentine army, two French lords tell Bertram that Parolles is a coward. The lords plan to capture Parolles when he tries to rescue the drum he has lost. They will pretend to be Sienese. The lords say Parolles will betray Bertram and Florence to save himself. Bertram takes one of the lords to meet Diana.

Scene 4.1: Outside the Florentine camp, a French lord and several Florentine soldiers ambush and blindfold Parolles, who believes he has been captured by soldiers loyal to Siena. To save his life, he promises to reveal "all the secrets of our camp" (l. 88). A lord sends a soldier to summon Bertram to witness Parolles's cowardice.

Scene 4.3: In the Florentine camp, two French lords discuss Bertram. They say Helena has died. With peace concluded between Florence and Siena, Bertram will return to France. Bertram watches as soldiers bring in Parolles, who reveals military secrets and speaks ill of Bertram and the Dumaine brothers, who are listening. Parolles promises to betray the Florentines and Bertram if the "Sienese" spare his life. A soldier removes Parolles's blindfold, and he sees Bertram and the Dumaine brothers, who leave him. They are followed by the soldiers who captured Parolles.

The Widow's House
Scene 3.7: Helena reveals her identity to the widow. Helena says Diana should agree to have sex with Bertram and ask for his ring. Helena will take Diana's place in bed, thereby getting his ring and his child, the two conditions he had set for being her husband in fact as well as in law. Helena offers Diana a dowry of three thousand crowns for helping her.

Scene 4.2: Bertram woos Diana. He gives her his ring, and she tells him to come to her room at midnight.

Scene 4.4: Helena prepares to return to France, having gotten Bertram's ring and become pregnant with his child.

Measure for Measure

AUSTRIA

Vienna

Situated on the Danube River, Vienna was settled by Celts circa 500 BCE. The Romans built a camp here (Vindobona) in the first century BCE. The Romans left in the fifth century CE and were succeeded by Lombards, Slavs, and Avars. By the eleventh century, Vienna had become an important trading center. Duke Henry II of Austria made Vienna his capital in 1155. Rudolf I established Habsburg rule here in 1276, and Vienna later served as the seat of the Holy Roman emperor. The city twice withstood Turkish sieges (1529 and 1683). After the 1529 siege, Ferdinand I leveled the suburbs to provide a clear field of fire against attackers. Shakespeare may have had this razing in mind when, in *Measure for Measure*, Pompey reports "All houses in the suburbs of Vienna must be plucked down" (1.2.98–99). Under Emperor Franz Joseph, who reigned from 1848 to 1916, the city became a commercial and cultural center. It is the capital of Austria.

Shakespeare's chief source for this play is George Whetstone's play *Promos and Cassandra* (1578), which is set "In the Cyttie of Iulio (sometimes vnder the dominion of Coruinus Kinge of Hungarie, and Boemia)." Whetstone in turn took his story from Giraldi Cinthio's *Hecatommithi* (1565), decade 8, novella 5, which takes place in Innsbruck. Shakespeare knew Cinthio's work, which he used as the basis of *Othello* (decade 3, novella 7). It is not clear why Shakespeare chose Vienna as his setting. His Vienna has much in common with London.

Angelo's House

Scene 2.2: The provost of the prison asks whether Angelo is certain Claudio should be executed. Angelo confirms the sentence and orders Juliet, pregnant by but not yet formally married to Claudio, to be sent to some suitable place. Anne Hathaway was three months pregnant when she married Shakespeare. About 30 percent of brides were pregnant in Shakespeare's day, and only about half were virgins. Contrary to Philip Larkin's "Annus Mirabilis," it is not true that "Sexual intercourse began / In nineteen sixty-three." The Puritan Philip Stubbes in his *Anatomy of Abuses* (1583) urged the death penalty for incest, adultery, and prostitution. Angelo is putting the Puritan agenda into practice in Vienna, a surrogate for London. The duke observes, "Lord Angelo is precise" (1.3.50). In his 1615 character of "A Precisian," that is, a Puritan, John Webster offers a good description of Angelo: "a demure creature, full of oral sanctity and mental impiety. . . . He will not stick to commit fornication or adultery so it be done in the fear of God."

A servant announces Isabella, who enters with Lucio. At first her plea for her brother is only half-hearted, but at Lucio's urging she becomes more fervent. She argues for mercy; Angelo, for justice. At length Angelo asks her to return the next day. Alone, Angelo acknowledges his lust for Isabella.

Scene 2.4: Angelo tells Isabella he will spare Claudio in exchange for sex. She refuses and threatens to expose Angelo's hypocrisy, but he says no one will believe her. He adds that, if she does not agree to his demand for sex, he will torture Claudio before killing him. Isabella leaves to talk to her brother.

Scene 4.4: Angelo and Escalus prepare to meet the duke. Alone, Angelo meditates on his misdeeds.

City Gate

Following the 1529 siege of Vienna by the Turks, the city's walls were rebuilt in 1548.

Scene 4.6: Isabella and Mariana prepare to confront Angelo. Friar Peter shows them where to stand to await the duke's return.

Scene 5.1: The duke arrives with Angelo, Escalus, Lucio, the provost, officers, and citizens. The duke congratulates Angelo on his just rule. When Isabella denounces Angelo, the duke seems to dismiss her accusations as madness, then as malice, and orders her arrest; she is led away. Friar Peter says Isabella did not, as she claimed, have sex with Angelo. He then produces Mariana, who says she slept with Angelo, who she claims is her husband, though he thought his partner was Isabella. Angelo thus has done what Claudio did, that is, slept with a woman to whom he was betrothed but to whom he was not formally married. Angelo denies her claim. Again, the duke seems to believe Angelo and denounces Friar Peter, Mariana, and Isabella. The duke sends the provost of the prison to fetch Friar Lodowick (the disguise the duke assumed), and the duke goes off. Escalus summons Isabella, who returns, as does the duke in his friar's habit. As Friar Lodowick he calls Angelo a villain. Esclaus orders Friar Lodowick's arrest, and Lucio denounces the friar. When Friar Lodowick resists being arrested, Lucio once more insults him and pulls off his cowl, thereby revealing his identity. Lucio now tries to sneak away, but the duke orders him held.

The duke takes Angelo's seat. Angelo confesses his crimes and asks to be executed. The duke orders him to marry Mariana at once. When Angelo and Mariana return, the duke orders Angelo to be executed for killing Claudio. Mariana pleads for him and asks Isabella to join her. The duke says Isabella will not beg the life of her brother's murderer, but she does. Still, the duke refuses to relent, and he dismisses the provost of the prison from his office for carrying out Claudio's execution. The provost says Barnardine can testify to the provost's remorse, and the duke sends the provost to fetch him.

The provost returns with Juliet, Barnardine, and a muffled figure. The duke pardons Barnardine, and the provost unmuffles Claudio, whom the duke pardons. The duke then asks Isabella for her hand in marriage. The duke orders Lucio to marry the woman who bore his child; meanwhile, he will be imprisoned. The duke tells Claudio to marry Juliet, and everyone leaves for the palace. Isabella never replies verbally to the duke's marriage proposal, so different productions have presented different endings: Isabella accepts the duke, or Isabella returns to her nunnery, or Isabella's response remains uncertain.

A Courtroom

Scene 2.1: Escalus pleads in vain with Angelo for Claudio. Angelo orders the provost of the prison to execute Claudio by nine o'clock the next morning. Officers enter with Elbow (a constable), Froth, and Pompey. Elbow accuses Froth of dishonoring his wife, which Froth and Pompey deny. The testimony becomes so tedious and convoluted that Angelo leaves, and Escalus releases Froth and Pompey.

The Duke's Palace
Michaelerkuppel, 1010

The Hofburg has served as the residence of the dukes of Austria since the thirteenth century. It has expanded over the centuries. It now contains the treasury, which contains the crown jewels of Austria, and the Spanish Riding School, as well as the residence and offices of Austria's president.

Scene 1.1: As Duke Vincentio prepares to leave Vienna for Poland, he entrusts the governing of the city to his deputy, the seemingly ascetic Angelo.

The Moated Grange of St. Luke

Mary Fitton, one of Queen Elizabeth's maids of honor and a candidate for Shakespeare's Dark Lady, had an affair with William Herbert, Third Earl of Pembroke, a candidate for the Fair Youth of Shakespeare's sonnets. In the sonnets the Fair Youth has an affair with the Dark Lady. She became pregnant and was dismissed from court. Pembroke refused to marry her (she had hoped he would), and in May 1601, after she gave birth to a boy who soon died, she retired to a moated grange (a country house surrounded by a moat) in Warwickshire, about twenty-five miles from Stratford, at the edge of Arbury Hall, Nuneaton (open to the public on bank holidays from April through August). She may be the model for Mariana. Mariana of the moated grange inspired paintings by Sir John Everett Millais and Edwin Austin Abbey and a poem by Tennyson.

Scene 4.1: The duke and Isabella tell Mariana of their plan for a bed trick. Angelo will have sex with Mariana but think she is Isabella.

A Monastery

Klosterneuburg Monastery was founded in 1114 by Margrave Leopold III. The Schottenstift, a Benedictine abbey, was established in 1155 by Henry II of Austria, who brought monks to Vienna from Ireland. Shakespeare may have had either (or neither) of these places in mind.

Scene 1.3: Duke Vincentio asks Friar Thomas to let him remain at the monastery. He explains that for fourteen years he has failed to enforce certain laws, such as those against fornication. (At 1.2.171 the period is nineteen years.) He has therefore placed Angelo in power to revive them. Disguised as a friar, the duke will watch Angelo's governance to see how precise he is.

A Nunnery

Scene 1.4: Isabella is about to enter the Order of St. Clare, noted for its austerity. She is as much an ascetic as Angelo wishes to be. Lucio tells Isabella of Claudio's arrest and pending death sentence for getting Juliet pregnant. At Lucio's urging she agrees to plead with Angelo for her brother.

Outside Vienna

Scene 4.5: The duke sends Friar Peter to deliver letters and summon certain people.

A Prison

Scene 2.3: The duke, disguised as Friar Lodowick, visits. When Juliet enters, the provost informs her of Claudio's sentence. The duke tells Juliet he is going to see her lover.

Scene 3.1: In the company of the provost, the duke (disguised as a friar) tries to prepare Claudio for death. Isabella arrives to speak with her brother; the duke and provost leave. Isabella informs Claudio of Angelo's offer to spare him if she will have sex with Angelo. At first Claudio tells his sister not to agree, but when he wavers she denounces her brother. The duke, having eavesdropped on their conversation, asks to speak to Isabella alone. She goes off, and the duke tells Claudio that Angelo was merely testing Isabella. Then he tells Isabella that Angelo was betrothed to Mariana but jilted her after her brother lost her dowry in a shipwreck. Mariana still loves Angelo. The duke instructs Isabella to agree to have sex with Angelo, but the duke will arrange for Mariana to take her place, and Isabella agrees.

Scene 3.2: Elbow and officers have arrested the bawd Mistress Overdone's servant, Pompey. When Pompey asks Lucio to post bail for him, Lucio refuses. After Elbow and the officers take Pompey away, Lucio speaks to the disguised duke, declaring Angelo is too ruthless. The duke, Lucio says, was lecherous himself and so was merciful to fornicators. Lucio also claims the duke was a drunkard and altogether a "very superficial, ignorant, unweighing [injudicious] fellow" (ll. 139–40). After Lucio departs, Escalus, the provost, and officers arrive with Mistress Overdone, who has been arrested. The duke asks Escalus his opinion of Vincentio (i.e., the duke, who wants to know whether Lucio's view is shared by others). Escalus praises the duke, then leaves to visit Claudio. In a rhyming soliloquy, the duke condemns Angelo's behavior.

Scene 4.2: To avoid imprisonment and whipping, Pompey agrees to serve as the executioner's assistant. The provost shows Claudio the warrant for his execution but hopes for a reprieve. The disguised duke arrives expecting Angelo's order to stop the execution because Angelo thinks he has had sex with Isabella. Angelo's messenger arrives but with confirmation of Claudio's sentence; Angelo has not kept his word, fearing Claudio would seek revenge if he lived. Barnardine, a dissolute criminal, is also scheduled for execution. The duke says to execute him and send his head to Angelo, claiming it is Claudio's.

Scene 4.3: Pompey recognizes many of his now-imprisoned former acquaintances from Mistress Overdone's brothel. Pompey summons Barnardine for execution, but Barnardine refuses to be killed. Fortunately, the pirate Ragazine has just died in the prison, so the duke and provost agree to send his head to Angelo. When Isabella comes to learn her brother's fate, the disguised duke tells her he was executed. He then informs her the duke is returning to Vienna the next day. Escalus and Angelo will meet him at the city gate, where she is to accuse Angelo of his misdeeds. Lucio enters and sympathizes with Isabella, saying Claudio would be alive if the "old fantastical Duke of dark corners" (ll. 156–57) had been governing. Lucio assures the disguised duke that Vincentio was a womanizer. He adds that he was once brought before the duke for impregnating a woman but denied the accusation to avoid being forced to marry her. The duke tries to get away from Lucio, but Lucio follows him.

A Street

Scene 1.2: As Lucio and two other gentlemen talk, the bawd Mistress Overdone comes to tell them Claudio has been arrested and sentenced to death for getting his fiancée,

Juliet, pregnant. Angelo's harsh rule has thus begun. Lucio and the gentlemen leave to investigate this story. Pompey enters to say that all the brothels in the Vienna suburbs are to be pulled down (but not the ones within the city's walls). In Shakespeare's London the houses of prostitution were located in the suburbs, where, like the theaters, they were outside the jurisdiction of the Puritanical city government. After Mistress Overdone and Pompey depart, the provost of the prison and officers bring in Claudio and Juliet. Lucio and the two gentlemen reenter. Claudio says he and Juliet are married in common law but have not yet wed in church, the same situation as Shakespeare's in 1582, when he had impregnated Anne Hathaway without benefit of clergy. Claudio asks Lucio to inform Claudio's sister Isabella, who is about to become a nun, about what is happening and ask her to intercede with Angelo.

TRAGEDIES

Titus Andronicus

ITALY

Rome

Two legends deal with the founding of Rome. One concerns the Trojan Aeneas, son of Anchises and the goddess Venus, who came to Italy after the destruction of Troy and whose son, Ascanius, founded Alba Longa. The other myth deals with Romulus and Remus, descendants of Aeneas, who were nursed by a she-wolf and built Rome. When Remus mocked Romulus's just-started wall, Romulus killed him. The name of the city supposedly derives from Romulus. Archeology shows settlements in what is now Rome dating from about 1000 BCE. By the seventh century BCE, the Forum had been established as a public meeting place. By the sixth century BCE, Rome was a powerful city-state. Rome was originally a monarchy. The last king, Tarquinus Superbus, was expelled in an aristocratic coup that created a republic (509 BCE). Shakespeare's *Coriolanus* is set just after the expulsion of the king; the play captures the concern of the citizenry regarding the possible return of tyranny. Romans had an aversion to the title of king (rex). It was the fear that Julius Caesar would make himself king that led to his assassination on March 15, 44 BCE, the subject of Shakespeare's best-known Roman play. No Roman emperor used the title of king.

During the period of the republic, Rome continued to expand. By 300 BCE it was the dominant power in Italy. In the third century BCE, Rome took Sicily from the Carthaginians (241 BCE) and then Sardinia (238 BCE). In the second century BCE, Rome conquered Greece and Macedonia, northern Africa, and Spain. The late second century BCE saw a rise in income inequality and the beginning of a century of political unrest that ended only with the defeat of Marc Antony at the Battle of Actium in 31 BCE and his death the next year in Egypt, leaving Octavius (to whom the Roman senate gave the title Augustus in 27 BCE) as sole ruler of the empire. These climactic events are depicted in Shakespeare's *Antony and Cleopatra*. By the late fourth century

CE, the empire was being attacked by Goths, who, together with Franks and Vandals, overran much Roman territory. Rome was sacked in 410 CE and again in 455. On September 4, 476, Romulus Augustus, the last Roman emperor in the west, was deposed by the German chieftain Odoacer. *Titus Andronicus* is set in the fourth century CE as the Western Roman Empire is under threat and has begun to decline. Shakespeare's play raises questions about who the barbarians really are and who is civilized.

In 210 CE Rome held about a million people. The population dramatically declined in the Middle Ages. By 1300 there were about 25,000 people living in the city. From the eighth century until 1870, Rome was ruled by popes as part of the papal states. In the fifteenth century, the popes helped fund the Renaissance. In 1871 Rome became the capital of a united Italy.

The Curia/Capitol
Roman senate house

The original curia is attributed to Tullus Hostilius, sixth king of Rome (672–641 BCE). The third curia was begun by Julius Caesar in 44 BCE and completed by Octavius in 29 BCE. Diocletian again rebuilt the curia after a fire in 283 CE. The Diocletian building survives nearly intact because, in the seventh century, it was converted into a basilica. However, the roof, part of the side walls, and rear façade date from the 1930s.

Scene 1.1: In front of the senate house, tribunes (representatives of the plebeians) and senators enter above. Below, Saturninus, son of the late Roman emperor, and his followers enter from one side of the stage, while his brother Bassianus and his followers enter from the other. Both brothers want to succeed their father. Marcus Andronicus says the people want Titus Andronicus to rule them. Saturninus and Bassianus seem to agree with this decision. The Roman Empire was repeatedly troubled with dynastic struggles because it lacked a method to determine succession. In late Elizabethan England, the same concern existed. By the early 1590s, when this play was written, it was clear Elizabeth would not produce an heir, and she refused to name a successor to avoid weakening her own hold on the throne.

Titus Andronicus returns from a successful war against the Goths. With him are Martius, Mutius, Lucius, and Quintus, the last sons remaining to him of twenty-five, the others having died fighting for Rome. Titus has brought to Rome as captives Tamora, queen of the Goths; her three sons (Alarbus, Chiron, and Demetrius); and her lover, Aaron the Moor. In Christopher Marlowe's *The Jew of Malta* (c. 1593), contemporary with this play, the Turkish slave is named Ithamore. Numbers 4.28 refers to Ithamore, the son of Aaron. Shakespeare may have taken Aaron's name from Marlowe's play, or Marlowe may have taken Ithamore's name from Shakespeare's. Aaron here, like Barabas in *The Jew of Malta*, is a Machiavellian figure.

The procession includes the coffin of one of Titus's sons. Lucius wants to sacrifice Tamora's oldest son, Alarbus, as an offering to Titus's dead children. Despite Tamora's pleas, Titus agrees. His sons lead Alarbus away and return with bloody swords. Romans did not engage in human sacrifice, but they were brutal to prisoners. At Aviracum in Gaul, Julius Caesar's army killed nearly all 40,000 residents when the town was captured by the Romans. The killing of Alarbus resembles the sacrifice of Hecuba's daughter Polixena and Andromache's son Astyanax to the shade of Achilles in Seneca's *Troades*, based on Euripides *Trojan Women*. Seneca is a key influence on and source for this play. Titus's daughter, Lavinia, arrives to greet her father.

When Marcus Andronicus tells his brother Titus that the people have chosen him emperor, Saturninus again claims the throne. Bassianus asks for Titus's support, but Titus urges the citizens to choose Saturninus, and they do. Saturninus now asks for Lavinia's hand in marriage. Titus consents, but Saturninus is also attracted to Tamora. Bassianus says Lavinia should be his, and Marcus Andronicus concurs. Bassianus and Marcus lead her away, and when Titus tries to pursue them, his son Mutius blocks his path. Titus kills him and orders Lucius to bring Lavinia back, but Saturninus now says he prefers Tamora. Saturninus also rejects Titus. Everyone leaves except Titus.

Titus initially refuses to allow Mutius to be buried in the family tomb, but he yields after Marcus and his remaining sons plead with him.

When Tamora, Saturninus, Bassianus, and Lavinia return with their followers, Tamora asks Saturninus to be reconciled with Titus but only so she can find a fitter time to be revenged on him and his family. Saturninus agrees to a general pardon and invites everyone to go hunting with him the next day.

Scene 2.1: In front of the senate house, Chiron and Demetrius argue over Lavinia. Aaron reconciles them by devising a plan for both of them to rape her, and they agree.

The Emperor's Palace
Via di San Gregorio

Various Roman emperors built large houses on the Palatine (the origin of the word *palace*), one of Rome's seven hills. Eventually the Palatine became the exclusive residence of the emperors. Only ruins remain of these palaces. At the time the play is set, the Palace of Domitian (also known as the Flavian Palace), completed in 92 CE, would have served as the imperial residence. The poet Statius described it thus: "Awesome and vast is the edifice, distinguished not by a hundred columns but by as many as could shoulder the gods and the sky if Atlas were let off" (*Silvae*, 4.2.18–20). Septimus Severus (emperor 193–211 CE) added to the building.

Scene 2.2: In front of the emperor's palace, Titus greets Saturninus and Tamora. Bassianus, Lavinia, Chiron, Demetrius, and their attendants go off to hunt, as do Saturninus and Tamora.

Scene 4.2: Young Lucius brings Chiron and Demetrius weapons from Titus's armory. He also gives them a scroll containing the text of Horace's Ode 1.22, lines 1–2: "*Integer vitae, scelerisque purus, / Non egat Mauri jaculis, nec arcu*" ("He who leads an upright life free from crime need not fear a Moor's javelin or bow").

Tamora gives birth to Aaron's child. A nurse enters with it and says Tamora wants to kill it because it is black and so will betray her affair with Aaron the Moor, but Aaron objects. Aaron also defends the child against Chiron and Demetrius, who want it dead. Aaron kills the nurse because she knows the child's color and plans to kill the midwife for the same reason. He will substitute the Goth Muliteus's baby for his own and take his baby to be raised by Goths.

Scene 4.3: Outside the emperor's palace, Titus, Marcus, Lucius, Publius, Sempronius, and Caius appear with bows and arrows. Attached to the arrows are prayers addressed to various gods asking for justice. They shoot the arrows into the courtyard, perhaps alluding to the reference to the bow in Horace's Ode 1.22 quoted in 4.2. A clown is passing by with pigeons. Titus instructs him to take the pigeons to the emperor, along with a knife and a petition.

Scene 4.4: Saturninus has found the arrows shot into his courtyard. The clown arrives with Titus's letter, accusing Saturninus of injustice. The emperor orders the clown hanged. Nuntius Aemilius enters with news of an invasion by the Goths under the command of Titus's son Lucius. Lucius's exile from and subsequent return to Rome at the head of a hostile army derives from Plutarch's "The Life of Caius Martius Coriolanus," which Shakespeare would mine more fully for a later tragedy about the Roman warrior. Line 4.4.68 refers to Coriolanus. Saturninus fears the Romans will revolt against him, but Tamora says she can pacify Titus. She tells Nuntius Aemilius to arrange a meeting between Lucius and Saturninus at Titus's house. She plans to convince Lucius to abandon the Goths.

Nuntius in Latin means "messenger." In his early plays, Shakespeare wears his classical learning on his sleeve, adapting Plautus's *Menaechmi* for *The Comedy of Errors* and filling his Senecan first tragedy here with classical quotations and allusions. In later plays the classicism is subtler though certainly present, as when he uses Ovid's story of Pyramus and Thisbe as the basis for the rude mechanicals' play in act 5 of *A Midsummer Night's Dream* or has Prospero quote from Medea's speech in Ovid's *Metamorphoses* in *The Tempest*, 5.1.33–57.

A Forest near Rome

Scene 2.3: Aaron buries a bag of gold under a tree. Tamora joins him and wants to have sex, but Aaron is focused on revenge. He gives her a letter for Saturninus.

Bassianus and Lavinia join Aaron and Tamora. After Aaron leaves to find Tamora's sons, they accuse Tamora of having an affair with Aaron. Bassianus says he will inform the emperor.

When Chiron and Demetrius arrive, Tamora claims Bassianus and Lavinia lured her into the forest to kill her, and she says they have insulted her. Her sons kill Bassianus, then put his body into a pit. They take Lavinia away to rape her. Aaron comes with Quintus and Martius, telling them he has found a panther. He lures them to the pit where Bassianus's body is lying. Martius falls in. Aaron then leaves to summon the emperor, who will conclude Quintus and Martius killed Bassianus. The emperor appears as Quintus is trying to rescue Martius. Tamora, Titus, and Lucius join them. Tamora gives Saturninus the letter Aaron had given her (which he has forged); it states that Quintus and Martius plan to kill Bassianus for a bag of gold, which Aaron "finds." Saturninus sentences the brothers to death. Titus pleads for his sons, but Saturninus refuses to relent. Tamora promises (falsely) to intercede for them.

Scene 2.4: Nearby, Chiron and Demetrius enter with the ravished Lavinia. They have cut off her hands so she cannot write to accuse them (or, like Philomel in myth, weave a tapestry revealing what happened) and have cut out her tongue so she cannot name them. They mock her before leaving. Marcus Andronicus finds her and takes her to Titus.

A Plain near Rome

Scene 5.1: As the Goths' army under Lucius nears the city, one of the Goths brings in Aaron and his child. Lucius orders their execution. Aaron promises to reveal secrets to Lucius if he will spare the infant, and Lucius agrees. Aaron informs Lucius that he fathered the child with Tamora; also, Chiron and Demetrius killed Bassianus and then raped and mangled Lavinia. He says he led Martius and Quintus to the pit where Bassianus's body lay, wrote the letter to Saturninus implicating Lucius's brothers in the murder, hid the gold that appeared to be the bribe to kill Bassianus, and deceived Titus into cutting off his hand. He regrets not accomplishing more evil deeds.

Nuntius Aemilius arrives from Rome to arrange a parley at Titus's house. Lucius agrees, and the army marches away toward Rome.

A Street

Scene 3.1: Titus pleads for Martius and Quintus as they are led to execution accompanied by judges, senators, and tribunes. He continues to ask for mercy for them even after he is left alone. Lucius tells him he (Lucius) has been banished for trying to rescue his brothers.

Marcus and Lavinia enter. Titus and Lucius bewail her injuries. Aaron arrives to say his sons will be pardoned if Titus cuts off his hand and sends it to the emperor. Lucius and Marcus each offer a hand to spare Titus and go off to find an ax. In their absence Titus asks Aaron to cut off his hand, which Aaron does and leaves with it. A messenger soon returns with the hand and the heads of Martius and Quintus. Titus sends Lucius to the Goths to raise an army against Rome and plans revenge on those who have wronged him.

Titus Andronicus's House

Scene 3.2: At a meal Titus laments to Marcus, Lavinia, and his grandson, young Lucius, the wrongs he and his family have suffered.

Scene 4.1: Lavinia is chasing young Lucius around Titus's garden. She wants his copy of Ovid's *Metamorphoses,* Shakespeare's favorite work. In book 6 she finds the story of Tereus's rape of Philomel, the model for Lavinia's rape in the play. She uses the text to reveal what has happened to her. Taking a stick, she uses her stumps to write the names of Chiron and Demetrius in the sand. Marcus, Titus, and young Lucius plot vengeance.

Scene 5.2: Tamora comes to Titus's courtyard disguised as Revenge, her sons as Murder and Rape. Titus, who recognizes them but pretends not to, says she should kill her sons, but she says they are her ministers. Titus welcomes them. She asks Titus to invite Lucius to dine with him. She will bring her sons and Saturninus to the meal, where Titus can do what he likes with them. Titus sends his brother Marcus to bring Lucius.

Tamora prepares to leave with her sons, but Titus asks the men to remain. Thinking Titus is fooled by their disguises, she agrees. Once she is gone, Titus summons Publius, Caius, and Valentine, who seize Chiron and Demetrius. Titus cuts their throats, and Lavinia catches their blood in a basin. Titus will prepare a pie (or pies) with their bones, blood, and heads. In Greek mythology Atreus killed the sons of his brother Thyestes (who was having an affair with Atreus's wife) and cooked them in a meal he served Thyestes. Scenes 5.2 and 5.3 owe much to Seneca's *Thyestes.* In Ovid's *Metamorphoses* Procne revenged Tereus's rape of her sister Philomel by killing Tereus's son Itys and serving the boy to his father in a meal.

Scene 5.3: In the courtyard of Titus's house, Lucius, Marcus, Goth soldiers, Aaron, and his son assemble. Saturninus, Tamora, Aemilius, senators, tribunes, and others join them. A table is brought in, and everyone sits. Titus, dressed as a cook, serves his guests. He asks whether Virginius was right to kill his daughter after she was raped. Shakespeare or Titus is changing the story to fit Lavinia's situation. In Livy (*Ab Urbe Condita Libri,* 3.44) and in Chaucer's "The Physician's Tale," Virginius kills his daughter to prevent her from being raped. When Saturninus approves of Virginius's action, Titus stabs Lavinia. Saturninus asks who raped Lavinia; Titus names Chiron and Demetrius. Saturninus orders them brought in. Titus replies they have been baked in his pie. Titus then stabs Tamora. Saturninus stabs him, and Lucius stabs Saturninus.

Lucius explains that Chiron and Demetrius killed Bassianus and raped Lavinia, and for Bassianus's murder Lucius's brothers were executed and he himself was banished.

Marcus adds that Aaron, lover of Tamora, instigated these crimes. Aemilius and the Romans hail Lucius as their new emperor. Lucius orders Aaron buried up to his chest and left to starve. Aaron remains unrepentant. Lucius orders the burial of all the dead except Tamora, whose body is to be left for beasts and birds to devour (like Jezebel in 1 Kings).

Romeo and Juliet

ITALY

Mantua

Located in Lombardy, Mantua has been occupied since about 2000 BCE. By the sixth century BCE, it was inhabited by Etruscans. The name may derive from the Etruscan deity Mantus or the mythical daughter of Tiresias, Manto. Virgil was born in a village (Virgilio) close enough to the city for Mantua to claim him. After the fall of the Roman Empire, Mantua was ruled by Ostrogoths, Lombards, and Franks, like so many other Italian cities. After being part of the Holy Roman Empire and being ruled by Tuscany, it achieved independence in the twelfth century. The three artificial lakes that surround the city were constructed in this period for defense. A fourth lake created at the same time was filled in during the eighteenth century. The Gonzaga family controlled the city from 1329 to 1708, when Mantua fell under Austrian rule and remained so, except during the Napoleonic period, until 1866, when it became part of the kingdom of Italy.

Leonarda da Vinci stayed here in the winter of 1499–1500 and drew a portrait of Isabella d'Este, wife of Francesco Gonzaga II; the portrait now hangs in the Louvre.

Shakespeare's chief source for this play is Arthur Brooke's poem *The Tragicall Historye of Romeus and Juliet* (1562). The poem, like the play, is set in Verona, and when Romeus is banished for killing Tybalt in the poem, he flees to Mantua, just as he does in Shakespeare's version.

Apothecary's Shop

Scene 5.1: Outside an apothecary's shop, Balthasar tells Romeo that Juliet is dead. Romeo resolves to return to Verona. He summons the apothecary and buys poison, which he intends to take that night in Juliet's tomb.

Verona

Located on the Adige River in the Veneto, seventy miles from Venice, Verona became a Roman colony in 89 BCE. It takes its name perhaps from its location on the road to Rome from the Alps (*versus Romae*, "toward Rome") or from the Adige River on which the city sits; the Adige was formerly called Vera, and *-ona* is a common Goth suffix. It fell to the Goths in 489 CE, and Theodoric built one of his palaces here. In 569 it became part of the Lombard kingdom. The Della Scala family ruled Verona from 1260 to 1387, when the Visconti of Milan annexed it, but in 1405 it fell under the control of Venice. In *Othello*, 2.1, a gentleman refers to a "noble ship of Venice" as a "Veronesa" (ll. 22, 26; i.e., a ship Verona provided to Venice). The city prospered in the Middle Ages. From 1814 to 1866, it was ruled by Austria, before becoming part of a united Italy.

Capulet's House
23 Via Cappella

This house, which belongs to the World Heritage Trust and is open to tourists, bears the coat of arms of the Cappelletti. It is known today as Casa di Giulietta. The house dates from the thirteenth century, though it has been renovated. It has a balcony (a repurposed sarcophagus), made famous by scene 2.2 of this play, but this feature was added in the early twentieth century. Elizabethan theaters had a balcony at the rear of the stage for such scenes as 2.2 in this play and *The Merchant of Venice*, 2.6.

Scene 1.3: Lady Capulet asks the nurse to summon Juliet to tell her that Paris wants to marry her. A servant announces that the guests are arriving for the party. Juliet and her mother leave to join them.

Scene 1.4: In front of the Capulet house, Romeo, Mercutio (related to the prince), Benvolio, and other revelers prepare to enter. Mercutio delivers a speech about Queen Mab (ll. 53–94). Despite Romeo's misgivings, they go inside.

Scene 1.5: Capulet welcomes his guests. As soon as Romeo sees Juliet, he falls in love with her. Tybalt, recognizing Romeo, wants to kill this Montague, but Old Capulet insists Tybalt leave Romeo alone. Romeo and Juliet compose a sonnet together in their conversation. As they begin another sonnet and Romeo kisses Juliet, the nurse interrupts them with a summons from Lady Capulet. The interrupted sonnet indicates the fate of their love affair, shattered by outside forces. The lovers never have an entire scene to themselves throughout the play. Romeo asks the nurse who Juliet's mother is; she identifies Juliet as a Capulet and later, alone with Juliet, informs her Romeo is a Montague.

Scene 2.1: Romeo hides in the Capulet orchard. Outside the orchard Benvolio and Mercutio call for him, but when he does not respond, they leave without him.

Scene 2.2: In the Capulet orchard, Romeo on the ground woos Juliet, who stands on her balcony. She proposes to him, and he agrees to marry her.

Scene 2.5: In the Capulet orchard, Juliet impatiently awaits the nurse's return. After many digressions the nurse gives Juliet Romeo's message to meet him at Friar Lawrence's cell that afternoon to be married.

Scene 3.2: Juliet eagerly awaits the consummation of her marriage. The nurse enters with a cord ladder Romeo is to use to ascend to Juliet's chamber that night. Shakespeare earlier used a cord ladder in *The Two Gentlemen of Verona*. The nurse reports a death. Juliet thinks she is speaking of Romeo, but eventually the nurse reveals Tybalt's death and Romeo's banishment. The nurse promises to bring Romeo to Juliet that night from his hiding place in Friar Lawrence's cell.

Scene 3.4: Old Capulet, his wife, and Paris talk. Old Capulet promises Paris that Juliet will marry him on Thursday.

Scene 3.5: After a night of lovemaking in Juliet's bedroom, Romeo prepares to flee Verona. The nurse enters to say that Lady Capulet is coming. Romeo kisses Juliet, descends into the orchard, and vanishes. Lady Capulet enters to inform Juliet of her

Casa di Giuletta, the supposed home of Shakespeare's Juliet, in the Piazza Erbe, Verona. While Juliet is, of course, a fictional character, the rival families of the Cappelletti and Montecchi were already known to Dante in the early fourteenth century, and this building bears the arms of the Cappelletti. The balcony is an early-twentieth-century addition because of Shakespeare's play. © iStock/StrenghtofFrame

father's decision that she should marry Paris on Thursday. Juliet refuses. Old Capulet enters and demands she obey. After her parents leave, Juliet tells the nurse to say she has repented of her disobedience and is going to Friar Lawrence's cell to confess her sins. She hopes the friar will find a way to prevent her unwanted bigamous marriage.

Scene 4.2: Returning home from her visit to Friar Lawrence, Juliet agrees to marry Paris.

Scene 4.3: In her bedroom Juliet drinks the potion Friar Lawrence gave her.

Scene 4.4: Preparations are underway for Juliet's wedding. Old Capulet sends the nurse to awaken Juliet.

Scene 4.5: In Juliet's bedroom the nurse tries unsuccessfully to wake Juliet. Old Capulet and his wife find Juliet, apparently dead. Friar Lawrence tells them to prepare for Juliet's funeral.

Friar Lawrence's Cell
2 Piazza San Zeno

Associated with the Basilica of St. Zeno is a Benedictine abbey dating from the ninth century (destroyed in the Napoleonic Wars, except for the cloisters and a tower). The crypt of the basilica is supposed to be the location for the (fictional) marriage of Romeo and Juliet. The Romanesque church dates from the tenth century, with later additions and modifications.

Scene 2.3: In his cell Friar Lawrence prepares to gather herbs. Romeo arrives to tell of his love for Juliet. Friar Lawrence agrees to marry the lovers to reconcile their feuding families. Whereas Shakespeare's source, Arthur Brooke's *The Tragicall Historie of Romeus and Juliet* (1562), condemns "superstitious friars (the naturally fit instruments of unchastity)," Shakespeare presents Friar Lawrence favorably despite the character's Catholicism. Brooke also takes a dim view of the "unfortunate lovers, thralling themselves to unhonest desire; neglecting the authority and advice of parents and friends." For Shakespeare, "passion lends them power" (prologue to act 2, line 13). His play sympathizes with the young lovers.

Scene 2.6: Romeo and Juliet meet and go off to be married.

Scene 3.3: The friar tells Romeo of his sentence of banishment. Romeo had fled the scene of Tybalt's murder and so was unaware of the prince's decree. The nurse arrives. Friar Lawrence tells Romeo to go to Juliet that night, then flee to Mantua until the time is right to reveal the marriage and have Romeo recalled to Verona. The nurse departs, and Romeo follows her.

Scene 4.1: Paris asks Friar Lawrence to marry him and Juliet on Thursday. Juliet arrives. After Paris leaves, the friar tells Juliet to pretend to agree to the wedding. On Wednesday night she is to drink a potion the friar gives her. She will seem dead for forty-two hours and be buried in the tomb of all the Capulets. Meanwhile, Friar

Lawrence will send a letter to Romeo to explain what is happening. Romeo will come to the Capulet tomb, Juliet will awake, and the couple will flee to Mantua. Juliet accepts this plan.

Scene 5.2: Friar John reveals he was unable to deliver to Romeo the letter explaining Juliet only appears to be dead. Friar Lawrence plans to go to the Capulet tomb, where Juliet will soon awake. He will write again to Romeo and will keep Juliet in his cell until Romeo returns from Mantua to claim her.

Juliet's Tomb
5 Via Luigi da Porto

Juliet's (fictional) tomb was originally located in the churchyard of the Convent of San Francesco del Corso. In a November 7, 1816, letter to Thomas Moore, Byron described the tomb as a "plain, open, and partly decayed sarcophagus, with withered leaves in it, in a wild and desolate conventual garden, once a cemetery, now ruined to the very graves. The situation struck me as very appropriate to the legend, being blighted as their love. I have brought away a few pieces of the granite, to give to my daughter and my nieces." In the 1930s the tomb was moved under the cloister. The convent is now the Museum of the Frescoes of Giovanni Battista Cavalcaselle.

Scene 5.3: Paris has come to place flowers on Juliet's tomb. Romeo and Balthasar arrive. Romeo intends to open the Capulet tomb (which Shakespeare envisioned as a crypt or mausoleum) to lie with Juliet in death. He dismisses Balthasar, who pretends to depart but hides nearby. As Romeo begins to open the Capulet tomb, Paris intercepts him. Romeo asks Paris to go away, but Paris tries to apprehend Romeo. They duel, and Paris is fatally wounded. Dying, Paris asks to be laid with Juliet, and Romeo takes his body into the tomb. He then drinks the poison he bought in Mantua and dies kissing Juliet.

Friar Lawrence enters the tomb and finds Paris and Romeo dead. Juliet awakes. The friar tries to lead her away but flees when he hears a noise. Juliet, finding Romeo dead, stabs herself with his dagger and, dying, falls on Romeo. Paris's servant and the watch (local constabulary) find the newly dead bodies. The prince, Capulet, Lady Capulet, and Montague arrive. Friar Lawrence reveals Juliet's marriage to Romeo, her taking the potion, the thwarting of his plan to inform Romeo that Juliet is not in fact dead, his discovery of the dead Paris and Romeo, and Juliet's suicide. Too late, Capulet and Montague reconcile. Montague promises to raise a golden statue to Juliet; Capulet says he will do the same for Romeo. A statue of Juliet stands in the courtyard of the Casa di Giulietta. The first statue, created in 1972 in bronze, suffered so much damage from affectionate tourists that it has been relocated to the Museum Castelvecchio.

Juliet's tomb. Originally located outside the convent of San Francesco al Corso, it now resides within the building, which is a museum. *Private Collection © Look and Learn/Bridgeman Images*

A Street

Scene 1.1: Samson and Gregory, servants of the Capulets, fight with Aaron and Balthasar, servants of the Montagues. Benvolio, nephew of Old Montague, enters and beats down the swords of the combatants. Tybalt, nephew of Lady Capulet, arrives. Benvolio tells him he is trying to keep the peace, but Tybalt draws his sword, and they fight.

Citizens with clubs enter and denounce both families. Old Capulet and his wife and Old Montague and his spouse appear. The old men want to fight each other. Prince Escalus arrives with his attendants. The prince orders the Capulets and Montagues to throw down their weapons. If another street brawl erupts, he says he will execute the heads of both families. He orders Old Capulet to come with him now to Free-town; Old Montague is to appear before him in the afternoon. He orders everyone to disperse on pain of death. Free-town is the Capulet castle in Arthur Brooke's *Romeus and Juliet,* but in the play it is a different location.

After everyone departs except Old Montague, his wife, and Benvolio, Montague asks how the fighting began, and Benvolio tells him. Lady Montague asks about her son, Romeo. Benvolio says he saw Romeo that morning in the woods. When Romeo appears, his parents withdraw so Benvolio can speak with him privately. Romeo says he is sad because he loves Rosaline, who does not share his feelings. While Romeo is viewed as the embodiment of true love, he forgets about Rosaline as soon as he sees Juliet in scene 1.5.

Scene 1.2: Old Capulet tells Paris, one of the prince's relatives, that both families are bound to keep the peace. Paris asks to marry Capulet's daughter Juliet, but Capulet says she is too young. Still, if Paris can get her consent, Capulet will agree to the match. Capulet invites Paris to a party at his house that night and sends a servant to deliver invitations. Capulet and Paris go off. The servant cannot read. Encountering Romeo and Benvolio, he asks for their help. Romeo learns that his beloved Rosaline will attend the party and resolves to go, as well.

Scene 2.4: As Benvolio and Mercutio talk, Romeo appears. They are joined by Juliet's nurse and her man, Peter. The nurse asks to speak with Romeo. After Benvolio and Mercutio leave, Romeo tells the nurse to have Juliet meet him that afternoon at Friar Lawrence's cell to be married.

Scene 3.1: Benvolio urges Mercutio to go inside because the day is hot and Capulets are roaming the streets. Tybalt, Petruchio, and others appear, followed by Romeo. Tybalt tries to provoke Romeo to fight, but Romeo refuses. Mercutio draws his sword and fights with Tybalt. As Romeo comes between them to try to stop the duel, Tybalt stabs Mercutio under Romeo's arm. Benvolio takes Mercutio away but soon returns to say Mercutio is dead. When Tybalt reappears, Romeo now duels with him and kills him, then flees. The prince enters with Old Montague, Old Capulet, and their wives. Hearing what just happened, the prince banishes Romeo from Verona.

Julius Caesar

GREECE

Philippi

Originally named Crenides (Greek for "fountains"), it was settled by colonists from Thrace in 360/359 BCE. Philip II, father of Alexander the Great, captured the city in 356 BCE and renamed it for himself. After the Third Macedonian War, the city came under Roman control (168 BCE). Following the Battle of Philippi in 42 BCE, the victors granted land here to their soldiers. The apostle Paul visited the city in 49 or 50 CE and again in 56 and 57; it was the first place in Europe where he preached, and he addressed an epistle to the Philippians (61–62 CE). In the early centuries CE, the city flourished, but an earthquake circa 619 nearly destroyed it. It was later contested by Bulgarians and Byzantines. In the thirteenth century, it fell to Serbs. At some point the city was abandoned. Modern Filippoi is located nearby. Because of the city's ruins and historical significance, it was designated a UNESCO World Heritage Site in 2016.

Scenes 5.1–5.5: The Battle(s) of Philippi. Two battles were fought here in October 42 BCE between the forces of Brutus and Cassius and those of Marc Antony and Octavius. In the first battle, fought in the first week in October, Brutus defeated Octavius, while Marc Antony defeated Cassius, who, believing Brutus also had been beaten, killed himself. In the second encounter, on October 23, Brutus was defeated and killed himself. Shakespeare conflates the two battles. In the play, Octavius and Marc Antony quarrel over who will take which position. Antony wants the more prestigious right flank, but Octavius claims it, foreshadowing the future rift between the triumvirs and Octavius's triumphing over Marc Antony. In Plutarch this argument occurs between Cassius and Brutus; Shakespeare transferred it ("Life of Marcus Brutus"). Thinking his forces defeated, Cassius asks Pindarus to kill him. When Titinius finds Cassius's body, he kills himself. After he loses the battle, Brutus asks Clitus, Dardanius, and Volumnius to kill him. All refuse. Strabo agrees to hold Brutus's sword while Brutus runs on it and so dies. The play ends with eulogies over Brutus's body spoken by Marc Antony and Octavius. The latter has the last speech, usually a sign in Shakespeare's plays of who is the dominant character (e.g., Duke Senior in *As You Like It*, Fortinbras in *Hamlet*), another foreshadowing of Octavius's eclipsing Marc Antony; Brutus's body is to rest in state in Octavius's tent, not in Marc Antony's, even though Marc Antony is the older and more experienced soldier and statesman. Antony wanted to cremate Brutus's body with full honors, but Octavius ordered Brutus's head cut off, sent to Rome, and cast at the feet of Caesar's statue.

ITALY

Rome

Two legends deal with the founding of Rome. One concerns the Trojan Aeneas, son of Anchises and the goddess Venus, who came to Italy after the destruction of Troy and whose son Ascanius founded Alba Longa. The other myth tells of Romulus and Remus, descendants of Aeneas, who were nursed by a she-wolf and built Rome. When Remus mocked Romulus's just-started wall, Romulus killed him. The name of the city supposedly derives from Romulus. Archeology shows settlements in what is now Rome dating from about 1000 BCE. By the seventh century BCE, the Forum had been established as a public meeting place. By the sixth century BCE, Rome was a powerful city-state. Rome was originally a monarchy. The last king, Tarquinus Superbus, was expelled in an aristocratic coup that created a republic (509 BCE). Shakespeare's *The Rape of Lucrece* (1594) treats the event that led to this coup, and *Coriolanus* is set just after the expulsion of the king; the play captures the concern of the citizenry regarding the possible return of tyranny. Romans had an aversion to the title of king (rex). It was the fear that Julius Caesar would make himself king that led to his assassination on March 15, 44 BCE, the subject of Shakespeare's best-known Roman play. No Roman emperor used the title of king.

During the period of the republic, Rome continued to expand. By 300 BCE it was the dominant power in Italy. In the third century BCE, Rome took Sicily from the Carthaginians (241 BCE) and then Sardinia (238 BCE). In the second century BCE, Rome conquered Greece and Macedonia, northern Africa, and Spain. The late second century BCE saw a rise in income inequality and the beginning of a century of political unrest that ended only with the defeat of Marc Antony at the Battle of Actium in 31 BCE and his death the next year in Egypt, leaving Octavius (to whom the Roman senate gave the title Augustus in 27 BCE) as sole ruler of the empire. These climactic events are depicted in Shakespeare's *Antony and Cleopatra*. By the late fourth century CE, the empire was being attacked by Goths, who, together with Franks and Vandals, overran much Roman territory. Rome was sacked in 410 CE and again in 455. On September 4, 476, Romulus Augustus, the last Roman emperor in the west, was deposed by the German chieftain Odoacer. *Titus Andronicus* is set in the fourth century CE as the Western Roman Empire is under threat and has begun to decline. Shakespeare's play raises questions about who the barbarians really are and who is civilized.

In 210 CE Rome held about a million people. The population dramatically declined in the Middle Ages. By 1300 there were about 25,000 people living in the city. From the eighth century until 1870, Rome was ruled by popes as part of the papal states. In the fifteenth century, the popes helped fund the Renaissance. In 1871 Rome became the capital of a united Italy.

Brutus's House

Probably located on the Aventine Hill near what was then the Temple of Diana, which was located on what is now the Via del Tempio di Diana.

Scene 2.1: In his garden, Brutus in a soliloquy convinces himself Caesar must die. Lucius, Brutus's servant, brings him a letter sent by Cassius, urging him to "Speak, strike, redress" (l. 47). The conspirators call on Brutus. Cassius wants to kill Marc Antony, as well as Caesar, but Brutus overrules him. As occurs repeatedly in the play, Cassius offers better advice, which Brutus rejects, leading ultimately to his defeat. After the conspirators leave, Brutus's wife, Portia (daughter of Cato the Younger), comes to ask what has been troubling him. Initially reluctant to tell her, he finally agrees to disclose to her the plot to assassinate Caesar. After she goes inside, a sick Caius Ligarius visits Brutus. Despite his illness, he agrees to join the conspiracy because Brutus is participating.

Scene 2.4: Portia sends Lucius to the capitol to check on her husband. She converses briefly with a soothsayer who plans to speak to Caesar on the way to the capitol.

The Curia/Capitol
Roman senate house

The original curia is attributed to Tullus Hostilius, sixth king of Rome (672–641 BCE). The third curia was begun by Julius Caesar in 44 BCE and completed by Octavius in 29 BCE. Diocletian again rebuilt the curia after a fire in 283 CE. The Diocletian building survives nearly intact because, in the seventh century, it was converted into a basilica. However, the roof, part of the side walls, and rear façade date from the 1930s.

Scene 2.3: Near the capitol Artemidorus reads over the warning he has written and plans to give to Caesar as he passes.

Scene 3.1: In front of the capitol, Caesar tells the soothsayer, who had warned Caesar, "Beware the ides of March" (1.2.23), "The ides of March are come," to which the soothsayer replies, "Ay, Caesar, but not gone" (3.1.1–2). In the Roman calendar, the ides fall on the fifteenth of March, May, July, and October and on the thirteenth of the other months. The ides corresponded to the full moon. Although Shakespeare seems to place the assassination of Julius Caesar at the capitol, he was in fact killed at the curia on the opposite end of the garden attached to the Theatre of Pompey, where the senate sometimes met. (See "A Street" in this chapter, scene 1.3, for details about the Theatre of Pompey.) Plutarch, Shakespeare's chief source for Roman history, in describing the assassination of Julius Caesar, refers to Pompey's porch but also to the senate. Shakespeare may not have understood that the senate sometimes met at the Theatre of Pompey.

Artemidorus gives Caesar his warning, which Caesar does not read. When the conspirators enter the capitol, Trebonius draws Marc Antony away, and the other plotters stab Caesar to death. Marc Antony returns and seems reconciled with Caesar's killers. He asks to speak at Caesar's funeral. Despite Cassius's objections, Brutus consents (another of Brutus's bad decisions). Left alone, Marc Antony predicts civil war will ensue. When the servant of Octavius Caesar, Julius Caesar's great-nephew and heir, reports his master is close to Rome, Marc Antony tells him Octavius should avoid the city for now.

Domus Publica, Via Sacra

The residence of the pontifex maximus, Rome's chief priest and overseer of the Vestal Virgins, it became Julius Caesar's residence in 62 BCE, when he assumed the priestly office. In 12 BCE it became part of the house of the Vestal Virgins when Augustus Caesar decided not to occupy it. The house was frequently rebuilt, but only ruins remain.

Scene 2.2: As a storm rages, Calpurnia urges Caesar not to go out that day, and they argue. A servant informs them the augurs say Caesar should stay home. After further arguing Caesar agrees to send Marc Antony to the senate to say Caesar is ill. Decius Brutus, who had promised the other conspirators to bring Caesar to the senate house, arrives. At first Caesar declares he is not venturing out, but Decius Brutus tells him the senate plans to make him emperor that day. The other conspirators come to attend on Caesar, and they set off.

The Forum

A plaza in the center of Rome between the Palatine and Velian Hills, the Forum was for centuries the focus of the city's daily life. The site was originally a marshy lake, which was drained by the Cloaca Maxima built by the Tarquins in the seventh century BCE. Augustus paved the Forum with travertine. The ruins of many temples are located here.

Scene 1.2: On the Feast of Lupercalia (February 15, 44 BCE) Caesar instructs his childless wife, Calpurnia, to stand where Marc Antony, one of the consuls, can touch her as he runs the ritual race, and he tells Antony to be sure to touch her to promote fertility. A soothsayer warns Caesar to beware the ides of March (March 15).

Left alone with Marcus Junius Brutus, Gaius Cassius Longinus seeks to enlist him in a conspiracy to kill Caesar because he is growing too powerful. As Caesar and his retinue cross the stage, Brutus plucks Publius Servilius Casca Longus by his toga. Casca remains to report what transpired. Casca says in the Forum Antony offered Caesar a crown three times, which Caesar three times refused. Casca also reports the tribunes Flavius and Marullus have been "put to silence" (l. 284), which may mean removed from office, exiled, or executed, for removing scarves from Caesar's images (and so dishonoring him). As the scene ends, Cassius says he will throw letters into Brutus's house warning of Caesar's ambition.

Scene 3.2: At Caesar's funeral Brutus addresses the citizens of Rome, who support him. Departing, Brutus urges them to listen to Marc Antony's speech. In his famous oration that begins "Friends, Romans, countrymen, lend me your ears" (l. 74), Marc Antony sways the citizens to attack Caesar's murderers. While, as noted previously, Shakespeare took much material in his Roman plays from Plutarch's *Lives of the Noble Grecians and Romans* translated by Thomas North (1579), he invented Marc Antony's speech. Plutarch writes only that Antony "mingled his oration with lamentable words, and by amplifying the matters did greatly move [his hearers'] harts and affections unto pitie and compassion." Plutarch describes Antony's showing "before the whole assembly the bloody garments of the dead, thrust through in many places with their swords, and called the malefactors, cruell and cursed murderers," just as Marc Antony does in this scene. Shakespeare again follows Plutarch in having the citizens of Rome attack the houses of the conspirators and in the servant's reporting the flight of Brutus and Cassius. In the play a servant tells Marc Antony that Octavius has arrived in Rome. In fact, Octavius was studying in Apollonia (now in Albania) when he learned of his great-uncle's assassination and returned to Rome only in late March. Shakespeare has Antony, Octavius, and Lepidus meeting at Caesar's house immediately after Marc Antony's funeral oration. Historically, Octavius and Marc Antony were initially enemies; the Second Triumvirate (the first had consisted of Julius Caesar, Pompey, and Crassus, formed in 60 BCE) was not created until November 27, 43 BCE.

Marc Antony's House

Scene 4.1: Octavius, Marcus Aemilius Lepidus, and Marc Antony decide who will die. The Second Triumvirate's proscriptions in fact were intended largely to raise money through bribes, though some of their opponents, including their own relatives, were executed. Most notable was Marcus Tullius Cicero, who had sided with Octavius against Antony before the two triumvirs reconciled. Antony wanted him killed, and Octavius agreed. After Lepidus leaves them, Marc Antony and Octavius prepare to confront the forces of Brutus and Cassius.

A Street

Scene 1.1: In October of 45 BCE, Caesar was granted a triumphal celebration for his victory over the sons of Pompey in Spain. The tribunes Flavius and Marullus, representatives of the plebeians and supporters of the defeated (and dead) Pompey, disperse a group of commoners who have gathered to observe the procession. This street may be located near the Forum, where 1.2 unfolds.

Scene 1.3: On March 14, 44 BCE, Casca tells Cicero of prodigies he has seen amid a violent storm that is raging. Cicero leaves, and Cassius appears. Casca and Cassius criticize Caesar. Cinna joins them on their way to Pompey's porch, the portico of the theater Pompey the Great built in 55 BCE. The Campo de' Fiori now sits on the site of the theater. The conspirators hope they can lure Brutus into joining their assassination plot.

Scene 3.3: A mob kills Cinna the poet because he has the same name as Cinna the conspirator. The citizenry do not come off well in Shakespeare's portrayal.

TURKEY

Sardis

The modern Sart, Sardis was the capital of Lydia. Here Croesus built the Temple of Artemis, one of the largest temples in the world. Only ruins remain. Later, the city was governed by the Persians and then fell to the Greeks under Alexander the Great (334 BCE). In 133 BCE Sardis came under Roman rule. The city was destroyed by Timur in 1402.

Scenes 4.2–4.3: Cassius with his army join Brutus and his forces. Inside Brutus's tent Cassius and Brutus quarrel, then reconcile. Brutus tells Cassius of Portia's death. Most contemporary historians place Portia's suicide after the second Battle of Philippi (October 23, 42 BCE), in which Brutus died. Some accounts, however, claim she died earlier, in June of 43 BCE. Shakespeare follows most Roman accounts in saying she committed suicide by swallowing hot coals. Some modern historians suggest she died of carbon monoxide poisoning by burning coals in a closed room. Plutarch repeats the story of suicide by hot coals but prefers the version in which she died of illness in 43 BCE. Gary Wills, in *Rome and Rhetoric: Shakespeare's "Julius Caesar"* (2011), agrees with Plutarch. Brutus also informs Cassius that Marc Antony and Octavius are going to Philippi, in what was eastern Macedonia (now Greece; see "Greece," earlier this chapter). Messala arrives to report the proscription of senators, including Cicero, and the death of Portia, which Brutus seems to dismiss. Brutus and Cassius debate whether to go to Philippi or await an attack by their opponents. Again, Brutus overrules Cassius, who favored staying in Asia Minor. As Brutus prepares to sleep, the ghost of Julius Caesar appears and says they will meet at Philippi.

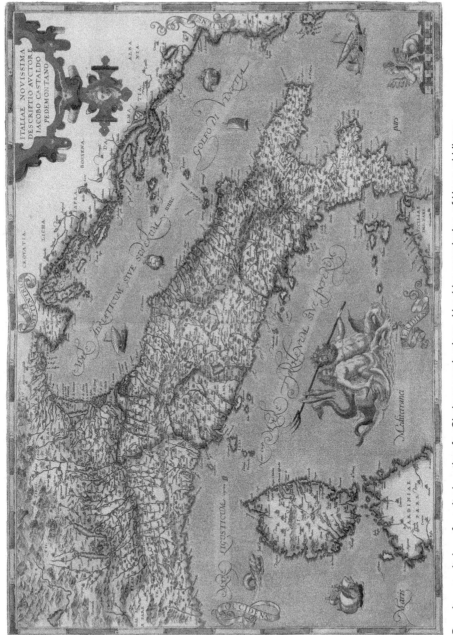

Renaissance Italy, a favorite location for Shakespeare's plays. *Used by permission of Harvard Library*

Hamlet

DENMARK

The Coast

Scene 4.4: Fortinbras passes with his army. Hamlet, on his way to his ship, talks with a Norwegian captain. Then, alone, he accuses himself of inaction and promises to take bloody revenge on Claudius.

Helsingør

Shakespeare's Elsinore is located in eastern Denmark. It takes its name from the Danish word *hais* ("neck") because it is located at the narrowest point of the Øresund (Øre Sound) between Helsingbord and Helsingør. By 1672 Helsingør was the third-largest city in Denmark. It was an important port. Saxo Grammaticus, whose Danish history provided the basis of *Hamlet,* was born here.

Although the story of Hamlet dates from the twelfth century, the modern city of Helsingør was founded in the 1420s by the Danish king Eric of Pomerania, who built the castle Krogen. Frederick II built an elaborate palace on the site in 1574–1585; the new palace incorporated some of Krogen. In setting *Hamlet* in the Renaissance palace of Kronborg, Shakespeare is indicating the title character is the ideal Renaissance prince as described by Baldassare Castiglione in *The Book of the Courtier.* Ophelia describes him as the "courtier's, soldier's, scholar's eye, tongue, sword, / The expectancy and rose of the fair state, / The glass of fashion, and the mold of form, / The observed of all observers" (3.1.152–55). Fynes Moryson described Elsinore in 1593 thus:

> This is a poor village, but much frequented by seafaring men, by reason of the straight [narrow] sea called the Sound, where the King of Denmark hath laid so great impositions upon ships and goods coming out of the Baltic Sea or brought into the same, as this sole profit passeth all the revenues of his kingdom. In this village a strong castle called Croneburg lyeth upon the mouth of the straight.

176

The palace now has a Shakespeare memorial tablet, and *Hamlet* is often staged here. In 1937 Laurence Olivier played Hamlet here, with Vivien Lee as Ophelia. Two years later John Gielgud assumed the role of Hamlet at Kronborg.

A Graveyard

Scene 5.1: Two gravediggers talk as they dig Ophelia's grave. Graves were reused in Shakespeare's day: hence his inscription over his tomb in Holy Trinity Church, Stratford (see "Holy Trinity Church" under "Stratford-upon-Avon" in appendix A), asking that his bones not be moved (as they have not been). Hamlet and Horatio enter and watch as the first gravedigger tosses skulls out of the hole he is making. When Hamlet asks about one of these, the gravedigger says it is the skull of Yorick, the former king's jester. Hamlet delivers a monologue about the jester, whom he knew when the prince was a child.

Claudius, Gertrude, Laertes, a priest, and lords arrive with the corpse of Ophelia as Hamlet and Horatio hide. The scene recalls the opening of Aeschylus's *Libation Bearers*. Philip Henslowe of the Rose Theatre paid Henry Chettle and Thomas Dekker for *Orestes' Furies* on May 2, 1599, and later that month he paid for *The Tragedy of Agamemnon*. Neither play survives, but they date from the time Shakespeare was composing this play. Hamlet had not known of Ophelia's death. After her body is placed in the grave (a space under the Globe stage with a trapdoor to provide access), Laertes leaps in after her. Hamlet reveals himself, leaps in after Laertes, and they fight in the grave. The stage direction for Hamlet to leap into the grave after Laertes appears only in the 1603 edition (Q1). It is omitted in the second quarto (Q2, 1604/1605) and the First Folio (1623). Shakespeare may have recognized the fight would be more visible if it occurred onstage rather than partially below it. Hamlet professes his love for Ophelia and former friendship toward Laertes. After Hamlet and Horatio depart, Claudius tells Laertes they will at once execute their plot against the prince.

Kronborg Castle

Named a UNESCO World Heritage Site (2000), the castle is located on the northeastern tip of the island of Zealand between Denmark and Sweden. King Frederick II rebuilt the original fifteenth-century fortification, turning it into a great Renaissance royal residence (1574–1585) with the largest banqueting hall in northern Europe. A fire in 1629 destroyed much of the castle, but King Christian IV rebuilt it. Swedes captured the castle in 1658. From 1739 to the early twentieth century, it served as a prison; Queen Caroline Mathilde was held here in 1772. It was opened to the public in 1938.

English actors played here in 1585, the first known performance by English actors on the Continent. In 1586 English players again performed here. Will Kempe was a comic actor in the troupe; other members included Thomas Pope and George Bryan.

All three later became part of the Lord Chamberlain's Men, Shakespeare's company, and may have provided Shakespeare with details about the castle. Even if Shakespeare knew specific details about the site, he took poetic license when he wrote about the "cliff / That beetles o'er the base of the castle" (1.4.70–71), indicating he was not familiar with the terrain or redesigned it for dramatic effect.

Scene 1.1: On the battlements of Kronborg Castle, Barnardo and Marcellus, accompanied by Horatio, relieve Francisco of guard duty. When they inform Horatio they have seen a ghost, he is skeptical, but soon the ghost, resembling the recently dead Old Hamlet, king of Denmark, appears. Horatio tries to speak with it, but it silently departs. Marcellus asks why Denmark is preparing for war, and Horatio explains that Fortinbras, son of Norway's former king who was killed by Old Hamlet, seeks to recover lands lost by his father to Denmark. In Shakespeare's day Norway was ruled by Denmark; it did not have its own king. However, in the early sixteenth century, Norway and Denmark had fought over Denmark's imposing the Protestant Reformation on mainly Catholic Norway. The ghost returns and seems about to speak, but a rooster crows, and the ghost again vanishes. Horatio says they should tell young Hamlet what they have seen.

Scene 1.2: In the Banqueting Hall, King Claudius holds court. Original audiences may have been surprised to see Claudius, young Hamlet's uncle, reigning rather than young Hamlet, son of the dead king. Denmark had an elected monarchy, but because England's monarchy was hereditary, the opening of this scene may have been intentionally disorienting, raising questions, as the entire play is written in the interrogative mode. Claudius dispatches Cornelius and Voltemand to the king of Norway to try to resolve the current crisis peacefully. Claudius then grants permission to Laertes, son of his Lord Chamberlain, Polonius, to return to his studies at the University of Paris (Catholic) but denies Hamlet's request to return to the University of Wittenberg (Protestant). Left alone, Hamlet delivers the first of his seven soliloquies. Horatio, Marcellus, and Barnardo arrive to tell Hamlet about the ghost; Hamlet resolves to watch with them on the battlements that night.

Scene 1.3: In Polonius's quarters Laertes bids farewell to his sister Ophelia. Polonius enters and, urging his son to depart at once, detains him with a long speech of advice. After Laertes leaves, Polonius orders Ophelia to stop seeing Hamlet.

Scene 1.4: On the battlements Hamlet, Horatio, and Marcellus await the ghost, while in the Banqueting Hall, Claudius and his court revel. The ghost appears and silently beckons Hamlet away. Repulsing the efforts of Horatio and Marcellus to restrain him, Hamlet leaves with the ghost.

Scene 1.5: On another part of the battlements, the ghost reveals himself as the spirit of Hamlet's father and declares Claudius, his brother, killed him. The ghost instructs Hamlet to avenge his death but not to punish Gertrude, Old Hamlet's widow, who has married Claudius. After the ghost departs, Horatio and Marcellus find Hamlet, who makes them promise not to disclose what has happened. Claudius's marrying his dead brother's wife would have reminded Shakespeare's audiences of Henry VIII's wedding Catherine of Aragon after the death of Henry's older brother, Arthur. The ghost calls that marriage incestuous, which was the excuse Henry VIII used to divorce Catherine in May 1533 after almost twenty-four years of marriage. Because Claudius is a murderer and the villain of the play, the parallel with Henry VIII is not flattering to that king, though the claim of incest here might support Henry's assertion that legitimized his marriage with the mother of Elizabeth, reigning when the play was first produced. While Shakespeare did not invent the plot about the medieval Danish prince Amleth, Elizabethan audiences would have detected the similarity with their own history.

Scene 2.1: From his quarters Polonius dispatches Reynaldo to give Laertes money and to spy on him. After Reynaldo leaves, Ophelia comes to report an unsettling silent visit from Hamlet. Polonius concludes Hamlet has gone mad because of his love for Ophelia. He resolves to tell Claudius.

Scene 2.2: In the Throne Room, Claudius and Gertrude welcome Hamlet's former school friends Rosencrantz and Guildenstern. In the 1590s two members of the Danish nobility, Frederick Rosenkrantz and Knud Gyldenstierne, visited London. Shakespeare may have met them. The royal couple hope these friends of Hamlet will learn why Hamlet has been behaving strangely. As soon as they go off, Polonius arrives to announce the return of Cornelius and Voltemand and declare he has discovered the cause of Hamlet's madness. Polonius brings in the ambassadors, who report a peaceful resolution for Denmark: Fortinbras has agreed to invade Poland rather than Denmark and seeks free passage through Claudius's realm to effect his purpose. In 1571 the Danish fleet seized eighteen ships belonging to the Polish-Lithuanian Commonwealth.

Once the ambassadors depart, Polonius tediously explains that Hamlet has gone mad because Polonius forbade Ophelia from seeing the prince. The king, queen, and Polonius agree to arrange a meeting between Hamlet and Ophelia to test this theory. Hamlet enters as the king and queen depart. He and Polonius talk, Hamlet putting on an antic disposition that shows his contempt for the old man. Polonius leaves, and Rosencrantz and Guildenstern come to try unsuccessfully to pluck out the heart of Hamlet's mystery. Rosencrantz informs the prince of the arrival of a troupe of strolling players. They have been forced from the city by the popularity of child acting companies, as the adult companies in London were threatened by them circa 1600, when the play was first performed. Hamlet greets the actors warmly and asks for a speech in which Aeneas tells of the death of King Priam of Troy; Shakespeare here rewrites part of Christopher Marlowe's *Dido, Queen of Carthage* (published 1594), 2.1, in which Aeneas describes the fall of Troy.

Hamlet commends the actors to the care of Polonius. After all but the leading actor depart, Hamlet asks him to stage *The Murder of Gonzago*, a play showing the crime the ghost claims Claudius committed, and to add a speech (never identified) that Hamlet will write for the production. Alone, Hamlet in a soliloquy berates himself for his inaction but says the play will reveal whether he should believe the ghost.

Scene 3.1: In the Great Hall, Claudius and Gertrude question Rosencrantz and Guildenstern about their conversation with Hamlet. The men report they have learned nothing, but Hamlet has arranged for the visiting actors to entertain the court; Polonius adds that Hamlet has asked him to invite the royal couple, and Claudius promises to attend. The king dismisses Rosencrantz and Guildenstern and then Gertrude. Claudius and Polonius hide to observe the encounter between Hamlet and Ophelia. Hamlet arrives and delivers his "To be or not to be" soliloquy (ll. 56+) and then verbally assaults Ophelia, perhaps because he knows he is being watched. After he and Ophelia leave, Claudius dismisses Polonius's theory of love-madness and resolves to send Hamlet to England, he says to collect taxes—much of England was ruled by Denmark in the early eleventh century, in which the original story of Amleth is set—but in fact to have him killed.

Scene 3.2: Hamlet instructs the players on the proper way to perform. The actors leave to prepare for their play, and Polonius arrives to say the royal couple are going to attend the performance. Polonius departs, and Hamlet's true friend Horatio joins the prince. Hamlet praises Horatio for his equanimity. To the flourish of trumpets, the king, queen, Polonius, Ophelia, Rosencrantz, Guildenstern, lords, and guards enter. Hamlet sits by Ophelia and talks with her bawdily until a trumpet sounds, followed by a dumb show. At Shakespeare's Globe, a trumpet announced the start of a play. At the beginning of this performance, the player queen swears eternal love for the player king, who lies down for a nap. Lucianus, nephew of the king, enters and pours poison in the king's ear as he sleeps, just as Claudius did to Old Hamlet. Claudius leaps from his chair and calls for light. All but Hamlet and Horatio leave, convinced now of the truth of the ghost's accusation. Rosencrantz and Guildenstern return to say the king is angry, and Gertrude wants to speak with Hamlet in her room. Polonius comes to echo that message. Everyone leaves but Hamlet, who goes to see his mother.

Scene 3.3: In the Kronborg chapel (inaugurated 1582), Claudius informs Rosencrantz and Guildenstern that they are to accompany Hamlet to England. After they depart, Polonius comes to say Hamlet is on his way to see Gertrude; Polonius will hide behind a tapestry to eavesdrop on their conversation. Left alone, Claudius confesses his guilt and tries to pray. Hamlet, passing the chapel on his way to his mother's room, sees the king on his knees. Hamlet considers killing the king then but decides to wait until Claudius is engaged in some activity that will guarantee his damnation. Is Hamlet here rationalizing his procrastination? Does Hamlet truly want to damn his uncle?

After Hamlet leaves, Claudius acknowledges his prayer is ineffectual because he does not intend to change his ways.

Scene 3.4: In Gertrude's chamber Polonius instructs Gertrude to be firm with Hamlet; he then retires behind a tapestry. When Hamlet arrives, Gertrude confronts him, and he in turn accuses her of killing Old Hamlet and incestuously marrying her first husband's brother. As the argument grows heated, Gertrude calls for help, as does Polonius. Hamlet stabs him through the tapestry, mistaking the Lord Chamberlain for Claudius. Later in the scene, the ghost of Old Hamlet appears for the last time to prompt Hamlet to avenge his murder and to comfort Gertrude. Hamlet asks his mother not to reveal he is sane and to stop sleeping with Claudius. In the 1603 first quarto of the play (Q1), she promises to help Hamlet. In subsequent editions her response, like so much else in the play, remains ambiguous. As the scene ends, Hamlet drags Polonius's body away.

Scene 4.1: In a corridor Gertrude tells Claudius that Hamlet has killed Polonius. Claudius knows he was the intended target. He summons Rosencrantz and Guildenstern to find Hamlet and to bring Polonius's body to the chapel.

Scene 4.2: Rosencrantz and Guildenstern try unsuccessfully to get Hamlet to reveal the location of Polonius's corpse. The prince warns them that Claudius will discard them once the king no longer needs them. He then flees, with Rosencrantz and Guildenstern in pursuit.

Scene 4.3: Hamlet has been caught. Brought before Claudius, Hamlet reveals he has hidden the body in the lobby. Claudius tells Hamlet he must go to England immediately. Alone, Claudius says he wants England to execute Hamlet.

Scene 4.5: Horatio persuades a reluctant Gertrude to speak with the mad Ophelia. Ophelia sings two songs, one of them bawdy. As soon as she exits, a messenger hurries in urging the king to flee a mob led by Laertes, who enters with supporters. Laertes orders his followers to wait outside while he confronts Claudius, who momentarily pacifies him. Ophelia returns to distribute herbs symbolically appropriate to the recipients and sings again before leaving. Claudius promises Laertes to explain the death of his father and to help him avenge Polonius's death.

Scene 4.6: A sailor gives Horatio a letter from Hamlet saying he was captured by pirates. The packet includes letters for Claudius and instructions to Horatio to go with the pirates to the king.

Scene 4.7: Claudius tells Laertes Hamlet killed Polonius. A messenger delivers Hamlet's letters, surprising the king, who thought Hamlet was dead or at least on his way to England. Now that Hamlet has returned to Denmark, Claudius plots with Laertes to kill the prince in a seemingly innocent fencing match. Gertrude arrives to report Ophelia's drowning. Shakespeare's narrative sources do not mention a drowning. In 1579 Katherine Hamlet drowned in the River Avon at Stratford, and a Jane Shaxspere (a relative of the playwright?) drowned near Stratford ten years earlier. These deaths may have prompted Shakespeare's killing of Ophelia, though Shakespeare's dramatic source of the play, an *Ur-Hamlet* from the late 1580s, perhaps by Thomas Kyd, no longer exists and may have included such an incident. Laertes leaves, followed by the king and queen.

Scene 5.2: Hamlet tells Horatio how on shipboard he stole and read Claudius's letter given to Rosencrantz and Guildenstern ordering Hamlet's execution. Hamlet exchanged that letter for another ordering the deaths of Rosencrantz and Guildenstern. The foppish courtier Osric enters to invite Hamlet to a fencing match with Laertes, and Hamlet agrees. In the Great Hall, Claudius, Gertrude, Laertes, Hamlet, and Horatio gather. Hamlet apologizes to Laertes for their encounter in the graveyard, and the match begins. Hamlet proves the better fencer, scoring two hits. Gertrude drinks the poisoned chalice Claudius had prepared for Hamlet; in different productions she knows or does not know Claudius has poisoned the wine intended for Hamlet. When the match resumes Laertes wounds Hamlet with the poisoned unbated foil. Hamlet scuffles with Laertes, gets the envenomed foil, and wounds Laertes. As Gertrude collapses she declares she has been poisoned. Dying, Laertes confesses the foil is poisoned, too. Hamlet stabs Claudius with it and forces him to drink the poisoned wine. The king and Laertes die. Horatio wants to join Hamlet in death by drinking from the

Kronborg Castle, Elsinore, Denmark, the setting for *Hamlet*. © *iStock/Arsty*

chalice, but Hamlet prevents him, urging him to explain how the tragedy occurred. Then Hamlet dies. The poison Claudius used to kill Old Hamlet thus spreads to engulf the entire royal family.

The sounds of a march are heard as Fortinbras returns triumphant from Poland. He arrives with the English ambassadors, who announce "Rosencrantz and Guildenstern are dead," (l. 373), giving Tom Stoppard the title of a play. Horatio promises to tell how this final scene of carnage came about. Fortinbras claims the Danish crown and orders a military funeral for Hamlet.

Othello

Located in the eastern Mediterranean, about 1,300 miles from Venice, it is the third-largest island in that ocean. It has been inhabited since the tenth millennium BCE. The origin of the name is unclear, but it may derive from the Sumerian word for copper, *Zubar*, which is plentiful on the island. The chemical symbol for copper is CU, for *cuprum*, the Latin word for the metal, short for *aes Cyprium*, "metal of Cyprus." Between 1571 and 1868, Cyprus was ruled by the Turks, who seized the island from Venice. The island gained independence in 1960 but remains contested between Greece and Turkey.

Cyprus is supposedly the birthplace of Venus, goddess of love, but in this play it is where hate triumphs and love is destroyed. Whereas Venice represents civilization in the play, Cyprus is wilder. It is also a contested and unsettled site, like Othello himself.

Famagusta

A city on the east coast of the island, Famagusta has the deepest harbor in Cyprus. The city was founded by Ptolemy II Philadelphus about 274 BCE and named for his sister Arsinoe. It flourished in the Middle Ages. In 1372 Genoa took the city, and in 1489 it fell to Venice; it was the last Venetian stronghold on the island to fall to Turkey in 1571. Othello's Castle dates from the fourteenth century. The castle takes its name from Shakespeare's play. In 1506 Christoforo Moro, a Moor like Othello, served as Venetian governor here.

A Cape

Scene 2.1: As Montano, the governor of Cyprus, and two gentlemen scan the horizon, a third gentleman says the recent storm must have scattered the Turkish fleet. While the scattering of the Turkish fleet here is counterfactual, it would recall for Shakespeare's audience the fate of the Spanish Armada in 1588. A medal struck to commemorate the English victory bears the inscription "FLAVIT י ה ו ET DISSIPATI SUNT," "God blew and they were scattered." On October 7, 1571, the Holy League, led by Venice and Spain, defeated a Turkish fleet off Lepanto, Greece. The Holy League had assembled the fleet to try to relieve the besieged port of Famagusta. In this effort they were unsuccessful; Famagusta had fallen to the Turks in August, and the victory at Lepanto did not alter the situation on Cyprus. In 1573 Venice ceded Cyprus to Turkey and paid 300,000 ducats indemnity.

This gentleman also reports the arrival of Othello's lieutenant, Michael Cassio, from Venice. Cassio enters, followed by Iago, Othello's ensign (a rank lower than lieutenant); Desdemona, Othello's wife; Emilia, Iago's wife and Desdemona's attendant; and Roderigo, disguised, in love with Desdemona. Othello lands and confirms the destruction of the Turkish fleet. All depart except Roderigo and Iago, who claims Desdemona loves Cassio. To remove Cassio, Iago instructs Roderigo to provoke a brawl with him, which will cause Othello to dismiss him. Iago wants Cassio's lieutenancy and is using Roderigo for his own purpose.

Othello's Castle

Built in the fourteenth century as a moated citadel to guard the harbor, the tower was remodeled in 1492 by the Venetian Niccolo Foscari. By the time of the play's setting, circa 1570, the castle was being used as a prison.

Scene 2.3: Othello instructs Cassio to oversee the guard that night, then leaves with Desdemona. Iago gets Cassio drunk; then Roderigo enters, angers Cassio offstage, and flees, pursued by Cassio, who beats him. When Montano tries to restrain the lieutenant, Cassio wounds him. An angry Othello arrives to inquire into the cause of the brawling. Iago, pretending to mitigate Cassio's guilt, makes it clear enough for Othello to deprive Cassio of his post.

Alone with Cassio, Iago urges him to appeal to Desdemona for the restoration of his lieutenancy. After Cassio leaves, Iago in a soliloquy says he will tell Othello that Desdemona is interceding for Cassio because she loves the disgraced lieutenant. The more she pleads, the more Othello will distrust her. Roderigo, upset over his beating, confronts Iago, who placates him by informing him Cassio has lost his lieutenancy. Once more alone, Iago plots to have Emilia ask Desdemona to help Cassio, and Iago will arrange for Othello to see Desdemona and Cassio together.

Scene 3.2: Othello gives Iago letters for the pilot and then goes with some gentlemen to inspect the city's fortifications.

Scene 3.3: In a garden in the citadel, Cassio asks Desdemona to help him regain his position. When Emilia announces Othello's approach, Cassio departs. Iago suggests Cassio has guiltily snuck away, thus planting the seed of suspicion in Othello's mind. Othello yields to Desdemona's plea for Cassio. When Iago and Othello are alone, Iago warns Othello against jealousy, thereby fostering it, and tells him to watch Cassio and Desdemona. Iago leaves, and Desdemona comes to call Othello to dinner. Othello complains of a pain in his forehead, alluding to a cuckold's horns; Desdemona tries to bind his head with her handkerchief decorated with strawberries, the first gift Othello gave her. The strawberry is a symbol of love—and of concealment because the plant grows low to the ground and snakes could hide beneath it; also, the strawberry itself can grow concealed, as the Bishop of Ely observes in *Henry V*, 1.1.60: "The strawberry grows underneath the nettle." Othello brushes the handkerchief away, and it falls to the ground. Emilia retrieves it after Othello and Desdemona go away. Iago has been asking her to steal that handkerchief. Emilia at first plans to have it copied, give her husband the duplicate, and restore the original to Desdemona. But Iago comes in, and she reluctantly hands it to him. Iago plans to leave it in Cassio's room; seeing Cassio with Desdemona's handkerchief will further inflame Othello's jealousy.

Othello appears, now consumed with jealousy. He warns Iago to prove Desdemona unfaithful, or Iago will face dire consequences. Iago invents a story about Cassio in his sleep kissing Iago while speaking of Desdemona. Iago says Desdemona has given her strawberry-spotted handkerchief to Cassio. Othello tells Iago to kill Cassio. Iago asks Othello to spare Desdemona, but Othello resolves to kill her, too. He makes Iago his lieutenant.

Scene 4.2: Othello questions Emilia about Desdemona and Cassio. Emilia assures him Desdemona is faithful, but he is past persuasion. Alone with his wife, Othello calls her a "cunning whore" (l. 89). After he leaves, Emilia brings Iago to comfort Desdemona. Left alone by the women, Iago is confronted by Roderigo; Iago convinces him to kill Cassio and promises to help with the deed.

Scene 5.2: In his bedroom Othello prepares to kill the sleeping Desdemona. When she awakes, he accuses her of sleeping with Cassio and giving him her strawberry-spotted handkerchief. She denies his allegations, but he retorts that Cassio has confessed and Iago has killed him. Desdemona weeps for him, and Othello, interpreting her tears as yet another proof of her love for Cassio, smothers her.

Emilia knocks on the door. When Othello admits her, she reports the death of Roderigo and the wounding of Cassio. Hearing a cry, Emilia goes to the bed and finds the dying Desdemona. Othello claims Desdemona was unfaithful, a charge Emilia again denies. Othello assures her Iago knew of the affair with Cassio.

Iago enters with Montano, Gratiano, and others. Emilia asks Iago to deny telling Othello that Desdemona was unfaithful; instead, Iago repeats his accusation. She then informs those assembled that Othello has killed his wife. He confirms the deed, adding he saw Cassio with Desdemona's handkerchief. Despite Iago's attempt to silence Emilia, she tells Othello she found that handkerchief and gave it to Iago. Iago says she is lying, but Othello now tries to stab Iago. Montano disarms Othello as Iago stabs Emilia and flees.

Othello and Emilia are left in the room. Emilia protests Desdemona's innocence as she dies. Lodovico, Cassio, Montano, and officers return with Iago. Othello wounds Iago, who, Lodovico reports, has partly confessed his villainy. Letters found on Roderigo and Roderigo's dying confession further confirm Iago's guilt. Lodovico arrests Othello, but Othello, after making one last speech, kills himself. Lodovico urges Cassio to torture Iago, while he himself will return to Venice to report what has happened.

A Street

Scene 2.2: A herald announces Othello has proclaimed a celebration for the defeat of the Turks.

Scene 3.1: Cassio asks Emilia to summon Desdemona.

Scene 3.4: Desdemona sends a message to Cassio to say she hopes she has succeeded in securing the restoration of his lieutenancy. She wonders aloud to Emilia where she lost her handkerchief. Othello enters and asks for it. When she says she cannot produce it, he tells her it has magic powers to keep a husband faithful. She tries to speak of Cassio, he of the handkerchief. Finally, he leaves in anger.

Iago and Cassio enter. Cassio asks Desdemona to plead for him. She promises to do so but says he must be patient. Iago goes to seek Othello as Desdemona and Emilia depart. When Cassio's lover, Bianca, enters, he gives her Desdemona's handkerchief, which he found in his room (where Iago placed it), and asks her to copy the work. They leave together.

Scene 4.1: Iago continues to fuel Othello's jealousy until Othello falls into a fit. When Cassio appears, Iago temporarily dismisses him. Once Othello recovers, Iago instructs him to hide while Iago gets Cassio to confess his affair with Desdemona. Iago speaks to Cassio about Bianca, causing Cassio to laugh, but Othello thinks Cassio is laughing about his relationship with Desdemona. Bianca comes, throws Desdemona's handkerchief at him, accuses him of receiving it from another lover, and then leaves, with Cassio in pursuit. Othello has seen the handkerchief, further convincing him of Desdemona's infidelity. He says he will poison her that night, but Iago persuades him to smother her in their bed.

Lodovico, arrived from Venice, enters with Desdemona and attendants and gives Othello a letter recalling Othello and naming Cassio as governor of Cyprus. Desdemona says she is glad, referring to their going home, but Othello thinks she rejoices in her lover's promotion and strikes her. She leaves, followed by Othello. Lodovico is surprised by Othello's behavior, but Iago tells him Othello is much changed and insinuates he is dangerous.

Scene 5.1: At night Roderigo attacks Cassio as he leaves Bianca's house. Cassio wounds Roderigo, and Iago wounds Cassio in the leg before fleeing. The wounded men call for help. Lodovico and Gratiano enter, followed by Iago, who mortally stabs Roderigo to silence him. When Bianca emerges, Iago accuses her of involvement in the attack on Cassio. Cassio and Roderigo are carried away, and Iago sends Emilia to inform Othello of what has occurred.

ITALY

Venice

Venice consists of many islands linked by bridges. The city takes its name from the Veneti, who settled in the area in the tenth century BCE. The First Doge (Duke) of Venice, Paolo Lucio Anafesto, was elected in 697 CE. Beginning in the ninth century CE, Venice became an important commercial city-state, as well as a powerful naval power; by the end of the thirteenth century, it was the most prosperous city in Europe and ruled many islands in the Mediterranean, including Crete and Cyprus. In Shakespeare's day the city's power was waning, but it still was an important commercial center.

Brabantio's House

A three-story palace with elaborate balconies on the Grand Canal purports to be Brabantio's.

Scene 1.1: In front of Brabantio's house, Iago, Othello's ensign, tells Roderigo that Othello has secretly married Brabantio's daughter, Desdemona, whom Roderigo loves. To vex Othello, Iago prompts Roderigo to arouse Brabantio and inform him of Desdemona's elopement. Brabantio will then try to arrest Othello and separate him from Desdemona, though Iago knows Brabantio will be unable to accomplish either. Iago tells Roderigo to lead Brabantio and his party to the Sagittary, the inn where Othello is staying. Like Don John in *Much Ado about Nothing*, an earlier, comic version of this play, Iago delights in making mischief. Whereas in Shakespeare's source (Giovanni Battista Giraldi, or Cinthio, *Gli Hecatommithi*, 3.7) Iago is motivated by Desdemona's rejecting his love for her, in this play Iago has no clear motive. Or rather, he has so many that he seems to be hunting for an excuse for his hatred: He suspects Othello has slept with his wife, Othello chose Cassio rather than Iago as his lieutenant, and Cassio "hath a daily beauty in his life / That makes me ugly" (5.1.19–20). Unvoiced motives include racism and perhaps a homoerotic attraction to Othello, Cassio, or both, as suggested by the story he tells Othello in 3.3 (see earlier) about the sleeping Cassio's kissing him, putting his leg over Iago's thigh, and holding Iago's hand. Shakespeare took his locations for this play from Cinthio's story.

The Doge's Palace

1 Piazza San Marco

The current Gothic palace was begun about 1340. A 1574 fire destroyed the Council Chamber, which was subsequently decorated by Andrea Palladio, Tintoretto, and Veronese, whose ceiling mural depicts good government.

Scene 1.3: In the Council Chamber, the doge and his advisors try to decide whether the Turks plan to invade Rhodes or Cyprus. Through reason and reports, they rightly choose Cyprus. In civilized Venice doubt is correctly resolved through logic. In the less-civilized Cyprus, where passion reigns, ambiguity results in false conclusions and tragedy. The Turks in fact seized Rhodes in 1522. In May 1570 they attacked Cyprus, which fell to them the following year. Brabantio, Othello, Cassio, Iago, Roderigo, and officers enter the Council Chamber, where Brabantio accuses Othello of stealing Desdemona with drugs and spells. Othello tells them to send for Desdemona. He says the only spells he has used were cast by his stories. (Writers since Homer have wanted to believe in the seductive powers of narrative.) Iago returns with Desdemona, who declares her love for Othello. He is placed in command of the Venetian forces and ordered away that night, even before his marriage can be consummated. Desdemona insists on accompanying him to war. As everyone is leaving, Brabantio warns Othello that Desdemona may deceive him as she did her father.

The Doge's Palace, Venice. *Courtesy of the Library of Congress, LC-DIG-ppmsc-06655*

Iago and Roderigo remain behind. Roderigo says he will kill himself because he cannot have Desdemona. Iago, planning to profit from this gullible, rich gentleman, urges him to get money and go to Cyprus in disguise. Iago promises to help Roderigo win Desdemona. Alone, Iago in a soliloquy declares he wants Cassio's lieutenancy, and because he suspects Othello has slept with his wife, Emilia, Iago wants to arouse Othello's jealousy.

The Sagittary

Shakespeare invented this inn; none of that name existed in Venice or London when the play was written. Shakespeare has Antipholus of Syracuse stay at the Centaur in *The Comedy of Errors*. It is not too much of a stretch to imagine the Centaur and Sagittary are male versions of the Mermaid Tavern, which Shakespeare supposedly frequented (see "Mermaid Tavern" under "London" in appendix A). In *The Comedy of Errors*, the inn's name has no thematic resonance, but reflecting the growth of Shakespeare's art, in *Othello* the image of half-man, half-beast, embodies the conflict within the protagonist. Iago's language is filled with animal imagery, and he appeals to the bestial in Othello. Desdemona embodies unconditional love. As in a medieval

Othello's Tower in Famagusta, Cyprus. The tower is named for Shakespeare's fictional character, who would have been based in this fifteenth-century fortress when he governed the island in Shakespeare's play. © iStock/koralex

morality play, Othello as Everyman is torn between Iago's hate and Desdemona's love. His choice of the former leads to tragedy. The theme of duality in humanity recurs in Shakespeare. In *Hamlet*, the tragedy that immediately precedes *Othello*, the prince reflects, "What a piece of work is a man, . . . in action how like an angel, in apprehension how like a god," but this same creature is also a "quintessence of dust" (2.2.311–16). In *King Lear*, the tragedy that follows *Othello*, the king claims, "Down from the waist they [women] are Centaurs, / Though women all above: / But to the girdle do the gods inherit, / Beneath is all the fiend's" (4.6.124–27).

Scene 1.2: Feigning friendship for Othello, Iago warns him that Brabantio will try to separate him from Desdemona. Cassio, Othello's lieutenant, arrives with officers to summon Othello to the duke because news has arrived that the Muslim Turks plan to invade Cyprus. As a Christian maritime power that controlled Cyprus since 1473, Venice will oppose the Turks, and Othello is to lead the expeditionary force to fight the invaders.

Brabantio, Roderigo, and officers come to arrest Othello. Both sides draw their swords, but Othello orders all to put up their weapons. All set off for the Council Chamber in the Doge's Palace.

King Lear

ENGLAND

Dover, Kent

The closest English port to France (twenty-five miles away), Dover, one of the Cinque Ports on the English Channel and famous for its white chalk cliffs, has been inhabited since the Stone Age, and by the Bronze Age it was used for shipping. The Romans called it Portus Dubris and used it as a base for their navy. The Pharos (lighthouse) at Dover Castle dates from circa 50 CE and may be the oldest structure in England. The city takes its name from the Dour River, which empties here into the English Channel. It remains an important port: The crossing from Dover to Calais is the busiest shipping channel in the world. One of the white cliffs is called Shakespeare's Cliff because it is supposedly where Gloucester in act 4, scene 6, of *King Lear* tries to kill himself by leaping from it.

Dover Castle dates from the eleventh century. In scene 5.1 of *King John*, the bastard announces that Kent has yielded to the invading French, but Dover Castle (under Hubert de Burgh) continued to resist. It held out for ten months. After his army was defeated at Lincoln and his navy destroyed near Dover, Louis of France abandoned his attempt to rule England. In World War II, the castle served as a command post; Admiral Sir Bertram Ramsey directed the Dunkirk evacuation from here. The castle is maintained by English Heritage and is open to the public.

Scene 4.3: At the French camp near Dover, a gentleman tells Kent that Cordelia wept when she heard of her father's mistreatment. Kent says Lear, who has been led to Dover, refuses to see Cordelia because he is ashamed of disinheriting her. Kent leads the gentleman to Lear. In Shakespeare's sources this reunion occurs in France. Shakespeare keeps the entire play in Britain.

Scene 4.4: At the French camp, Cordelia sends an officer to find Lear. A messenger reports the approach of the British forces.

Scene 4.6: Edgar tells Gloucester they are climbing the cliffs of Dover. Gloucester imagines he jumps from the top of the cliffs, and Edgar tells him he has miraculously survived his fall. Lear enters, mad, and meets Gloucester. Their conversation ends abruptly when Cordelia's agents try to capture Lear, who flees. As Edgar guides Gloucester away, they encounter Oswald, who wants to murder the earl but is killed by Edgar. Dying, he gives Edgar a letter for Edmund in which Goneril declares her love for him and asks him to kill her husband during the upcoming battle so she can marry Edmund. Hearing a drum announcing imminent battle, Edgar leaves with Gloucester.

Scene 4.7: In a tent in the French camp, Lear awakes and recognizes Cordelia.

Scene 5.1: In the British camp, Regan woos Edmund. Albany and Goneril arrive with their forces. Edgar comes to give Albany Goneril's letter to Edmund and tells the duke that, if the British forces triumph, Albany should summon Edgar with a trumpet. Alone, Edmund reflects he has promised himself to both Regan and Goneril. He also declares his intention to thwart Albany's intention to pardon Cordelia and Lear if they are taken prisoner.

Scene 5.2: On a field near Dover, Cordelia's forces are defeated. Shakespeare changed the outcome of the battle; in his sources Lear regains his kingdom and reigns for two or three years. After he dies Cordelia succeeds him and reigns for five years. Her nephews then rebel and capture her; she kills herself in prison. In 1681 Nahum Tate produced his *History of King Lear*, which ends with Lear's restoration, and Cordelia survives. This version of the play was the *Lear* theater audiences saw for more than 150 years. Critics have never liked Tate's version. Samuel Johnson was an exception; he argued Cordelia's death was too terrible to see: "And if my sensations could add anything to the general suffrage, I might relate that I was many years ago so shocked by Cordelia's death that I know not whether I ever endured to read again the last scenes of the play till I undertook to revise them as an editor." Tate's version has been revived occasionally as a curiosity.

According to Geoffrey of Monmouth and *King Leir*, the French king leads the invading forces. In the 1608 quarto (Q1), the king of France comes to England, then returns to his country, leaving the Marshal of France, Monsieur la Far, in charge of his forces (scene 17). Shakespeare in the Folio version of the play follows Holinshed in having Cordelia lead the invasion—her husband remains in France—to diminish the sense of a foreign attack on British soil.

Edgar leads Gloucester to safety; Edmund orders Lear and Cordelia away to prison and gives a captain the order to kill them. Albany, Goneril, and Regan enter with their forces. Albany demands Lear and Cordelia from Edmund, who refuses to surrender them. Albany reminds Edmund he is not a commander, but Regan and Goneril both support Edmund. Feeling ill, having been poisoned by Goneril, Regan announces she plans to marry Edmund, but Albany arrests him for treason. Albany has read Goneril's letter asking Edmund to kill the duke.

Albany orders the sounding of a trumpet to summon Edgar, and Albany challenges Edmund to a duel. Regan, growing sicker, departs. Edgar arrives and challenges Edmund to a duel, and in the ensuing combat, Edmund is mortally wounded. Albany confronts Goneril with her letter, and she leaves. Edgar reveals his identity and describes his recent adventures and Gloucester's death.

A gentleman enters with a bloody knife that Goneril, in despair over Edmund's death, used to kill herself. Kent arrives and asks for Lear. The dying Edmund repents and reveals his order to kill the king and his daughter. Edgar rushes off with Edmund's sword as a token of the prisoners' reprieve, but as Edgar exits Lear enters with Cordelia's dead body in his arms. Albany wants to restore the crown to Lear, but Lear dies. Albany now offers the kingdom to Kent and Edgar, but Kent refuses, saying he will soon follow Lear in death. In the 1608 quarto version of the play, Albany delivers the last lines, indicating he will become king, but in the 1623 Folio, Edgar speaks them, suggesting he will assume the throne. If the Duke of Albany, ruler of Scotland, assumes the throne of Britain, he will be foreshadowing or imitating James VI of Scotland assuming the throne of Britain in 1603. Edgar as king would also compliment James. Edgar (c. 934–975) became king of all England in 959 and so, like James, was a unifier, and Edgar was known as "the Peaceful." James envisioned himself as a peacemaker. While Shakespeare took the plot of Gloucester, Edgar, and Edmund from Sir Philip Sidney's *Arcadia* (1590), the name *Edgar* does not appear there.

Gloucester, Gloucestershire

The Welsh Caerloyw (*caer* being a "fort") and the Roman Colonia Nervia Gelvensium (founded 97 CE during the reign of Emperor Nerva), Gloucester sits on the River Severn near Wales. Gloucester fell to the Celts after the Romans withdrew. Later it was part of the Anglo-Saxon kingdom of Wessex and then Mercia. In the Middle Ages, it thrived because of the wool trade—the Cotswolds were and remain noted for sheep—and fishing. Parliament sometimes met in the cathedral. It is not clear in the play whether the Earl of Gloucester is meant to be living in Gloucester. See W. W. Greg, "Time, Place, and Politics in *King Lear*."

Earl of Gloucester's Castle

Scene 1.2: Edmund, alone, schemes to have his older and legitimate brother, Edgar, disinherited. When Gloucester appears, Edmund shows him a forged letter indicating Edgar wants to kill his father. After Gloucester leaves, Edgar arrives. Pretending to befriend his brother, Edmund warns Edgar his father is angry with him. Gloucester refers to "These late eclipses in the sun and moon" (ll. 106–7). There was a solar eclipse on September 27, 1605, followed by a lunar eclipse on October 2, 1605, so this allusion may help date the play's composition.

Scene 2.1: Edmund continues his plotting against his brother. The Duke of Cornwall and Regan arrive.

Scene 2.2: Oswald and Kent confront each other, and Kent beats Oswald. Cornwall orders Kent put in the stocks, even though doing so shows disrespect for Lear, whom Kent represents.

Scene 2.3: Edgar, proclaimed an outlaw, disguises himself as Tom O'Bedlam.

Scene 2.4: When Lear arrives and finds Kent in the stocks, he refuses to believe Cornwall and Regan are responsible. He complains to Regan of Goneril's behavior, but she sides with her sister. Goneril joins the group. The sisters tell Lear he can have none of the hundred knights he had reserved for himself when he surrendered the throne. Lear, Kent, and the fool exit into a storm; Cornwall orders Gloucester to lock his doors.

Scene 3.3: Gloucester tells Edmund of his concern for the king's treatment. He repeats the news Kent reports in scene 3.1 (later) that the Dukes of Cornwall and Albany are at odds with each other and the French are planning to invade to help Lear. Gloucester says he and his son must support the king. After Gloucester exits to search for Lear, Edmund declares he will inform the Duke of Cornwall of Gloucester's views.

Scene 3.5: Edmund pretends to regret informing the Duke of Cornwall about Gloucester's siding with Lear. The duke promises Edmund his father's earldom and sends him to seek Gloucester.

Scene 3.6: Gloucester has brought Kent, Lear, Edgar, and the fool to a farmhouse adjoining the castle. After he leaves, Lear imagines he is arraigning his daughters. Gloucester returns to send Lear, Kent, and the fool to the safety of Dover because Cornwall wants to kill the king. All leave. This is the last scene in which the fool appears. He may have doubled as Cordelia, not only so the play will require one less actor but also to link the two truth-telling characters devoted to Lear.

Scene 3.7: Cornwall sends Goneril back to her husband to prepare to confront the French invasion led by Cordelia, and he sends Edmund with her. Oswald reports Lear's flight. When Gloucester is brought in, Cornwall has him tied to a chair, and Regan plucks hairs from his beard. Ignoring Gloucester's reminding them he is their host, Cornwall and Regan interrogate him about his support for Lear. Initially he equivocates but then declares his loyalty to the king. Cornwall cuts out one of Gloucester's eyes and is about to cut out the other when a servant intervenes. The servant wounds Cornwall; Regan then kills the servant. Though wounded, Cornwall cuts out Gloucester's other eye. Gloucester calls on Edmund to avenge him, but Regan informs him it was Edmund who betrayed him. She and Cornwall order Gloucester thrown out into the storm. After Goneril and Regan exit, two servants pursue Gloucester to help him.

Scene 4.5: Regan tries to learn from Oswald about the relationship between Goneril and Edmund, declaring she, being widowed, is a better match for him than her married sister. She promises to reward Oswald for killing Gloucester.

The Heath

Although this location is now as famous and traditional as Juliet's balcony, it was not noted in a stage direction until Nicholas Rowe added it to his 1709 edition of the play. No seventeenth-century edition of *King Lear* as Shakespeare wrote it included a mention of a heath. Rowe probably took this location from Nahum Tate's version of the play or from *Macbeth*, which has a heath. See Henry S. Turner, "*King Lear* Without: The Heath." At the beginning of 3.1, Tate has the stage direction, "*A desert heath. Enter Lear and Kent in the storm.*"

Scene 3.1: Kent tells a gentleman of a rift between the Dukes of Cornwall and Albany and of an impending invasion by the French. Kent sends the gentleman to Dover to report Lear's mistreatment by his daughters. Kent and the gentleman go off in different directions in search of the king.

Scene 3.2: Lear rages against the storm. Kent finds him and leads him toward a hovel for shelter.

Scene 3.4: Lear at first refuses shelter. The fool enters the hovel, then rushes out because Edgar as Poor Tom is within. Edgar, seemingly mad, emerges wearing only a blanket. Lear begins to tear off his clothes in imitation of Edgar. Gloucester finds them. He fails to penetrate his son's disguise and leads them to shelter.

Scene 4.1: Edgar comes upon his blinded father being led by an old man. Gloucester calls upon Edgar, unaware of his presence, then dismisses the old man and asks Poor Tom to lead him to Dover, where he plans to kill himself by jumping off a cliff.

Leicester, Leicestershire

Leicester sits on the bank of the River Soar. The city was the Roman Ratae Corieltauvorum or Ratiscorion and the Anglo-Saxon Ligora-caestra (*Ligora* being the name of the river and *caestra* from the Latin *castrum*, "fortified military camp"). The 1086 Domesday Book calls it Ledecestre. Romans found an Iron-Age settlement here. In the Middle Ages, the city was part of the kingdom of Mercia and then part of the Danelaw, ruled by Vikings. The castle, originally built by Hugh de Grandmesnil (1032–1098), served as a royal residence under the Lancastrians, and three parliaments met here. Part of the hall and two of the gateways remain. Thomas Cook in 1841 arranged his first railway excursion from Leicester to Loughborough and back. In 2012 Richard III's remains were discovered under the ruins of Greyfriars Abbey (under what is now a parking lot) near Leicester, and in 2015 these remains were buried in Leicester Cathedral. Cardinal Thomas Wolsey died in Leicester in 1530 and is buried in the Abbey

Park. Leicester is also the traditional home of King Lear and his daughters, though Shakespeare's play about them does not mention the city. Geoffrey of Monmouth's twelfth-century *Historia Regum Britanniae* (*History of the Kings of Britain*; c. 1135) called Leicester by its old Welsh name Kaerleir, Lear's city. Leir derives from the Brittonic name for the River Soar: Leir, Liger, or Ligora.

As noted there, the Welsh name for the city was Kaerleir, prompting Geoffrey of Monmouth in his *Historia Regum Britanniae* to propose King Lear as its founder. According to Raphael Holinshed's *Chronicles*, Lear was the son of Bladud and came to the throne in the eighth century BCE. Holinshed says Lear reigned at the same time as King Joash of Judah, who came to the throne circa 836 BCE. Holinshed records Lear's death occurred fifty-four years before the founding of Rome, traditionally dated 753 BCE, so Lear died in 801 BCE.

Although Lear is now viewed as a mythical ruler, Shakespeare took many details of his play from Holinshed, and the first printed edition calls the play not a tragedy but *The True Chronicle Histories of the Life and Death of King Lear and His Three Daughters* (1608). Another source of this work is the play *The True Chronicle History of King Leir*, written perhaps by Robert Greene, Thomas Kyd, and Thomas Lodge and performed by actors from Queen Elizabeth's Men and Sussex's Men at the Rose Theatre in April 1594; it was entered in the Stationers' Register on May 14, 1594, to be printed. This play was published in 1605. Although Shakespeare felt free to change the ending he found in his sources, indicating he may have had reservations about the historical accuracy of the accounts he used, *King Lear* and *Macbeth* should be viewed as part of his exploration of British history. Prior to the accession of King James I, Shakespeare focused on English history. James sought to unite England and Scotland politically, and in support of that agenda, Shakespeare's historical plays after 1603 (except for *Henry VIII*) deal with Britain rather than England.

King Lear's Palace

Scene 1.1: The Earl of Gloucester introduces his illegitimate son Edmund to the Earl of Kent. King Lear enters and announces his plan to divide his kingdom among his three daughters and retire as ruler. As noted earlier, James I wanted to unite his two kingdoms of Scotland and England, and the play supports James's political agenda by showing the disastrous results of dividing a kingdom. Lear stages a love contest among his three daughters to determine who will get the best portion of his kingdom, though he has already drawn up the boundaries of each new realm. His two older daughters, Goneril and Regan, effusively protest their great love for their father, but Cordelia, his favorite and youngest, refuses to flatter. Enraged, Lear disinherits her. When Kent speaks for her, the king banishes him. The Duke of Burgundy and the king of France, suitors of Cordelia enter. Burgundy refuses to marry Cordelia without a dowry, but

France regards her as dowry enough and accepts her. After Cordelia leaves, Goneril and Regan plot against their father.

SCOTLAND

In Shakespeare's source play *King Leir* (published 1605), Goneril is married to the Duke of Cambria (Wales). However, according to Geoffrey of Monmouth and Holinshed's *Chronicles*, she married the Duke of Albania (i.e., Albany/Scotland). Because Elizabeth ruled Wales but not Scotland, perhaps the authors of *King Leir* changed Albania to Cambria, whereas Shakespeare chose Albany rather than Cambria to flatter the Scottish King James (Albany is presented favorably in the play) and to stress the danger of dividing England and Scotland, as discussed under "Leicester, Leicestershire" earlier this chapter. W. W. Greg's article, cited earlier, notes that none of the locations in this play, except for Dover, are precisely identifiable. In *Shakespearean Tragedy* (1904) A. C. Bradley notes the "vagueness of the scene where the action takes place" (lecture 7).

Duke of Albany's Castle

Scene 1.3: Goneril complains to her steward Oswald about the behavior of Lear and his knights; Lear has retained a hundred knights for his attendants. She instructs Oswald to be less accommodating to them than he has been heretofore.

Scene 1.4: Kent, disguised, returns to serve Lear even though Lear has banished him. Oswald, following Goneril's admonition, shows no respect for the old king. Lear's fool speaks bitter truths. Goneril appears and tells her father she wants to reduce his knightly retinue from the previously agreed one hundred. As he prepares to go to Regan, whom he expects to find kinder, Lear curses Goneril. He discovers she has already dismissed fifty of his knights. Goneril sends Oswald to her sister to acquaint her with her concerns.

Scene 1.5: Lear sends Kent with letters to Gloucester's castle, where Regan and her husband are staying.

Scene 4.2: In front of the Duke of Albany's palace, Goneril dispatches Edmund back to Regan to hasten the mustering of troops while she gathers an army as well. She gives him a love token and a kiss before he departs. When her husband arrives, the duke denounces her, and she, him. A messenger reports the death of the Duke of Cornwall and the blinding of Gloucester. Goneril worries Regan may now take Edmund as her lover or husband; Albany vows to avenge Gloucester.

Macbeth

ENGLAND

London

According to Geoffrey of Monmouth's *Historia Regum Britanniae* (c. 1136), London was founded by Brutus, great-grandson of Aeneas, about 1100 BCE. His settlement was called Caer Troia ("fortress or citadel of Troy") or Troia Nova. One of London's early legendary kings was Lud, who allegedly renamed the town Caer Ludein, the supposed origin of the city's name. Cymbeline refers to London as "Lud's Town" (*Cymbeline*, 5.5.181). When Julius Caesar's army arrived at what is now Southwark, they found no settlement here (55–54 BCE), but by the time of the second Roman invasion in 43 CE, a small port and commercial center had risen on the site. The Romans built a bridge across the Thames and established an administrative center on the north bank, calling it Londinium (50 CE). Boudica destroyed the Roman city in about 60 CE, but it was quickly rebuilt. In the second century CE, Londinium replaced Colchester as the administrative center of Roman Britain. Between 180 and 225 CE, the Romans built a wall around London; remains of this wall can still be seen. It encircled what is now essentially the City, London's financial district.

The Romans abandoned England in 410 CE and were replaced by the Middle Saxons, hence the county name of Middlesex. They named the settlement Lundenwic, the *wic* denoting a trading center. Vikings sacked the city in 842 and 851, and the Danes held the city from 871 to 886 and again early in the eleventh century until 1042. Under the Normans London replaced Winchester as England's capital, and it has grown and prospered over the centuries. In Shakespeare's time it held about 200,000 people (c. 1600) and was, as it still is, the cultural as well as the political and commercial center of the country.

Palace of Westminster

North bank of the Thames [Underground stop: Westminster]

Originally built for Edward the Confessor, the Palace of Westminster served as a royal residence until Henry VIII made Whitehall Palace his chief residence in 1512 after the Palace of Westminster was damaged by fire. It has also been the meeting place of Parliament since the thirteenth century. In 1834 a fire destroyed most of the building. Only St. Mary Undercroft (the crypt under St. Stephen's Chapel), Westminster Hall (dating from 1097), the Cloisters, and the Jewel Tower (1365) survived. The current Gothic building was designed by Sir Charles Barry and Augustus Pugin. Construction began in 1837. Most of the restoration was completed by 1860, though work continued until 1870. The House of Commons was destroyed in the Blitz of 1940–1941; it was restored by Sir Giles Gilbert Scott after World War II during the period 1945–1950.

Scene 4.3: In front of King Edward the Confessor's palace, Macduff tries to persuade Malcolm to lead an army against Macbeth. Distrustful of Macduff, Malcolm tests him before telling him Old Siward (Earl of Northumberland, historically the uncle of Malcolm, though the play does not mention this detail) is about to invade Scotland with ten thousand men. A doctor enters, and the three men discuss Edward the Confessor's touching people to cure them of the King's Evil (scrofula). The Stuarts in England continued this practice. Ross enters to report the slaughter of Macduff's family. Malcolm, Ross, and Macduff set off to join Old Siward's forces. Historically, in 1046 Siward launched an unsuccessful attempt to unseat Macbeth. In 1054 he forced Macbeth to yield territory in southern Scotland. In a battle fought at Dunsinane, Siward's oldest son, Osbjorn, was killed (as Young Siward is killed in 5.7). Siward died in 1055, two years before Macbeth. Shakespeare conflates this 1054 invasion with the August 15, 1057, Battle of Lumphanan in Aberdeenshire, in which Macbeth was killed by forces loyal to the future Malcolm III.

SCOTLAND

Birnam Wood, Perthshire

Located on the south bank of the River Tay. All that remains of Birnam Wood are two trees: the Birnam Oak and the Birnam Sycamore. The Birnam Oak is believed to be at least six hundred years old; the Birnam Sycamore is about three hundred years old. In 1599 English actors came to Scotland at the request of James VI (future James I of England) and visited Birnam.

Scene 5.4: Malcolm orders his soldiers to cut branches from the trees in Birnam Wood to disguise their numbers.

According to Holinshed's *Chronicles*,

Malcolme following hastilie after Makbeth, came the night before the battell vnto Birnane wood, and when his armie had rested a while there to refresh them, he commanded euerie man to get a bough of some tree or other of that wood in his hand, as big as he might beare, and to march foorth therewith in such wise, that on the next morrow they might come closelie and without sight in this manner within view of his enimies. On the morow when Makbeth beheld them comming in this sort, he first maruelled what the matter ment, but in the end remembred himselfe that the prophesie which he had heard long before that time, of the comming of Birnane wood to Dunsinane castell, was likelie to be now fulfilled.

Dunsinane Hill, Perthshire

The name means "an anthill." Located near the village of Collace, Perthshire, in eastern Scotland, it is the site of two early forts. Ramparts are still visible. Birnam Wood is twelve miles away. It is more than one thousand feet high. As noted previously, Siward defeated Macbeth here on July 27, 1054, but Macbeth survived. Holinshed reports that Macbeth built a castle here, ten miles from Perth.

Scene 5.2: Near Dunsinane, Menteith, Caithness, Angus, Lennox, and soldiers prepare to join with the English forces under Siward.

Scene 5.6: The English throw down their boughs.

Scene 5.7: Macbeth fights and kills Young Siward. Macduff seeks Macbeth. Malcolm tells Old Siward that Dunsinane has surrendered and Macbeth's soldiers have switched sides.

Scene 5.8: Macbeth and Macduff meet. Macbeth refuses to fight with Macduff, having killed his family. Macbeth declares his invincibility: No one born of woman can kill him. Macduff replies he was born by cesarean section. Again, Macbeth refuses to fight, now because he knows he will be defeated. Macduff then orders him to surrender, which Macbeth will not do. They exit fighting. According to Holinshed, Macduff pursued Macbeth to Lunfannaine, where Macbeth was killed.

Scene 5.9: Malcolm notes Macduff and Young Siward are missing. Ross reports the death of the latter. Macduff enters with Macbeth's head and hails Malcolm as king of Scotland. Malcolm announces he will create Scotland's first earls and will recall those exiled. The play ends with his inviting everyone to attend his coronation at Scone.

Macbeth's Castle

Scene 5.1: A gentleman tells a doctor about Lady Macbeth's sleepwalking. She enters with a candle and washes her hands, which she seems unable to get clean. In her sleep she urges Macbeth to put on his nightgown and go to bed, and she says someone is knocking at the gate, thus reliving the end of scene 2.2.

Scene 5.3: Macbeth declares he wants to hear no more accounts of the English invaders, but a servant reports ten thousand English soldiers are marching toward Dunsinane. Macbeth, preparing for battle, says he will not fear until Birnam Wood comes to Dunsinane.

Scene 5.5: As Macbeth prepares to withstand a siege by the English, he hears a cry. Seyton goes to learn its cause; he returns to report the death of Lady Macbeth. Historically, Queen Gruoch, wife of Macbeth, was the granddaughter of King Kenneth III. By a previous marriage, she had a son, Lulach mac Gille Coemgáin (i.e., son of Gille Coemgáin); Lulach reigned as king of Scotland following Macbeth from 1057 to 1058. Malcolm III killed him and assumed the crown. Although Lady Macbeth says, "I have given suck" (1.7.54), indicating she had at least one child, Macduff states Macbeth "has no children" (4.3.216). Macbeth and Queen Gruoch had no children of their own.

Macbeth delivers his "Tomorrow, and tomorrow, and tomorrow" speech (ll. 19–28). A messenger declares a grove is coming to Dunsinane. Macbeth understands the witches have equivocated with him, but he resolves to confront the English in open battle.

Fife

A peninsula between the Firth of Tay on the north and the Firth of Forth on the south, Fife was the seat of the Macduff clan.

Macduff's Castle

Located near East Wemyss, Fife. The Earls of Macduff built a castle here during the reign of Macbeth (1040–1057), but nothing of that structure survives. In the fourteenth century, their descendants, the Wemyss family, began a castle; Edward I of England visited here in 1304. The property still belongs to the Wemyss family. Only ruins remain.

Scene 4.2: As Macbeth resolved in scene 4.1, he sends murderers to kill Macduff's family. A messenger, as mysterious as the third murderer in scene 3.3, warns Lady Macduff to flee with her children, but as soon as the messenger departs, the murderers arrive and kill her and everyone else in the castle. According to Holinshed's *Chronicles*, Shakespeare's chief source for this play, Macbeth himself led the attack on Macduff's castle.

Forres

Mentioned in Claudius Ptolemy's second-century-CE *Geography*, it was the site of a royal castle since the ninth century CE. Forres became a royal borough in 1140. It is situated on the Moray coast between Inverness (the location of Macbeth's castle in acts 1–2) and Elgin. Sueno's Stone is located here. It was probably carved by Picts to celebrate a victory against Norse invaders. Sueno is mentioned in scene 1.2 of *Macbeth*. A hill here is named Macbeth's Hillock for Shakespeare's character.

A Cave

Scene 4.1: Hecate joins the three witches who met Macbeth in scene 1.3. After Macbeth arrives he encounters three apparitions. The first, an armed head, warns him to beware of Macduff. The second, a bloody child, assures him that no man born of woman can harm him, and the third, a crowned child holding a tree, declares Macbeth's throne is secure until Birnam Wood comes to Dunsinane Hill. In response to Macbeth's asking whether Banquo's children will rule in Scotland, the witches show him a line of eight kings, the eighth holding a mirror showing an endless procession of more rulers, and Banquo appears, pointing at them to show that they are his descendants. The eight kings are Robert II, Robert III, and James I–VI of Scotland, thus culminating in England's current monarch, James VI of Scotland and James I of England. Shakespeare omitted Mary, Queen of Scots.

Seeing Macbeth's discontent caused by this vision, the witches dance for him and then vanish. Lennox arrives to inform Macbeth of Macduff's flight to England. Macbeth resolves to attack Macduff's castle and kill his wife, children, and everyone else related to him.

A Heath

In scene 1.3 Banquo asks, "How far is't called to Forres" (l. 39), indicating the heath is near this town.

Scene 1.1: Three witches gather and plan to meet Macbeth after the battle that is now raging. A heath still exists near Forres.

Scene 1.3: The three witches converse before Macbeth and Banquo arrive. They greet the two men, hailing Macbeth as Thane of Glamis, his current title, but also Thane of Cawdor and future king. They promise Banquo his children will be kings. After the witches vanish, Ross and Angus arrive to greet Macbeth as Thane of Cawdor: Duncan has conferred this title on Macbeth after the execution of the rebel thane. The new Thane of Cawdor will also prove to be a rebel. Banquo warns Macbeth against trusting in the witches' prophecies, but Macbeth is rapt with contemplation of their words. Recovering, he goes with Banquo, Ross, and Angus to Duncan's camp.

Scene 3.5: Hecate chides the witches for consorting with Macbeth. She instructs them to meet her the next morning at the pit of Acheron, where Macbeth will come to learn his fate. Hecate will go to the moon to get a "vap'rous drop profound" (l. 24) that she will use to raise visions that will lead to Macbeth's destruction.

This scene was probably written by Thomas Middleton.

King Duncan's Camp

Located near the royal castle at Forres. Duncan reigned from 1034 to 1040 CE. Shakespeare conflates Macdonwald's rebellion and the Norwegian invasion under Sueno. Shakespeare used (and altered) Raphael Holinshed's *Chronicles of England, Scotland and Ireland* (1577; second edition, 1587) as his source. Shakespeare also conflates the murder of Duncan and that of one of his predecessors, Duff, by Donwald in 968 CE; Donwald was encouraged by his wife to commit regicide. He arranged for the murder of Duff at Forres and made the chamberlains drunk. When the king's body was discovered, Donwald rushed in and killed the chamberlains. The voices Macbeth hears after killing Duncan come from yet another incident: After King Kenneth kills his nephew, he hears a voice threatening him, and he cannot sleep. Holinshed links Banquo and Macbeth in the killing of Duncan, but King James I, reigning when Shakespeare wrote this play, descended from Banquo, so Shakespeare exonerates him. Shakespeare also condenses Macbeth's seventeen-year reign into what seems like months, a technique he employed in his English history plays, as well.

Scene 1.2: A bleeding sergeant who saved the life of Malcolm, King Duncan's older son, reports about the bravery of Macbeth and Banquo in fighting the rebel Macdonwald and the invading Norwegians. Too weak from loss of blood to continue his tale, he is taken away. Ross and Angus, Scottish noblemen, report the defeat of the Norwegians and their ally, the Thane of Cawdor, at Fife.

King Duncan's (Later Macbeth's) Palace

A motte-and-bailey castle, it was demolished in 1297. Later rebuilt, it was burned by Alexander Stewart, Earl of Buchan, in 1390. Again rebuilt, it belonged to the Dunbars of Westfield until the seventeenth century. Nothing of the castle remains aboveground.

Scene 1.4: Duncan warmly greets Macbeth when the thane arrives with Banquo, Ross, and Angus. The king names Malcolm his heir. Scotland was not a strictly hereditary monarchy at this time; as Duncan's cousin, Macbeth should have inherited the throne after Duncan's death if Malcolm was not yet of age. Duncan says he plans to spend the night at Macbeth's castle at Inverness, twenty-five miles west of Forres.

Scene 3.1: Banquo in a soliloquy expresses his suspicion that Macbeth killed Duncan, but the fulfillment of the witches' prophecies for Macbeth gives him hope his children will be kings. Macbeth, Lady Macbeth, Lennox, Ross, and attendants enter. Macbeth announces a feast that night and invites Banquo, whom he questions about his plans for the afternoon. All depart except for Macbeth and a servant, whom Macbeth dispatches to bring to him two murderers he has engaged to kill Banquo and Fleance. Macbeth promises to inform them where to conduct their ambush.

Scene 3.2: Macbeth tells his wife his mind is unquiet. He hints at a bloody deed to come but does not tell Lady Macbeth about his plan to kill Banquo and Fleance.

Scene 3.3: In a park near the palace, a mysterious third murderer joins the other two. The murderers kill Banquo, but Fleance escapes.

The identity of the third murderer has provoked much debate, and directors have responded in a variety of ways. See John Addis, "Was Macbeth the Third Murderer of Banquo?"; Gilbert Bennett, "The Third Murderer"; George Walton Williams, "The Third Murderer in *Macbeth*"; and Theodore Halbert Wilson, "The Third Murderer." Roman Polanski in his 1971 film version has Ross as the third murderer. In the BBC's 1983 *Macbeth* directed by Jack Gold, Macbeth's servant Seyton is the third killer. In this production, after Banquo is slain, Seyton kills the other two murderers, though in the text the first murderer appears in the next scene.

Scene 3.4: In the Banqueting Hall, Macbeth, Lady Macbeth, Ross, Lennox, lords, and attendants gather for the feast. The first murderer comes to the door to tell Macbeth that Banquo is dead but Fleance has escaped. Macbeth dismisses the murderer, then publicly laments Banquo's absence. When Macbeth tries to sit, he finds Banquo's bloody ghost in his chair. As Macbeth points to the ghost that only he can see and he yells at it, Lady Macbeth initially attempts to gloss over this odd behavior but at length dismisses everyone. Macbeth declares he will visit the witches the next day to learn what the future holds.

Scene 3.6: Lennox and a lord discuss Macbeth's tyrannous reign. The lord informs Ross that Malcolm is living in England at the court of Edward the Confessor (reigned 1043–1066), and Macduff has gone there to raise an army to liberate Scotland from Macbeth's rule.

Inverness

Scottish Gaelic Inbhir Nis ("mouth of the River Ness"), Inverness is the northernmost city in the United Kingdom and is situated where the River Ness empties in the Moray Firth. The eleventh-century battle of Blàr nam Fèinne against the Norwegians occurred near here. The Battle of Culloden (1746), marking the last attempt of the Stuarts to regain the British throne, was fought nearby. The present castle was built in 1835 on the site of the one erected by Malcolm III (reigned 1058–1093), son of Duncan, after he destroyed Macbeth's castle about a half-mile away.

Glamis Castle, some five miles from Forfar, is the ancestral seat of the Earls of Strathmore and Kinghorne since 1372 and was the childhood home of Queen Elizabeth the Queen Mother (Lady Elizabeth Bowes-Lyon) and the birthplace of Princess Margaret. The current castle dates from about 1400, with major seventeenth-century renovations. Many interiors date from the eighteenth and nineteenth centuries. It claims to be the site of King Duncan's murder and the most haunted castle in Britain.

The poet Thomas Gray visited here in 1765 and wrote to Dr. Thomas Wharton, "The house from the height of it, the greatness of its mass, the many towers atop, the spread of its wings, has really a very singular and striking appearance, like nothing I ever saw."

Macbeth's Castle

Scene 1.5: Lady Macbeth reads a letter from her husband relating his encounter with the witches. She fears he will be reluctant to kill Duncan even though he wants to be king. A messenger announces Duncan's imminent visit. When Macbeth arrives, she tells him of her plan to kill Duncan.

Scene 1.6: Duncan prepares to enter Macbeth's castle.

Scene 1.7: Macbeth ponders regicide. He tells his wife they will not proceed with their plot, but Lady Macbeth convinces him to kill Duncan.

Scene 2.1: Banquo gives Macbeth a diamond from Duncan for Lady Macbeth. They discuss the witches' prophecies. Alone, Macbeth sees a bloody dagger that leads him to Duncan's bedroom. A bell rings, summoning Macbeth to kill the king. Holinshed places the killing of Duncan at Inverness, though he notes "some say" the regicide occurred at Botgosuane.

Scene 2.2: Macbeth returns from killing Duncan and describes the scene to his wife. He claims he heard a voice saying he would not sleep again. Lady Macbeth dismisses his fears. Then, noticing the bloody daggers in his hand, she tells him he must return them to the scene of the crime. When he refuses, she takes them. She says she will smear blood on the drunken sleeping grooms to make them appear guilty of the murder. Upon her return, there is a knocking at the gate. They retire as the knocking continues. Thomas De Quincey wrote a seminal essay "On the Knocking at the Gate in *Macbeth*," which first appeared in the *London Magazine* of October 1823.

Scene 2.3: In the only humorous scene in the play, a drunken porter inside the gate hears the knocking and imagines he is the gatekeeper of hell. His lines "Knock, knock, knock! Who's there, i' th' name of Beelzebub?" (ll. 3–4) suggest that the knock-knock joke was extant by 1606, or perhaps Shakespeare created it. (*Hamlet* begins with a truncated version of this opening: "Who's there?") At length he admits Macduff and Lennox. When Macbeth appears, Macduff goes to wake Duncan; he returns, horrified to announce the king's murder. As Macduff calls for the ringing of the alarm bell, Macbeth and Lennox go to Duncan's chamber. Lady Macbeth and Banquo enter. Macbeth and Lennox return with Ross; they are joined by Duncan's sons, Malcolm and Donalbain. Macbeth's claim that he regrets killing the grooms, the apparent murderers, rouses Macduff's suspicion. As Macbeth tries to explain his action, Lady Macbeth faints or seems to, distracting attention from her husband. She is carried out, and Macbeth summons everyone to gather in the hall. Fearing for their lives, Malcolm and Donalbain flee, the former for England, the latter for Ireland. Both men probably sought refuge with their uncle Siward, Earl of Northumberland.

Scene 2.4: Outside Macbeth's castle, Ross and an old man discuss recent disturbances in nature, always a harbinger of political disruption. Macduff arrives to report the rumor that Malcolm and Donalbain suborned the grooms to kill their father. He says Macbeth has been declared king and has gone to Scone (in Perth and Kinross), the traditional site for the crowning of Scottish kings from at least the ninth century CE, while Duncan's body has been sent to the island of Iona, where Scottish kings were buried. Ross plans to attend Macbeth's coronation, but Macduff is returning to his castle in Fife. Macduff's failure to attend Macbeth's coronation is a slight to the new king.

Antony and Cleopatra

EGYPT

Alexandria

Founded by Alexander the Great at the mouth of the Nile River in 332 BCE after he took Egypt from the Persians. His successors, the Ptolemies, made this city their capital. It had the largest library in antiquity, and its lighthouse was one of the seven wonders of the ancient world. The lighthouse stood on the island of Pharos, opposite Alexandria, and rose to a height of 400 feet (the Great Pyramid at Giza stands at 455 feet, though it was probably about 480 feet tall when it was built). Julius Caesar captured Alexandria in 47 BCE. Egypt became a Roman province in 30 BCE after the death of Antony and Cleopatra VII. Alexandria grew to become the second-largest city in the Roman Empire, with a population of 500,000. In Shakespeare's time it was an important port. In Christopher Marlowe's *The Jew of Malta*, Barabas has an "argosy from Alexandria / . . . / Laden with riches and exceeding store / Of Persian silks, of gold, and orient pearl" (1.1.85–88).

Antony's Camp

Scene 4.5: When a soldier informs Antony that Enobarbus has defected to Octavius, Antony orders Enobarbus's treasure sent after him to the enemy camp. According to Plutarch, Enobarbus defected before the Battle of Actium.

Scene 4.8: Cleopatra joins Antony to celebrate his victory.

The Battlefield

Scene 4.7: Antony's forces defeat Octavius.

Scene 4.10: Following Octavius's naval victory over Antony at Actium in 31 BCE, in August of 30 BCE, Antony prepares to fight Octavius by sea again.

Scene 4.11: Octavius prepares for battle.

Scene 4.12: Antony announces his fleet has surrendered to Octavius. He blames Cleopatra for betraying him; when she arrives he denounces her, and she leaves.

Cleopatra's Palace

Located on the island of Antirhodos, the palace, dating from the third century BCE, was destroyed by an earthquake and tsunami in 365 CE and now lies under about sixteen feet of water.

Scene 1.1: Philo complains to Demetrius about Antony's infatuation with Cleopatra. Antony and Cleopatra enter with their attendants, followed by a messenger from Rome. Because Cleopatra mocks Antony for being at the beck and call of his wife, Fulvia, or Octavius Caesar, he refuses to listen to the messenger.

Scene 1.2: Charmian, Iras, and Alexas seek to learn their futures from a soothsayer. Cleopatra enters, looking for Antony. She is about to send Enobarbus to seek him when he enters; she leaves with Enobarbus and the others. Antony finally learns from the messenger that Fulvia and Antony's younger brother, Lucius, who had been enemies, joined forces against Octavius and were defeated. This was the Perusine War of 41–40 BCE. Also, Quintus Labienus with an army from Parthia is capturing Roman territory in Asia that Antony should be guarding. Another messenger announces the death of Fulvia (40 BCE). Antony resolves to leave Egypt. He has heard that Sextus Pompeius, son of Pompey the Great, controls the seas around Italy and has defied Octavius. In 40 BCE Sextus Pompeius's admiral Menas seized Sardinia from Octavius's governor Marcus Lurius.

Scene 1.3: When Antony tries to take his leave of Cleopatra, she feigns illness. Reluctant for him to depart, she at length accepts his decision and wishes him success.

Scene 1.5: Cleopatra speaks of Antony to Charmian and the eunuch Mardian. Alexas brings greetings and a pearl from Antony to Cleopatra, who goes off to write to Antony.

Scene 2.5: When a messenger informs Cleopatra of Antony's marriage to Octavia, she slaps him, drags him up and down the room, and orders him whipped. He begs for mercy, but when he repeats his news, she draws a knife to kill him, and he flees. Calmer, she summons him back. Yet again he says that Antony has married Octavius's sister. Cleopatra dismisses him and asks her attendants to take her to her bedroom.

Scene 3.3: Cleopatra asks the messenger to describe Octavia, and he is clever enough to disparage her. Cleopatra rewards him with gold and prepares to send him to Antony with letters.

Scene 3.11: Having been defeated at Actium, Antony offers his wealth to his attendants and dismisses them. Cleopatra arrives with Charmian, Eros, and Iras. She and Antony reconcile.

Scene 3.13: Antony's ambassador reports Octavius's rejection of Antony's request to live in peace. Antony leaves with the ambassador to challenge Octavius to single combat. Enobarbus resolves to defect to Octavius. When Thidias arrives from Octavius, Cleopatra says she will yield her crown to him, but Antony, returning, orders Thidias whipped, and Antony berates Cleopatra. Antony sends Thidias back to Caesar. He and Cleopatra again reconcile, and Antony resolves to fight Caesar.

Scene 4.2: Antony and Cleopatra plan to feast before the battle with Octavius.

Scene 4.3: As Antony's soldiers gather before Cleopatra's palace, they hear music in the air and belowground, which one of the soldiers interprets as the god Hercules abandoning Antony. Plutarch records in his "Life of Antony,"

> During this night, it is said, about the middle of it, while the city was quiet and depressed through fear and expectation of what was coming, suddenly certain harmonious sounds from all sorts of instruments were heard, and the shouting of a throng, accompanied by cries of Bacchic revelry and satyric leapings, as if a troop of revelers, making a great tumult, were going forth from the city; and their course seemed to lie about through the middle of the city toward the outer gate which faced the enemy, at which point the tumult became loudest and then dashed out. Those who sought the meaning of the sign were of the opinion that the god to whom Antony always most likened and attached himself was now deserting him.

Constantine P. Cavafy in 1911 wrote a poem inspired by this incident, "The God Abandons Antony":

> When suddenly, at midnight, you hear
> an invisible procession going by
> with exquisite music, voices,
> don't mourn your luck that's failing now,
> work gone wrong, your plans
> all proving deceptive—don't mourn them uselessly.
> As one long prepared, and graced with courage,
> say goodbye to her, to Alexandria who is leaving.
> Above all, don't fool yourself, don't say
> it was a dream, your ears deceived you:
> don't degrade yourself with empty hopes like these.
> As one long prepared, and graced with courage,
> as is right for you who proved worthy of this kind of city,
> go firmly to the window
> and listen with deep emotion, but not
> with the whining, the pleas of a coward;
> listen—your final pleasure—to the voices,

to the exquisite music of that strange procession,
and say goodbye to her, to the Alexandria you are losing.

Scene 4.4: Antony summons Eros to arm him. Cleopatra helps. Antony goes off to battle.

Scene 4.13: Fearing Antony's anger, Cleopatra prepares to flee to the tomb she has prepared for herself and sends Mardian to inform Antony she has killed herself, dying with Antony's name on her lips.

Scene 4.14: When Antony arrives at Cleopatra's palace, Mardian tells him Cleopatra has killed herself, her last words being "Antony, most noble Antony" (l. 30). Antony asks Eros to kill him; instead, Eros kills himself. Antony now falls on his sword, mortally wounding himself, but he does not die at once. He asks guards and then the just-arrived Diomedes to kill him. Diomedes replies he was sent by Cleopatra from her tomb, where she has hidden from Antony. She sent Diomedes to contradict the report of her death, fearing Antony would commit suicide. Antony asks the guards to take him to Cleopatra's tomb.

Cleopatra's Tomb

The location of Cleopatra's tomb is uncertain. Zahi Hawass and Kathleen Martinez think they have located it at Taposiris Magna in a western suburb of Alexandria. There was a temple to Osiris here, of which the outer wall and pylons remain.

Scene 4.15: Antony is lifted onto Cleopatra's tomb. He dies, and Cleopatra faints. Upon reviving, she resolves to kill herself. All depart bearing Antony's body, which Plutarch says was cremated.

Scene 5.2: When Proculeius arrives, Cleopatra asks that her son be allowed to govern Egypt. Proculeius assures her Caesar will be kind, but Roman soldiers enter with Gallus and capture her. Proculeius disarms her when she tries to stab herself. She declares she will never be part of Octavius's triumphal procession. Dolabella comes from Caesar, and Proculeius leaves with the soldiers. Cleopatra delivers a paean to Antony. Dolabella tells her Caesar will display her in his Roman triumph. Octavius, Proculeius, Gallus, Maecenas, and others visit Cleopatra. Octavius says, if Cleopatra kills herself, he will kill her children.

Octavius in fact killed her son by Julius Caesar, Caesarion (Ptolemy XV Philopator Philometor Caesar) because the boy would have been a rival, being more closely related to Julius Caesar than was Octavius. Cleopatra's children by Antony were taken to Rome and displayed in Octavius's triumph. Cassius Dio records only the twins reached Rome, so Ptolemy Philadelphus may have died en route. The twins were raised by Octavia, Antony's former wife. The daughter, Cleopatra Selene, was married to King Juba of Numidia; the couple were sent to govern Mauritania. The fate of her twin brother, Alexander Helios, is unknown after his arrival in Rome.

Dolabella tells Cleopatra that Octavius plans to leave Egypt in three days and intends to send Cleopatra and her children ahead of him. A rustic clown whom Cleopatra asked Charmian to summon enters with a basket containing asps. Cleopatra dresses as a queen. Iras dies. Cleopatra puts an asp to her breast, another on her arm, and she dies, followed by Charmian. When Octavius arrives, he finds them dead and orders Cleopatra and Antony be buried together, as in fact they were.

Octavius Caesar's Camp

Scene 3.12: Antony has sent his schoolmaster to Octavius to request permission to live peacefully in Egypt or Athens, and Cleopatra asks for her children to be her heirs. Caesar rejects Antony's request but promises to agree to Cleopatra's if she banishes or kills Antony. He sends Thidias to negotiate with Cleopatra.

Scene 4.1: Caesar, Agrippa, and Maecenas prepare to confront Antony's forces.

Scene 4.6: Octavius orders Agrippa to begin the battle against Antony (July 31, 30 BCE). All leave except Enobarbus, who notes Octavius does not trust Antony's former supporters, like him, who have deserted Antony. Antony's messenger delivers Enobarbus's treasure from Antony. Instead of fighting, Enobarbus, ashamed of his ingratitude, resolves to find a ditch in which to die.

Scene 4.9: Calling on Antony, Enobarbus dies. Two soldiers find his body and carry him off.

Scene 5.1: Decretas arrives with Antony's sword and reports Antony's suicide. Agrippa, Maecenas, and Octavius lament his death. An Egyptian messenger from Cleopatra asks for Octavius's instructions, which Octavius promises to provide. After the messenger leaves, Octavius sends Proculeius and Gallus to reassure her of his goodwill lest she kill herself and so deny him the opportunity to display her in his triumphal procession in Rome.

GREECE

Actium

Situated at the mouth of the Ambracian Gulf, western Greece. A few years after his victory here, Octavius enlarged Apollo's temple and dedicated ten ships to the god. He also revived the Actian games, held every five years.

Scene 3.7: Enobarbus urges Cleopatra to leave lest she distract Antony, who insists on fighting Octavius at sea despite protests from members of his army.

Scene 3.8: Octavius tells Titus Statilius Taurus not to attack Antony's army by land until the conclusion of their naval engagement.

Scene 3.9: Antony instructs Enobarbus on the disposition of troops.

Scene 3.10: Shakespeare could not show the naval battle of Actium (September 2, 31 BCE), so he has Enobarbus report the flight of the Egyptian fleet. Antony pursued Cleopatra, abandoning the battle, which Octavius's admiral Marcus Vipsanius Agrippa won. Publius Canidius Crassus, Antony's general, says he will surrender his legions to Octavius, just as six kings have done already. He actually returned to Egypt and joined Antony. Captured by Octavius, he either was killed or committed suicide.

Athens

An important Mycenean center, the city-state in the eighth century BCE was aristocratic. In 508 BCE Cleisthenes created a form of democracy in Athens, though broader democracy did not arrive until the 460s. Women and foreign residents still were not allowed to vote. Of a population of some 100,000, probably only about 10,000 could. Sacked by a Persian army in 480 BCE shortly before the Athenian navy defeated Persia at the Battle of Salamis (September 480 BCE), in 478 BCE Athens became an imperial city-state when it assumed leadership of the Delian League. Throughout the fifth century BCE, Athens and Sparta battled for hegemony in the First Peloponnesian War (461–446 BCE), followed by the Second Peloponnesian War (431–404 BCE), which ended in the defeat of Athens. The city quickly recovered, resumed its democracy in 403 BCE, and established a second Athenian Confederacy in 378 BCE. Following Philip of Macedon's victory at the Battle of Chaeronea (338 BCE), Greece came under Macedonian rule. In the Hellenistic period, Athens became a cultural center of the Mediterranean world under the rule of Alexander the Great's successors, the Antigonids, and remained so into the sixth century CE. After 146 BCE Greece was ruled by Rome. Later, Greece became part of the Ottoman Empire. When Greece gained independence in the nineteenth century, Athens became its capital.

Antony's House

Scene 3.4: Antony complains to Octavia about her half-brother, who has resumed his war against Sextus Pompeius and publicly spoken against Antony. Octavia will go to Rome to try to reconcile her brother and husband (37 BCE).

Scene 3.5: Eros reports Octavius has removed Lepidus from the triumvirate (September 26, 36 BCE).

ITALY

Messina, Sicily

Founded by Greek settlers in the eighth century BCE, Messina, located in northeast Sicily, was originally named Zancle, from the Greek word for *scythe*, the shape of its natural harbor. Anaxilas of Rhegium renamed it Messene in the early fifth century

BCE after a Greek mainland city. Before becoming part of Italy, it was ruled successively by Romans, Goths, the Byzantine Empire, Arabs, Normans, and the Spanish, under the last of which Messina prospered. Spain seized Sicily in 1282, after the islanders massacred their French rulers in the Sicilian Vespers. Don Pedro I of Aragon was offered the crown by the Sicilians. In 1571 Don John of Austria, illegitimate stepbrother of King Philip II of Spain, commanded the Christian fleet that defeated the Turks at the Battle of Lepanto. In Shakespeare's day Messina was one of the greatest cities in Europe. Prone to earthquakes, the city has been repeatedly destroyed. It is now the third-largest city on the island of Sicily.

Sextus Pompeius's House

Scene 2.1: Sextus Pompeius, Menecrates, and Menas meet. Menas reports Octavius and Lepidus have mustered forces against them. Sextus Pompeius does not believe him, and he hopes Antony will stay in Egypt. Varrius comes to announce that Antony is expected daily in Rome. Sextus Pompeius and his allies leave to prepare to confront the triumvirate.

Miseno

In classical times known as Misenum, the city is located on the Bay of Naples and was an important port in antiquity, serving as the largest base of the Roman navy. It was also a luxury resort for rich Romans. The city is named for the Trojan Misenus, trumpeter of Aeneas, who was drowned near here after challenging the sea god Triton to a trumpeting competition (*Aeneid*, book 6); Misenus was supposedly buried here. The emperor Tiberius died in Misenum.

Scene 2.6: Sextus Pompeius and Menas, Octavius, Antony, Lepidus, Enobarbus, Maecenas, and Agrippa meet. The triumvirs offer Sextus Pompeius Sicily and Sardinia, in exchange for which he will, like his father, Pompey the Great, before him, rid the Mediterranean of pirates and will send wheat to Rome, Sicily being a source of grain. Sextus Pompeius accepts these terms, and all set off to feast on Sextus Pompeius's galley, except for Menas and Enobarbus. In their conversation Enobarbus declares Antony will return to Cleopatra and thus provide Octavius an excuse to make war against him. The scene ends with their going off to join the festivities.

In 39 BCE the triumvirs concluded the Treaty or Pact of Misenum with Sextus Pompeius. The terms are largely as Shakespeare describes them. The treaty was short-lived because Antony refused to cede Achaea. When hostilities resumed, Sextus Pompeius was defeated in the naval Battle of Naulochus (September 3, 36 BCE).

Scene 2.7: As Octavius, Antony, Lepidus, Agrippa, Maecenas, Enobarbus, Menas, and Sextus Pompeius feast, Menas urges Sextus Pompeius to kill the triumvirs and make himself ruler of the Roman world. Sextus Pompeius replies that Menas should have acted without telling him because his honor will not allow him to consent. Lepidus is carried off the galley, drunk. The revelry continues until all but Menas and Enobarbus depart; these two go off to Menas's cabin.

Rome

Two legends deal with the founding of Rome. One concerns the Trojan Aeneas, son of Anchises and the goddess Venus, who came to Italy after the destruction of Troy and whose son, Ascanius, founded Alba Longa. The other myth deals with Romulus and Remus, descendants of Aeneas, who were nursed by a she-wolf and built Rome. When Remus mocked Romulus's just-started wall, Romulus killed him. The name of the city supposedly derives from Romulus. Archeology shows settlements in what is now Rome dating from about 1000 BCE. By the seventh century BCE, the Forum had been established as a public meeting place. By the sixth century BCE, Rome was a powerful city-state. Rome was originally a monarchy. The last king, Tarquinus Superbus, was expelled in an aristocratic coup that created a republic (509 BCE). Shakespeare's *Coriolanus* is set just after the expulsion of the king; the play captures the concern of the citizenry regarding the possible return of tyranny. Romans had an aversion to the title of king (rex). It was the fear that Julius Caesar would make himself king that led to his assassination on March 15, 44 BCE, the subject of Shakespeare's best-known Roman play. No Roman emperor used the title of king.

During the period of the republic, Rome continued to expand. By 300 BCE it was the dominant power in Italy. In the third century BCE, Rome took Sicily from the Carthaginians (241 BCE) and then Sardinia (238 BCE). In the second century BCE, Rome conquered Greece and Macedonia, northern Africa, and Spain. The late second century BCE saw a rise in income inequality and the beginning of a century of political unrest that ended only with the defeat of Marc Antony at the Battle of Actium in 31 BCE and his death the next year in Egypt, leaving Octavius (to whom the Roman senate gave the title Augustus in 27 BCE) as sole ruler of the empire. These climactic events are depicted in Shakespeare's *Antony and Cleopatra*. By the late fourth century CE, the empire was being attacked by Goths, who, together with Franks and Vandals, overran much Roman territory. Rome was sacked in 410 CE and again in 455. On September 4, 476, Romulus Augustus, the last Roman emperor in the west, was deposed by the German chieftain Odoacer. *Titus Andronicus* is set in the fourth century CE as the Western Roman Empire is under threat and has begun to decline. Shakespeare's play raises questions about who the barbarians really are and who is civilized.

In 210 CE Rome held about a million people. The population dramatically declined in the Middle Ages. By 1300 there were about 25,000 people living in the city. From the eighth century until 1870, Rome was ruled by popes as part of the papal states. In the fifteenth century, the popes helped fund the Renaissance. In 1871 Rome became the capital of a united Italy.

Lepidus's House

According to Pliny the Elder, Lepidus's father decorated this house in a grand style: "M. [Marcus Aemilius] Lepidus, who was consul with Q. Catulus [78 BCE], was the first to have the lintels of his house made of Numidian marble, a thing for which he was greatly censured." The triumvir was also named Marcus Aemilius Lepidus.

Scene 2.2: Antony and Octavius meet. Lepidus hopes the two will resolve their differences. Antony denies responsibility for his brother and wife's warring against Octavius and explains that he ignored Octavius's messenger because he (Antony) was engaged with three kings. He apologizes for not helping Octavius when he was asked. Lepidus, Maecenas, and Enobarbus urge Octavius to reconcile with Antony. Agrippa suggests Antony marry Octavius's half-sister Octavia, and Antony agrees (40 BCE). All leave except Agrippa, Maecenas, and Enobarbus, who describes, in words taken almost verbatim from Plutarch, the first meeting between Antony and Cleopatra. He says Antony will never abandon her.

Octavius Caesar's House

Located on the Palatine Hill next to the Hut of Romulus, it had two stories and did not use marble. The walls were painted in reds, yellows, and blues. The house was opened to tourists in 2008 after lying underground for centuries. Octavius lived here for forty years. This house postdates the Battle of Actium, so the scenes set in the house of Octavius would have occurred in a different building.

Scene 1.4: Octavius disparages Antony to Lepidus, the third member of the triumvirate. A messenger reports the strength of Sextus Pompeius and his allies and of the pirates Menecrates and Menas.

Scene 2.3: The Egyptian soothsayer tells Antony to return to Egypt, and Antony decides to follow that advice. He dispatches Publius Ventidius Bassus to Parthia. In fact, Antony sent him to fight the Parthians (whom he defeated) in 39 BCE after the conclusion of the Pact of Misenum shown in scene 2.6.

Scene 3.2: Antony prepares to leave Rome and go to Athens with Octavia.

Scene 3.6: Octavius denounces Antony to Maecenas and Agrippa for making Cleopatra ruler of Egypt, lower Syria, and Lydia. To their older son, Alexander Helios, Antony gave Media, Parthia, and Armenia, and to their younger son, Ptolemy Philadelphus, Syria, Cilicia, and Phoenicia (Donation of Alexandria, 34 BCE). Octavius says Antony replied to these charges that he had not received any part of Sicily or any of the revenues that had been Lepidus's share of the triumvirate. Octavius agrees to share his conquests if Antony will do the same. Octavia arrives to try to make peace between Antony and Octavius, but Octavius tells her Antony has returned to Cleopatra and is

The Roman Empire. Shakespeare's Roman plays range from the early days of the republic in *Coriolanus* to the latter days of the empire in *Titus Andronicus*. *Used by permission of Harvard Library*

preparing for war against Octavius. Shakespeare conflates Octavia's two visits to her brother to try to reconcile Octavius and Antony.

A Street

Scene 2.4: Lepidus, Maecenas, and Agrippa prepare for war against Sextus Pompeius.

SYRIA

Gindarus

Site of a battle between the Parthians led by Pacorus and the Romans under Ventidius in 38 BCE.

Scene 3.1: Venditius has defeated the Parthian forces under Pacorus and appears with Pacorus's body carried before him. Silius urges him to pursue the Parthians, but Ventidius fears being too successful and so falling from favor. He intends to credit Antony with the victory.

Coriolanus

Antium

Founded by the Tyrrhenians and Pelasgians, it was a port in Latium, about thirty miles south of Rome. It served as the Volscian capital. The Romans captured the city in 468 BCE and tried to colonize it, but it revolted in 459 BCE. Rome captured the city again in 338 BCE. It became a favorite resort for rich and aristocratic Romans. Caligula and Nero were born here, and the Apollo Belvedere (in the Vatican) and the Borghese Gladiator (in the Louvre) were discovered in the ruins of villas in Antium. Remains of many Roman villas are visible here, including the palace of Nero. Modern Anzio, the site of heavy fighting in World War II, occupies the site of ancient Antium.

Cominius's Camp
Located somewhere between Antium and Corioli (see "Corioli" later this chapter).

Scene 1.6: Caius Martius (Coriolanus) arrives after Cominius's forces have withdrawn from battle. Caius Martius asks permission to attack Tullus Aufidius and his army. When Caius Martius asks for volunteers, all the Roman soldiers agree to follow him.

Scene 1.8: Near the Roman encampment, during the battle between Roman and Volscian forces, Caius Martius defeats Tullus Aufidius and those who come to help him.

Scene 1.9: The Romans triumph. Cominius praises Caius Martius and offers him an oak garland, a horse, and a tenth of all the spoils. Martius declines the horse and the booty. In Plutarch he accepts the horse though not a tenth of the spoils. Shakespeare's character is either humbler or prouder than Plutarch's. Cominius grants him the name Coriolanus to commemorate his deeds at Corioli. Martius asks Cominius to free a Volscian prisoner who helped him inside the city, but he cannot remember the man's name. This forgetting is not included in Plutarch; Shakespeare added it perhaps to show Coriolanus's absentmindedness or to show Coriolanus's indifference to others, especially the lower classes. In Plutarch the Volscian helper is rich, but Shakespeare makes him poor. Earlier, Coriolanus could not recall the names of all the tribunes. Hotspur in *1 Henry IV*, another impulsive character who devotes himself exclusively to honor and war, is similarly forgetful.

House of Tullus Aufidius

Scene 4.4: As Tullus Aufidius feasts with Volscian nobles, Coriolanus in disguise prepares to enter Aufidius's house.

Scene 4.5: Servants try to evict the disguised Coriolanus. When one of them fetches Aufidius, Coriolanus reveals his identity and offers his services to fight Rome. Aufidius embraces him and gives him command of half the Volscian forces. Coriolanus fled to the Volsci in 491 BCE and attacked Rome in 488 BCE. Shakespeare condenses this period.

Road to Antium

Scene 4.3: The Roman Nicanor tells the Volscian Adrian about the banishment of Coriolanus and the dissension in Rome between plebeians and patricians that has ensued.

Corioli

Situated south of Rome and north of the Volscian capital of Antium. The precise location of the city was already lost in antiquity.

Scene 1.2: In the Volscian senate house, the Volscian senators put Tullus Aufidius in charge of the Volscian army (493 BCE).

Scene 1.4: Before Corioli, the Volsci beat back a Roman army, which counterattacks and drives the Volsci into their city. Caius Martius follows the retreating Volsci and is shut in when the Volsci lock their gates. The Romans assume he will be killed, but he emerges, bleeding, and the Roman army pours through the gates he has opened.

Scene 1.5: Within Corioli Caius Martius tells Titus Lartius to secure the city while he and his followers join Cominius in fighting Tullus Aufidius. Titus Lartius tries to dissuade the wounded Caius Martius from further fighting, but Caius Martius insists.

Scene 1.7: Before the gates of Corioli, Titus Lartius prepares to join Cominius.

Scene 5.6: In a public place, the lords of the city welcome Aufidius. Followed by citizens of Corioli, Coriolanus enters and presents the peace treaty he has concluded with Rome. Aufidius accuses Coriolanus of treason and calls him "boy of tears" (l. 100). Coriolanus responds by boasting of his victory over the Volsci in 493, and the citizenry call for his death. The lords try to keep the peace, but Aufidius's henchmen kill Coriolanus. Remorseful, Aufidius orders Coriolanus's body be borne off respectfully. Shakespeare here follows Plutarch. Livy writes, "I find in Fabius, by far the oldest authority, that Coriolanus lived on to old age."

Rome

Two legends deal with the founding of Rome. One concerns the Trojan Aeneas, son of Anchises and the goddess Venus, who came to Italy after the destruction of Troy and whose son, Ascanius, founded Alba Longa. The other myth deals with Romulus and Remus, descendants of Aeneas, who were nursed by a she-wolf and built Rome. When Remus mocked Romulus's just-started wall, Romulus killed him. The name of the city supposedly derives from Romulus. Archeology shows settlements in what is now Rome dating from about 1000 BCE. By the seventh century BCE, the Forum had been established as a public meeting place. By the sixth century BCE, Rome was a powerful city-state. Rome was originally a monarchy. The last king, Tarquinus Superbus, was expelled in an aristocratic coup that created a republic (509 BCE). Shakespeare's *Coriolanus* is set just after the expulsion of the king; the play captures the concern of the citizenry regarding the possible return of tyranny. Romans had an aversion to the title of king (rex). It was the fear that Julius Caesar would make himself king that led to his assassination on March 15, 44 BCE, the subject of Shakespeare's best-known Roman play. No Roman emperor used the title of king.

During the period of the republic, Rome continued to expand. By 300 BCE it was the dominant power in Italy. In the third century BCE, Rome took Sicily from the Carthaginians (241 BCE) and then Sardinia (238 BCE). In the second century BCE, Rome conquered Greece and Macedonia, northern Africa, and Spain. The late second century BCE saw a rise in income inequality and the beginning of a century of political unrest that ended only with the defeat of Marc Antony at the Battle of Actium in 31 BCE and his death the next year in Egypt, leaving Octavius (to whom the Roman senate gave the title Augustus in 27 BCE) as sole ruler of the empire. These climactic events are depicted in Shakespeare's *Antony and Cleopatra*. By the late fourth century CE, the empire was being attacked by Goths, who, together with Franks and Vandals, overran much Roman territory. Rome was sacked in 410 CE and again in 455. On September 4, 476, Romulus Augustus, the last Roman emperor in the west, was deposed by the German chieftain Odoacer. *Titus Andronicus* is set in the fourth century CE as the Western Roman Empire is under threat and has begun to decline. Shakespeare's play raises questions about who the barbarians really are and who is civilized.

In 210 CE Rome held about a million people. The population dramatically declined in the Middle Ages. By 1300 there were about 25,000 people living in the city. From the eighth century until 1870, Rome was ruled by popes as part of the papal states. In the fifteenth century, the popes helped fund the Renaissance. In 1871 Rome became the capital of a united Italy.

Caius Martius Coriolanus's House

Scene 1.3: Volumnia, mother of Caius Martius, rejoices in her son's military exploits, while his wife, Virgilia, cringes at the thought of blood. When Valeria visits, Volumnia praises her own grandson's violent nature. Valeria wants Volumnia and Virgilia to visit a woman who has just delivered a baby, but Virgilia refuses to leave her house until her husband returns from the war. The other two women leave without her.

Scene 3.2: Menenius, a senator, and even Volumnia urge Coriolanus to apologize for criticizing the plebeians, and he reluctantly agrees.

A City Gate

Scene 4.1: Coriolanus bids farewell to Volumnia, Virgilia, Menenius, Cominius, and young Roman nobles. Plutarch records Coriolanus was much admired by the younger Roman patricians. In Shakespeare's chief source for this play, Plutarch's "Life of Caius Martius Coriolanus," Coriolanus takes leave of his wife and mother at home.

Scene 4.2: Near the city gate, Volumnia curses Brutus and Sicinius; Menenius vainly tries to pacify her.

Scene 5.4: On a street near the city's gate, Menenius doubts Coriolanus will spare Rome even at the solicitation of his wife and mother. A messenger tells Sicinius the plebeians have assaulted Brutus and swear they will kill the tribunes if Coriolanus attacks Rome. Another messenger reports the women's success in saving the city, and Romans celebrate their reprieve.

Scene 5.5: Volumnia, Virgilia, Valeria, senators, and lords process across the stage as a senator praises the women.

The Curia/Capitol

Curia (Roman senate house)

The original curia is attributed to Tullus Hostilius, sixth king of Rome (672–641 BCE). The third curia was begun by Julius Caesar in 44 BCE and completed by Octavius in 29 BCE. Diocletian again rebuilt the curia after a fire in 283 CE. The Diocletian building survives nearly intact because in the seventh century it was converted into a basilica. However, the roof, part of the side walls, and rear façade date from the 1930s.

Scene 2.2: Patricians, tribunes, Coriolanus, Menenius, and Cominius arrive for the election of a consul. Coriolanus departs to avoid hearing Cominius praise him. When Coriolanus returns, Menenius tells him the senate wants him to serve as consul, but he must address the plebeians. Because Coriolanus does not wish to do so, Menenius asks the tribunes to forego this exercise. Alone, the tribunes plan to speak to the citizens of Rome.

The Forum

A plaza in the center of Rome between the Palatine and Velian Hills, the Forum was for centuries the focus of the city's daily life. The site was originally a marshy lake, which was drained by the Cloaca Maxima built by the Tarquins in the seventh century BCE. Augustus paved the Forum with travertine. The ruins of many temples are located here.

Scene 2.3: Citizens debate whether to accept Coriolanus as consul. He enters, wearing a gown of humility, a detail Shakespeare took from Plutarch. Menenius urges him to speak nicely to the citizens, then leaves. When citizens approach Coriolanus, he is at first barely polite, but they accept him as consul. Menenius returns with the tribunes; Menenius takes Coriolanus away to the senate house, while the tribunes remain behind to incite the crowd against Coriolanus, and the plebeians leave resolved to deny him the consulship.

Scene 3.3: Sicinius and Brutus prepare to incite the plebeians against Coriolanus. He enters with Menenius, Cominius, senators, and patricians. An aedile (one of two, later four, Roman magistrates responsible for public buildings and maintaining public order) brings the plebeians. Menenius seeks to calm the citizens, but Sicinius accuses Coriolanus of treason. Menenius asks Coriolanus to respond moderately. Instead, he rebukes the commoners and the tribunes, who order Coriolanus be banished. He leaves with Cominius, Menenius, senators, and patricians as the plebeians rejoice. According to Plutarch, Coriolanus incited the ire of the masses in 491 BCE when he opposed giving them grain until they agreed to surrender their newly granted right to have tribunes, and the plebeians banished him for life.

Scene 4.6: Sicinius tells Brutus the patricians are disappointed Coriolanus's banishment has had no ill effects. An aedile enters to announce the Volsci have invaded Roman territory. At first the tribunes refuse to believe this report, but a messenger confirms it and adds that Coriolanus has joined Aufidius. Still, the tribunes reject the news as false. Yet another messenger confirms the account, and Cominius arrives to tell the tribunes they have destroyed Rome, against which Coriolanus is leading the Volscian army. Citizens claim they banished Coriolanus against their will; Shakespeare's mobs are always fickle. Menenius and Cominius go to the senate, as do the tribunes after they send the citizens home.

Scene 5.1: Menenius initially refuses to intercede with Coriolanus to spare Rome because Cominius has been rebuffed, but the tribunes persuade him to try. After Menenius departs, Cominius predicts Coriolanus will not be swayed.

A Street

Scene 1.1: During a food shortage, the plebeians prepare to riot. As Shakespeare was writing this play in 1607, England was experiencing grain shortages. Uprisings occurred in Northamptonshire, Leicestershire, and Shakespeare's native Warwickshire, where three thousand people gathered at Hill Norton, broke down enclosures, and tilled the land before being driven off. At Cottesbich, five thousand people gathered. During an earlier grain shortage in England in 1598, Shakespeare was prosecuted for hoarding eighty bushels of malt. Though the play is set at the dawn of the Roman Republic, it reflects social and political tensions in early Jacobean England that would culminate in the English Civil War.

In Livy's history of Rome, *Ab Urbe Condita*, one of Shakespeare's sources for this play, the food shortage in scene 1.1 occurred in 492 BCE, following the defeat of the Volsci shown later in this act. As Shakespeare so often does in his histories, he here telescopes and inverts events for dramatic effect.

The first citizen claims the patricians are hoarding grain and criticizes Caius Martius, but the second citizen defends him. Menenius Agrippa arrives to pacify the mob. Caius Martius appears and denounces the plebeians, who, he reports, have been granted five tribunes to represent them. The plebeians, suffering from debt, had left the city for the Mons Sacer, and Agrippa Menenius Lanatus, whom the plebeians liked, had persuaded them to return to the city if they were granted two (or perhaps five) tribunes (494 or 493 BCE). By 470 BCE the number of tribunes was five. According to Livy, Agrippa Menenius succeeded by telling the fable of the stomach in 1.1.97+.

A messenger announces the Volsci are preparing to attack Rome. In the early fifth century BCE, the Volsci, coming from the Apennines, overran southern Latium and would repeatedly attack Rome until 431 BCE. They were Romanized in the fourth and third centuries BCE. The tribunes Sicinius Velutus and Junius Brutus enter with the generals Cominius and Titus Laertius and senators. Lucius Sicinius Vellutus was one of the first tribunes. Plutarch names Brutus as another leader of the populace. Caius Martius agrees to assist Cominius, and he tells the plebeians that the Volsci have grain, which they can obtain by joining the army. Instead, the plebeians slink away. The two tribunes remain behind to criticize Caius Martius after everyone else leaves.

Scene 2.1: Shakespeare invented this scene. The tribunes Sicinius and Brutus tell Menenius that Coriolanus is proud; he replies they are, as well. Volumnia, Virgilia, and Valeria inform Menenius that Coriolanus is approaching Rome. Volumnia is glad her son has been wounded because he will have more scars to show the populace when he seeks votes to serve as consul.

Flanked by Cominius and Titus Lartius, Coriolanus enters with his oak garland. Left alone, the tribunes plot to prevent Coriolanus's election as consul. As the scene ends, a messenger reports that Coriolanus is receiving an enthusiastic reception.

Scene 3.1: Coriolanus, Cominius, Titus Lartius, and senators gather. Sicinius and Brutus warn them not to proceed to the Forum. Menenius urges calm as Coriolanus and the tribunes rail against each other, and the senators try to silence Coriolanus.

He criticizes the senators for granting tribunes to the plebeians, whom he disparages. When the tribunes try to arrest Coriolanus for treason, a melee ensues, and Coriolanus and his supporters drive away their opponents. The senators, Menenius, and Cominius instruct Coriolanus to go home, and he reluctantly leaves with Cominius and others. Brutus and Sicinius return with a mob, determined to execute Coriolanus. Menenius pacifies them and promises to bring Coriolanus to the Forum.

Volscian Camp

Scene 1.10: Near Corioli, Tullus Aufidius, now five times defeated by Coriolanus, expresses his hatred for the Roman and declares his desire for revenge.

Scene 4.7: Near Rome, one of Aufidius's lieutenants tells him Coriolanus is overshadowing him. Aufidius vows revenge.

Scene 5.2: Two guards bar Menenius from seeing Coriolanus. When Coriolanus appears with Aufidius, Menenius appeals to him to spare Rome; Coriolanus orders him away. According to Plutarch, Rome sent four embassies to Coriolanus. To the first he granted a thirty-day truce, to the second, a three-day respite. Coriolanus refused to see a delegation of Roman priests. The fourth delegation included his wife and mother, as shown in scene 5.3. Shakespeare condenses the action here and makes Coriolanus more implacable, rendering his yielding to his mother more powerful.

Scene 5.3: Virgilia, Volumnia, young Martius, and Valeria come to Coriolanus's tent to plead with him. Adamant initially, he at last yields to his mother and agrees to conclude a treaty with Rome rather than destroy the city.

Timon of Athens

GREECE

Athens

An important Mycenean center, the city-state in the eighth century BCE was aristocratic. In 508 BCE Cleisthenes created a form of democracy in Athens, though broader democracy did not arrive until the 460s. Women and foreign residents still were not allowed to vote. Of a population of some 100,000, probably only about 10,000 could. Sacked by a Persian army in 480 BCE shortly before the Athenian navy defeated Persia at the Battle of Salamis (September 480 BCE), in 478 BCE Athens became an imperial city state when it assumed leadership of the Delian League. Throughout the fifth century BCE, Athens and Sparta battled for hegemony in the First Peloponnesian War (461–446 BCE), followed by the Second Peloponnesian War (431–404 BCE), which ended in the defeat of Athens. The city quickly recovered, resumed its democracy in 403 BCE, and established a second Athenian Confederacy in 378 BCE. Following Philip of Macedon's victory at the Battle of Chaeronea (338 BCE), Greece came under Macedonian rule. In the Hellenistic period, Athens became a cultural center of the Mediterranean world under the rule of Alexander the Great's successors, the Antigonids, and remained so into the sixth century CE. After 146 BCE Greece was ruled by Rome. Later, Greece became part of the Ottoman Empire. When Greece gained independence in the nineteenth century, Athens became its capital.

Athens's Walls

The Themistoclean walls (named for the Athenian general Themistocles) were erected after the Persian invasion of Greece in 480–478 BCE. The walls were repeatedly rebuilt.

Scene 4.1: Outside the walls of Athens, Timon curses the city.

Scene 5.2: Before the walls of Athens, two senators await news about Timon. The senators who visited Timon in scene 5.1 arrive to report Timon is not returning to the city.

Scene 5.4: Alcibiades and his army arrive at the walls of Athens. The senators plead with him, and he agrees to spare the city. He will punish only his enemies and Timon's. A soldier announces the death of Timon.

Lucullus's House

Scene 3.1: Lucullus thinks Timon's servant Flaminius has come to give him a gift. When Flaminius instead asks for fifty talents, Lucullus gives him three solidares to say he did not see Lucullus. Flaminius throws back the money.

A Public Place

Scene 3.2: When strangers tell Lucius of Timon's financial problems and Lucullus's refusal to help, Lucius says he would give Timon money if he were asked. Servilius comes from Timon to request fifty talents, which Lucius declines to provide. After Lucius leaves, the strangers decry Lucius's ingratitude.

Sempronius's House

Scene 3.3: Asked for money for Timon, Sempronius first says Timon should ask Lucius, Lucullus, and Ventidius. Told Timon did ask them, Sempronius claims he is angry that Timon did not ask him first. He leaves without giving any money for Timon.

The Senate House

The old bouleuterion was built on the west side of the Agora circa 450 BCE. It became a temple (the Metroon, devoted to Cybele) after a new bouleuterion was built in the late fifth century BCE west of the old bouleuterion.

Scene 3.5: Alcibiades pleads with senators to pardon a friend of his convicted of murder, but the senators insist on executing the man. When Alcibiades persists in pleading, he is banished. He resolves to assemble his army to seek revenge on the city.

Alcibiades (451–404 BCE) was a prominent Athenian general in the ill-fated Sicilian expedition in 415 BCE. Accused of sacrilege by the Athenians, he defected to Sparta and aided Athens's enemy until he fell out with the Spartans, as well, and defected to Persia in 412 BCE. His allies in Athens effected his recall in 411 BCE, and he again served as an Athenian general. After the Athenian defeat at the Battle of Notium in 406 BCE, Alcibiades again went into exile and took refuge in Phrygia, where he was killed in 404 BCE, perhaps at the instigation of Sparta.

A Senator's House

Scene 2.1: Aware of Timon's many debts, a senator sends his servant Caphis to collect what Timon owes him.

Timon's Cave

Scene 4.2: In the woods near the sea, Timon curses humanity. Digging for roots to eat, he discovers gold, which he calls the perverter of everything, but he retains some. Alcibiades arrives with his mistresses, Phrynia and Timandra. Timandra was named by Lucian as Alcibiades's lover. Phrynia was an Athenian courtesan but not traditionally linked with Alcibiades. Timon hopes Timandra will infect her Athenian lovers with venereal diseases and gives Alcibiades gold to help him fight Athens and kill its inhabitants. He also gives gold to Timandra and Phrynia and charges them to spread disease. As noted at the end of *Troilus and Cressida*, London's theaters were located near brothels and were frequented by prostitutes, one of the reasons Puritans objected to playhouses. Alcibiades leaves with his lovers. Apemantus finds Timon, who curses him. They argue and denounce each other. After Apemantus leaves, thieves arrive, having heard Timon has found treasure. Timon gives them gold and urges them to continue thieving and killing. When they depart, Flavius, Timon's loyal former steward, arrives. Timon gives him gold as well, and instructs him to hate people. Flavius wants to stay with Timon, but Timon sends him away.

Scene 5.1: The poet and painter are seeking Timon because they have learned he has gold. He gives them some, then chases them away. Flavius returns with two senators, who ask him to return to Athens to defend the city against Alcibiades. Timon replies he does not care how many Athenians Alcibiades kills. He offers Athenians a tree on which to hang themselves.

Scene 5.3: A soldier finds Timon dead and buried.

Timon's House

Pausanius (*Description of Attica*) places Timon's tower near Plato's academy. Lucian (*Timon, or the Misanthrope*) places his residence at the foot of Mouth Hymettus.

Scene 1.1: A painter, poet, jeweler, and merchant come to offer their wares to Timon. (Because Burbage was a painter, as well as an actor, and Shakespeare a poet, their appearance may be an in-joke, especially if Shakespeare played the poet. He had probably stopped acting by 1608, when the play was first staged, but he may have assumed this role for the humor of it.) Timon enters with a messenger from Ventidius, who has been imprisoned for a debt of five talents, which Timon agrees to pay. An

Athenian talent was worth twenty-six kilograms of silver. In 2017 that would have been a bit over $14,000. An old Athenian asks Timon to stop Timon's servant Lucilius from courting the man's only daughter because Lucilius is poor. Timon promises to match the daughter's dowry if the old man will consent to their marriage, which he does. The cynic Apemantus appears and denounces the poet, painter, jeweler, and merchant. Timon invites everyone to dine with him.

Alcibiades arrives with some twenty attendants. All go off with Timon, leaving only Apemantus, who denounces two lords who come to join the feast.

Scene 1.2: In Timon's banqueting hall, Timon, Athenian lords, Alcibiades, and Ventidius prepare to dine. Apemantus joins them. Timon refuses Ventidius's offer to repay him for rescuing him from debtor's prison. Cupid introduces a masque of ladies dressed as Amazons. The lords dance with them before the masquers leave. Timon receives gifts of horses and greyhounds, which he reciprocates, though his steward Flavius tries to warn him he has no money left. After Flavius leaves, Timon gives presents to the lords who have dined with him. Alone with Timon, Apemantus tells him he is too generous, but Timon ignores his advice.

Scene 2.2: In front of Timon's house, Flavius, holding many bills, laments Timon's extravagance. Caphis enters with servants of other usurers seeking to collect money Timon owes them. When Timon appears with Alcibiades and lords, the servants ask for money. Alcibiades and the lords depart. Timon asks Flavius why he is being hounded for debts. Flavius promises the servants that he will explain the situation, and the two men go off.

Apemantus arrives with the fool and mocks the servants waiting for money. A slave comes with letters and asks Apemantus to read the addresses, then leaves. The fool and Apemantus return to criticizing the usurers' servants. As the two men leave, Timon and Flavius return. Timon blames Flavius for not reining in expenses, but Flavius replies Timon never listened to him. Now Timon owes more than twice what he has. Timon assures Flavius that he can borrow what he needs and sends his servants to Lucius, Lucullus, and Sempronius for fifty talents each and tells Flavius to ask the senators for additional funds; Flavius replies that the senators have already refused. Timon now sends Flavius to Ventidius, who so recently offered to repay the money Timon provided to free him from debtor's prison.

Scene 3.4: The servants of Timon's creditors assemble. Flavius tells them Timon has no money, then leaves. Servilius tries to dismiss the creditors' servants, but they remain. When Timon appears, they present their bills. After telling them he has no money, Timon leaves, and the creditors' servants do, as well. Timon instructs Flavius to invite his friends to another dinner.

Scene 3.6: In the banqueting room, Timon's friends, senators, and lords gather. Timon enters with attendants. He curses his guests, then has their dishes uncovered to reveal warm water, which he tosses in their faces, after which he throws the dishes at them.

Scene 4.2: Flavius shares his wealth with Timon's servants, who depart. Flavius resolves to find Timon and continue to serve him.

ROMANCES

Pericles, Prince of Tyre

Mytilene

The capital of the island of Lesbos, Mytilene was founded in the eleventh century BCE. Located on the island's eastern shore, in classical times it had an excellent harbor. It was the home of Sappho and Alcaeus. Captured by the Romans in 81 BCE, it prospered under Roman rule. It became part of the Byzantine Empire and then was ruled by Genoa and the Ottomans. Longus's second-century-CE romance *Daphnis and Chloe* is set around Mytilene. Daphnis undergoes some of the same misadventures as Marina, including being kidnapped by pirates. Daphnis and Chloe are finally reunited with their parents and marry, just as happens to Marina.

The locations throughout the play derive from Shakespeare's two main sources: John Gower's *Confessio Amantis* (1393), book 8, and Laurence Twine's *The Patterne of Painefull Aduentures* (1576; reprinted 1607).

A Brothel

Scene 4.2: Pander, Pander's servant Boult, and a bawd lament the lack of prostitutes. Boult goes to search the market and returns with Marina and the pirates, from whom the bawd buys Marina. Boult then advertises Marina in the town. Marina resolves to kill herself rather than lose her virginity.

Scene 4.5: Two gentlemen discuss Marina's preaching and resolve never to visit a brothel again.

Scene 4.6: Pander, Boult, and a bawd regret bringing Marina to their brothel because she is harming their trade with her prayers and preaching. Lysimachus, governor of Mytilene, comes to the brothel and is offered Marina. Alone with the governor, she criticizes him for frequenting a brothel; he gives her money and promises to help her. Angry that Marina has driven away Lysimachus, Pander and the bawd want Boult to rape her. She gives Boult gold and offers to "sing, weave, sew, and dance" (l. 187) and teach others to do so as well to earn money for her captors. Boult agrees to ask Pander and the bawd if they will consent to her proposition.

The Coast
Scene 5.1: Near the coast of Mytilene, Lysimachus boards Pericles's ship. Helicanus greets Lysimachus and reports that Pericles has been silent for three months, ever since learning of the death of his daughter, Marina. A lord brings Marina to him (whom Pericles does not initially recognize), and she gets him to speak. As she relates her life's story to him, he discovers she is his daughter. While Pericles sleeps, the goddess Diana visits him in a dream and directs him to Ephesus. When Pericles awakes, he sets sail for that city.

LEBANON

Tyre
An island city in southern Phoenicia that became a rich commercial center in the ancient world, with trading ties extending from Spain to Persia. Herodotus dates its founding to about 2750 BCE. It became part of the Achaemenid (Persian) Empire in 539 BCE. Captured by Alexander the Great in 332 BCE, who connected it to the mainland, it was ruled by the Ptolemies and then, after 198 BCE, the Seleucids. In 126 BCE it became a free city-state. Under Roman rule it served as the capital of Syria Phoenicia. It produced a rare dye, Tyrian purple, used only by royalty and the nobility. The city fell to the Arabs in 638 CE. It was part of the kingdom of Jerusalem after it was captured by the First Crusade on July 7, 1124. The Mamluks retook the city in 1291, and it was part of the Ottoman Empire from 1516 to World War I. It became part of modern Lebanon when that state was created in 1920.

The Governor's House
Scene 2.4: Helicanus informs Escanes that Antiochus and his daughter, while seated in a chariot, were killed by a bolt of lightning. Some lords, believing Pericles dead, want to name Helicanus king. He asks them to wait a year and to use that time to seek Pericles. They agree.

Palace of Pericles
Scene 1.2: Helicanus urges Pericles to travel to avoid Antiochus's efforts to kill him. Pericles resolves to go to Tarsus, leaving Helicanus in charge of Tyre.
     Scene 1.3: Thaliard arrives in Tyre, seeking to kill Pericles. Thaliard claims he has a message for Pericles; finding Pericles flown, Thaliard prepares to leave.

LIBYA

Pentapolis

The name means "five cities" in Greek, and the location included Cyrene, Apollonia, Arsinoe (or Taucheria), Euesperides (or Berenice), and Barce (or Ptolemais). It became part of the Persian Empire after Persia conquered Egypt in 525 BCE. Alexander took Egypt in 332 BCE, and after his death Pentapolis was controlled by the Ptolemies. Under the Romans it was known as Cyrenaica. It was ruled by Arabs and the Ottoman Empire before becoming part of Libya.

Palace of Simonides

Scene 2.2: In the tiltyard six knights process before Simonides and Thaisa. Each has an impresa with a motto. In 1613 Shakespeare and Richard Burbage designed an impresa for Francis Manners, Sixth Earl of Rutland, for which each received forty-four shillings. Rutland carried this device (an image with brief text) at a tournament to celebrate James I's accession day on March 24, 1613.

Scene 2.3: In the banqueting hall, Simonides, Thaisa, the marshal of the tourney, lords, ladies, and knights sit at a feast. Thaisa presents the wreath of victory to Pericles. (Shakespeare could not show the actual jousting onstage.) Simonides asks Thaisa to ask Pericles to identify himself; Pericles replies he is a gentleman of Tyre who was shipwrecked at Pentapolis. Following the meal, the knights and ladies dance, then retire to bed.

Scene 2.5: Thaisa chooses Pericles as her husband. Simonides favors the match but pretends to believe Pericles has bewitched his daughter before agreeing to the wedding.

The Seacoast

Scene 2.1: Sailing from Tarsus, Pericles is shipwrecked on the coast of Pentapolis. Fishermen tell him the next day is the birthday of Thaisa, the daughter of their ruler, Simonides, who is holding a joust for her hand. In their net the fishermen catch Pericles's rusty armor, which Pericles requests of them so he can compete for Thaisa's hand. The fishermen give him the armor and a pair of pleated skirts knights wore on horseback.

TURKEY

Antioch

An important city in ancient Syria, founded in 300 BCE by Seleucis I Nicator, one of Alexander the Great's generals, who named the city for his father, Antiochus. It was located on the eastern shore of the Orontes River, near the site of modern Antakya, Turkey. Pompey annexed the city to the Roman Empire in 64 BCE. The city served as the capital of the Roman province of Syria. With a population of 250,000, it was the third-largest city in the east, behind Alexandria and Seleucia. It was an important trading center on the route between Asia and the Mediterranean, and the city's patriarchs played important roles in the early Christian Church. Arabs captured the city in 637 CE.

Palace of Antiochus

Scene 1.1: Pericles has come to woo Antiochus's daughter. If a suitor solves the riddle Antiochus sets him, he wins his daughter; if the suitor fails, his head is cut off. Pericles decodes the riddle, which indicates Antiochus and his daughter are incestuous lovers. Pericles hints he understands this relationship. Antiochus invites Pericles to remain in Antioch, but Pericles decides to leave immediately. After Pericles departs, Antiochus orders Thaliard, one of his lords, to kill Pericles. When a messenger reports Pericles's flight, Antiochus tells Thaliard to pursue him and not return until he has killed Pericles.

Ephesus

Ephesus, in present-day Turkey, was settled by Greek colonists in the tenth century BCE on the site of the former capital of Arzawa. It was an important port on the Aegean Sea until the harbor silted up. Today the old harbor is three miles inland. It came under Roman rule in 129 BCE. The Temple of Artemis (Diana) here was one of the seven wonders of the ancient world, and it figures in the final act of this play. The temple was rebuilt three times before an earthquake destroyed the last structure on the site in 401 CE. Augustus made Ephesus the capital of proconsular Asia. Strabo described Ephesus as second only to Rome in size and importance.

Ephesus became an important center of early Christianity. Paul lived here in 52–54 CE and later wrote his epistles of the Ephesians while imprisoned in Rome (62 CE). The Gospel of John may have been written here (c. 90–100 CE), and it is one the seven cities addressed in the Book of Revelation. A legend claims Jesus's mother spent her last years here.

Cerimon's House

Scene 3.2: Cerimon's servants bring him the chest containing Thaisa's body with a note from Pericles identifying her as his queen. Cerimon revives her.

Scene 3.4: Thinking her husband dead and ignorant of the fate of her daughter, Thaisa resolves to become a priestess of Diana in the goddess's temple at Ephesus.

The Temple of Diana/Artemis

Scene 5.2: Marina, Lysimachus, Helicanus, Pericles, and a lord enter. As instructed by Diana, Pericles recounts his life. Thaisa, hearing him, faints. Cerimon explains he brought Thaisa back to life. When Thaisa recovers, she recognizes Pericles's ring. Because Thaisa's parents have died, she and Pericles will go to Pentapolis. There Lysimachus will marry Marina, and the young couple will rule Tyre, while Pericles and Thaisa stay at Pentapolis. The fourteenth-century poet John Gower, who serves as the play's chorus, ends the play by reporting the death of Cleon and Dionyza.

Tarsus

Located at the mouth of the Burden River in southern Turkey, Tarsus was ruled by Hittites (the city's name is Hittite), Assyria, and Persia before becoming part of the Seleucid and then the Roman Empire. The capital of Roman Cilicia from 72 CE, it was a prosperous commercial as well as philosophical center of the ancient world. Cleopatra and Marc Antony met here in 41 BCE, and it is the birthplace of St. Paul. St. Paul was shipwrecked on Malta (Acts 27), just as Pericles is shipwrecked at Pentapolis. The city contains many ancient ruins.

Cleon's House

Scene 1.4: Cleon, governor of Tarsus, laments to his wife, Dionyza, over the famine gripping his city. When a lord reports the arrival of a fleet, Cleon fears an invasion from a power taking advantage of the city's weakened condition, but the ships belong to Pericles, who is bringing grain to the inhabitants.

Scene 3.3: Pericles prepares to depart from Tarsus, leaving behind Marina, named for the sea where she was born. Cleon and Dionyza promise to care for her.

Scene 4.3: Dionyza has told her husband about the murder of Marina by Leonine, whom Dionyza then poisoned. Cleon laments the killing of Marina, while Dionyza defends her action. Cleon and Dionyza erect a monument to Marina.

The Coast

Scene 3.1: As Pericles is returning to Tyre, a storm at sea near Tarsus causes Thaisa to give birth to a girl. Thaisa apparently dies in childbirth, and the sailors insist on throwing her body overboard to quiet the storm. She is placed in a waterproof chest and cast into the sea. Pericles asks the sailors to land at Tarsus, where he plans to leave the baby with Cleon.

Scene 4.1: Dionyza has hired Leonine to kill the fourteen-year-old Marina because Marina outshines Dionyza's daughter Philoten. Leonine is about to kill Marina when pirates appear. Leonine flees, and the pirates take Marina. Leonine says he will tell Dionyza he killed Marina.

The pirates in this play and in others—Ragozine in *Measure for Measure*, the pirates who kill William de la Pole in *2 Henry VI*, Antonio in *Twelfth Night* (accused of being a pirate), Sextus Pompeius in *Antony and Cleopatra*, and the pirates (offstage) in

Southwark Cathedral. Shakespeare's brother Edmund (1580–1607) is buried here, as are John Fletcher, with whom Shakespeare collaborated on several plays, and John Gower, who serves as the chorus of *Pericles* and whose *Confessio Amantis* is a source for that play. © *iStock/ tupungato*

Hamlet—may have inspired Marc Norman and Tom Stoppard to have Shakespeare working on a pirate-themed play (*Romeo and Ethel, the Pirate's Daughter*) at the beginning of their 1998 movie *Shakespeare in Love*.

Monument to Marina

Scene 4.4: Pericles has returned to Tarsus to retrieve his daughter, only to discover the monument commemorating her death. Mourning, he leaves Tarsus.

Cymbeline

ENGLAND

A Battlefield

Because this battle is Shakespeare's invention, it is impossible to localize it. According to Geoffrey of Monmouth's highly romanticized twelfth-century *Historia Regum Britanniae*, Guiderius and Arviragus fought the Emperor Claudius's invasion of Britain. After Guiderius was killed, Arviragus continued the battle against the Romans; Arviragus may be modeled on Caratacus, who fought the Romans for a decade.

Scene 5.2: Posthumus, disguised as a British peasant, disarms Jachimo and then leaves. Cymbeline is captured by the Romans, then rescued by Belarius, Guiderius, and Arviragus. Posthumus joins them, and all go off together. Lucius, Jachimo, and Imogen (or Innogen—much ink has been spilled in the debate over her name) appear briefly before exiting.

Scene 5.3: Posthumus recounts how Belarius and his sons stopped the Roman advance and rallied the British forces. Posthumus had hoped to die in the fighting. Posthumus now surrenders to the British as a Roman and is turned over to a jailor.

The British Camp

Scene 5.4: Asleep in prison, Posthumus dreams that his dead parents and siblings pray to Jupiter for him. Jupiter appears and hurls a thunderbolt. The ghosts kneel. Jupiter promises them a happy resolution to Posthumus's woes, drops a tablet, and ascends to heaven. The ghosts thank him and vanish after placing the tablet on Posthumus's chest. When Posthumus awakes he reads the tablet. A jailer comes to execute Posthumus, but a messenger arrives to say he is to be taken to the king.

Scene 5.5: At Cymbeline's tent the king thanks and knights Belarius, Guiderius, and Arviragus for saving him; knighting is an anachronism in this play. Cymbeline wishes he could find the fourth man who fought beside them. Cornelius enters to report the queen's death. He says the queen confessed she never loved Cymbeline, had planned to murder him so that her son Cloten could become king, and had also wanted to kill Imogen.

Lucius, Jachimo, the soothsayer, Leonatus, Imogen, and other Roman prisoners enter. Cymbeline declares his intention to execute them. Lucius pleads for his page Fidele, the disguised Imogen. Cymbeline, thinking the youth looks familiar, agrees to take "him" into his service and to let "him" choose a prisoner to pardon. Lucius expects Fidele to select him, but "he" asks to speak to Cymbeline in private about another. When Fidele and the king return, "he" asks for Jachimo, who is wearing the ring Imogen gave Posthumus; Fidele wants to know how he got it. He confesses his villainy. Posthumus reveals his identity and confronts Jachimo. When Fidele tries to calm him, Posthumus strikes "him." Pisanio identifies Fidele as Imogen, who revives to accuse Pisanio of poisoning her. Cornelius explains the queen admitted giving the unwitting Pisanio a box of what she thought were fatal herbs, which Cornelius made certain were only soporific. Belarius, Guiderius, and Arviragus recognize Imogen as their Fidele, whom they thought dead. She embraces Posthumus. Cymbeline asks about Cloten. Pisanio tells of Cloten's pursuit of Imogen, and Guiderius says he killed Cloten. When Cymbeline orders Guiderius executed, Belarius reveals that Guiderius and Arviragus are the king's sons. Cymbeline now pardons all the prisoners. Posthumus asks Lucius to summon the soothsayer Philharmonus (aptly named as lover of harmony) to interpret the tablet Jupiter left him, which the soothsayer does. Cymbeline agrees to continue paying tribute to Rome and blames the queen for his revolt.

Colchester, Essex

Located about fifty miles northeast of London. A Bronze-Age settlement existed on this site circa 1100 BCE. The *chester* part of the name derives from the Latin *castra*, or "military fortification." The *Col* may come from the Celtic *Colne* or Roman *Colonia*, a type of Roman settlement. Cunobelinus, Shakespeare's Cymbeline, ruled from Camulodunum (Colchester). Geoffrey of Monmouth has him reigning from 33 BCE to 2 CE. According to Holinshed he came to the throne in 23 BCE. In either case, he ruled at the time of Augustus in Rome and also at the time of the birth of Jesus, both associated with peace. While this play deals with war, it ends with a peaceful resolution between Britain and Rome. James I, ruling at the time of this play, regarded himself as a peacemaker and hoped even to reconcile Protestant Britain with the pope. Seutonius called Cunobelinus "Britannorum rex," analogous to James I of England, who ruled Scotland, as well as England and Wales, and wanted to unite Scotland with England politically. Thus, while Shakespeare found little about Cymbeline in Holinshed or Geoffrey of Monmouth, he chose this king's reign for its symbolic values.

The Romans conquered Britain in 43 CE (after the death of Cunobelinus) and established a fortification here. Shakespeare has Cymbeline rule Britain as a Roman tributary. The Romans used Camulodunum as a provincial capital, but after Boudica destroyed the city in 61 CE, the Romans moved the capital of Britannia to London (Londinium). Many Roman ruins are visible in Colchester, including the remains of two theaters and a circus (chariot race track). Colchester was part of the Danelaw from circa 880 to 917 CE. The Normans erected Colchester Castle in the eleventh century; it has the largest keep in Europe. In the Middle Ages and Tudor period, the city prospered because of its cloth manufacturing. It is a candidate for being Arthur's Camelot.

Palace of Cymbeline

Scene 1.1: Two gentlemen discuss the recent marriage between Cymbeline's daughter, Imogen, and Posthumus Leonatus, who is poor but worthy. The queen (who is nameless) wanted Imogen to marry her son, Cloten. Although Cymbeline raised Posthumus, the king has now banished him because of his marriage.

The gentlemen leave as the queen, Imogen, and Posthumus enter. The queen promises to intercede for Posthumus, then leaves the newlyweds. Imogen notes the queen's hypocrisy. Posthumus, who is going to Rome to live with Philario, promises to be faithful to Imogen. He gives her a bracelet, and she gives him a diamond ring.

The queen has told Cymbeline where to find the lovers. He orders Posthumus away and criticizes Imogen's choice of husband, whom Imogen defends. After the king departs, Pisanio, Posthumus's servant, reports Cloten drew his sword on Posthumus, but no one was hurt. Posthumus leaves Pisanio in Britain to serve Imogen.

Scene 1.2: In the palace grounds, Cloten asks two gentlemen whether he hurt Posthumus in their duel. The first lord flatters Cloten by assuring him he must have, while in asides the second lord observes that Cloten had the worst of the encounter. The first lord also criticizes Imogen's choice of Posthumus over Cloten, but the second lord in further asides praises her decision.

Scene 1.3: Pisanio describes Posthumus's sailing away. The queen sends a messenger to summon Imogen.

Scene 1.5: The queen wishes to poison Pisanio. The physician Cornelius, suspecting her designs, has given the queen herbs that will merely induce sleep, and she gives Pisanio a box she thinks contains poison, claiming the contents are a sovereign cure for illness. She promises him advancement if he will advocate for Cloten with Imogen, but she knows he will remain loyal to Posthumus.

Scene 1.6: Pisanio introduces Jachimo to Imogen. Jachimo claims Posthumus is reveling in Rome. He flatters Imogen and asserts that Posthumus is unfaithful to her. He says she should avenge herself by sleeping with him. When Imogen condemns him, he replies he was only testing her and assures her Posthumus is faithful. He asks her to keep a chest in which he says is stored a plate for the Roman emperor. She agrees to leave it in her bedroom overnight.

Scene 2.1: On the palace grounds, Cloten complains to two lords about losing a game of bowls and being rebuked for swearing. As in scene 1.2, the first lord flatters Cloten, while in asides the second lord mocks him. Cloten and the first lord go off to meet Jachimo.

Scene 2.2: As Imogen sleeps in her bedroom, Jachimo emerges from the chest she has stored here. He makes an inventory of the room, takes the bracelet Posthumus gave her, and notes a mole on her left breast. He sees she has been reading Shakespeare's favorite poet, Ovid, book 6, the story of the rape of Philomel, which Shakespeare had used in *Titus Andronicus.* While Jachimo does not actually rape Imogen, his behavior is a visual ravishing. In line 12 he even compares himself to Tarquin, who raped Lucrece, the subject of Shakespeare's 1594 narrative poem. Jachimo then returns to his trunk. With the details he has collected and the bracelet, he will be able to convince Posthumus he has slept with Imogen.

Scene 2.3: Cloten has summoned musicians to play outside Imogen's bedroom. They perform "Hark, hark, the lark at heaven's gate sings" (ll. 20+), then leave. Cymbeline and his queen enter. A messenger tells them Caius Lucius has come from Rome. After they depart, Cloten knocks on Imogen's door. When she appears, he tries to woo her, but she rebuffs him, saying she values Posthumus's "meanest garment" more than she does Cloten (l. 133). He is stung by her words, which he keeps repeating. Imogen requests Pisanio to ask her lady Dorothy to search for her missing bracelet; Pisanio leaves to look for it as well. She leaves Cloten still muttering, "His meanest garment" (l. 156).

Scene 3.1: Cymbeline, the queen, and Cloten tell Caius Lucius that Britain will no longer pay tribute to Rome. Caius Lucius declares war on Britain.

Scene 3.2: Pisanio reads a letter from Posthumus accusing Imogen of adultery and instructing Pisanio to kill her. Posthumus has also written to Imogen, saying he awaits her at Milford Haven in Wales and asking her to join him there. His intention is to lure her away from court so Pisanio can kill her. Imogen is eager to set off, while Pisanio, understanding Posthumus's design, tries to discourage her. Colchester is located near the east coast of England; Milford Haven, on the west coast of Wales; the distance between them is about 324 miles.

Scene 3.5: Lucius takes his leave of Cymbeline, the queen, and Cloten. As Cymbeline prepares for war, he notes Imogen's absence and sends a messenger for her. He returns to say her door is locked, and she is not responding. Cymbeline and Cloten go to seek her. The queen notes Pisanio is also missing, a consequence, she hopes, of the herbs she gave him. Cloten returns to report Imogen's absence and the king's anger. When Pisanio returns, Cloten asks him where Imogen is. He gives Cloten

Posthumus's letter summoning her to Milford Haven. Cloten asks him to serve him as he has served Posthumus, and Pisanio deceives him by agreeing. Cloten requests some of Posthumus's clothes, recalling Imogen's saying she preferred Posthumus's meanest garment to him. He plans to dress as Posthumus, go to Milford Haven, kill Posthumus, and rape Imogen.

Scene 4.3: Cymbeline laments his daughter's disappearance, his queen's illness, and Cloten's absence. A lord informs him the Romans have invaded Britain. Shakespeare has the Romans landing at Milford Haven. The precise site of the actual Roman invasion in 43 CE under Aulus Plautius is unclear; Kent or Southampton in Hampshire are the likeliest locations. Julius Caesar's invasions of 55 and 54 BCE occurred in Kent.

The Roman Camp

Scene 5.1: Posthumus contemplates the bloody cloth Pisanio sent him as proof of Imogen's murder. He laments his order to kill Imogen and resolves to abandon the Roman army to fight for Britain.

ITALY

Rome

Two legends deal with the founding of Rome. One concerns the Trojan Aeneas, son of Anchises and the goddess Venus, who came to Italy after the destruction of Troy and whose son, Ascanius, founded Alba Longa. The other myth deals with Romulus and Remus, descendants of Aeneas, who were nursed by a she-wolf and built Rome. When Remus mocked Romulus's just-started wall, Romulus killed him. The name of the city supposedly derives from Romulus. Archeology shows settlements in what is now Rome dating from about 1000 BCE. By the seventh century BCE, the Forum had been established as a public meeting place. By the sixth century BCE, Rome was a powerful city-state. Rome was originally a monarchy. The last king, Tarquinus Superbus, was expelled in an aristocratic coup that created a republic (509 BCE). Shakespeare's *Coriolanus* is set just after the expulsion of the king; the play captures the concern of the citizenry regarding the possible return of tyranny. Romans had an aversion to the title of king (rex). It was the fear that Julius Caesar would make himself king that led to his assassination on March 15, 44 BCE, the subject of Shakespeare's best-known Roman play. No Roman emperor used the title of king.

During the period of the republic, Rome continued to expand. By 300 BCE it was the dominant power in Italy. In the third century BCE, Rome took Sicily from the Carthaginians (241 BCE) and then Sardinia (238 BCE). In the second century BCE, Rome conquered Greece and Macedonia, northern Africa, and Spain. The late second century BCE saw a rise in income inequality and the beginning of a century of political unrest that ended only with the defeat of Marc Antony at the Battle of Actium in

31 BCE and his death the next year in Egypt, leaving Octavius (to whom the Roman senate gave the title Augustus in 27 BCE) as sole ruler of the empire. These climactic events are depicted in Shakespeare's *Antony and Cleopatra*. By the late fourth century CE, the empire was being attacked by Goths, who, together with Franks and Vandals, overran much Roman territory. Rome was sacked in 410 CE and again in 455. On September 4, 476, Romulus Augustus, the last Roman emperor in the west, was deposed by the German chieftain Odoacer. *Titus Andronicus* is set in the fourth century CE as the Western Roman Empire is under threat and has begun to decline. Shakespeare's play raises questions about who the barbarians really are and who is civilized.

In 210 CE Rome held about a million people. The population dramatically declined in the Middle Ages. By 1300 there were about 25,000 people living in the city. From the eighth century until 1870, Rome was ruled by popes as part of the papal states. In the fifteenth century, the popes helped fund the Renaissance. In 1871 Rome became the capital of a united Italy.

Philario's House
Scene 1.4: Jachimo and a Frenchman belittle Posthumus to Philario. When Posthumus arrives, the Frenchman tells of an argument between Posthumus and a citizen of Orleans caused by Posthumus's claim that Imogen is more beautiful, virtuous, and constant than any woman in France. Jachimo denies Imogen can excel the women of Italy and bets Posthumus ten thousand ducats against the ring Posthumus is wearing he can seduce her. Philario tries in vain to prevent the bet.

Scene 2.4: Philario and Posthumus discuss Cymbeline's lapsed payment of tribute to Rome. Philario thinks Cymbeline will pay, but Posthumus believes Britain will fight Rome. Jachimo arrives, claiming he slept with Imogen. The details he provides of her room and body and the bracelet he has stolen cause Posthumus to believe him.

Scene 2.5: In a soliloquy Posthumus denounces Imogen and women in general.

A Public Place
Scene 3.7: Two Roman senators and tribunes discuss Lucius's planned invasion of Britain.

WALES

Milford Haven, Pembrokeshire
On the west coast of Pembrokeshire in southwest Wales. The town of Milford itself dates from 1793. William Camden wrote of Milford Haven,

> From here runneth the shore along not many miles continuate, but at length the land shrinketh back on both sides giving place unto the sea, which encroaching upon it a great

way, maketh the Haven which Englishmen call *Milford Haven*, than which there is not another in all Europe more noble or safer, such variety it hath of nouked Bayes, and so many coves and creekes, for harbour of ships, wherewith the bankes are on every side indented, and that I may use the Poets words:

> Hic exarmatum terris cingentibus aquor,
> Clauditur & placidem discit servare quietem.
> The sea disarmed here of windes, within high banke and hill,
> Enclosed is and learnes thereby to be both calme and still.

Neither is this haven famous for the secure safeness thereof more, than for the arrival therein of King Henrie the Seventh a Prince of most happy memory, who from hence gave forth unto England then hopeless the first signall to hope well, and raise it selfe up, when as now it had long languished in civill miseries and domesticall calamities, within it selfe.

In 1610 James's older son, Henry, was invested as Prince of Wales. This investiture was celebrated May 31 to June 6, 1610, with plays. Just as *The Merry Wives of Windsor* may well be a Garter play, *Cymbeline* may be an investiture play, thus accounting for Shakespeare's setting part of this work in Wales.

Scene 3.3: In front of the cave of Belarius near Milford Haven, Belarius praises the rustic life, but Guiderius and Arviragus find it confining. Belarius, who had served Cymbeline until he was banished twenty years earlier, informs them of the evils of court life. He sends the youths up the mountain to hunt deer, while he remains below. Alone, Belarius reveals he kidnapped the two youths, Cymbeline's sons, in revenge for his unjustified banishment. The young men think Belarius is their father.

Scene 3.4: Pisanio shows Imogen Posthumus's letter to him accusing her of adultery and instructing him to kill her. Imogen tells Pisanio to obey Posthumus's order, but he refuses. Why, then, she asks, has Pisanio brought her to Milford Haven? He replies Lucius will arrive there. She is to disguise herself as a man and serve him. She will then be able to travel to Rome to be near Posthumus. Pisanio gives Imogen the box of herbs the queen gave him, claiming it will cure any ills she may suffer, though actually the contents are a powerful soporific that produces a deathlike slumber.

Scene 3.6: Seeking Milford Haven, Imogen, dressed as a man, enters Belarius's cave. When Belarius, Guiderius, and Arviragus return from hunting, they find her. She introduces herself as Fidele and says she is going to Milford Haven. Because night is near, they welcome her to stay with them and share their food.

Scene 4.1: Near the cave of Belarius, Cloten repeats his intention to kill Posthumus and rape Imogen.

Scene 4.2: Before the cave of Belarius, Imogen is ill but refuses the aid of Guiderius or Arviragus. She takes some of Pisanio's herbs and goes inside the cave. When Cloten arrives, Guiderius confronts him, and they exit fighting. Guiderius returns with Cloten's head. Arviragus enters the cave to find Fidele apparently dead. They lament "his" death and sing "Fear no more the heat o' th' sun" (ll. 258+). After they leave, Imogen awakes and sees Cloten's body. Because of the clothes, she thinks the body is Posthumus's and blames Pisanio for betraying her.

Lucius arrives with captains and a soothsayer, who predicts a Roman victory. They find Imogen with Cloten's body. She claims the dead man was her master, Richard du Champ (i.e., Richard Field, Shakespeare's friend from Stratford who moved to London and printed and published *Venus and Adonis*, 1593, and printed *The Rape of Lucrece*, 1594, and "The Phoenix and Turtle," 1601). Richard Field's father was a tanner in Stratford. As a glover, Shakespeare's father would have bought leather from him, and the two families lived close to each other, Richard's on Bridge Street, Shakespeare's on Henley Street. In London, Field was apprenticed to Thomas Vautrollier; after Vautrollier's death in 1587, Field married his widow (1589). Together they published works Shakespeare used in his plays, including Thomas North's translation of Plutarch's *Lives*, Robert Greene's *Pandosto* (the source of *The Winter's Tale*), and editions of Ovid. Shakespeare may have used Field's printing and publishing establishment as a library. Field called himself Ricardo del Campo, the Spanish version of Richard du Champ.

Fidele agrees to accompany Lucius after Cloten is buried.

Scene 4.4: Belarius wants to flee the approaching Roman legions; he does not want to fight for the king who banished him. His sons, however, want to join the British army, and Belarius agrees to accompany them.

The Winter's Tale

BOHEMIA

Located in the western part of the Czech Republic, Bohemia was a kingdom in the Holy Roman Empire and later part of the Habsburgs' Austro-Hungarian Empire. It was the Roman Boiohaemum, first mentioned in Tacitus's *Germania*, *Boi* for the Celtic tribe Boii, plus *haimaz* (German *heimat*, "home"). In 1613 James I's daughter Elizabeth married the elector Palatine, ruler of Bohemia. As part of the celebration, *The Winter's Tale* was performed at court in February of that year. The astrologer Simon Forman saw the play at the Globe on May 15, 1611, and it was performed at court on November 5 of that year.

The Coast

Ben Jonson (and many after him) objected to Shakespeare's giving Bohemia a seacoast. Jonson mocked, "Shakespeare in a play brought in a number of men saying they had suffered shipwreck in Bohemia, where [there] is no Sea near, by some 100 miles." As with Delphos (see scene 2.1 later in this chapter), the error derives from the play's source, Robert Greene's *Pandosto* (1588). Greene's romance is set in Sicily and Bohemia. Shakespeare reversed the locations: What happens in *Pandosto* in Sicily occurs in Shakespeare's play in Bohemia and vice versa. Also, this is a play in which wonders seem familiar. If a statue can come to life, Bohemia can have a seacoast. As Paulina declares, "It is required / You do awake your faith" (5.3.94–95), faith being, according to St. Paul (for whom Paulina in the play is named), the "substance of things hoped for, and the evidence of things unseen" (Hebrews 11:1).

Scene 3.3: Guided by a dream, Antigonus has landed on the coast of Bohemia. In that dream Hermione tells him he will never see his wife again. Dreams figure prominently in Shakespeare's romances. See Marjorie Garber, *Dream in Shakespeare* (1974). Antigonus leaves the infant with a scroll and a bundle that contains gold. A storm begins, and Antigonus exits, "pursued by a bear," Shakespeare's most famous stage direction, perhaps the most famous stage direction in theater history. There has been much throwing about of brains regarding the original staging of this incident. Might a real bear have been used? In a view of London often wrongly attributed to Wenceslaus Hollar, the Globe is identified at the Bear Garden and vice versa. Bearbaiting, a popular sport in Shakespeare's time, occurred near the Globe. Some venues were used for both play-acting and bearbaiting. Given the risk, though, the use of a real bear here seems unlikely. In 1598 the inventory of the Lord Admiral's Men included a "beares skynne" (Philip Henslowe's *Diary* for March 10, 1598). Perhaps the King's Men borrowed it for this play or had one of their own. Over the centuries directors have used various alternatives, from an actor in a bear suit to a shadow.

A shepherd enters looking for two lost sheep and finds the baby. His son appears and reports the death of Antigonus and the sinking of the ship that brought the baby to Bohemia. The shepherd and his son take the baby (Perdita; i.e., "lost one") home.

The Palace of Polixenes

Scene 4.2: Sixteen years have passed since the end of act 3, as Time explains in scene 4.1. Camillo longs to return to Sicily, but Polixenes refuses to part with him. Polixenes asks about his son Florizel, who has been absent from court and has been spending time with the shepherd who found Perdita, and with her as well. Camillo and Polixenes plan to disguise themselves and visit the shepherd.

A Road

Scene 4.3: Near the shepherd's cottage, the shepherd's son is calculating the revenue from his sheep shearing. His figures reveal Shakespeare's familiarity with the wool trade in which his father illegally engaged during the playwright's youth. Bits of wool have been found at Shakespeare's birthplace in Stratford; the right half of the building (which was a separate edifice in Shakespeare's time) is called the woolshop. The youth is also contemplating what he needs to buy for the upcoming sheep-shearing feast. The son finds the rogue Autolycus groveling on the ground as though he has been robbed and beaten. As the shepherd's son helps him, Autolycus picks his pocket. Shakespeare named Autolycus for the grandfather of Odysseus, who "excelled all men in thievery and shifty oaths" (*Odyssey*, book 19); no such character exists in the play's source. This encounter between the shepherd's son and Autolycus offers an ironic twist on the parable of the Good Samaritan (Luke 10:25–37).

The Shepherd's Farm

Scene 4.4: At the sheep-shearing festival such as Shakespeare would have known in rural England, Florizel, Polixenes's son, praises Perdita, who worries that their difference in rank will prevent their marriage. (As is often the case, however remote a play's supposed setting, such as the woods outside ancient Athens in *A Midsummer Night's Dream* or the Vienna of *Measure for Measure*, Shakespeare actually is depicting life in Elizabethan and Jacobean England.) Florizel reassures Perdita, promising to be hers. The shepherd, his son, the shepherdesses Dorcas and Mopsa, and servants enter, along with Camillo and Polixenes in disguise. Perdita entertains the two visitors, and they observe Florizel with her. Autolycus comes selling ballads and ribbons, clothing and perfume. Although the festival is held in Bohemia, it is very English, as Autolycus is a very English peddler, selling the various "fairings" (items sold at fairs) an English peddler would offer, including ballads. The shepherd's son buys ballads for Dorcas and Mopsa, both of whom are in love with him. The two shepherdesses sing a ballad with Autolycus, then leave. Twelve men disguised as satyrs dance. After this entertainment, Polixenes asks Florizel about Perdita, and the shepherd joins the hands of the lovers. As Robert L. Greaves writes in *Society and Religion in Elizabethan England* (1981), such handfasting "had the force of a contract in canon law" and was the equivalent of marriage (180). Polixenes says Florizel should request his father's permission to marry, but Florizel replies he intends to keep this relationship secret from him. Polixenes now reveals himself and insists the lovers part. After Polixenes leaves, Florizel assures Perdita he will remain faithful to her. Camillo, who has stayed behind, advises him to go to Sicily. When Autolycus returns from selling all his wares, Camillo has Florizel exchange clothes with the rogue so the prince can flee Bohemia undetected. Camillo plans to inform Polixenes of the couple's flight and thus return to Sicily himself.

The shepherd's son urges his father to reveal to Polixenes that Perdita is not really his daughter. Because she is a foundling, the youth reasons, the shepherd and his son cannot be blamed for Perdita's and Florizel's love. Autolycus reappears, now richly dressed in Florizel's clothes; he pretends to be a courtier and promises to help them gain access to the king. The shepherd gives him gold as a bribe. After the shepherd and his son leave, Autolycus says he will take the men to Florizel, whom he once served and who may reward him.

ITALY

Sicily

A Court of Justice

Scene 3.2: Confronting Leontes, Hermione denies his accusations of adultery and treason. This trial scene would have reminded Shakespeare's audiences of the divorce trial of Henry VIII's first wife, Catherine of Aragon. Like Hermione's daughter, Catherine of Aragon's daughter, Mary, was declared illegitimate. L. C. Knight points out the parallel in *The Crown of Life* (1947). Officers bring in Cleomenes and Dion, who present the sealed message of the oracle of Delphos; it proclaims Hermione is innocent and

Leontes will die without an heir if the baby is not recovered. The oracle's statement might serve as a commentary on Henry VIII's divorce of Catherine. Leontes rejects the oracle's declaration. Immediately afterward a servant enters the court to announce the death of Mamilius. In 1596 Shakespeare's son, Hamnet/Hamlet died. The actor who played Mamilius might have taken the role of Perdita in acts 4 and 5 of this play, effecting a resurrection of sorts. In all Shakespeare's romances except *The Two Noble Kinsmen*, a child presumed dead is found alive. In *The Brothers Karamazov*, written shortly after the death of Fyodor Dostoevsky's son Alexei, it is the significantly named Fyodor Karamazov who is killed and his son Alexei who lives. The losses of life are repaired in literature.

Hermione faints at the news of her son's death. Paulina and attendants remove Hermione, while Leontes, thinking her alive, promises to reconcile with her, as well as with Polixenes and Camillo. Paulina returns to say Hermione is dead. Leontes will bury his queen and son together, and he pledges to visit their grave daily. In scene 2.1, before Hermione is taken away, Mamilius begins to tell a scary story, "There was a man. . . . / Dwelt by a churchyard" (2.1.29–30). That man is Leontes.

Palace of Leontes

Neither Shakespeare nor his source for this play, Robert Greene's *Pandosto* (1588), gives a specific location for the palace.

Scene 1.1: Archidamus, a Bohemian lord, and Camillo, a Sicilian lord, discuss the visit of Polixenes, the king of Bohemia, is paying Leontes, king of Sicily; the two monarchs have been friends since childhood.

Scene 1.2: Polixenes prepares to return home after spending nine months, the gestation period for a fetus, in Sicily. Shakespeare added this detail about the duration of the visit. *Pandosto* does not indicate its length. In the play, Hermione is about to deliver a baby, and Polixenes has been in Sicily just long enough for him to be the father. As Iago says in *Othello*, which bears similarities to this work, "Trifles light as air / Are to the jealous confirmations strong / As proofs of Holy Writ" (3.3.319–21). When Leontes asks him to stay longer, he refuses, but when, at Leontes's bidding, his wife, Hermione, asks Polixenes to remain, he agrees. Leontes now suspects Hermione and Polixenes are lovers. Camillo tries to disabuse him of his suspicions, but Leontes rejects his advice and orders Camillo to poison Polixenes. While seeming to consent, Camillo warns Polixenes of Leontes's homicidal intention and urges Polixenes to flee at once. Camillo and Polixenes leave Sicily.

Scene 2.1: As Hermione relaxes with two of her ladies and her son Mamilius, Leontes enters with Antigonus and other Sicilian lords and their attendants. Informed of Polixenes's flight, Leontes takes Mamilius from Hermione and claims she is carrying Polixenes's child. Although she denies the charge, Leontes orders her imprisoned.

After she leaves, Antigonus and another lord assure Leontes that Hermione is faithful, but he refuses to believe them. He has, however, sent Cleomenes and Dion to Apollo's temple at Delphos (2.1.184), the place name Greene uses in *Pandosto*, to confirm his suspicion. The famous oracle of Apollo was at Delphi, which Shakespeare (and Greene) may intend. Following Greene's *Pandosto*, Shakespeare makes Delphi, if Delphi is meant, an island, which it is not. There was a shrine to Apollo on the island of Delos, Apollo's birthplace; Delos was also called Delphos. Shakespeare's knowledge of and concern about geography was limited, as appears, for example, in *The Tempest* (see headnote to that play). In *The Two Gentlemen of Verona*, Valentine sails from Verona to Milan (1.1.71), which cannot be done. In *The Winter's Tale*, however, Shakespeare's geographical errors should be attributed to Robert Greene, who may have confused or conflated Delphi and Delos because both have Apollonian associations.

Scene 2.3: Paulina arrives with Hermione's newborn. Despite Paulina's insistence, Leontes denies the child is his. She leaves the baby when he forces her from the room. The king first orders the baby burned, but a lord dissuades him. Instead, Leontes commands Paulina's husband, Antigonus, to take the infant away from Sicily and abandon it on some foreign shore. After Antigonous leaves with the infant, a messenger announces the return of Cleomenes and Dion from Delphos. Leontes orders the convening of a court to try Hermione.

Scene 5.1: Cleomenes urges Leontes to forgive himself for the wrongs he committed sixteen years earlier. Paulina reminds him he killed Hermione and accuses Cleomenes and Dion of wanting Leontes to marry again to produce an heir. Leontes agrees not to remarry without Paulina's permission, which she says she will not grant until Hermione lives again.

A servant announces the arrival of Florizel and his princess (Perdita). Leontes sends Cleomenes and Dion to escort them to him. Florizel claims he is visiting Leontes on his father's behalf after wedding Perdita, daughter of the king of Libya. This reference to Libya anticipates the offstage marriage of Claribel, daughter of Alonso, king of Naples, to the king of Tunis in Shakespeare's next play, *The Tempest*.

A lord enters to say Polixenes has come to Sicily and asks Leontes to detain Florizel, who understands Camillo has betrayed him. Florizel admits he and Perdita are not married, and Leontes agrees to intercede for the young lovers.

Scene 5.2: In front of the palace of Leontes, three gentlemen recount to Autolycus the revelation that Perdita is Leontes's lost daughter. The third gentleman also relates the reunion of Polixenes and Leontes. They then go off to Paulina's house to see a statue of Hermione executed by Julio Romano (1498/1499–1546). Romano studied with Raphael and was a noted architect as well as a painter. He also sculpted. Why Shakespeare chose Romano here is unclear. See Piero Boitani, "Julio Romano," Marie-Madelaine Martinet, "*The Winter's Tale* et Julio Romano," and Richard Studing, "'That Rare Italian Master'—Shakespeare's Julio Romano."

After they leave, the shepherd and his son enter. They have been made gentlemen. The son says he was a gentleman born before his father. Shakespeare is alluding to his securing a coat of arms for his father and hence himself in 1596, after his father had failed to secure one decades earlier. By securing the coat of arms for his father rather than himself, he made himself a "gentleman born" (l. 139). Shakespeare also refers to acquiring a coat of arms at the beginning of *The Merry Wives of Windsor* (c. 1597). In *Every Man out of His Humour*, performed by Shakespeare's company, the Lord Chamberlain's Men, in 1599, the country bumpkin Sogrialdo boasts of his recently purchased coat of arms. Another character suggests he should choose as his motto "Not without Mustard," a reference to the motto on Shakespeare's coat of arms, "*Non Sans Droit*," "not without right." Shakespeare was just as ready as Ben Jonson to laugh at his social aspirations at the same time that he had them. In "The Crack-Up" (*Esquire Magazine*, February 1936) F. Scott Fitzgerald wrote, "The test of a first rate intelligence is the ability to hold two opposed ideas in the mind at the same time, and still retain the ability to function." Shakespeare exemplifies the truth of Fitzgerald's observation.

Autolycus asks the shepherd and his son to plead for him with Florizel, and they agree. They then go to Paulina's house to join the others.

Paulina's House

Scene 5.3: Leontes, Polixenes, Florizel, Perdita, Camillo, Paulina, and lords gather to see Hermione's statue. Paulina says she can make the statue move, but first the viewers must "awake [their] faith" (l. 95). To the sound of music, Hermione descends from her pedestal and embraces Leontes, who urges Paulina to marry Camillo. The statue's coming alive recalls the story of Pygmalion and Galatea in Ovid's *Metamorphoses*, book 10, Shakespeare's favorite work. The scene also continues the theme in Shakespeare's romances of the dead coming back to life.

A Prison

Scene 2.2: When Paulina comes to visit Hermione, the jailor will not admit her but agrees to summon Hermione's lady-in-waiting Emilia, who reports Hermione has delivered a daughter. Paulina asks to be allowed to take the baby to Leontes in the hope that seeing the child will soften him.

Desdemona's attendant in *Othello* is also named Emilia. Emilia Bassano Lanier is a candidate for being the Dark Lady of Shakespeare's sonnets. Might she be the inspiration for Shakespeare's choice of these women's name? In *The Two Noble Kinsmen*, Emily/Emilia is the sister of Hippolyta, but Shakespeare found that name in Geoffrey Chaucer's "The Knight's Tale," the first of the *Canterbury Tales* and the source of that play.

A Road

Scene 3.1: Cleomenes and Dion describe their experience at Delphos.

The Tempest

PROSPERO'S ISLAND

Prospero's is an island of the mind, no more real than the islands of Circe and Calypso in the *Odyssey*. Still, just as scholars have sought to give to these Homeric airy nothings a local habitation and a name, there have been attempts to find Prospero's enchanted realm. In *New Illustrations of the Life, Study, and Writings of Shakespeare* (1845), Joseph Hunter identified Prospero's island as Lampedusa. It is accessible from both Tunis, from where Alonso and his companions are returning after the marriage of Claribel, Alonso's daughter, to the king of Tunis, and from Naples, the ship's destination when it is wrecked by the storm Prospero raises. It was also largely uninhabited and is associated with storms and St. Elmo's fire (1.2.198–201), and mariners called it the Enchanted Island. It had many pines, in one of which Ariel was confined (1.2.277), and it supplied wood for Malta, so Ferdinand would have many logs to gather in scene 3.1. Other Mediterranean islands proposed are Corsica and Pantelleria. Tunisia is visible from Pantelleria on a clear day and lies on the sea route from there to Naples.

While logically Prospero's island should lie in the Mediterranean, *The Tempest* was inspired by a shipwreck in the Atlantic Ocean. On July 28, 1609, the *Sea Venture*, the flagship of a nine-ship expedition bound for Jamestown, Virginia, under Sir George Somers, was wrecked off the coast of Bermuda with 150 men onboard. The ship was presumed lost; the other vessels, like those accompanying Alonso back from Tunis, continued on to their destination. Bermuda was uninhabited and had been envisioned as enchanted. As its name "Isle of Devils" indicates, it was regarded as dangerous. Sylvester Jourdain, in *A Discovery of the Bermudas, Otherwise Called the Isle of Divels, by Sir Thomas Gates, Sir George Sommers, and Captayne Newport, with Divers Others* (1610), reported, however, that the shipwrecked Englishmen found the "AYRE SO TEMPERATE and the COUNTRY SO ABUNDANTLY FRUIT-FULL" that, though the provisions they had onboard their ship were spoiled, they survived for nine months and were able to carry away food when, after they built two pinnaces, they sailed to Virginia, arriving in Jamestown on May 23, 1610. Their reappearance would have seemed like something out of a Shakespearean romance: Those lost and presumed dead were found alive. In addition to Jourdain's published account, another, *A True Reportory of the Wreck and Redemption of Sir Thomas Gates, Knight, upon and from the Islands of the Bermudas: His Coming to Virginia and the Estate of That Colony Then and After, under the Government of the Lord La Warr, July 15, 1610, Written by William Strachey, Esquire,* existed in manuscript. It was published in 1625, but Shakespeare could have seen this work. The Third Earl of Southampton, to whom Shakespeare dedicated *Venus and Adonis* and *The Rape of Lucrece,* was named to the council of the Virginia Company in 1609, and the Third Earl of Pembroke, a dedicatee of the First Folio, was a member of the company. Shakespeare was moving in a circle familiar with English exploration. Ariel refers to the "still-vexed Bermoothes" (1.2.229), and Caliban's name suggests both cannibals and the Carib(bean). Gonzalo Fernández de Oviedo y Valdés wrote the earliest description of Bermuda. His first and second names provided the names, respectively, of Alonso's adviser (Gonzalo) and son (Ferdinand). Gonzalo's description of his ideal commonwealth in scene 2.1 derives from Miguel de Montaigne's essay "De Cannibals," dealing with the natives of the New World. The play thus relates to British exploration and colonization. As deformed and depraved as Caliban is, he has been enslaved by the European Prospero, his island stolen from him. As he declares, "This island's mine by Sycorax my mother, / Which thou tak'st from me" (1.2.333–34). He also notes, "I am all the subjects that you have, / Which first was mine own king" (1.2.343–45). Caliban taught Prospero "all the qualities of the isle" (1.2.339). At first Prospero treated him well, as the English did the Native Americans, before enslaving and killing them. Ariel, too, must serve Prospero. When Ariel asks to be free, Prospero threatens, "If thou more murmur'st, I'll rend an oak / And peg thee in his knotty entrails till / Thou hast howled away twelve winters" (1.2.295–97). Perhaps the most magical aspect of Prospero's island is that, at the end of the play, all the Europeans sail away, leaving it to its original inhabitant, Caliban, and Ariel is freed.

On the grounds of Grotto Bay Beach resort in Bermuda is Prospero's Cave (previously called Island Cave), named for Shakespeare's magus. It contains stalactites and stalagmites and a subterranean blue lake. It now also includes a spa. It was discovered in 1609 by Sir George Somers, the first cave found in Bermuda. It is open only to guests of the resort.

Scene 1.1: As Alonso, king of Naples; his brother, Sebastian; Antonio, Prospero's brother and usurping duke of Milan; Alonso's son, Ferdinand; Alonso's councilor, Gonzalo; and others are sailing back to Italy from the marriage of Alonso's daughter, Claribel to the king of Tunis, a storm arises off the coast of Prospero's island, and their ship splits.

Scene 1.2: Observing the storm and shipwreck, Miranda begs her father, Prospero, deposed duke of Milan, to stop the tempest. He assures her all is well and explains why he has caused the ship to wreck on his island. He recounts his brother's treachery in seizing the dukedom, Gonzalo's assistance to Prospero, and his first arrival with Miranda on the island. Now, Prospero says, fortune has brought his enemies to his shore and will allow him to recover his dukedom.

While Miranda sleeps, Prospero's sprite Ariel appears. He reports he has fulfilled Prospero's demands, forcing Alonso's ship to land but harming no one and letting the other ships in the fleet sail toward Naples. He has separated Ferdinand from his father and attendants and has left the ship's crew asleep below hatches. When Ariel asks to be set free, as Prospero has promised, Prospero reminds him that he was imprisoned in a pine tree for twelve years by the witch Sycorax, who had been banished to the island from Algiers. She died, leaving her son, the monster Caliban, to whom she gave birth on the island, its only other inhabitant. Prospero freed Ariel from his arboreal confinement and enslaved Caliban after Caliban tried to rape Miranda. Ariel agrees to serve Prospero willingly. Prospero now instructs Ariel to assume the shape of a sea nymph, and the sprite exits.

After awakening Miranda, Prospero and his daughter visit Caliban. Ariel reappears in the guise of a sea nymph; Prospero whispers instructions to him, and Ariel departs. Caliban curses Prospero, whom he accuses of stealing his island from him. He recalls how Prospero initially treated him kindly, and Caliban showed him the island's springs and fertile places, but now Caliban is imprisoned in a cave and forced to work for Prospero. Prospero orders Caliban to fetch fuel.

Caliban goes off, and Ariel returns with Ferdinand, whom Prospero intends for Miranda's husband. She falls in love at first sight, as does he. Prospero pretends to be angry with Ferdinand to avoid making their union too easy and so unappreciated (see *The Fantasticks*). He accuses Ferdinand of being a traitor. Miranda pleads for Ferdinand, but Prospero does not relent. She reassures Ferdinand as they all exit.

Scene 2.1: Gonzalo tries to cheer Alonso, who rejects Gonzalo's efforts to comfort him. Sebastian and Antonio mock Gonzalo. Sebastian criticizes his brother for marrying Claribel to an African and blames him for Ferdinand's apparent death. To distract Alonso, Gonzalo explains how he would govern the island so all would be equal and happy. Ariel enters to play music that puts everyone to sleep except Sebastian and Antonio. Antonio says he will kill Alonso, and Sebastian should kill Gonzalo. Then Sebastian will rule in Naples, and Antonio will no longer have to pay tribute to that kingdom. As the two prepare to execute their plot, Ariel reappears to awaken Gonzalo, who then wakes Alonso. They see Sebastian and Antonio with their swords drawn. The would-be assassins claim they heard lions roaring. All go off to search for Ferdinand; Ariel leaves to report to Prospero.

Scene 2.2: As Caliban is gathering fuel, Trinculo, a jester, appears. Caliban, having never seen anyone but Prospero, Miranda, and Sycorax, thinks Trinculo is a spirit sent by Prospero to torment him. To avoid detection, Caliban falls to the ground. Another storm seems about to begin, so Trinculo hides under Caliban's cloak. As soon as he does so, Stephano, Alonso's drunk butler, enters and thinks he has found a monster with four legs, which he will take back to Naples to present to some ruler, as natives (as well as plants and animals) were brought back from the New World to be shown as curiosities. When Caliban cries out, Stephano gives him liquor from the bottle he is carrying. Recognizing Stephano's voice, Trinculo calls to him, and Stephano drags him out from under Caliban's cloak. Caliban rises and swears to be Stephano's subject.

Scene 3.1: As Ferdinand is gathering logs at Prospero's command, Miranda enters, as does Prospero, unseen. She offers to help Ferdinand, who declines her assistance. Prospero is pleased to witness their profession of love for each other.

Scene 3.2: Ariel overhears Caliban's urging Stephano to kill Prospero. Imitating Trinculo's voice, Ariel keeps repeating, "Thou liest," causing Stephano to beat Trinculo.

Scene 3.3: Alonso, Sebastian, Antonio, Gonzalo, the lords Adrian and Francesco, and others are weary from searching for Ferdinand. Sebastian and Antonio say they will kill Alonso and Gonzalo that night. Prospero has spirits bring food and a table. As the men prepare to eat, Ariel enters as a harpy, makes the food vanish, and declares, "You are three men of sin" (l. 53), Alonso for supporting Antonio's usurpation of the dukedom of Milan; Antonio for usurping the dukedom, setting Prospero and Miranda adrift in a leaky boat, and now plotting to kill Alonso and Gonzalo; and Sebastian for joining this new conspiracy. Ariel says they are now being punished for their seizing Prospero's dukedom and banishing Prospero and Miranda. Prospero praises Ariel's performance. Alonso goes off to drown himself. The others exit. This scene owes much to book 3 of the *Aeneid*, and in book 1 of that work, Aeneas's ship is forced by a storm onto the coast of Tunis separate from the other nineteen vessels in his fleet. After the shipwreck, Aeneas falls in love with Dido, and she, with him, just as Ferdinand and Miranda fall in love, but in Shakespeare's play the lovers end more happily than in Virgil's poem. The storm in book 1 of the Aeneid is caused by Juno, seeking revenge against the Trojans because the Trojan Paris said Venus was more beautiful than she, just as Prospero has raised the tempest against those who wronged him.

Scene 4.1: Prospero agrees to the marriage of Ferdinand and Miranda but warns Ferdinand against premarital sex: "If thou dost break her virgin-knot before / All sanctimonious ceremonies may / With full and holy right be minist'red / No sweet aspersion shall the heavens let fall / To make this contract grow; but barren hate, / Sour-eyed disdain, and discord shall bestrew / The union of your bed with weeds so loathly / That you shall hate it both" (ll. 15–22). Anne Hathaway was pregnant by Shakespeare when they married. Was Shakespeare writing from experience here?

Prospero instructs Ariel to bring Alonso and his party to him. Meanwhile, he will stage a masque to celebrate the union of the lovers. Iris, Ceres, and Juno (goddess of weddings, hence the popularity of weddings during her month of June) bless them. Iris, messenger of the gods, goes off and returns with dancing nymphs. Remembering Caliban's plot against him, Prospero starts, and the masque abruptly ends. Prospero reassures the lovers, whom he sends to his cave.

Ariel reports he has left Caliban, Stephano, and Trinculo in a dirty pool. Prospero instructs Ariel to fetch gaudy clothes from Prospero's cave and hang them on a line. When Stephano and Trinculo take the garments, Prospero and Ariel set spirit dogs on the plotters, who flee.

Scene 5.1: Ariel has led Alonso and his companions to a grove in front of Prospero's cave and left them paralyzed there. Prospero instructs Ariel to bring the men to him. While Ariel is gone, Prospero delivers his "Ye elves of hills" speech, translated from Ovid's *Metamorphoses*, book 7. This speech is often viewed as Shakespeare's farewell to the theater. Although he subsequently wrote three more plays with John Fletcher (*Henry VIII*, *The Two Noble Kinsmen*, and *Cardenio*), *The Tempest* is his last independent work.

Prospero places the men in a charmed circle. He has Ariel bring his duke's robes from his cave and dress him. Then he sends Ariel to the ship to bring the ship's master and boatswain. Prospero breaks the spell on Alonso and his companions and reveals himself. Alonso restores the dukedom of Milan to Prospero, who welcomes Gonzalo and in an aside informs Sebastian and Antonio he knows of their plot to kill Alonso. When Alonso mourns the death of his son, Prospero replies he himself has lost a daughter (he means through marriage), then shows Ferdinand and Miranda playing chess in his cell.

Ariel fetches the master of the ship and the boatswain, who reports the ship is yare and fully rigged. Prospero tells Ariel to free Caliban, Trinculo, and Stephano and bring them. Prospero orders Caliban to prepare his cave to receive his guests before all the Europeans sail back to Italy. Ariel will provide "calm seas, auspicious gales" (l. 315) and then be free. And Caliban will once again be lord of his island.

The Two Noble Kinsmen

GREECE

Athens

An important Mycenean center, the city-state in the eighth century BCE was aristocratic. In 508 BCE Cleisthenes created a form of democracy in Athens, though broader democracy did not arrive until the 460s. Women and foreign residents still were not allowed to vote. Of a population of some 100,000, probably only about 10,000 could. Sacked by a Persian army in 480 BCE shortly before the Athenian navy defeated Persia at the Battle of Salamis (September 480 BCE), in 478 BCE Athens became an imperial city-state when it assumed leadership of the Delian League. Throughout the fifth century BCE, Athens and Sparta battled for hegemony in the First Peloponnesian War (461–446 BCE), followed by the Second Peloponnesian War (431–404 BCE), which ended in the defeat of Athens. The city quickly recovered, resumed its democracy in 403 BCE, and established a second Athenian Confederacy in 378 BCE. Following Philip of Macedon's victory at the Battle of Chaeronea (338 BCE), Greece came under Macedonian rule. In the Hellenistic period, Athens became a cultural center of the Mediterranean world under the rule of Alexander the Great's successors, the Antigonids, and remained so into the sixth century CE. After 146 BCE Greece was ruled by Rome. Later, Greece became part of the Ottoman Empire. When Greece gained independence in the nineteenth century, Athens became its capital. Shakespeare's Athens is, like its ruler, Theseus, mythical rather than historical. Shakespeare would have found accounts of Theseus and Hippolyta in Thomas North's translation of Plutarch's *Lives*, first published in 1579, and in Chaucer's "The Knight's Tale," a source for this play, as well as for *A Midsummer Night's Dream*. Though born in Troezen, Theseus, son of Aegeus, king of Athens, came to Athens as an adult and succeeded his father as ruler of that city, which celebrated him in the Theseia each October.

A Midsummer Night's Dream took the wedding of Theseus and Hipployta from Chaucer's "The Knight's Tale" and then wandered off on its own. *The Two Noble Kinsmen* follows Chaucer's poem.

Altars of Mars, Venus, and Diana

Scene 5.1: Arcite and Palamon enter with their knights. The cousins embrace, then Palamon and his knights leave. Arcite and his knights pray to Mars, the god of war, for victory and receive a sign of success. They depart, and Palamon and his knights pray to Venus, goddess of love, for victory. They, too, receive a sign of success. After they exit, Emilia prays to Diana, goddess of chastity and asks that the cousin who loves her most should triumph or she be allowed to remain unwed. In response she hears music, and a rose drops from a tree that has magically arisen, indicating she will have to marry.

Athens's Gates

Scene 1.3: Before the gates of Athens, Pirithous, Theseus's friend and general, resolves to join Theseus even though Theseus asked him to remain in the city (1.1.222–23). After he departs, the sisters Emilia and Hippolyta discuss the love the two men have for each other, and Emilia tells of her love for the dead Flavina. Emilia claims she will never love a man, but Hippolyta doubts her resolve. Emilia's statement reflects her Amazon nature. It is also yet another example of homoeroticism in Shakespeare.

Country near Athens

In *A Midsummer Night's Dream*, the woods outside Athens are enchanted. The landscape outside Athens here is darker, containing madness and strife. It is what the woods in *A Midsummer Night's Dream* would be like without fairies and with only one woman for the two men, Lysander and Demetrius.

Scene 2.3: Arcite, freed from prison but banished from Theseus's realm, envies the still-confined Palamon because he thinks Palamon can still see Emilia, while he himself cannot. He resolves to stay near Athens. He encounters four countrymen going to a festival to celebrate Emilia's birthday and decides to attend in disguise and compete in the games there. If he does well, he hopes to be able to see Emilia regularly.

Scene 3.1: On May Day Palamon encounters Arcite. Arcite promises to bring Palamon food and free him from his chains. Arcite will also bring Palamon a sword and armor so they can fight to determine who will love Emilia.

Scene 3.2: The jailer's daughter seeks unsuccessfully for Palamon and laments her separation from him.

Scene 3.3: Arcite brings Palamon food, wine, files, and clothes. As Palamon eats, they fondly recall former loves, but then they argue about Emilia. Arcite promises to return with a sword and armor for Palamon so the two can fight each other.

Scene 3.4: The jailer's daughter has gone mad because of her loss of Palamon.

Scene 3.5: Master Gerald the schoolmaster, five morris dancers, five women, and Timothy the tabor player practice to perform for Theseus but are missing Cicely. The mad jailer's daughter enters, singing, and becomes Cicely's replacement. On June 13, 1587, while the Queen's Men were at Thame, the actors John Towne and William Knell argued, and Towne killed Knell. The company went on to perform at Stratford but lacked a player. Samuel Schoenbaum has suggested in *Shakespeare, the Globe and the World* (1979, p. 43) that this is how Shakespeare got his start in the theater. It has also been suggested Shakespeare was a schoolmaster and actor in Lancashire (see "Hoghton, Lancashire" in appendix A). In his last play, Shakespeare may be reflecting on his theatrical beginnings. This scene is attributed to Fletcher, but Shakespeare might have introduced some autobiographical elements. A similar situation occurs in Shakespeare's other Athenian play, *A Midsummer Night's Dream*, when the rude mechanicals fear Bottom has been transported, thus preventing them from performing "The most lamentable comedy, and most cruel death of Pyramus and Thisbe" (1.2.11–13) for Theseus's wedding festivities. In that play Bottom reappears, and the play goes forward.

Everyone leaves except Gerald, who greets Theseus, Pirithous, Hippolyta, Emilia, Arcite, and their attendants when they appear hunting a stag. The schoolmaster introduces the dancers, whom Theseus rewards for their performance before proceeding with the hunt.

Scene 3.6: Arcite arrives with swords and armor for Palamon and himself. As they dress each other—one needs help donning armor—they praise each other's previous military deeds. When they begin to fight, they hear Theseus's hunting horns. Arcite urges Palamon to hide because he is an escaped prisoner, but Palamon insists on continuing their battle. Theseus, Hippolyta, Emilia, Pirithous, and attendants find the combatants; Theseus orders them executed for fighting without his permission. Palamon reveals himself and explains they are fighting over Emilia. Hippolyta, Emilia, and Pirithous beg Theseus to spare them. Emilia suggests Theseus banish the cousins and make them promise not to fight about her. Both men refuse to give her up. Theseus asks Emilia to choose one of them for her husband, but she says she cannot. Theseus now orders the cousins to return to Thebes and gather three knights each, then return to Athens to fight for Emilia. The winner will marry Emilia, and the loser will be beheaded.

Scene 5.3: Theseus, Hippolyta, Emilia, Pirithous, and attendants arrive at the site of the battle between Palamon and Arcite. Emilia refuses to watch. Alone, she meditates on her two lovers. From the field of battle come shouts for Palamon, then for Arcite; the play does not show the actual combat. Theseus, Hippolyta, and Pirithous present Arcite to Emilia as the victor.

Scene 5.4: Palamon and his knights enter, bound, along with the jailer, executioner, and guard. Facing execution, Palamon and his knights present their purses to the jailer, a common custom in Elizabethan England for upper-class people facing execution. As Palamon lays his head on the block, a messenger rushes in shouting, "Hold, hold!" (l. 40). He reports that Arcite, riding in Athens, was fatally hurt when his horse fell on top of him. Theseus, Hippolyta, and Emilia arrive with the injured Arcite in a chair. Arcite yields Emilia to his cousin and dies. Theseus says that Arcite acknowledged Palamon, having seen Emilia first, had the better claim to her. Theseus declares a period of mourning for Arcite, to be followed by Palamon's marriage to Emilia. Palamon's knights are pardoned.

Palace of Theseus

Scene 2.1: In the palace garden, adjacent to the prison, a wooer (unnamed in the play), wants to marry the jailer's daughter, who is in love with Palamon and Arcite, whom Theseus has imprisoned.

Scene 2.5: Arcite has won a garland at the festival's games. When he asks to serve Theseus, Pirithous assigns him to attend on Emilia.

Scene 4.2: Emilia contemplates the portraits of Palamon and Arcite. A gentleman reports their arrival, and a messenger and Pirithous describe the knights Palamon and Arcite have brought. All go to look at them. Emilia laments that one of the cousins must die because of his love for her.

The Prison

Scene 2.2: Palamon and Arcite lament their captivity but rejoice at being together and declare their mutual love. Then Emilia enters the garden near the jail; both fall instantly and passionately in love with her. Palamon declares he saw her first, so he has the right to love her, but Arcite counters he prefers to love Emilia than remain friends with Palamon. Thus, the cousins become enemies. Renaissance theory claimed male-male friendship was stronger than male-female love—there was no interest in female-female friendship. Shakespeare's plays, like life, repeatedly explode this idea, showing love always triumphs over friendship.

The jailer takes Arcite away to Theseus and returns to announce Arcite's perpetual banishment. Palamon is to be moved, so he will no longer see Emilia.

Scene 2.4: The jailer's daughter declares her love for Palamon.

Scene 2.6: The jailer's daughter relates she has freed Palamon and hidden him in the woods until she can bring him food and a file to remove his chains. She hopes he will return her love.

Scene 4.1: A friend tells the jailer that Palamon has cleared him of involvement in the escape, and the jailer's daughter has been pardoned. The wooer comes to say the jailer's daughter is mad. He heard her by the lake singing about Palamon and the jailer. She fled when she saw the wooer, but her uncle caught her. When her uncle brings her, she continues to sing and speak madly.

Scene 4.3: After the jailer's daughter leaves, a doctor tells the jailer and wooer that, to cure her, the wooer must pretend to be Palamon.

Scene 5.2: The doctor inquires of the wooer whether his advice has worked, and the wooer replies it has. The doctor tells the wooer to do whatever the jailer's daughter wants; when she asks to sleep with him, he agrees (following doctor's orders). The play here takes a different attitude toward premarital sex than Shakespeare's other works do, but this scene is attributed to John Fletcher. As the scene ends, the jailer and doctor go off to watch the combat between Palamon and Arcite.

A Temple

Scene 1.1: Theseus prepares to wed Hippolyta, queen of the Amazons, whom Theseus has defeated in battle. Three queens interrupt the procession and beg Theseus's aid against Creon, king of Thebes, who will not let them bury their dead husbands. Although Theseus wants to marry before dealing with Creon, Hippolyta and her sister, Emilia urge him to delay his marriage, and he agrees. Whether Hippolyta and Emilia are motivated by compassion for the queens or Hippolyta's eagerness to delay the marriage is unclear. In the opening of *A Midsummer Night's Dream*, Theseus thinks the four (actually three) days until his wedding are passing slowly, indicating his eagerness to marry, while Hippolyta thinks they are going by swiftly, revealing her reluctance. As Rosalind observes in *As You Like It*, centuries before Einstein, "Time travels in divers paces with divers persons" (3.2.308–9).

Thebes

Located in Boeotia in central Greece, there has been a settlement here since the Bronze Age. By the fourteenth century BCE, Thebes was an important center of the Mycenaean world, with a palace, a wall around the city, and an extensive cemetery that included a royal tomb. Homer refers to it as "seven-gated Thebes," as distinct from "hundred-gated Thebes" in Egypt. It was supposedly founded by Cadmus, the walls self-constructed through the music of Amphion's lyre. The city is the mythical birthplace of Hercules and Dionysus. Pindar was born here about 522 BCE. Under Epaminondas and Pelopidas, Thebes briefly held the hegemony of Greece in the fourth century BCE, but after the Battle of Chaeronea (338 BCE), the city played a small role in Hellenistic affairs. In 335 BCE Alexander destroyed the city after it rebelled against him; he spared only Pindar's house. The city was rebuilt by Cassander in 315 BCE. It came under Roman rule in 146 BCE. In the Byzantine period, it was the largest silk producer in the empire. It remains a market town with many ruins from antiquity.

Thebes is the center of many Greek myths and the setting for many Greek tragedies, including *Oedipus* and *Antigone*; the latter centered on King Creon's refusal to grant burial to Polynices, one of the sons of Oedipus, after he is killed in his attempt to capture the city from his brother Eteocles. In Chaucer's "Knight's Tale," the source of *The Two Noble Kinsmen*, a similar situation causes Theseus to fight and defeat Creon.

A Battlefield

Scene 1.4: On the battlefield before Thebes, Theseus defeats Creon and tells the queens to bury their husbands. A herald brings in the wounded Palamon and Arcite, and Theseus orders them treated by surgeons.

A Cemetery

Scene 1.5: The queens bury their dead husbands.

Creon's Palace

Scene 1.2: The cousins Palamon and Arcite, nephews of King Creon (these cousins do not appear in *Antigone* but are central to "The Knight's Tale"), plan to leave the court because of Creon's tyranny. When Valerius reports Theseus's invasion, they decide to fight for their city, not their king.

POEMS

The Rape of Lucrece

ITALY

Ardea

An ancient settlement founded in the eighth century BCE, located about twenty miles from Rome and two miles from the Mediterranean coast. In 509 BCE Lucius Tarquinius Superbus (i.e., "the proud," which is not a flattering epithet in Roman culture) besieged this capital of the Rutuli but was deposed before he could capture it. Under the Romans the town declined in importance and population. Remains of the ancient town are visible in the modern one. Shakespeare expanded his version from Ovid's *Fasti*, 2.721–852, using the locations he found in that work. Chaucer's *The Legend of Good Women* also used that source; Shakespeare may have drawn on Chaucer's dream vision as well.

As *The Rape of Lucrece* begins, the Romans are besieging Ardea. Sextus Tarquinius, son of the Roman king Lucius Tarquinius Superbus, sets off for the house of Lucrece in Collatium; he has fallen in lust with her either from seeing her ("The Argument") or hearing about her (the poem itself). "The Argument" derives from Livy's account of this incident (*Ab Urbe Condita Libri*, book 1, chaps. 57–58), the poem itself from Ovid's *Fasti*.

Collatium/Collatia

Nothing remains of this capital of the Sabines, ten miles from Rome, captured by the Romans in 585 BCE.

Sextus Tarquinius is welcomed by Lucrece when he comes to her house. Her husband, Lucius Tarquinius Collatinus, a kinsman of Sextus Tarquinius, is at Ardea with the Roman army. After dinner Sextus Tarquinius rapes her, threatening that, if she does not yield to him, he will kill her and a servant and put them together in bed so it will appear she was having an affair. After he departs, Lucrece sends for her husband.

When Collatinus arrives with others, including her father, Lucrece reveals what happened and asks the men to kill her attacker. She then kills herself so no woman can use her example as an excuse for being unchaste. Her husband and father lament her death, and Lucius Junius Brutus, heretofore regarded as a fool, urges them to swear vengeance.

Rome

Two legends deal with the founding of Rome. One concerns the Trojan Aeneas, son of Anchises and the goddess Venus, who came to Italy after the destruction of Troy and whose son Ascanius founded Alba Longa. The other myth deals with Romulus and Remus, descendants of Aeneas, who were nursed by a she-wolf and built Rome. When Remus mocked Romulus's just-started wall, Romulus killed him. The name of the city supposedly derives from Romulus. Archeology shows settlements in what is now Rome dating from about 1000 BCE. By the seventh century BCE, the Forum had been established as a public meeting place. By the sixth century BCE, Rome was a powerful city-state. Rome was originally a monarchy. The last king, Tarquinus Superbus, was expelled in an aristocratic coup that created a republic (509 BCE). Shakespeare's *Coriolanus* is set just after the expulsion of the king; the play captures the concern of the citizenry regarding the possible return of tyranny. Romans had an aversion to the title of king (rex). It was the fear that Julius Caesar would make himself king that led to his assassination on March 15, 44 BCE, the subject of Shakespeare's best-known Roman play. No Roman emperor used the title of king.

During the period of the republic, Rome continued to expand. By 300 BCE it was the dominant power in Italy. In the third century BCE, Rome took Sicily from the Carthaginians (241 BCE) and then Sardinia (238 BCE). In the second century BCE, Rome conquered Greece and Macedonia, northern Africa, and Spain. The late second century BCE, saw a rise in income inequality and the beginning of a century of political unrest that ended only with the defeat of Marc Antony at the Battle of Actium in 31 BCE and his death the next year in Egypt, leaving Octavius (to whom the Roman senate gave the title Augustus in 27 BCE) as sole ruler of the empire. These climactic events are depicted in Shakespeare's *Antony and Cleopatra*. By the late fourth century CE, the empire was being attacked by Goths, who, together with Franks and Vandals, overran much Roman territory. Rome was sacked in 410 CE and again in 455. On September 4, 476, Romulus Augustus, the last Roman emperor in the west, was deposed by the German chieftain Odoacer. *Titus Andronicus* is set in the fourth century CE as the Western Roman Empire is under threat and has begun to decline. Shakespeare's play raises questions about who the barbarians really are and who is civilized.

In 210 CE Rome held about a million people. The population dramatically declined in the Middle Ages. By 1300 there were about 25,000 people living in the city. From the eighth century until 1870, Rome was ruled by popes as part of the papal states. In the fifteenth century, the popes helped fund the Renaissance. In 1871 Rome became the capital of a united Italy.

Collatinus and Brutus take the body of Lucrece to Rome to expose Sextus Tarquinius's crime. The citizens banish Tarquin and establish the Roman Republic (509 BCE). The title of king became so abhorrent to Romans that, after the republic ended, emperors called themselves imperator, a military term for "commander," but never rex, "king."

"The Phoenix and Turtle"

This enigmatic sixty-seven-line poem begins,

> Let the bird of loudest lay
> On the sole Arabian tree
> Herald sad and trumpet be,
> To whose sound chaste wings obey.

The first five four-line stanzas summon birds to mourn the death of the phoenix and turtle. The next eight four-line stanzas offer a eulogy filled with paradoxes for the dead birds. In the final five three-line stanzas, Reason, which was confounded by the eulogy, presents its lament.

The phoenix has a long association with Arabia. In *The Tempest*, 3.3.21–24, Sebastian declares,

> Now I will believe
> That there are unicorns; that in Arabia
> There is one tree, the phoenix' throne, one phoenix
> At this hour reigning there.

Herodotus described the bird as being about the size of an eagle, red (or purple; *phoenix* means "purple") and gold in color. Every five hundred years, the phoenix would fly from Arabia to Heliopolis in Egypt to bring its aged parent to the Temple of the Sun, where the old bird would be covered in myrrh. In medieval bestiaries the phoenix is unique. In these accounts, when the bird gets old, it builds a funeral pyre, turns toward the sun, flaps its wings, and sets itself on fire. On the third or ninth day, a new bird rises from the ashes. The word *phoenix* means "palm tree," as well as "purple";

the pyre was believed to be built in a palm tree, the "sole Arabian tree" of line 2 of the poem. Given the bird's resurrection on the third day, it became a symbol for Christ. It also symbolized resurrection more generally and the Virgin Mary (because it gives birth without having sex). The bird's motto is *semper eadem* ("always the same"), which was that of Queen Elizabeth I, as well. The Phoenix Jewel (a gold pendant with enameled border dating from c. 1570–1580, housed in the British Museum, Museum number SLMisc. 1778) shows the profile of the queen on one side, the phoenix on the other, and she was often depicted with that bird. In *Henry VIII* Thomas Cranmer calls Elizabeth the "bird of wonder . . . , the maiden phoenix" (5.4.40).

The turtle of the poem is the turtledove. The dove symbolizes love, the Holy Ghost, Christ, the Virgin Mary, innocence, spiritual love, peace, chastity, and (because of its red feet) martyrdom. It also represents fertility and is the bird of Venus. Like the phoenix (which was used as a sign by some fire-fighting and fire-insurance companies), it is associated with fire. In Daniel 3:13–26 it appears above Shadrach, Meshach, and Abednego when they are in the fiery furnace, and at Pentecost the spirit of God descended on Jesus's disciples in tongues of flame.

Shakespeare's poem appeared in Robert Chester's *Love's Martyr, or Rosalin's Complaint, Allegorically Showing the Truth of Love, in the Constant Fate of the Phoenix and Turtle*. This anthology of poems includes pieces by Ben Jonson, John Marston, and George Chapman, as well as Shakespeare's contribution. The book was published in honor of the knighting of Sir John Salusbury on June 14, 1601, and the book is dedicated to him. He and his wife are candidates for being the phoenix and dove, as are the Earl and Countess of Bedford. Chester's "Love's Martyr" compares Elizabeth to the phoenix, and the Second Earl of Essex, once a favorite of the queen, has been proposed as the dove. If that was the intended meaning of the book, its publication was ill timed: Essex was executed on Elizabeth's order on February 25, 1601, a few months before the work appeared.

Perhaps the confusion over the poem's meaning reflects the inexplicability of love. In "The Canonization" John Donne wrote, "The phoenix riddle hath more wit / By us: we two being one, are it." Shakespeare's poem similarly describes love as this arithmetical muddle: "two distincts, division none: / Number there in love was slain" (ll. 27–28), and later, "Single nature's double name / Neither two nor one was called" (ll. 39–40). Love confounds reason.

The "Threnos" Reason utters to conclude the poem presents a bleak world in which "Truth and Beauty buried be" (l. 64). This dark mood coincides with the zeitgeist at the end of Elizabeth's reign. In his 1611 "The Anatomy of the World," John Donne wrote,

> And new philosophy calls all in doubt,
> The element of fire is quite put out;

> The sun is lost, and th' earth, and no man's wit
> Can well direct him where to look for it. . . .
> Tis all in pieces, all coherence gone[.]

In *Troilus and Cressida* (c. 1602), chivalry and heroism have yielded to cynicism. *Twelfth Night* (c. 1602) ends with Feste's doleful song, with its refrain, "For the rain it raineth every day." While the specific meaning of the poem remains elusive, it clearly captures the sense of an era's ending.

Sonnets 153 and 154

Bath, Somerset

Bath is located on the River Avon. Bath was supposedly founded by Bladud, father of King Lear. A leper, he saw his leprous pigs regain their health by bathing in the warm mud in the area. He did likewise and recovered. About 54 CE the Romans established baths here at what they called Aquae Sulis, from Sul, a local deity the Romans likened to Minerva. The Romans built a temple, now under the Pump Room, dedicated to Sulis Minerva. The West Saxons captured the town in 577, naming it Akemanceaster and then Aet Bath. In the Middle Ages, the town was a center of the cloth trade; Chaucer's Wife of Bath is a clothier. The city reached its pinnacle of fashion in the eighteenth century. In 1705 Beau Nash became master of ceremonies in the town and brought order to the city's social life. John Wood Sr. designed and John Wood Jr. used Bath stone to build the Circus (1754–1770s) and then the Crescent. Jane Austen lived in Bath from 1801 to 1806, and her first and last novels, *Northanger Abbey* and *Persuasion* (both published together in 1817), are set here. The Jane Austen Centre is located at 40 Gay Street.

Sonnets 153 and 154 are known as the Bath Sonnets for their setting. They describe the origin of the hot-water baths there from the attempt by nymphs to extinguish Cupid's love torch by submerging it in water. The torch was Cupid's emblem before the bow and arrow. The water cannot extinguish love (Song of Solomon, 8.7: "Many waters cannot quench love"); rather, Cupid's torch makes the waters perpetually hot. In addition to referring to the Song of Solomon, these two sonnets draw on the *Greek Anthology*. In the translation of John William Mackail, *Select Epigrams from the Greek Anthology* (1900):

> Here beneath the plane-trees, overborne by soft sleep, Love slumbered, giving his torch
> to the Nymphs' keeping; and the Nymphs said one to another, "Why do we delay? And

would that with this we might have quenched the fire in the hearts of mortals." But now, the torch having kindled even the waters, the amorous Nymphs pour hot water thence into the bathing pool.

In these two sonnets, the narrator goes to Bath to be cured, either of his love or of venereal disease caught from his love, but finds no remedy for either complaint.

Appendix A

Other Shakespearean Sites

Barton-on-the Heath, Warwickshire

Seventeen miles south of Stratford.

Shakespeare's maternal aunt and uncle Joan and Edmund Lambert lived here. In 1579 John Shakespeare mortgaged land from Mary Arden's dowry to the Lamberts for forty pounds. The money was never repaid. In 1588 and again in 1597, the Shakespeares sued to recover the land but never did. Shakespeare refers to this village in the induction of *The Taming of the Shrew*.

Bidford-on-Avon, Warwickshire

Seven miles southwest of Stratford-upon-Avon.

According to Stratford schoolmaster Joseph Greene (1712–1790), Shakespeare went to Bidford-on-Avon to drink at the Falcon Inn (now a house) on Church Street. The drunk Shakespeare went to sleep beneath a crab-apple tree; a descendant of that tree is still called Shakespeare's Tree. The next morning Shakespeare's companions wanted to resume drinking, but Shakespeare declined, bidding farewell to

> Piping Pebworth, Dancing Marston
> Haunted Hillboro, Hungry Grafton,
> Dodging Exhall, Popish Wixford,
> Beggarly Broom and Drunken Bidford.

The poem appears in the December 1794 *Gentleman's Magazine* (64: 1068) in a piece signed "M. E.," who wrote, "The epithets are strongly characteristic of his manner, being peculiarly and happily adapted to the several villages whence the miscellaneous group of Sippers had resorted to Bidford."

Billesley, Warwickshire

Church of All Saints

Three miles west of Stratford-upon Avon.

Although the current building dates from 1692, a church has stood on the site for a thousand years. Shakespeare may have been married here in 1582, and his granddaughter may have married her second husband here as well (June 5, 1649). Church records of the period are not extant.

Charlecote, Warwickshire

Charlecote House

Four miles east of Stratford.

The house was largely refurbished in Tudor style in the 1820s and 1830s by George Hammond and Mary Elizabeth Lucy, but it was initially built in 1558 by Sir Thomas Lucy. The Elizabethan Revival Library was added in 1830–1837, designed by Charles S. Smith. This library contains ivory-inlaid ebony furniture—eight chairs, two cabinets, and a sofa—thought to have been given by Queen Elizabeth I to Robert Dudley, Earl of Leicester, though in fact it came from India in the seventeenth century.

The surrounding deer park extends for 185 acres along the River Avon. Shakespeare is supposed to have poached deer, rabbits, or both here. Richard Davies (d. 1708), chaplain of Corpus Christi College, wrote that Shakespeare was

> much given to all unluckiness in stealing venison and rabbits particularly from Sr. Lucy who had him oft whipped and sometimes imprisoned and at last made him fly his native country to his great advancement. But his revenge was so great that he is his Justice Clodpate [Shallow in *2 Henry IV* and *The Merry Wives of Windsor*] and calls him a great man and that in allusion to his name bore three louses rampart for his arms.

According to the seventeenth-century Reverend William Fulman of Gloucestershire, Lucy, a justice of the peace, had Shakespeare whipped and imprisoned for poaching. In 1584 Lucy introduced a bill into Parliament making poaching a felony. In *The Merry Wives of Windsor*'s scene 1.1, Slender claims his dimwitted uncle Justice Robert Shallow has the "dozen white luces" in his ancient coat of arms (l. 15). A luce is a pike. The Lucy coat of arms includes three luces, but the Lucy tomb at Warwick displays a dozen. The Welsh parson Sir Hugh Evans responds, "The dozen white louses do become an old coat well" (l. 17). Shallow may thus be modeled on Sir Thomas Lucy. Also, Justice Shallow wants to bring a Star Chamber case against Falstaff because he has "beaten my men, killed my deer, and broke open my lodge" (1.1.106–7), as the young Shakespeare may have done. In *The Winter's Tale*, the shepherd observes, "I would there were no age between ten and three-and-twenty, or that youth would sleep out the rest; for there is nothing in the between but getting wenches with child, wronging the ancientry, stealing, fighting" (3.3.58–62). At eighteen Shakespeare got Anne Hathaway with child, and he may have wronged Sir Thomas Lucy, stolen Lucy's game, and fought with Lucy's gamekeepers. At twenty-three Shakespeare may have joined the Queen's Men when they passed through Stratford lacking an actor because of a recent duel at Thame, Oxfordshire, in which William Knell was killed (1587).

Nicholas Rowe, Shakespeare's first biographer (1709), claimed that, in retaliation for Lucy's treatment, Shakespeare wrote a satirical ballad against him. In the 1680s Joshua Barnes recorded a version:

> Sir Thomas was too covetous
>   To covet so much deer,
> When horns enough upon his head
>   Most plainly did appear.
>
> Had not his worship one deer left?
> What then? He had a wife
> Took pains enough to find him horns
> Should last him during life.

Thomas Jones (d. 1703) provided a different text:

> A parliament member, a justice of peace,
> At home a poor scare-crow, at London an ass,
> If lousy is Lucy, as some volke miscall it,
> Then Lucy is lousy whatever befall it:
> He thinks himself great,
> Yet an ass is his state,
> We allow by his ears but with asses to mate.
> If Lucy is lousy, as some volke miscall it,
> Sing lousy Lucy, whatever befall it.

Shakespeare supposedly affixed the poem to the gates of Charlecote House. Lucy then sought to prosecute Shakespeare, who fled to London.

Lucy was noted for his prosecution of Catholics. Some scholars believe Shakespeare and his family adhered to the old religion, in which case Shakespeare may have left Stratford to escape Lucy for that reason.

The property belongs to the National Trust and is open to the public.

Charlecote House, home of Sir Thomas Lucy. *Private Collection © Look and Learn/Bridgeman Images*

Hoghton, Lancashire

In his August 13, 1581, will, Alexander Hoghton of Lea Hall near Preston left to his half-brother Thomas his costumes if Thomas wanted to maintain players. If Thomas did not, Sir Thomas Hesketh of Rufford Old Hall (200 Liverpool Road, Rufford) was to have the clothes. And he asked Sir Thomas "to be ffreyndlye unto ffoke Gyllome and William Shakeshafte now dwellynge with me and eyther to take them vnto his Servyce or els to helpe theyme to some good master as my truste ys he will." Is William Shakespeare "William Shakeshafte"? Did Shakespeare, after leaving school in about 1579, serve as tutor to Hoghton's children? The Stratford schoolmaster John Cottam from Lancashire had ties to the Hoghtons and might have recommended Shakespeare to them.

Fernando Strange, Fifth Earl of Derby, lived nearby. He was patron to Lord Strange's Men, who performed four of Shakespeare's early plays: *Titus Andonicus* and the three parts of *Henry VI*. Might Lord Strange have met Shakespeare at Rufford Old Hall in the early 1580s? Is this how Shakespeare got his start in the London theater?

Hoghton Tower, dating from 1560–1565, though much renovated, was one of Alexander Hoghton's homes. The other was nearby at Preston (see "Preston, Lancashire"

in this appendix). Hoghton Tower is sometimes open to the public and is adminis-
tered by the Hoghton Tower Preservation Trust.

Kenilworth, Warwickshire

Kenilworth Castle

Occupied by the Romans, in the 1086 Domesday Book, the area is called Chinewrde
("the farm of a woman named Cynehild").

Kenilworth Castle was begun in the 1120s by Geoffrey de Clinton. Among its owners was John of Gaunt, father of Henry IV, who added the Strong Tower, Banqueting
Hall, and southern rooms. From 1399 to 1563, it served as a royal residence. In 1563
Queen Elizabeth gave the castle to Robert Dudley, Earl of Leicester, who enlarged the
castle. He entertained her here in 1565, 1568, 1572, and 1575. The festivities for this
last royal visit were the most elaborate. Sir Walter Scott described them in his novel
Waverley (1814). Among the displays was a water pageant, with Arion riding on a dolphin's back, which Shakespeare mentions in *A Midsummer Night's Dream* (2.1.148–
54) and again in *Twelfth Night* (1.2.15). The story of Arion charming a dolphin with
his music is recounted in Ovid's *Fasti*, 3.83–118, from which Shakespeare could have

Kenilworth Castle. *Courtesy of the Library of Congress, LC-DIG-ppmsca-52391*

drawn his allusion. Still, it is pleasant to imagine that in July 1575 the eleven-year-old Shakespeare went to Kenilworth, about eleven miles from Stratford-upon-Avon, and saw Dudley's aquatic entertainment. Because Shakespeare's father was a prominent Stratford citizen, he may even have been invited to the festivities. In *A Midsummer Night's Dream*, Shakespeare also mentions Cupid's aiming his arrow "At a fair vestal thronèd by the west," but the "imperial vot'ress passed on, / In maiden meditation, fancy free" (2.1.158, 163–64), perhaps a reference to Dudley's unsuccessful attempt to win Elizabeth's hand at this 1575 celebration.

In 1611 the castle again became a royal possession. Charles II gave the castle to Edward Hyde, Earl of Clarendon, whose descendants owned the property until 1937. The extensive ruins of the castle and its Elizabethan garden are maintained by English Heritage, and the site is open to the public.

London

Bell Inn

Carter Lane, off Gracechurch Street [Underground stops: Liverpool Street, Aldgate East]

One of four inns where plays were staged in the Elizabethan period from 1576 to 1594, when the city banned plays in these locations. On January 2, 1567, the brothel-keeper John Shawe claimed that "little Margaret," a prostitute, lived "at the Bell beyond Shoreditch church," where Lawrence Dutton, an actor, "kepes her." In 1576 the prostitute Godlyfe White attended a play at the Bell Inn with a tailor and a Mr. Wally's wife. Afterward they went to a house where the tailor had sex with her. In 1578 Elizabeth Everys attended a play here and met Benjamin Gunston, who gave her five shillings with which to buy a pair of gloves for his sake.

The inn dates from 1424 and ceased operations in 1708. On October 25, 1598, Richard Quiney, whose son Thomas would marry Shakespeare's younger daughter, Judith, in 1616, wrote the only known letter to Shakespeare. Quiney, in London on Stratford town business, had incurred expenses and asked Shakespeare for a loan (or to arrange a loan) of thirty pounds. Because the letter was found among Quiney's papers, it may never have been sent, though Shakespeare might have returned it with an answer.

Bel Savage Inn

68 Ludgate Hill [Underground stops: St. Paul's, Blackfriars]

Used by a variety of acting companies, it was one of four inns within the city licensed for a time to stage plays. It probably takes its name from the Savage family, fifteenth-century owners of the inn. Plays were performed here from at least 1575. From 1583 the Queen's Men used this location, as well as the Black Bull Inn (see the next entry in this appendix). Whereas the Black Bull stage was outdoors, the Bel Savage had an enclosed space for performance. Shakespeare may have acted here. The antiquarian

William Lambarde in 1596 wrote of the Bel Savage as a place to see "bear-baiting, interludes or fence-play," that is, fencing. According to the Puritan play-hating William Prynne, the devil once appeared here during a production of Christopher Marlowe's *Dr. Faustus*.

The inn dates from at least 1420. The *Bel* may derive from the sign of a bell marking its location or from its proximity to the Old Bailey. In 1616 Pocahontas stayed here. The building was destroyed in the 1666 Great Fire of London but was rebuilt by 1676. A 1674 advertisement claimed it had forty rooms and stables for one hundred horses, making it an important coaching inn. In 1852 John Cassell's publishing house took over part of the site, and the next year it took over the entire inn. The building was demolished for a railway viaduct in 1873. Cassell built new offices behind the old location. In 1940 German bombs destroyed this building and a million books within. In 1967 the site was cleared for a garden. In *The Pickwick Papers*, Tony Weller begins and ends his journeys from and to London here.

Black Bull Inn
92 Bishopsgate Street Within [Underground stops: Liverpool Street, Aldgate, Bank]

This inn had a permanent stage. The Queen's Men played here, and Shakespeare may have acted here. In 1584 the city of London licensed four inns to stage plays: Bel Savage Inn, the Black Bull Inn, the Bell Inn, and the Cross Keys Inn. A decade later the Privy Council banned plays within the city. The building was demolished in 1866.

Blackfriars Theatre
[Underground stop: Blackfriars]

The theater takes its name from the Dominican priory, founded in 1276, that occupied this location until the dissolution of the monasteries under Henry VIII. The Dominicans wore black robes that gave them their nickname. In 1529 a court met here to hear Henry VIII's divorce case against Catherine of Aragon (the "King's Great Matter"), and in November of that year, Parliament met here to bring a bill of attainder against Cardinal Thomas Wolsey (who had failed to get Henry the divorce he wanted).

In 1538 the monastery was dissolved. Most of the buildings were demolished, but in 1556–1584 and again in 1597–1642, the refectory was used as a theater. The Children of the Chapel performed here (1577–1584 and 1600–1608). In 1596 James Burbage bought this location for six hundred pounds to serve as an indoor venue for the Lord Chamberlain's Men (Shakespeare's company) because the Theatre (see "The Theatre" under "London" in this appendix) was open to the air. Hence, the Theatre was cold in the winter and relied on natural lighting. Local residents objected to an adult acting company's using this space—theaters attracted prostitutes and pickpockets, as well as crowds blocking the streets. Their petition stated, "A common playhouse . . . will grow to be a very great annoyance and trouble, not only to all noblemen and gentlemen near thereabout inhabiting, but also a general inconvenience to all the inhabitants of the same precinct, by reason of the gathering together of all manner of lewd and vagrant persons." They also objected to the noise. Among those who signed the petition was George Carey, Second Lord Hunsdon, who would soon become Lord Chamberlain, the licenser of plays and patron of Shakespeare's company. Richard Field, Shakespeare's friend from Stratford who published *Venus and Adonis* and printed *The Rape of Lucrece*, also signed. The Children of the Chapel, a boys' acting company, were allowed to use the Blackfriars Theatre from 1600 to 1608, when the King's Men (formerly Lord Chamberlain's Men) were given permission to perform here. The boys' company had offended the French ambassador with their production of George Chapman's *The Conspiracy and Tragedy of Charles, Duke of Byron* (1608). As a result, the boys' company was suppressed. The King's Men continued to perform here until the Puritans closed the theaters in 1642.

This theater was sixty-six feet long and forty-six feet wide, with two or three galleries. The seating capacity was six hundred to one thousand. Prices began at sixpence, six times the cost of a place to stand in the pit of an open-air theater like the Globe. According to one account, the King's Men "got, and yet doth, more in one winter in the said great hall by a thousand pounds than they were used to get on the Bankside" (i.e., at the Globe). Neighbors still objected to the crowds the theater drew, complaining, "Inhabitants cannot come to their houses, nor bring in their necessary provisions of beer, wood, coal or hay, nor the tradesmen or shopkeepers utter their wares, nor the passengers go to the common water stairs without danger of their lives and limbs."

Because the stage used artificial lighting, actors could achieve more special effects, and because the higher ticket prices attracted a more educated audience, plays performed here could be more sophisticated. Because the candles had to be trimmed, music was played between acts. The five-act structure of plays may have resulted from this need to trim candles periodically during performances. The new Globe Theatre (see "The Globe Theatre" under "London" in this appendix) now includes an indoor acting space (Sam Wanamaker Theatre) that replicates the experience of seeing a play at the Blackfriars. The Sam Wanamaker Theatre is smaller than the Blackfriars and, unlike the Globe, does not try to reconstruct the earlier acting space. But productions are lit exclusively with candles, and audiences sit on backless benches.

On March 10, 1613, Shakespeare bought Blackfriars' Gatehouse in Ireland Yard for £140. Henry Walker had bought the gatehouse from Matthew Bacon in 1604, and Walker sold it to Shakespeare. The Gatehouse had connections to Catholic missionaries and to Catholic members of the Gunpowder Plot, who sought refuge here after the plot failed. (See *The Times* [London], April 23, 1928, p. 15) Shakespeare rented the gatehouse to John Robinson, who lived here until 1639. Robinson's brother Edward studied at the Catholic seminary of the English College in Rome. The refectory was torn down in 1655 (August 6), and the Great Fire of London (1666) destroyed the remains of the monastery, except for part of a wall that survives in Ireland Yard. Playhouse Yard stands at the site of the former theater.

British Library
96 Euston Road [Underground stop: King's Cross St. Pancras]
Opened in 1997 in a building designed by Sir Colin St. John Wilson, it was the largest public building erected in Britain in the twentieth century. It houses over 16 million books and can seat 1,200 readers. The library's origins go back to the founding of the British Museum in 1753. In that year the museum bought Sir Hans Sloane's book collection for £20,000. Robert Cotton's manuscripts, given to the nation in 1700, and those collected by two generations of the Harley family, bought for £10,000, joined these volumes. In 1757 King George II donated the Old Royal Library and made the British Museum a copyright depository so it would receive a copy of every copyrighted book printed in Britain. George IV gave the museum 65,000 printed volumes in 1823. The British Library was established as a separate entity in 1973.

In 1757 the English actor David Garrick commissioned a marble statue of William Shakespeare from the French sculptor Louis-François Roubiliac for his Palladian Temple to Shakespeare at Hampton. Garrick himself posed for the statue. It was bequeathed, along with Garrick's books, to the British Museum in 1779; in 2005 it was transferred to the British Library. The library also houses a copy of Shakespeare's First Folio (1623), the first collected edition of Shakespeare's plays, which includes eighteen works not previously printed, as well as many other Shakespeare rarities, including one of only two copies of the 1603 first printed edition (Q1) of *Hamlet*. The British Library copy lacks the title page. The other copy, at the Huntington Library in San Marino, California, is missing the last leaf.

Christopher Mountjoy's House
Corner of New London Wall and Noble Street [Underground stops: St. Paul's, Barbican, Moorgate]
From about 1603 to 1605, Shakespeare lived with the Huguenot family of Christopher Mountjoy in a house that stood at the corner of Silver and Muggle (Monkwell) Streets opposite St. Olave's Churchyard. The three-story house was probably timber-framed and had pitched gables. The ground floor was the Mountjoy workshop, where he made tires, fancy headdresses for women. Among his customers was James I's wife, Queen Anne. The building was destroyed in the Great Fire of London, but a large house was rebuilt on the site. This structure ran sixty-three feet along Silver Street and the same along Monkwell. By the mid-nineteenth century the Cooper's Arms, a

public house, stood here. The German bombing attack of December 29, 1940, reduced the area to rubble. In the 1960s the Barbican development was erected here. Charles Nicholl in *The Lodger* (2007) places the Mountjoy house in the current London Wall carpark.

Shakespeare was involved in a Mountjoy family drama. On May 11, 1612, he testified at the Court of Requests, Westminster, in the case of *Belott v. Mountjoy*. Stephen Belott, former apprentice to Christopher Mountjoy, was suing his one-time master over what Belott claimed was a sixty-pound dowry Mountjoy had promised to pay him on the day he married Mountjoy's daughter Mary, whom Belott had wed in 1604. Belott also said Mountjoy had promised to leave the couple two hundred pounds in his will. Mountjoy denied both claims.

According to the court record, Mountjoy's wife, Marie, "did solicit and entreat this deponent [Shakespeare] to move and persuade the said complainant [Belott] to effect the said marriage, and accordingly this deponent did move and persuade the complainant thereunto." Another witness stated Shakespeare performed a troth-plighting or handfasting, in which the couple would give "each other's hand to the hand," a form of betrothal, even marriage, in Elizabethan England. In *The Winter's Tale*, 4.4.386, the shepherd performs this rite for his daughter Perdita and Prince Florizel. In *As You Like It*, 4.1.121, Rosalind takes Orlando's hand and asks Celia to marry them.

In his testimony Shakespeare said, "The defend[an]t [Mountjoy] promised to geue the said complainant a porcion in marriadg with Marye his daughter. but what certayne porcion he Rememberithe not. Nor when to be payed nor knoweth that the defendant promised the plaintiff twoe hundred poundes with his daughter Marye at the tyme of his decease." He also stated, "he can saye noth[ing] touching any parte or poynte of the same Interrogatory for he knoweth not what Implementes and necessaries of household stuffe the defendant gaue the plaintiff in marriadge wth his daughter Marye."

Records from the Court of Requests and the French Church (to which the case was referred) indicate Belott never got his sixty pounds. Belott seems to have reduced his demand to ten pounds, which arbitration further cut to twenty nobles (six pounds, six shillings, sixpence), but Mountjoy refused to pay even that sum. Church records also show Mountjoy took his maid Isabel as his lover after his wife died in the fall of 1606. On February 27, 1614, Mountjoy was suspended from the church. He married Isabel on August 21, 1615. In his will, dated January 26, 1620, he left his daughter and son-in-law a quarter of his estate, bequeathing the rest to his wife.

City of London School
Victoria Embankment [Underground stops: Embankment, Charing Cross]

This prestigious school for boys aged ten to eighteen has a stone figure of Shakespeare by John Daymond and Son (1882).

Cross Keys Inn

16 Gracechurch Street [Underground stops: Liverpool Street, Aldgate East]

One of the four city inns where plays could be staged, it was used by the Lord Chamberlain's Men, Shakespeare's company, and perhaps Lord Strange's Men, as well. In October 1594 Lord Hunsdon, the Lord Chamberlain, wrote to the Lord Mayor of London,

> Where my now company of players have been accustomed for the better exercise of their quality, and for the service of her Majesty if need so require, to play this winter time within the City at the Cross Keys in Gracious [Gracechurch] Street, these are to require and pray your Lordship to permit and suffer them to do so.

In 1594 the Privy Council, prompted by the Lord Mayor, banned the performance of plays within the city. Plays had been performed here since at least 1576. The building dated from 1309, when it was the home of Sir Hugh Nevill. In the fifteenth century, Dick Whittington, Lord Mayor of London, lived here.

The Cross Keys burned down in the 1666 Great Fire of London, was rebuilt, and burned again in 1734. Again rebuilt, it was a popular coaching inn in the early nineteenth century, with some forty coaches arriving and leaving each day. In Charles Dickens's *Great Expectations*, chapter 20, Pip reports, "The journey from our town to the metropolis, was a journey of about five hours. It was a little past mid-day when the four-horse stage-coach by which I was a passenger, got into the ravel of traffic frayed out about the Cross Keys, Wood-street, Cheapside, London." Dickens himself arrived here from Rochester as a boy. In chapter 12 of *The Uncommercial Traveller* he recalled,

> As I left Dullborough in the days when there were no railroads in the land, I left it in a stage-coach. Through all the years that have since passed, have I ever lost the smell of the damp straw in which I was packed—like game—and forwarded, carriage paid, to the Cross Keys, Wood-street, Cheapside, London? There was no other inside passenger, and I consumed my sandwiches in solitude and dreariness, and it rained hard all the way, and I thought life sloppier than I had expected to find it.

Railings with crossed keys on them mark the site of the old inn. The inn was adjacent to the church of St. Peter Cheap in Wood Street, which was destroyed in the 1666 Great Fire of London and not rebuilt. The crossed keys are St. Peter's.

The current Crosse Keys Pub is located at 9 Gracechurch Street.

Curtain Theatre

18 Hewett Street [Underground stops: Old Street, Shoreditch, Liverpool Street]

A curtain is part of a wall between two bastions. The Curtain Theatre, named for this feature, was London's second playhouse, built in 1577 and located two hundred yards south of the Theatre (see "The Theatre" under "London" in this appendix). It was located a mile north of the city walls and so outside the jurisdiction of the city's Puritan council, which hated plays. It did not have a theater curtain. All London's early theaters had thrust stages, which did not isolate the acting space from the audience. Unlike the Theatre and the Globe (see "The Globe Theatre" under "London" in this appendix), it was rectangular rather than polygonal. In 1578 L. Grenade wrote of the two theaters in Shoreditch,

> At one end of this meadow are two very fine theatres [the Curtain and the Theatre], one of which is magnificent in comparison with the other and has an imposing appearance on the outside [probably the Theatre]. This theatre can hold from 4 to 5,000 people [probably about 3,000] and it is said that a great Lord had it erected. Now, both of these were erected and dedicated for the performance of some plays and other spectacles, most of which comprise actions made up for pleasure rather than ones that have actually taken place.

In 1592 Henry Lanham, owner of the Curtain, agreed to share the theater's profits with James Burbage, owner of the Theatre, and his brother-in-law John Brayne. Between 1597 and 1599, Shakespeare's company used this venue because the Theatre was closed as a result of a dispute with the owner of the land (Giles Allen) on which that building sat. *2 Henry IV* was staged here. John Marston mentions *Romeo and Juliet* being applauded at the Curtain (*Scourge of Villanie*, 1598).

Thomas Platter, a visitor from Switzerland, described London's theaters in 1599:

> These places are built in such a fashion that the players perform on a raised stage so that every one can see what happens. Nevertheless there are different gangways and places where one sits more comfortably, but then you have to pay more. If you stand below you pay one English penny, but if a seat is required you have to go through another door and pay an extra penny. If you wish to sit on cushions in the most comfortable seat, so that you can not only see everything but can be seen yourself, you enter by yet another door and pay a further penny.

Stephen Gosson in *Playes Confuted* (1582) claimed,

> In the playhouses at London, it is the fashion of youths to go first into the yard, and to carry their eye through every gallery, then like ravens, where they spy the carrion thither they fly, and press as near to the fairest as they can . . . they give them apples, they dally with their garments to pass the time, they minister talk upon odd occasions, and either bring them home to their houses on small acquaintance, or slip into taverns when the plays are done.

Elephant Inn

119 Newington Causeway [Underground stops: Elephant and Castle, Kennington]

Shakespeare refers to this place in *Twelfth Night*, 3.3.39 and 48–49. Unlike some other inns, such as the Sagittary in Othello (1.1.155), this one was real. The current inn on this site postdates Shakespeare's time, so the actual location of Shakespeare's Elephant is uncertain. Shakespeare puts it in Southwark ("in the south suburbs") and so not far from the Globe.

Garrick Club

15 Garrick Street [Underground stops: Covent Garden, Leicester Square]

Founded in 1831, the club's members have included many of England's leading actors, though membership is not limited to thespians. English actor David Garrick, for whom the club is named, commissioned Louis-François Roubiliac to carve a bust of Shakespeare for the Shakespeare Jubilee in 1769. This bust now resides in the Garrick Club. Another such bust resides at the British Library, and a plaster version is held by the Shakespeare Memorial Library, Stratford-upon-Avon.

The Globe Theatre

21 New Globe Walk [Underground stops: Blackfriars, Mansion House, St. Paul's, London Bridge, Southwark]

Nicholas Brend, a friend of John Heminge of the Lord Chamberlain's Company, inherited land near the Rose Theatre (see "Rose Theatre" under "London" in this appendix) in Southwark. Shakespeare's company took a lease on this land, and on December 28, 1598, the Burbages (Richard, the great actor, and his brother Cuthbert), the carpenter Peter Street (who built the Fortune Theatre and also worked on the Blackfriars Theatre), and workers began dismantling the Theatre north of the river and transporting the timbers across the Thames. Members of the company took shares in the new theater. The Burbages got 50 percent; Shakespeare, John Heminge, Henry Condell, Augustus Philips, and William Sly each got 10 percent. The building had twenty sides, was one hundred feet across, and had a stage almost fifty feet wide. It could hold as many as 3,500 people. Construction was finished by May 16, 1599, but the company waited for an auspicious day to stage its first production. The Globe opened on June 12, which in the Julian calendar then in use in England was the summer solstice. (Protestant England rejected the Gregorian calendar until 1752 because the calendar had been created by a Catholic pope.) The first play staged here may have been *Henry V*, though *Julius Caesar* and *As You Like It* are other candidates for this distinction.

This first Globe burned down on June 29, 1613, during a production of *Henry VIII*. Henry Wotton described what happened in a letter to Edmund Bacon dated July 2, 1613:

> The Kings Players had a new Play called *All Is True*, representing some principal pieces of the Reign of Henry 8, which was set forth with many extraordinary circumstances of Pomp and Majesty, even to the matting of the stage; the Knights of the Order, with their Georges and Garter, the Guards with their embroidered Coats, and the like: sufficient in truth within a while to make greatness very familiar, if not ridiculous. Now, King *Henry* making a masque at the Cardinal *Wolsey's* House, and certain Canons [*sic*] being shot off at his entry [scene 1.4], some of the Paper, or other stuff wherewith one of them was stopped, did light on the Thatch, where being thought at first but an idle smoak, and their eyes more attentive to the show, it kindled inwardly, and ran round like a train, consuming within less than an hour the whole House to the very grounds.
>
> This was the fatal period of that vertuous Fabrique; wherein yet nothing did perish, but wood and straw, and a few forsaken Cloaks; only one man had his Breeches set on fire, that would perhaps, have broyled him, if he had not by the benefit of a provident wit put it out with bottle ale.

The theater was rebuilt the next year with a tiled rather than a thatched roof and was closed in 1642 by the Puritans, who then demolished the building. The third Globe opened in 1997. It is the only thatched building in London. The American actor Sam Wanamaker was a leading advocate for rebuilding the Globe. In 1970 he founded the Shakespeare Globe Trust. The indoor theater at the Globe, modeled on such Jacobean indoor theaters as the Blackfriars (see "Blackfriars Theatre" under "London" in this appendix), is named for him. The new Globe stands 750 feet from the site of the original. The site of Shakespeare's Globe is now mostly under 67-70 Anchor Terrace, which is a listed (protected) building.

For a penny (the cost of a loaf of bread in 1600), the groundlings could stand around the stage. Seating in the lower galleries cost twopence; a cushion cost another penny, as did seating in the upper gallery. The most expensive place from which to watch the play was the stage itself, where gallants sat as much to be seen as to see. The theater relied on natural lighting.

The Globe takes its name from the Latin tag *totus mundus agit histrionem*, which Shakespeare loosely translated in *As You Like It* (2.7.138–39) as "All the world's a stage, / And all the men and women merely players." When a play was to be performed, the theater would fly a flag, on which that motto was printed, along with the image of Hercules holding up the globe of the world. In *Hamlet*, discussing the "tragedians of the city" who are visiting Elsinore, Hamlet asks whether the boy actors

The interior of the reconstructed Globe Theatre. © *James Brittain/Bridgeman Images*

now "carry it away." Rosencrantz replies, "Ay, that they do, my lord—Hercules and his load, too," referring to the Globe's emblem.

Gray's Inn
Gray's Inn Road [Underground stops: Chancery Lane, Holborn]

The building dates from the late thirteenth or early fourteenth century. The inn takes its name from Reginald de Grey. The Greys of Wilton owned the property in the fourteenth century. In Shakespeare's day this was the largest and most fashionable of the four Inns of Court, where lawyers were educated. (See also "Middle Temple" in *1 Henry VI*.) Gray's Inn was especially popular among prominent Catholic families, and its members included Henry Wriothesley, Third Earl of Southampton, to whom Shakespeare dedicated *Venus and Adonis* (1593) and *The Rape of Lucrece* (1594). Francis Bacon and William Cecil, First Baron Burghley (chief adviser to Queen Elizabeth), were also members. Bacon designed its gardens.

Masques were performed here from at least 1527. On December 28, 1594, Shakespeare's *The Comedy of Errors* was staged at Gray's Hall (built 1556).

In *2 Henry IV*, 3.2.34, Robert Shallow recalls fighting with Samson Stockfish behind Gray's Inn.

Hampton Court Palace
Richmond

Located fifteen miles southwest of London on the banks of the Thames. Thomas Wolsey bought this site in 1514 from the Order of St. John of Jerusalem. Here he built a palace with 280 rooms for guests. In 1528 he gave the palace to Henry VIII in an unsuccessful effort to regain the king's favor, lost because of Wolsey's inability to secure for Henry papal nullification of his marriage to Catherine of Aragon so he could marry Anne Boleyn. The next year Henry seized Wolsey's lands and goods. Henry enlarged the building and installed the astronomical clock by Nicholas Oursian (1540); the clock still works. All of Henry's wives except for Catherine of Aragon lived here. Katherine Howard, Henry's fifth wife, was arrested here for infidelity; her ghost supposedly roams the "Haunted Gallery."

Elizabeth I always celebrated Christmas at Hampton Court. Celebrations included plays, and the Great Hall is the oldest surviving Elizabethan theater in England. The King's Men performed for James I here during Christmas 1603–1604. In 1590 the Duke of Württemberg described Hampton Court as the "most magnificent royal palace of any that may be found in England, or indeed in any other Kingdom."

In the late seventeenth century, William and Mary commissioned Sir Christopher Wren to demolish the Tudor palace and replace it with a new Versailles. Because of the death of Queen Mary in 1694 and lack of funds, only Henry VIII's state apartments were destroyed, and four new ranges were built in the neoclassical style. George II was the last monarch to live here, and Queen Victoria opened the palace to the public (1851).

Leicester Square
[Underground stop: Leicester Square]
In this little oasis near the National Gallery and National Portrait Gallery and amid the West End theaters and a discount theater ticket booth stands a marble statue of Shakespeare by Giovanni Fontana. Fontana adapted William Kent's design, executed by Peter Scheemakers, for the Shakespeare memorial in Poets' Corner, Westminster Abbey.

Liberty of the Clink
Shoreditch, Clink Street [Underground stop: London Bridge]
By 1599 Shakespeare was living in the Liberty of the Clink near the newly built Globe Theatre. He remained here until about 1603. The Liberty of the Clink belonged to the Bishop of Winchester. In the sixteenth century, the Clink Prison was his, as well. The prison was destroyed in the 1780 Gordon Riots. A museum at 1 Clink Street now shows the history of the prison.

Mermaid Tavern
29-30 Bread Street [Underground stops: Mansion House, St. Paul's]
In a verse epistle to Ben Jonson, his fellow dramatist Francis Beaumont wrote,

> What things have we seen
> Done at the Mermaid? Heard words that have been
> So nimble, and so full of subtle flame,
> As if that every one from whence they came
> Had meant to put his whole wit in a jest,
> And had resolv'd to live a fool, the rest
> Of his dull life. (*Master Francis Beaumont's Letter to Ben Jonson*)

The Mermaid Tavern, Cheapside, was located at the corner of Bread and Friday (now Cannon) Streets. It dated back to at least 1411. Thomas Coryate in *Traveller for the English Wits* (1616) wrote of a "right Worshipfull Fraternitie of Sirenical Gentlemen, that meet the first Friday of every Month, at the sign of the Mermaid in Bread Street." *Sirenical* derives from the Latin for "sea cow." The order Sirenia includes manatees, which have been mistaken for mermaids.

In his posthumously published *The History of the Worthies of England* (1662), Thomas Fuller claimed,

> Many were the wit-combats betwixt him [Shakespeare] and Ben Jonson: which two I behold like a Spanish great Galleon and an English man of war. Master Jonson (like the former) was built far higher in learning: solid, but slow in his performances. Shakespeare, with the English man of war, lesser in bulk, but lighter in sailing, could turn with all tides, tack about, and take advantage of all winds, by the quickness of his wit and invention.

According to William Gifford, in his 1816 edition of the works of Ben Jonson,

> Sir Walter Raleigh, previously to his unfortunate engagement with the wretched Cobham and others, had instituted a meeting of beaux esprits at the Mermaid, a celebrated tavern in Friday-street. Of this Club, which combined more talent and genius, perhaps, than ever met together before or since, our author [Jonson] was a member; and here, for many years, he regularly repaired with Shakespeare, [Francis] Beaumont, [John] Fletcher, [John] Selden, [Sir Robert] Cotton, [Thomas] Carew, Martin, [John] Donne, and many others. . . . Here, in the full flow and confidence of friendship, the lively and interesting "wit combats" took place between Shakespeare and our author; and hither, in probable allusion to them, Beaumont fondly lets his thoughts wander, in his Letter to Jonson, from the country.

Keats wrote "Lines on the Mermaid Tavern." The first stanza reads,

> Souls of Poets dead and gone,
> What Elysium have ye known,
> Happy field or mossy cavern,
> Choicer than the Mermaid Tavern?
> Have ye tippled drink more fine
> Than mine host's Canary wine?
> Or are fruits of Paradise
> Sweeter than those dainty pies
> Of venison? O generous food!
> Drest as though bold Robin Hood
> Would, with his maid Marian,
> Sup and bowse from horn and can.

In "Shakespeare and the Host of the Mermaid" (1933), Leslie Hotson showed that Shakespeare knew William Johnson, the Mermaid's proprietor. In 1613 Johnson was a trustee for Shakespeare when he purchased the Blackfriars Gatehouse. There is no evidence Shakespeare was one of the Sirenical gentlemen who gathered at the Mermaid, but if he was not, he should have been. I. A. Shapiro, in "The Mermaid Club" (1950), takes a jaundiced view of the stories linking Shakespeare to this group but surveys the accounts that place him here.

The tavern was destroyed in the 1666 Great Fire of London.

Mitre Tavern
37 Fleet Street [Underground stops: Temple, Blackfriars, St. Paul's]

A plaque marks the site of the Mitre Tavern, which Shakespeare is supposed to have patronized. Samuel Johnson and James Boswell frequented the Mitre. Boswell wrote of one visit shortly after they first met in 1763,

> We had a good supper, and port-wine, of which he (Johnson) sometimes drank a bottle. The orthodox high-church sound of The Mitre—the figure and manner of the celebrated Samuel Johnson—the extraordinary power and precision of his conversation, and the pride arising from finding myself admitted as his companion, produced a variety of sensations, and a pleasing elevation of mind, beyond what I had ever experienced.

Newington Butts Theatre
Newington Butts [Underground stops: Elephant and Castle, Kennington]

Located a mile south of London Bridge, this outdoor theater was the first playhouse built south of the Thames (c. 1575). *Butts* may refer to archery targets that stood in the area. In 1592 riots and then plague closed the London theaters for twenty months, except for two brief periods in winter. Finances and patron deaths caused the old acting companies to fold. Two new companies formed in their stead: the Lord Admiral's Company and the Lord Chamberlain's Company. Shakespeare's was the latter. In June 1594 both companies played at Newington Butts for ten days, the first known performances of Shakespeare's troupe. On June 9, 1594, they staged a version of *Hamlet*, probably by Thomas Kyd. This revenge play includes a ghost; Shakespeare drew on this now-lost version for his tragedy. The take was a mere eight shillings. The theater was too far from London to attract large crowds. The Lord Admiral's men soon moved to the Rose Theatre (see "Rose Theatre" under "London" in this appendix). Nothing remains of the Newington Butts playhouse, which was pulled down in 1600.

Paris Garden
Southwark [Underground stop: Southwark]

The name is a corruption of "Parish Garden." The land was granted to the Knights Templar by Bermondsey Abbey in the early Middle Ages, and when the Templars were disbanded in 1324, the land passed to the Hospitallers, the knights of St. John of Jerusalem. After the Reformation William Baseley bought the lease to the manor house and grounds. Holland's Leaguer, a brothel named for its madame, Bess Holland, was located here. *Leaguer* means "a military camp." It modeled itself on the Schoen Majken in Brussels and was noted for its Dutch prostitutes, good food, and clean linen. Among the brothel's clients were King James I and George Villiers, First Duke of Buckingham. Another brothel was the Elephant, on the corner of Horseshoe Alley on the river. Shakespeare refers to it in *Twelfth Night* as being "in the south suburbs" (3.3.39) of Illyria, as it was in London. Antonio says it's a good place to live. Shakespeare moved to Paris Garden in 1596. Did he agree with Antonio about the desirability of lodging at the Elephant? Paris Garden was largely rural apart from such establishments. An amphitheater was built here for bull- and bearbaiting in the early 1500s. During the reign of King James I, this site was used for plays as well. This theater, like all others, was closed in 1642 by the Puritans. It reopened during the Restoration in 1660 and closed in 1687.

Porpentine Inn
Bankside, near Boar's Head Alley [Underground stops: Southwark, London Bridge]

Some of the inns mentioned in Shakespeare's plays did not exist, but this one did. It is mentioned five times in *The Comedy of Errors* (3.1.116, 3.2.167, 4.1.49, 5.1.222, 5.1.276) and in an exchequer document of 1624. It may have been a brothel, like the Elephant (see "Elephant Inn" under "London" in this appendix) mentioned in *Twelfth Night*, 3.3.48. Bankside, outside the jurisdiction of the London Council, was noted for its brothels. A porpentine is a porcupine (see *Hamlet*, 1.5.20).

Richmond Palace
Richmond

Formerly the Palace of Shene, which began as a manor house dating from at least 1125. Edward III expanded the house. It was the favorite residence of Richard II and Anne of Bohemia. After Anne's death in 1394, Richard, according to Raphael Holinshed's *Chronicles*, "caused it [the manor] to be thrown down and defaced; whereas the former kings of this land, being wearied of the citie, used customarily thither to resort as to a place of pleasure, and serving highly to their recreation." Henry V had the palace repaired, and Henry VII preferred it to all his other palaces. A fire in 1497 destroyed it, but Henry VII rebuilt it and renamed it Richmond Palace. Henry VII died here in 1509. In 1540 Henry VIII gave it to Anne of Cleves, his fourth wife, as part of their divorce settlement.

Elizabeth I liked to winter here, as it was the warmest of her palaces, and hunted in what is now the Old Deer Park. She died here on March 24, 1603. Shakespeare's company performed for her here, the last time on February 2, 1603. James gave the palace to his son Prince Henry, and then, after Henry's death in 1612, to Charles, who in turn gave it to Queen Henrietta Maria. Under Cromwell the palace was largely destroyed, and efforts by Charles II and James II to rebuild it were unavailing. All that remains are the gateway with the arms of Henry VII and, in the Old Palace Yard, restored buildings of the Wardrobe, Trumpeter's House, and Gate House (which dates from 1501).

Rose Theatre
Rose Alley [Underground stops: Southwark, St. Paul's, London Bridge]

Built by Philip Henslowe and John Cholmley in 1587–1588, it was the first London theater south of the Thames (excluding Newington Butts; see "Newington Butts Theatre" under "London" in this appendix). The theater's name derives from a rose garden that had stood on the site or from a house called the Rose there. The wooden building was octagonal. Lord Strange's Men played here; that company may have included Shakespeare. *1 Henry VI* and *Titus Andronicus* were first staged at the Rose, and *2* and *3 Henry VI* may have been as well. The building was demolished in the early seventeenth century after Henslowe's lease expired in 1605. In 1989 the theater's foundations were found, and they remain partly visible.

Shakespeare's Head Public House
29 Great Marlborough Street [Underground stop: Oxford Circus]

This pub has a bust of Shakespeare looking out a second-story window. The Shakespeare's Head, built in 1735, was originally owned by Thomas and John Shakespeare, who were distant relatives of the poet. It is named for them, not their famous ancestor. The bust lacks a hand as a result of German bombing in World War II.

Somerset House
Strand [Underground stop: Temple]

In 1547 Edward Seymour, Duke of Somerset, began building a palace for himself on the Thames. The palace was nearly complete when he was executed at the Tower in 1552, and the palace became a Crown possession. Elizabeth I lived here from 1553 to 1558. In 1603 Anne of Denmark moved here; the palace was renamed Denmark House. She and Charles I's queen, Henrietta Maria, engaged Inigo Jones to redesign parts of the building; Jones died here in 1652. In 1645 the building's name reverted to Somerset House when Henrietta Maria left England for the Netherlands because of the English Civil War. Christopher Wren undertook renovations after the Restoration. After Catherine of Braganza (widow of Charles II) left the palace in 1693 to become regent of Portugal, it ceased to be a royal residence, serving as grace and favor apartments until 1775, when the old building was demolished and a new one begun. The building has served as government offices and now houses the Courtauld Institute, the Gilbert Collection, and the Hermitage Rooms, modeled on the Winter Palace, St. Petersburg.

The King's Men (Shakespeare's company) attended on the Spanish ambassador here during peace negotiations with James I, August 9–27, 1604.

Southampton House
Corner of Holborn and Chancery Lane [Underground stop: Chancery Lane]

The London home of the Third Earl of Southampton, Shakespeare's patron, to whom he dedicated *Venus and Adonis* (1593) and *The Rape of Lucrece* (1594). Southampton is probably the Fair Youth of the sonnets. Southampton was part of the Earl of Essex's faction at court that opposed the Cecils. Shakespeare's plays tend to support Essex. Polonius has been seen as a satire on William Cecil, First Baron Burghley (d. 1598), Queen Elizabeth's chief adviser, and Hamlet is modeled on Essex. *Love's Labor's Lost* may satirize Sir Walter Raleigh and his circle; Raleigh and Essex were political rivals. In *Henry V* Shakespeare compares Essex to the eponymous king (chorus before act 5), and on the day before Essex's ill-fated uprising against Elizabeth in February 1601, Shakespeare's company staged *Richard II* at Essex's request. The play shows the deposing of a rightful but ineffective monarch by a younger, more capable man, as Essex hoped to do, though he may have intended to put James VI of Scotland on the English throne rather than himself; the Essex faction had ties to King James VI of Scotland. One of the first acts of King James when he assumed the English crown in 1603 was to make Shakespeare's acting company the King's Men. James also freed the Third Earl of Southampton from the Tower of London, where Elizabeth had imprisoned him for his role in Essex's uprising.

In the summer of 1604, Sir William Cope wrote to Robert Cecil, Viscount Cranborne,

> I have sent and been all this morning hunting for players, jugglers and such kinds of creatures, but find them hard to find. Wherefore leaving notes for them to seek me, [Richard] Burgage is come and says there is no new play that the Queen has not seen. But they have revived one called *Love's Labour's Lost*, which for wit and mirth, he says, will please her exceedingly. And this is appointed to be played tomorrow night at my Lord of Southampton's, unless you send writ to remove the *corpus cum causa* to your house in The Strand.

Corpus cum causa is a legal term for a writ demanding that the prisoner and the cause for which he is committed be brought before a judge. Here it means the actors and the play.

A. L. Rowse (1965) believes *Love's Labor's Lost* was first staged at Southampton House. Don Armado in that play may be based on John Florio, Italian tutor to the Third Earl of Southampton. Rowse also claims *A Midsummer Night's Dream* was composed for the second marriage of the earl's mother, Mary Browne, Countess of Southampton. The location of the wedding is uncertain, but it may have occurred at Southampton House, in which case that play would have been premiered there as well if Rowse is correct. See his *Shakespeare's Southampton: Patron of Virginia* (1965). Nothing of Southampton House remains.

Southwark Cathedral
Montague Close [Underground Stop: London Bridge]
The Cathedral Church of St. Saviour and St. Mary Overie (i.e., over the river). It has been a cathedral since 1905. Parts of the current church, the fourth on this site, date from the twelfth century. This is the oldest Gothic church in London and may have been Shakespeare's parish church for a time. The south aisle contains a memorial to Shakespeare carved by Henry McCarthy in 1912. Above the sculpture is the Shake-speare window (unveiled 1954, created by Christopher Webb), replacing an earlier set of memorial windows destroyed in a Nazi air raid in mid-February 1941. The central panel shows Prospero and Ariel. The left panel depicts characters from the comedies; the right panel displays characters from the tragedies. The church celebrates Shake-speare's birthday on April 23 each year. While Shakespeare definitely died on April 23, 1616, his birthdate is uncertain. April 23 is St. George's Day, celebrating England's patron saint, so it is pretty to believe Shakespeare, England's secular patron saint, was born on that date. Shakespeare was christened on April 26, 1564; hence he would have been born a few days earlier.

Shakespeare's youngest brother, Edmund, an actor, was buried in this church on December 31, 1607, age twenty-seven. Also buried here are John Fletcher, with whom Shakespeare collaborated for *Henry VIII*, *The Two Noble Kinsmen*, and the lost *Cardenio*; the playwright Philip Massinger; and Lawrence Fletcher, a co-lessee of the Globe Theatre. The medieval poet John Gower, a benefactor of the church, is buried here. Shakespeare brings him onstage as the narrator in *Pericles*.

St. Helen's Bishopsgate
Great St. Helens Place [Underground stops: Aldgate, Bank, Liverpool Street]
London's largest parish church, it was Shakespeare's parish church when he lived in Bishopsgate, his first known London address, which was near the Theatre. The church is dedicated to the Emperor Constantine's mother, St. Helena. The church dates from the twelfth century. William Fitzwilliam founded a Benedictine nunnery here circa 1204. In 1385 the Benedictine nuns here were reprimanded for keeping small dogs,

perhaps the inspiration for Chaucer's observation about the prioress in the prologue to the *Canterbury Tales*:

> Of smale houndes hadde she, that she fedde
> With rosted flesh, or milk and wastrel-breed.
> But soore weep she if oon of hem were deed,
> Or if men smoot it with a yerde smerte.

The church escaped the Great Fire of London, but Irish Republican bombs that exploded nearby in 1993 and again in 1994 damaged the building, which has been fully restored. It contains a Shakespeare memorial window donated by a Mr. Prentice, an American, in 1884. The window shows the playwright full length.

St. Mary Aldermanbury Garden
Love Lane [Underground stops: St Paul's, Moorgate, Bank]

John Heminge and Henry Condell, two of Shakespeare's fellow actors and the men who arranged for the printing of the First Folio, the first collected edition of Shakespeare's plays, in 1623, were buried in the church, which was destroyed in the Great Fire of London in 1666 and again, after Sir Christopher Wren rebuilt it, in the Blitz of 1940. Only the garden remains. The garden contains a bronze-and-granite monument to Heminge and Condell sculpted by Charles John Allen in 1895. It displays a model of the First Folio (showing the title page and part of the introduction by Heminge and Condell) and includes a bust of Shakespeare.

St. Olave's Church
London Wall and Noble Street [Underground stops: Barbican, St. Paul's, Moorgate]

The church stood opposite the Christopher Mountjoy House (see "Christopher Mountjoy's House" under "London" in this appendix) where Shakespeare lived in the early seventeenth century and so may have been where he worshiped. It dated from at least the twelfth century. John Stow in his *Survey of London* described it as small and lacking any noteworthy monuments. It was destroyed in the Great Fire of 1666 and not rebuilt. A plaque marks the site of the building.

Swan Theatre
Paris Garden [Underground stop: Southwark]

Built in 1595 by Francis Langley, it held three thousand spectators. It was made of flint concrete. Johannes de Witt, a Dutch visitor to London circa 1596, described it as the finest of the London theaters:

teltum

porticus

sedilia

orchestra

ingressus

mimorum
aedes.

proscænium.

planities siue arena.

Ex obseruationibus Londinensibus
Johannis de witt

Sketch by Johannes de Witt, circa 1595, of a performance at the Swan Theatre, London. *Private Collection © The Stapleton Collection/Bridgeman Images*

There are four amphitheatres in London of notable beauty, which from their diverse signs bear diverse names. In each of them a different play is daily exhibited to the populace. The two more magnificent of these are situated to the southward beyond the Thames, and from the signs suspended before them are called the Rose and the Swan. The two others are outside the city towards the north on the highway which issues through the Episcopal Gate, called in the vernacular Bishopgate. There is also a fifth [de]voted to the baiting of beasts, where are maintained in separate cages and enclosures many bears and dogs of stupendous size, which are kept for fighting, furnishing thereby a most delightful spectacle to men. Of all the theatres, however, the largest and the most magnificent is that one of which the sign is a swan, called in the vernacular the Swan Theatre; for it accommodates in its seats three thousand persons, and it is built of a mass of flint stones (of which there is a prodigious supply in Britain), and supported by wooden columns painted in such excellent imitation of marble that it is able to deceive even the most cunning. Since its form resembles that of a Roman work, I have made a sketch of it above. (Joseph Quincy Adams, *Shakespearean Playhouses*, 1920, p. 167)

The Globe Theatre also has wooden columns painted to look like marble. De Witt's sketch is the only contemporary image extant of the interior of an Elizabethan theater.

In the winter of 1596–1597, when the Lord Chamberlain's Men were disputing with their landlord at the Theatre, they may have performed here. The theater was plagued by controversies and was used only occasionally for plays in the early seventeenth century. In 1632 Nicholas Goodman in *Holland's Leaguer* described it as "now fallen into decay, and, like a dying swan, hangs her head and sings her own dirge."

The Theatre
86 and 88 Curtain Road [Underground stop: Old Street]

The first London purpose-built theater, it was erected in 1576 by James Burbage (whose son Richard was the leading actor in Shakespeare's plays) in Shoreditch at a cost of seven hundred pounds on land that had been a nunnery until the dissolution of the monasteries by Henry VIII; it witnessed the opening of many of Shakespeare's plays. The polygonal half-timbered open-air theater had three galleries and a thrust stage. In 1578 John Stockwood complained in a sermon about the "gorgeous playing-place erected in the fields . . . a shew-place of all beastly and filthy matters." It had a tiled roof and two external staircases. Its frontage was nearly a hundred feet. Because of a dispute with the landlord, Giles Alllen, the Lord Chamberlain's Men (Shakespeare's company) stopped using this venue in 1597. In December 1598 workmen disassembled the building, transported the timbers across the Thames, and built the Globe (see "The Globe Theatre" under "London" in this appendix).

The neighborhood was dangerous. A February 1580 report noted unlawful assemblies of the people to hear and see certain interludes called plays exercised by the said James Burbage and divers other persons unknown of a certain place called the Theatre in Holy Well in the aforesaid county. By reason of which unlawful assembling of the people great affrays[,] assaults[,] tumults[,] and quasi-insurrections and divers other misdeeds and enormities have been then and there done by very many ill-disposed persons to the great disturbance of the peace.

Elizabethan theaters performed a different play each day. In a season there would be about thirty different works presented at each theater, half of them new, thus creating great demand for writers to produce new or at least revised plays.

According to John Aubrey, Shakespeare lived nearby in Holywell Lane (the nunnery had a holy well on the premises) or Norton Folgate. Christopher Marlowe lived at the latter location.

The Vine
Near the Clink, Southwark [Underground stops: Southwark, London Bridge]

Edmund Shakespeare, William's youngest brother and also an actor, lived here, as did Shakespeare's fellow actor Lawrence Fletcher. The Vine was located near the Globe; Shakespeare may have lived here. According to the Agas map, an aerial view of London named for the surveyor Ralph Agas (c. 1540–1621), the building had two stories and two chimneys, as well as two gabled windows.

Westminster Abbey
[Underground stops: Westminster, St. James Park]

Poet's Corner contains a marble statue of Shakespeare. The monument was designed by William Kent and executed by Peter Scheemakers, and both signed it, with the date 1740. The carved heads of Queen Elizabeth I, Henry V, and Richard III appear on the base of the pedestal. The figure of the poet, about five feet, six inches in height, stands with his right leg crossed in front of his left, leaning his elbow on a pile of three books (untitled). A wreath of bays, signifying immortality, with a dagger (symbol of tragedy) and a dramatic mask are also carved above the head of Richard III. The group stands in front of a pedimented architectural frame. Shakespeare's left index finger points to a scroll hanging from the pedestal, on which is painted a variant of Prospero's lines from *The Tempest*, 4.1.152–56:

> The Cloud capt Tow'rs,
> The Gorgeous Palaces,
> The Solemn Temples,
> The Great Globe itself,
> Yea all which it Inherit,

Shall Dissolve;
And like the baseless Fabrick of a Vision
Leave not a wreck behind.

Luddington, Warwickshire

Seven miles southwest of Stratford-upon-Avon.

The village's name derives from Anglo-Saxon for "Lud's farm." The Old House (or the Cottage) stands on the site of the old church, where Shakespeare may have married Anne Hathaway in 1582. The village's current church was built in the nineteenth century in a different location.

Oxford, Oxfordshire

Crown Inn
3 Corn Market

In Shakespeare's time John Davenant, a vintner, owned a tavern (called the Taverne) here. Shakespeare stayed with John Davenant and his wife, Jane/Jennet (b. 1568), when he traveled between London and Stratford. In 1606 William Davenant was born here; Shakespeare was his godfather. William Davenant later encouraged the belief that Shakespeare was his father. According to John Aubrey,

> Mr. William Shakespeare was wont to go into Warwickshire once a year, and did commonly in his journey lie at this house [the Crown] in Oxon, where he was exceedingly respected. . . . Now Sir William [Davenant] would sometimes, when he was pleasant over a glass of wine with his most intimate friends—e.g. Sam Butler, author of *Hudibras*, etc., say, that it seemed to him that he writ with the very spirit that did Shakespeare, and seemed contented enough to be thought his Son. He would tell them the story as above, in which way his mother had a very light report, whereby she was called a Whore.

The Taverne/Crown was not an inn, though the Cross Inn was adjacent to it, and Shakespeare might have stayed with the Davenants rather than at the inn.

The poet Thomas Carew wrote of himself and Davenant, "[W]e of the adulterate mixture . . . / (So, oft the bastard nobler fortune meets, / Than the dull Issue of the lawfull sheets)," implying Davenant was not John's son. Anthony Wood claimed John Davenant was an "admirer and lover of plays and playmakers, especially Shakespeare, who frequented his house in his journeys between Warwickshire and London." Wood describes Jane as a "very beautiful woman, of a good wit and conversation." The late-seventeenth-century antiquarian Thomas Hearne related that one day young William Davenant, who was dashing through the streets of Oxford, was stopped by the master of New College, who asked him why he was running so fast.

"To greet my Godfather [Shakespeare]," said William.

"Do not take the name of the thy God in vain," replied the master.

It has also been suggested that Sonnet 126, which begins "O thou, my lovely boy, who in thy power / Dost hold Time's fickle glass, his sickle hour," is addressed to William Davenant. No evidence supports this conjecture, but like so many other stories about Shakespeare, it is pretty to believe.

William Davenant owned the Chandos portrait of Shakespeare and was the source of the story, first reported by Nicolas Rowe in his 1709 biography of Shakespeare, that the Third Earl of Southampton gave Shakespeare a thousand pounds "to go through with a purchase which he had a mind to." This story is doubted by scholars. Davenant is also the source of the story that, when Shakespeare first came to London, he held horses outside the theater.

Preston, Lancashire

Lea Hall belonged to Alexander Hoghton, who also owned Hoghton Tower, Hoghton (see "Hoghton, Lancashire" in this appendix). He may have employed Shakespeare as a tutor to his children.

Only the farmhouse, dating from the sixteenth or seventeenth century, remains. It is a private residence on the Blackpool Road.

Rufford, Lancashire

In the early 1580s, Shakespeare may have acted at Rufford Old Hall, the home of Sir Thomas Hesketh (see "Preston, Lancashire" in this appendix). The Hall (dating from c. 1530), at 200 Liverpool Road, belongs to the National Trust.

Shottery, Warwickshire

Anne Hathaway's Cottage

22 Cottage Lane, one mile west of Stratford-upon-Avon.

The twelve-room half-timbered thatched farmhouse was begun in the fourteenth century and expanded in the sixteenth. The house was known as Hewlands Farm in Shakespeare's day and sat on more than ninety acres. It contains a bed in which Shakespeare's future wife was supposedly born in 1556 and a settle on which Shakespeare allegedly courted Anne. Anne Hathaway lived here until she married Shakespeare in 1582. The orchard dates from the sixteenth century. The cottage remained in the Hathaway family until 1846. The grounds were restored in the 1920s by Ellen Willmott. Anne's father, Richard, sold fleeces to Shakespeare's father, which may be how they met.

The cottage was acquired by the Shakespeare Birthplace Trust in 1892.

Anne Hathaway's cottage, Shottery, a mile from Stratford, where Shakespeare may have courted his future wife. © *iStock/Andy Roland*

Snitterfield, Warwickshire

Five miles northeast of Stratford.

In the 1520s Shakespeare's paternal grandfather, Richard Shakespeare, leased eighty acres from Thomas Arden, father of Mary (Shakespeare's mother), on what is now Bell Lane and farmed here for some thirty-five years. John Shakespeare, the playwright's father, was born here circa 1530. A house on this site incorporates part of a Tudor farmhouse. In *2 Henry IV*, Davy asks Shallow to judge a dispute between "William Visor of Woncot" and "Clement Perks o' the Hill" (5.1.39–40). Perks was a common name in Snitterfield.

Stratford-upon-Avon, Warwickshire

Located 101 miles northwest of London, Stratford-upon-Avon takes its name from the Old English *straet*, "street," and *ford*, "a shallow place along the River Avon." The street began as a Roman road. The town was first settled by Anglo-Saxons in the seventh century CE. The nearby Cotswolds was an important sheep-growing area, so Stratford prospered in the Middle Ages because of the wool trade. (The Cotswolds takes its name from *sheep-cote* and *wold*, or "wooded area," though *wold* can also mean "rolling hills" or "an open field.") The characteristic sheep of the Cotswolds is

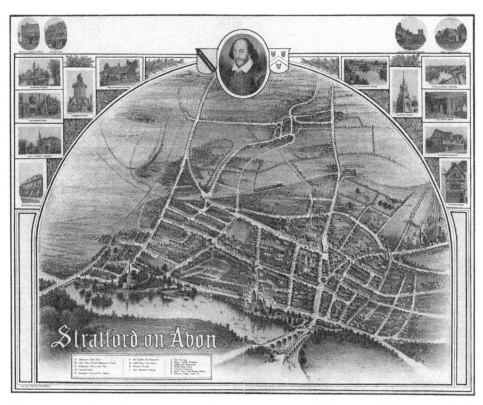

Stratford-upon-Avon, Shakespeare's native town. *Courtesy of the Library of Congress, G5754. S85E65 1908*

the Cotswold lion, brought to England by the Romans. As noted in "The Birthplace" under "Stratford-upon-Avon" in this appendix, wool played an important part in John Shakespeare's early prosperity. The town had 217 houses in 1590 and 429 by 1670. Its major industry now is tourism.

The Birthplace
Henley Street

The Birthplace is a sixteenth-century half-timbered house with three gables. Now one building, in Shakespeare's time it consisted of two separate structures. The western building, the Birthplace, was the family's residence; the eastern one, known as the Woolshop, was a workplace or warehouse where John Shakespeare made gloves and illegally dealt in wool; bits of wool have been found here. John Shakespeare was living on Henley Street by April 29, 1552, when he was fined a shilling for keeping a dung heap in front of his residence. He bought the Woolshop from Edward West in October 1556; he bought the Birthplace in 1575. All of John Shakespeare's children were born

Shakespeare's birthplace, Stratford-upon-Avon, and Shakespeare's Stratford home until 1596. *Courtesy of the Library of Congress, LC-DIG-ppmsc-08872*

here, and it was William's Stratford residence until 1597. Here his three children were born, and here his only son, Hamnet (or Hamlet), died in 1596. By 1603 the eastern building had become an inn run by Lewis Hiccox. In 1647 it was the Maidenhead Inn. Shakespeare added to the Birthplace a house at the western edge, now called Joan Hart's Cottage. Shakespeare's sister Joan lived here with her husband, William Hart.

A pilgrimage site by the nineteenth century, Sir Walter Scott, Thomas Carlyle, and other famous visitors have left their signatures in the window of the room where Shakespeare was supposedly born. The Shakespeare Birthplace Trust, which maintains this and other Stratford properties with Shakespearean associations, acquired the building in 1847 for three thousand pounds. It is open to the public.

Hall's Croft
Chestnut Walk, Old Town

A half-timbered Tudor house with later additions. Most of the building dates from 1613. This was the home of Dr. John Hall and Susanna Shakespeare, the playwright's older daughter, who married Dr. Hall on June 5, 1607, at Holy Trinity Church. Its enclosed garden, which contains herbs Hall might have used in his medical practice, is in keeping with the house's name, a croft being a farm or enclosed field. After Shakespeare died in 1616, the Halls moved to New Place (see "New Place" under "Stratford-upon-Avon, Warwickshire" in this appendix).

The property belongs to the Shakespeare Birthplace Trust, which acquired it in 1949.

Holy Trinity Church
Mill Lane

Stratford's oldest building is located in Mill Lane. Part of the church dates from 1210. Shakespeare was baptized here on April 26, 1564, and buried here in the chancel on April 25, 1616. The church contains a monument to Shakespeare dating from shortly after his death. On his grave is carved the epitaph

> GOOD FRIEND FOR JESUS SAKE FOREBEAR,
> TO DIGG THE DVST ENCLOSED HERE.
> BLESTE BE YE MAN YT SPARES THESE STONES,
> AND CURSED BE HE YT MOVES MY BONES.

As shown in *Hamlet*, 5.1, graves in Shakespeare's time were reused, the old bones being removed and placed in a charnel house. Shakespeare's epitaph saved his remains from this fate. Shakespeare's wife, Anne, is buried next to him. His son, Hamnet/Hamlet, and two daughters, Susanna and Judith, are buried in Holy Trinity Churchyard, as are Susanna's husband, John Hall, and Judith's husband, Thomas Quiney. Susanna, Shakespeare's first child, was christened here on May 26, 1583; Shakespeare's twins, Judith and Hamnet, were christened here on February 2, 1585. The twins' godparents were Shakespeare's Catholic neighbors Hamnet and Judith Sadler.

The monument to Shakespeare was erected near his grave sometime between 1616 and 1623. It was carved by Gheerhart Janssen and presents one of the two reliable images of the playwright, the other being the Droeshout portrait in the First Folio. The monument was painted, but in 1793 the otherwise-admirable Shakespeare scholar Edmond Malone had it whitewashed. Color was restored in 1861.

King Edward VI's School
Corner of Church Street and Chapel Lane

Located in the Guildhall (built 1417). There has been a school on this site since the thirteenth century. In 1553 King Edward VI granted the school a charter. Shakespeare attended the school, which is still in operation, from the age of seven to the age of fourteen. By the time students entered this school, they were expected to be able to

Holy Trinity Church, Stratford-upon-Avon, where Shakespeare and his children were baptized and where he and his wife are buried inside, his children outside. *Courtesy of the Library of Congress, LC-DIG-ppmsc-08870*

read and write English and to have a rudimentary knowledge of Latin. These skills were taught at petty schools, which children attended from age five to seven. The grammar taught at this school was Latin (and some Greek), not English. Roger Ascham observed in *The Schoolmaster* (1570), "All men covet to have their children speak Latin." The school day began at 6:00 a.m. in summer; 7:00 a.m., in winter. Classes continued until 11:00 a.m. or noon, when students would be allowed to go home to lunch. Classes resumed at 1:00 p.m. and continued until 5:00 or 6:00 p.m. All ages were taught in the same room. School was in session six days a week throughout the year, with holidays for Christmas, Easter, and Whitsuntide. Before the Reformation, saints' days were also holidays. There were occasional "remedies," days off for no reason. Corporal punishment was rife. Teachers were well educated: Shakespeare's were graduates of Oxford. But they were not well paid. The average salary for a grammar school master was seven pounds a year, more than a choirmaster (five pounds, seven shillings) but less than a parish priest (twenty-five pounds).

Here Shakespeare would have read the classics from which he drew in his writings, and he would have acted in plays, which were part of the humanist curriculum of the period. Among the playwrights Shakespeare would have encountered here were Plautus, whose *Menaechmi* is the basis of *The Comedy of Errors*, and Seneca, whose bloody tragedies are models for *Titus Andronicus*. He would have read Ovid, his favorite poet. In *Titus Andronicus* Lucius's son has a copy of Ovid he received from his mother (4.1), as Shakespeare may have. Ovid's theme of metamorphosis and his stories, like Pyramus and Thisbe (the subject of the rude mechanicals' play in act 5 of *A Midsummer Night's Dream*) and Tereus and Philomel (model for the rape of Lavinia in *Titus Andronicus*), pervade Shakespeare's plays. Virgil, another school text, supplied the harpies and other elements in *The Tempest*. Homer (which Shakespeare read in translation), Virgil, and Ovid tell of the Trojan War, as does Shakespeare's *Troilus and Cressida*. In William Lyly's school text, he would have found Horace's "Integer vitae scelerisque purus / Non eget Mauris iaculis neque arcus" (ode 1.22), which Shakespeare quotes in *Titus Andronicus*, 4.2.20–21. Ben Jonson famously wrote in his poem introducing the First Folio that Shakespeare had "small Latin and less Greek," but graduates of an Elizabethan grammar school would have put any modern college classics major to shame because they were immersed in the language. At school they were allowed to speak only Latin or Greek. Here Shakespeare also would have learned the rhetorical tropes he uses repeatedly in his plays. The school building was used by touring acting companies. In 1587 the Queen's Men, Sussex's Men, Essex's Men, and Leicester's Men performed here.

Thomas Jenkins, master of this school from 1575 to 1579, was Welsh. He may have been the model for Sir Hugh Evans, the parson in *The Merry Wives of Windsor*, who in 4.1 examines the suggestively named young William on his Latin.

Nash's House
Chapel Street

Located next to New Place (see "New Place" under "Stratford-upon-Avon, Warwickshire" in this appendix), this half-timbered Tudor house dating from about 1600 was the home of Shakespeare's granddaughter Elizabeth and her husband, Thomas Nash. A property of the Shakespeare Birthplace Trust since 1876, it houses Stratford's local history museum.

New Place
22 Chapel Street (Corner of Chapel Street and Chapel Lane)

This, the second-largest house in Stratford in the 1590s, had been built in the 1480s by Hugh Clopton, a rich dealer in textiles, who became Lord Mayor of London. Clopton donated the money for building a stone bridge over the River Avon and also for decorating the Guild Chapel. The three-story brick-and-timber house, fronting on Chapel Street, had five gables, three bays, ten fireplaces, twenty to thirty rooms, a courtyard, two gardens, two orchards, and two barns. It was sixty feet long and seventy feet deep. Shakespeare bought the house from William Underhill in 1597 for about £120. The bill of sale put the price at £60, but real estate dealings were not always what they seemed, even in the sixteenth century. The house was in need of repairs, but the purchase allowed Shakespeare's wife and two children to move away from his parents on Henley Street. Shakespeare died here in 1616. His daughter Susanna Hall and then her daughter, Elizabeth, inherited the property. Elizabeth, Shakespeare's last direct descendant, died in 1670, and her husband, John Barnard, died in 1674, after which the house again was owned by the Cloptons, who replaced the half-timbered building with a brick house. (In 1675 Sir Edward Walker bought New Place. His daughter married John Clopton.) According to Reverend Joseph Greene, who served as headmaster of Stratford Grammar School in the eighteenth century, when the Cloptons reacquired the property they found

> several little epigrams on familiar subjects . . . upon the glass of the house windows, some of which were written by Shakespeare, and many of them the product of his own children's brain: the tradition being, that he often in his times of pleasantry thus exercised his and their talents, and took great pleasure when he could trace in them some pretty display of that genius which God and Nature had blessed him with.

In 1759 the owner, the (not very) Reverend Francis Gastrell, having already chopped down a mulberry tree supposedly planted by Shakespeare on the property, demolished the house because of a tax dispute with city authorities, and he may have been tired of tourists wanting to see Shakespeare's house.

In 1861 the property was acquired by the Shakespeare Birthplace Trust, which has planted Elizabethan-style gardens on the property.

Royal Shakespeare Theatre
Waterside

The first permanent Shakespeare theater was built on the banks of the Avon in 1879. After this building burned down in 1926, its replacement was designed by Elisabeth Scott and opened in 1932. It has a thrust stage, typical of theaters in Shakespeare's time; Scott's design had a proscenium arch, which was altered in 2007–2010. The theater holds about one thousand people.

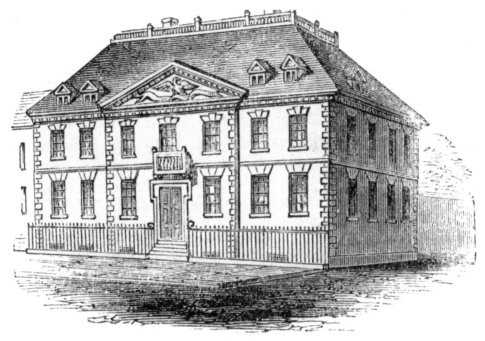

New Place, Stratford-upon-Avon, Shakespeare's Stratford home after 1596. *Samuel Orchart Beeton, Shakespeare Memorial. London: S. O. Beeton, 1864.*

Shakespeare Center
Henley Street

Opened in 1964, the four-hundredth anniversary of Shakespeare's birth, the center serves as the headquarters of the Shakespeare Birthplace Trust. Its library is a valuable resource for scholars, with material dealing with Shakespeare's life, theater, work, and times, as well as the history of Stratford. It includes a copy of the First Folio (1623), the first collected edition of Shakespeare's plays.

Swan Theatre
Waterside

Opened in 1986 next to the current Royal Shakespeare Theatre (see "Royal Shakespeare Theatre" under "Stratford-upon-Avon" in this appendix) on the site of the 1879 Royal Shakespeare Theatre that burned down in 1926. It has a thrust stage and, with a seating capacity of 450, is more intimate than the larger facility next door. It is named for the Elizabethan-era Swan Theatre in London (see "Swan Theatre" under "London" in this appendix).

Temple Grafton, Warwickshire

Five miles west of Stratford.

Shakespeare probably married Anne Hathaway here, perhaps on December 1, 1582. According to a church commissioners' report of 1586, the vicar here, John Frith, was an old "priest and Unsound in religion, he can neither preach nor read well, his chiefest trade is to cure hawkes that are hurt or diseased, for which purpose many do usually repair to him." In *As You Like It*, 3.3, Touchstone asks Sir Oliver Mar-text, an unsound priest, to marry him and Audrey. Is Shakespeare thinking about his own marriage almost twenty years earlier? Jaques tells Touchstone to find a "good priest" (3.3.84).

Shakespeare's parents were married as Catholics. Perhaps Shakespeare was, too. The seventeenth-century Anglican archdeacon Richard Davies claimed "He dyed a Papyst."

Warwick, Warwickshire

Warwick Castle

A fortification has stood on this site overlooking the River Avon since the tenth century. In 1068 William the Conqueror built a motte-and-bailey castle here with timber. In 1260 the castle was rebuilt with stone. Thomas de Beauchamp, Eleventh Earl of Warwick, added Caesar's Tower and Guy's Tower in the fourteenth century. Further additions were made in the next century. In the sixteenth century, the castle fell into decay, but later owners refurbished it. In 1751 Horace Walpole, creator of a castle of his own at Twickenham (Strawberry Hill), praised the building and its grounds, which are open to the public. The Earls of Warwick have played important roles in English history, and Richard Neville, Sixteenth Earl of Warwick, looms large in Shakespeare's *Henry VI* plays.

Welford-on-Avon, Warwickshire

Bell Inn

Binton Road, four miles southwest of Stratford-upon-Avon.

According to the Stratford-upon-Avon vicar John Ward (1629–1681), a week before Shakespeare died on April 23, 1616, "Shakespear, [Michael] Drayton and Ben Jonson had a merry meeting [at Welford-on-Avon], and it seems, drank too hard, for Shakespear died of a feavour there contracted." The Bell Inn, built in the seventeenth century, is still a pub.

Ward mentioned Shakespeare five times in his diary, including a note to himself to read the plays. Ward also reported, "I have heard that Mr. Shakspeare was a natural wit, without any art at all; hee frequented the plays all his younger time, but in his elder days lived at Stratford, and supplied the stage with two plays every year, and for itt had an allowance so large, that hee spent att the rate of 1,000 l [pounds] a-year, as I have heard."

Wilmcote, Warwickshire

Glebe House

Station Road, four miles north of Stratford.

Robert Arden, Shakespeare's maternal grandfather, was born in Wilmcote circa 1490; his daughter Mary, Shakespeare's mother, circa 1535. Mary Arden, Shakespeare's mother, lived in the Glebe House. The house has a Victorian brick veneer but is Tudor. The house was built circa 1514 and is fifty-five feet long, with a central open hall. It is owned by the Shakespeare Birthplace Trust, which maintains it as a working Tudor farm.

Wilton, Wiltshire

Wilton House

King Egbert founded a priory on this site near Wilton circa 871. After the dissolution of the monasteries in 1536, Henry VIII gave the property to William Herbert, who became First Earl of Pembroke in 1542. He built a Tudor mansion on the site, of which only the Holbein porch (which may have been designed by the artist) and the great tower in the middle of the east façade survive. In the 1630s the fourth earl built a Palladian mansion to replace the Tudor structure, and the eleventh earl added Gothic elements to the house. While the Herberts continue to live in the house, it is open to the public.

Sir Philip Sidney's sister lived here, and he wrote much of his *Arcadia* at Wilton House. That work provides the Gloucester plot for *King Lear*. William Herbert, the third earl, is a candidate for Shakespeare's Fair Youth of the sonnets, and the First Folio was dedicated to him and his brother Philip. On December 2, 1603, while plague kept King James from London and kept the theaters closed, Shakespeare's company performed for him here and received thirty pounds. The play may have been *As You Like It*. The King's Men also played for the town of Wilton, for which they received sixty-five shillings. In 1604 the King's Men performed a masque at the wedding of the earl's brother Philip to Susan de Vere.

Worcester, Worcestershire

Public Records Office

Worcestershire Archive and Archaeology Service, The Hive, Sawmill Walk, The Butts

Worcestershire's archives contain two documents relating to Shakespeare's marriage. In Elizabethan times the normal procedure was for banns to be read three times, that is, on three successive Sundays before the wedding, at the engaged couple's parish church to allow for objections to be raised. Shakespeare and Anne Hathaway married by special license. An Episcopal register entry for November 27, 1582, says a license was issued for Shakespeare to marry Anne Whateley of Temple Grafton: "Anno Domini 1582 . . . Novembris . . . 27 die eiusdem mensis. Item eodem die supradicto emanavit Licentia inter Wm Shaxpere et Annam Whateley de Temple Grafton." The other document, dated November 28, 1582, is a bond for forty pounds' surety for Shakespeare to marry Anne Hathaway of Stratford-upon-Avon. The bond was to protect the Bishop of Worcester, who issued the license, from liability in case some impediment to the marriage should be discovered later. The bond was signed by Fulke Sandalls and John Richardson of Stratford; these men were supervisors of the will of Richard Hathaway, Anne's father, who had died in September 1581. The discrepancy in the bride's name has prompted speculation, though the most widely accepted (and least interesting) explanation is that *Whateley* is a clerical error in the register. However, in his 1970 *Shakespeare* Anthony Burgess wrote,

> It is reasonable to believe that Will wished to marry a girl named Anne Whateley. The name is common enough in the Midlands and is even attached to a four-star hotel in Horse Fair, Banbury. Her father may have been a friend of John Shakespeare's, he may have sold kidskin cheap, there are various reasons why the Shakespeares and the Whateleys, or their nubile children, might become friendly. Sent on skin-buying errands to Temple Grafton, Will could have fallen for a comely daughter, sweet as May and shy as a fawn. He was eighteen and highly susceptible. Knowing something about girls, he would know that this was the real thing. Something, perhaps, quite different from what he felt about Mistress Hathaway of Shottery. But why, attempting to marry Anne Whateley, had he put himself in the position of having to marry the other Anne? I suggest that, to use the crude but convenient properties of the old women's-magazine morality-stories, he was exercised by love for the one and lust for the other.

There is no evidence an Anne Whateley existed, but speculation is delightful.

Wroxall, Warwickshire
Thirteen miles north of Stratford-upon-Avon.

In the fifteenth century, Wroxall Abbey had as its abbess Dame Isabella Shakespeare. She may have given her name to the heroine in *Measure for Measure*, who is named Cassandra in Shakespeare's source. Shakespeare's paternal grandfather, Richard, was born in Wroxall circa 1500 and served as bailiff before leaving the village for Snitterfield (see "Snitterfield, Warwickshire" in this appendix).

Appendix B
Works by Location

ARABIA

"The Phoenix and Turtle"

AUSTRIA

Vienna.

    Angelo's House. *Measure for Measure*, 2.2, 2.4, 4.4

    City Gate. *Measure for Measure*, 4.6, 5.1

    A Courtroom. *Measure for Measure*, 2.1

    The Duke's Palace. *Measure for Measure*, 1.1

    The Moated Grange of St. Luke. *Measure for Measure*, 4.1

    A Monastery. *Measure for Measure*, 1.3

    A Nunnery. *Measure for Measure*, 1.4

    Outside Vienna. *Measure for Measure*, 4.5

    A Prison. *Measure for Measure*, 2.3, 3.1, 3.2, 4.2, 4.3

    A Street. *Measure for Measure*, 1.2

BERMUDA

See Prospero's Island.

BOHEMIA

The Coast. *The Winter's Tale*, 3.3

The Palace of Polixenes. *The Winter's Tale*, 4.2

A Road. *The Winter's Tale*, 4.3

The Shepherd's Farm. *The Winter's Tale*, 4.4

CYPRUS

Famagusta.

> A Cape. *Othello*, 2.1
>
> Othello's Castle. *Othello*, 2.3, 3.2, 3.3, 4.2, 5.2
>
> A Street. *Othello*, 2.2, 3.1, 3.4, 4.1, 5.1

DENMARK

The Coast. *Hamlet*, 4.4

Helsingør.

> A Graveyard. *Hamlet*, 5.1
>
> Kronborg Castle. *Hamlet*, 1.1, 1.2, 1.3, 1.4, 1.5, 2.1, 2.2, 3.1, 3.2, 3.3., 3.4, 4.1, 4.2, 4.3, 4.5, 4.6, 4.7, 5.2

EGYPT

Alexandria.

> Antony's Camp. *Antony and Cleopatra*, 4.5, 4.8
>
> The Battlefield. *Antony and Cleopatra*, 4.7, 4.10, 4.11, 4.12
>
> Cleopatra's Palace. *Antony and Cleopatra*, 1.1, 1.2, 1.3, 1.5, 2.5, 3.3, 3.11, 3.13, 4.2, 4.3, 4.4, 4.13, 4.14
>
> Cleopatra's Tomb. *Antony and Cleopatra*, 4.15, 5.2
>
> Octavius Caesar's Camp. *Antony and Cleopatra*, 3.12, 4.1, 4.6, 4.9, 5.1

ENGLAND

Barnet, Hertfordshire. *3 Henry VI*, 5.2, 5.3

Bath, Somerset. Sonnets 153 and 154

A Battlefield. *Cymbeline*, 5.2, 5.3

Berkeley Castle, Gloucestershire. *Richard II*, 2.3

Bosworth Field, Leicestershire. *Richard III*, 5.3, 5.4, 5.5

Bristol Castle, Bristol. *Richard II*, 3.1

The British Camp. *Cymbeline*, 5.4, 5.5

Bury St. Edmunds, Suffolk. *2 Henry VI*, 3.1, 3.2; *King John*, 5.2

Cade Street, East Sussex. *2 Henry VI*, 4.10

Chertsey, Surrey. *Richard III*, 1.2

Clitheroe, Lancashire. *3 Henry VI*, 3.1

Colchester, Essex.

>   Palace of Cymbeline. *Cymbeline*, 1.1, 1.2, 1.3, 1.5, 1.6, 2.1, 2.2, 2.3, 3.1, 3.2, 3.5, 4.3

Coventry, Warwickshire. *1 Henry IV*, 4.3; *3 Henry VI*, 5.1; *Richard II*, 1.3

Daventry, Northamptonshire. *3 Henry VI*, 5.1

Dover, Kent. *2 Henry VI*, 4.1; *King Lear*, 4.3, 4.4, 4.6, 4.7, 5.1, 5.2

Gadshill, Kent. *1 Henry IV*, 2.2

Gaultree Forest, Yorkshire. *2 Henry IV*, 4.1, 4.2, 4.3

Gloucester, Gloucestershire.

>   Earl of Gloucester's Castle. *King Lear*, 1.2, 2.1, 2.2, 2.3, 2.4, 3.3, 3.5, 3.6, 3.7, 4.5

>   The Heath. *King Lear*, 3.1, 3.2, 3.4, 4.1

Gloucestershire. *2 Henry IV*, 3.2, 5.1, 5.3

Kenilworth Castle, Warwickshire. *2 Henry VI*, 4.9

Kimbolton Castle, Huntingdonshire. *Henry VIII*, 4.2

Kings Langley Castle, Hertfordshire. *Richard II*, 3.4, 5.2

Leicester, Leicestershire. *Richard III*, 5.2

> King Lear's Palace. *King Lear*, 1.1

Lincoln, Lincolnshire. *King John*, 5.3, 5.4, 5.5

London.

> Baynard's Castle. *Richard III*, 3.7
>
> Blackfriars. *Henry VIII*, 2.4
>
> Blackheath. *2 Henry VI*, 4.2, 4.3
>
> Boar's Head Tavern, Eastcheap. *1 Henry IV*, 2.4, 3.3; *2 Henry IV*, 2.4, 5.4; *Henry V*, 2.1, 2.3
>
> Cannon Street. *2 Henry VI*, 4.6
>
> Church of the Observant Friars, Greenwich. *Henry VIII*, 5.4
>
> Crosby House (or Crosby Place). *Richard III*, 1.2
>
> Duke of Gloucester's House. *See* London, Palace of Placentia, Greenwich
>
> Duke of York's Gardens. *2 Henry VI*, 2.2
>
> Eltham Palace, Greenwich. *1 Henry VI*, 1.1
>
> Ely Palace. *Richard II*, 1.2, 2.1
>
> Fulham Palace. *3 Henry VI*, 4.8
>
> Lord Hastings's House. *Richard III*, 3.2
>
> Middle Temple. *1 Henry VI*, 2.4
>
> Palace of Placentia, Greenwich. *2 Henry VI*, 1.2, 1.4; *Henry VIII*, 1.1, 1.2, 1.3, 2.2, 2.3, 3.1, 3.2, 5.1, 5.2, 5.3
>
> Palace of Westminster. *Edward III*, 1.1; *1 Henry IV*, 1.1, 1.2, 1.3, 3.2; *2 Henry IV*, 3.1, 5.2; *Henry V*, 1.1, 1.2; *1 Henry VI*, 3.1, 5.5; *2 Henry VI*, 1.1, 1.3, 4.4; *3 Henry VI*, 1.1, 3.2, 4.1, 4.4, 5.7; *Henry VIII*, 2.1; *King John*, 1.1, 4.2, 5.1; *Macbeth*, 3.1, 4.3, 5.5; *Richard II*, 1.4, 4.1; *Richard III*, 1.3, 2.1, 2.2, 2.4, 4.2, 4.3, 4.4
>
> Palace of Whitehall (Former York Palace). *Henry VIII*, 1.4
>
> Sir William Stanley's House. *Richard III*, 4.5

Winchester, Hampshire.

    Wolvesey Castle. *2 Henry VI*, 3.3

Wincot, Warwickshire (Formerly Gloucestershire). *The Taming of the Shrew*, Induction, 1, 2, 3

Windsor, Berkshire.

    Dr. Caius's House. *The Merry Wives of Windsor*, 1.4

    A Field outside Windsor. *The Merry Wives of Windsor*, 2.3

    A(nother) Field outside Windsor. *The Merry Wives of Windsor*, 3.1

    Ford's House. *The Merry Wives of Windsor*, 3.3, 4.2, 4.4

    Garter Inn. *The Merry Wives of Windsor*, 1.3, 2.2, 3.5, 4.3, 4.5, 4.6, 5.1

    Page's House. *The Merry Wives of Windsor*, 1.1, 1.2, 2.1, 3.4

    A Street. *The Merry Wives of Windsor*, 3.2, 4.1

    Windsor Castle. *Richard II*, 1.1, 2.2, 5.3, 5.4, 5.6

    Windsor Park. *The Merry Wives of Windsor*, 5.2, 5.3, 5.4, 5.5

York, Yorkshire. *3 Henry VI*, 1.4, 2.2, 4.7

    Bishopthorpe Palace. *1 Henry IV*, 4.4; *2 Henry IV*, 1.3

FRANCE

Agincourt, Artois. *Henry V*, 3.7, 4.1, 4.2, 4.3, 4.4, 4.5, 4.6, 4.7, 4.8, 5.1

Angiers. *1 Henry VI*, 5.2, 5.3, 5.4; *King John*, 2.1, 3.1, 3.2, 3.3, 3.4

Auvergne. *1 Henry VI*, 2.3

Bordeaux. *1 Henry VI*, 4.2

    The Duke's Palace. *As You Like It*, 1.2, 1.3, 2.2, 3.1

    Oliver de Boys's House. *As You Like It*, 1.1, 2.3

Brittany. *Edward III*, 4.1

Calais. *Edward III*, 4.2, 5.1

Castillon-le-Bataille. *1 Henry VI*, 4.5, 4.6, 4.7

GREECE

Athens's Gates. *The Two Noble Kinsmen*, 1.3

Athens's Walls. *Timon of Athens*, 4.1, 5.2, 5.4

Country near Athens. *The Two Noble Kinsmen*, 2.3, 3.1, 3.2, 3.3, 3.4, 3.5, 3.6, 5.3, 5.4

Lucullus's House. *Timon of Athens*, 3.1

Palace of Theseus. *A Midsummer Night's Dream*, 1.1, 5.1; *The Two Noble Kinsmen*, 2.1, 2.5, 4.2

Peter Quince's House. *A Midsummer Night's Dream*, 1.2, 4.2

The Prison. *The Two Noble Kinsmen*, 2.2, 2.4, 2.6, 4.1, 4.3, 5.2

A Public Place. *Timon of Athens*, 3.2

Sempronius's House. *Timon of Athens*, 3.3

The Senate House. *Timon of Athens*, 3.5

A Senator's House. *Timon of Athens*, 2.1

A Temple. *The Two Noble Kinsmen*, 1.1

Timon's Cave. *Timon of Athens*, 4.2, 5.1, 5.3

Timon's House. *Timon of Athens*, 1.1, 1.2, 2.2, 3.4, 3.6, 4.2

The Woods outside Athens. *A Midsummer Night's Dream*, 2.1, 2.2, 3.1, 3.2, 4.1

Mytilene.

A Brothel. *Pericles, Prince of Tyre*, 4.2, 4.5, 4.6

The Coast. *Pericles, Prince of Tyre*, 5.1

Philippi. *Julius Caesar*, 5.1, 5.2, 5.3, 5.4, 5.5

Thebes.

A Battlefield. *The Two Noble Kinsmen*, 1.4

A Cemetery. *The Two Noble Kinsmen*, 1.5

Creon's Palace. *The Two Noble Kinsmen*, 1.2

ILLYRIA

The Coast. *Twelfth Night*, 1.2, 2.1

The Duke's Palace. *Twelfth Night*, 1.1, 1.4, 2.4

Olivia's House. *Twelfth Night*, 1.3, 1.5, 2.2, 2.3, 2.5, 3.1, 3.2, 3.4, 4.1, 4.2, 4.3, 5.1

A Street. *Twelfth Night*, 3.3

ITALY

Antium.

    Cominius's Camp. *Coriolanus*, 1.6, 1.8, 1.9

    House of Tullus Aufidius. *Coriolanus*, 4.4, 4.5

    Road to Antium. *Coriolanus*, 4.3

Ardea. *The Rape of Lucrece*

Belmont. *The Merchant of Venice*, 1.2, 2.1, 2.7, 2.9, 3.2, 3.4, 3.5, 5.1

Collatium/Collatia. *The Rape of Lucrece*

Corioli. *Coriolanus*, 1.2, 1.4, 1.5, 1.7, 5.6

Florence.

    The Duke's Palace. *All's Well That Ends Well*, 3.1, 3.3

    Outside Florence. *All's Well That Ends Well*, 3.5, 3.6, 4.1, 4.3

    The Widow's House. *All's Well That Ends Well*, 3.7, 4.2, 4.4

Mantua.

    Apothecary's Shop. *Romeo and Juliet*, 5.1

    Forest of Mantua. *The Two Gentlemen of Verona*, 4.1, 5.3, 5.4

Messina, Sicily. *See* "Sicily" under "Italy."

Milan.

    The Duke's Palace. *The Two Gentlemen of Verona*, 2.1, 2.4, 2.6, 3.1, 3.2, 4.2, 4.3, 4.4, 5.2

Friar Patrick's Cell. *The Two Gentlemen of Verona*, 5.1

A Street. *The Two Gentlemen of Verona*, 2.5

Miseno. *Antony and Cleopatra*, 2.6, 2.7

Padua.

Baptista Minola's House. *The Taming of the Shrew*, 1.1, 2.1, 3.1, 3.2, 4.2, 4.4

Hortensio's House. *The Taming of the Shrew*, 1.2

Lucentio's House. *The Taming of the Shrew*, 5.1, 5.2

Road to Padua. *The Taming of the Shrew*, 4.5

Rome. *The Rape of Lucrece*

Brutus's House. *Julius Caesar*, 2.1, 2.4

Caius Martius Coriolanus's House. *Coriolanus*, 1.3, 3.2

The Capitol. *See* "The Curia/Capitol."

A City Gate. *Coriolanus*, 4.1, 4.2, 5.4, 5.5

The Curia/Capitol. *Coriolanus*, 2.2; *Julius Caesar*, 2.3, 3.1; *Titus Andronicus*, 1.1, 2.1

Domus Publica, Via Sacra. *Julius Caesar*, 2.2

The Emperor's Palace. *Titus Andronicus*, 2.2, 4.2, 4.3, 4.4

A Forest near Rome. *Titus Andronicus*, 2.3, 2.4

The Forum. *Coriolanus*, 2.3, 3.3, 4.6, 5.1; *Julius Caesar*, 1.2, 3.2

Julius Caesar's House. See "Domus Publica, Via Sacra."

Lepidus's House. *Antony and Cleopatra*, 2.2

Marc Antony's House. *Julius Caesar*, 4.1

Octavius Caesar's House. *Antony and Cleopatra*, 1.4, 2.3, 3.2, 3.6

Philario's House. *Cymbeline*, 1.4, 2.4, 2.5

A Plain near Rome. *Titus Andronicus*, 5.1

A Public Place. *Cymbeline*, 3.7

Senate House. See "The Curia/Capitol."

A Street. *Antony and Cleopatra*, 2.4; *Coriolanus*, 1.1, 2.1, 3.1; *Julius Caesar*, 1.1, 1.3, 3.3; *Titus Andronicus*, 3.1

Titus Andronicus's House. *Titus Andronicus*, 3.2, 4.1, 5.2, 5.3

Volscian Camp. *Coriolanus*, 1.10, 4.7, 5.2, 5.3

Sicily.

A Court of Justice. *The Winter's Tale*, 3.2

Messina.

A Church. *Much Ado about Nothing*, 4.1, 5.3

Leonato's House. *Much Ado about Nothing*, 1.1, 1.2, 1.3, 2.1, 2.2, 2.3, 3.1, 3.2, 3.4, 3.5, 5.1, 5.2, 5.4

A Prison. *Much Ado about Nothing*, 4.2

Sextus Pompeius's House. *Antony and Cleopatra*, 2.1

A Street. *Much Ado about Nothing*, 3.3

Palace of Leontes. *The Winter's Tale*, 1.1, 1.2, 2.1, 2.3, 5.1, 5.2

Paulina's House. *The Winter's Tale*, 5.3

A Prison. *The Winter's Tale*, 2.2

A Road. *The Winter's Tale*, 3.1

Venice.

Brabantio's House. *Othello*, 1.1

Court of Justice. *The Merchant of Venice*, 4.1

The Doge's Palace. *Othello*, 1.3

The Sagittary. *Othello*, 1.2

Shylock's House. *The Merchant of Venice*, 2.3, 2.5, 2.6

A Street. *The Merchant of Venice*, 1.1, 1.3, 2.2, 2.4, 2.8, 3.1, 3.3, 4.2

Verona.

Antonio's House. *The Two Gentlemen of Verona*, 1.3

Capulet's House. *Romeo and Juliet*, 1.3, 1.4, 1.5, 2.1, 2.2, 2.5, 3.2, 3.4, 3.5, 4.2, 4.3, 4.4., 4.5

Friar Lawrence's Cell. *Romeo and Juliet*, 2.3, 2.6, 3.3, 4.1, 5.2

Julia's House. *The Two Gentlemen of Verona*, 1.2, 2.2, 2.7

Juliet's Tomb. *Romeo and Juliet*, 5.3

Petruchio's House. *The Taming of the Shrew*, 4.1, 4.3

A Street. *Romeo and Juliet*, 1.1, 1.2, 2.4, 3.1; *The Two Gentlemen of Verona*, 1.1, 2.3

Volscian Camp. *Coriolanus*, 1.10, 4.7, 5.2, 5.3

LEBANON

Tyre.

The Governor's House. *Pericles, Prince of Tyre*, 2.4

Palace of Pericles. *Pericles, Prince of Tyre*, 1.2, 1.3

LIBYA

Pentapolis.

Palace of Simonides. *Pericles, Prince of Tyre*, 2.2, 2.3, 2.5

The Seacoast. *Pericles, Prince of Tyre*, 2.1

PROSPERO'S ISLAND

The Tempest, 1.1, 1.2, 2.1, 2.2, 3.1, 3.2, 3.3., 4.1, 5.1

SCOTLAND

Birnam Wood. *Macbeth*, 5.4

Duke of Albany's Castle. *King Lear*, 1.3, 1.4, 1.5, 4.2

Dunsinane Hill, Perthshire. *Macbeth*, 5.2, 5.6, 5.7, 5.8, 5.9

Macbeth's Castle. *Macbeth*, 5.1, 5.3, 5.5

Fife.

Macduff's Castle. *Macbeth*, 4.2

Forres.

>A Cave. *Macbeth*, 4.1

>A Heath. *Macbeth*, 1.1, 1.3, 3.5

>King Duncan's Camp. *Macbeth*, 1.2

>King Duncan's (Later Macbeth's) Palace. *Macbeth*, 1.4, 3.1, 3.2, 3.3, 3.4, 3.6

Inverness.

>Macbeth's Castle. *Macbeth*, 1.5, 1.6, 1.7, 2.1, 2.2, 2.3, 2.4

Roxburghshire.

>Roxburghe Castle. *Edward III*, 1.2, 2.1, 2.2

SPAIN

Navarre. *Love's Labor's Lost*, 1.1, 1.2, 2.1, 3.1, 4.1, 4.2, 4.3, 5.1, 5.2

SYRIA

Gindarus. *Antony and Cleopatra*, 3.1

TURKEY

Antioch.

>Palace of Antiochus. *Pericles, Prince of Tyre*, 1.1

Ephesus.

>Cerimon's House. *Pericles, Prince of Tyre*, 3.2, 3.4

>House of Antipholus of Ephesus. *The Comedy of Errors*, 2.1, 3.1, 3.2, 4.2

>The Marketplace. *The Comedy of Errors*, 1.2, 2.2, 4.1, 4.3, 4.4

>The Phoenix. *See* "The House of Antipholus of Ephesus" under "Ephesus" under "Turkey."

>A Priory/Temple of Artemis. *The Comedy of Errors*, 5.1

>A Public Square. *The Comedy of Errors*, 1.1

>The Temple of Diana/Artemis. *Pericles, Prince of Tyre*, 5.2

The Greek Camp near Troy.

>Achilles's Tent. *Troilus and Cressida*, 2.1, 2.3, 3.3, 5.1

>Agamemnon's Tent. *Troilus and Cressida*, 1.3, 4.5

>Calchas's Tent. *Troilus and Cressida*, 5.2

The Plain between the Greek Camp and Troy. *Troilus and Cressida*, 5.4, 5.5, 5.6, 5.7, 5.8, 5.9, 5.10

Sardis. *Julius Caesar*, 4.2, 4.3

Tarsus.

>Cleon's House. *Pericles, Prince of Tyre*, 1.4, 3.3, 4.3

>The Coast. *Pericles, Prince of Tyre*, 3.1, 4.1

>Monument to Marina. *Pericles, Prince of Tyre*, 4.4

Troy.

>Calchas's House. *Troilus and Cressida*, 3.2, 4.2, 4.3, 4.4

>Priam's Palace. *Troilus and Cressida*, 2.2, 3.1, 5.3

>A Street. *Troilus and Cressida*, 1.2, 4.1

>Troilus's House. *Troilus and Cressida*, 1.1

WALES

Flint, Flintshire.

>Flint Castle. *Richard II*, 3.3

Merionethshire.

>Harlech Castle. *1 Henry IV*, 3.1; *Richard II*, 3.2

Milford Haven, Pembrokeshire. *Cymbeline*, 3.3, 3.4, 3.6, 4.1, 4.2, 4.4; *Richard II*, 2.4

Bibliography

EDITIONS OF SHAKESPEARE'S WORKS

Allen, Michael J. B., and Kenneth Muir, eds. *Shakespeare's Plays in Quarto: A Facsimile of Copies Primarily from the Henry E. Huntington Library*. Berkeley: University of California Press, 1981.

Barnet, Sylvan, ed. *The Complete Signet Classic Shakespeare*. New York: Harcourt Brace Jovanovich, 1972.

Bevington, David, ed. *The Complete Works of Shakespeare*. 7th ed. Boston: Pearson, 2014.

Brockbank, Philip, ed. *The New Cambridge Shakespeare*. Cambridge, UK: Cambridge University Press, 1984 .

Brooke, C. F. Tucker, ed. *The Shakespeare Apocrypha: Being a Collection of Fourteen Plays Which Have Been Ascribed to Shakespeare*. Oxford, UK: Clarendon Press, 1918.

Brooks, Harold F., and Harold Jenkins, eds. *The New Arden Shakespeare*. Cambridge, MA: Harvard University Press, 1951.

Cowl, Richard, and Arthur Eustace Morgan, eds. *1 Henry IV*. London: Methuen, 1914.

Evans, G. Blackmore, ed. *The Riverside Shakespeare*. 2nd ed. Boston: Houghton Mifflin, 1997.

Furness, Horace Howard, et al., eds. *A New Variorum Edition of Shakespeare*. Philadelphia: J. B. Lippincott, 1871.

Harbage, Alfred, ed. *William Shakespeare: The Complete Works*. New York: Penguin Books, 1977.

Harrison. G. B. *Shakespeare: The Complete Works*. New York: Brace and World, 1948.

Hinman, Charlton, ed. *The First Folio of Shakespeare: The Norton Facsimile*. New York: W. W. Norton, 1968.

Ribner, Irving, and George Lyman Kittredge, eds. *The Complete Works of Shakespeare*. Rev. ed. Waltham, MA: Ginn, 1971.

Wells, Stanley, and Gary Taylor. *William Shakespeare: The Complete Works*. London: Oxford University Press, 1986.

SOURCES

Brooke, Arthur. *The Tragicall History of Romeus and Juliet*. London: Richard Tottell, 1562.

Bullough, Geoffrey, ed. *Narrative and Dramatic Sources of Shakespeare*. 8 vols. New York: Columbia University Press, 1957–1975.

Burrow, Colin. *Shakespeare and Classical Antiquity*. Oxford, UK: Oxford University Press, 2013.

Dessen, Alan C. *Shakespeare and the Late Moral Plays*. Lincoln: University of Nebraska Press, 1986.

Donaldson, E. Talbot. *The Swan at the Well: Shakespeare Reading Chaucer*. New Haven, CT: Yale University Press, 1985.

Gesner, Carol. *Shakespeare and the Greek Romance: A Study of Origins*. Lexington: University Press of Kentucky, 1970.

Gillespie, Stuart. *Shakespeare's Books: A Dictionary of Shakespeare's Sources*. London: Continuum, 2001.

Hamlin, Hannibal. *The Bible in Shakespeare*. Oxford, UK: Oxford University Press, 2013.

Hankins, John Erskine. *Shakespeare's Derived Imagery*. Lawrence: University of Kansas Press, 1953.

Hart, Alfred. *Shakespeare and the Homilies: And Other Pieces of Research into the Elizabethan Drama*. Melbourne, Australia: Melbourne University Press, 1934.

Holinshed, Richard. *Chronicles of England, Scotland, and Ireland*. London: John Hunne, 1577; 2nd ed., London: Finished in Ianuarie 1587, and the 29 of the Queenes Maiesties reigne, with the full continuation of the former yeares, at the expenses of Iohn Harison, George Bishop, Rafe Newberie, Henrie Denham, and Thomas Woodcocke; Henry Denham in Aldersgate street at the signe of the Starre, 1587.

Hosley, Richard, ed. *Shakespeare's Holinshed: An Edition of Holinshed's Chronicles, 1587*. New York: G. P. Putnam's Sons, 1968.

Jones, Emrys. *The Origins of Shakespeare*. Oxford, UK: Clarendon Press, 1977.

Lodge, Thomas. *Rosalynde: Eupheus' Golden Legacie*. London: Thomas Orwin for T. G. and John Busbie, 1590.

Mackail. John William. *Select Epigrams from the Greek Anthology*. London: Longman's, Green, 1900.

Martindale, Charles, and Michelle Martindale. *Shakespeare and the Uses of Antiquity: An Introductory Essay*. London: Routledge, 1990.

Martindale, Charles, and A. B. Taylor, eds. *Shakespeare and the Classics*. Cambridge, UK: Cambridge University Press, 2004.

Miola, Robert S. *Shakespeare's Reading*. Oxford, UK: Oxford University Press, 2000.

Muir, Kenneth. *The Sources of Shakespeare's Plays*. New Haven, CT: Yale University Press, 1978.

Noble, Richmond. *Shakespeare's Biblical Knowledge and Use of the Book of Common Prayer, as Exemplified in the Plays of the First Folio*. New York: Macmillan, 1935.

Ovid. *Metamorphoses*. 8 CE.

Potts, Abbie Findlay. *Shakespeare and "The Faerie Queene."* Ithaca, NY: Cornell University Press, 1958.

Satin, Joseph. *Shakespeare and His Sources*. Boston: Houghton Mifflin, 1966.

Shaheen, Naseeb. *Biblical References in Shakespeare's Plays*. Newark: University of Delaware Press, 1999.

Spencer, Terence J. B. *Shakespeare's Plutarch*. Harmondsworth, UK: Penguin Books, 1964.

Swift, Daniel. *Shakespeare's Common Prayers: The Book of Common Prayer and the Elizabethan Age*. Oxford, UK: Oxford University Press, 2012.

Taylor, A. B., ed. *Shakespeare's Ovid: "The Metamorphoses" in the Plays and Poems*. Cambridge, UK: Cambridge University Press, 2000.

Thompson, Ann. *Shakespeare's Chaucer: A Study in Literary Origins*. New York: Barnes and Noble Books, 1978.

Thomson, J. A. K. *Shakespeare and the Classics*. London: George Allen and Unwin, 1952.

The Troublesome Raigne of John King of England. London: Samson Clarke, 1591.

Virgil. *Aeneid*. 30–19 BCE.

Whitaker, Virgil. *Shakespeare's Use of Learning: An Inquiry into the Growth of His Mind and Art*. San Marino, CA: Huntington Library, 1953.

BIOGRAPHIES

Ackroyd, Peter. *Shakespeare: The Biography*. New York: Doubleday, 2005.

Bate, Jonathan. *Soul of the Age: A Biography of the Mind of William Shakespeare*. New York: Random House, 2009.

Bradbrook, Muriel C. *Shakespeare: The Poet in His World*. New York: Columbia University Press, 1978.

Burgess, Anthony. *Shakespeare*. New York: Alfred A. Knopf, 1970.

Chambers, Edmund Kerchever. "A Blackfriars House." *The Times* (London), April 23, 1928, p. 15.

Chambers, E. K. *William Shakespeare: A Study of Facts and Problems*. 2 vols. Oxford: Clarendon Press, 1930.

Dawson, Giles E. *The Life of William Shakespeare*. Washington, DC: Folger Shakespeare Library, 1958.

Greenblatt, Stephen. *Will in the World*. New York: W. W. Norton, 2004.

Halliday, F. E. *The Life of Shakespeare*. Rev. ed. London: Duckworth, 1964.

Holden, Anthony. *William Shakespeare: The Man behind the Genius: A Biography*. Boston: Little, Brown, 1999.

Honan, Park. *Shakespeare: A Life*. New York: Oxford University Press, 1998.

Hunter, Joseph. *New Illustrations of the Life, Study, and Writings of Shakespeare*. London: J. B. Nichols and Son, 1845.

Potter, Lois. *The Life of William Shakespeare: A Critical Biography*. Malden, MA: Blackwell, 2012.

Quennell, Peter. *Shakespeare: A Biography*. Cleveland, OH: World, 1963.

Rowe, Nicholas. "Some Account of the Life &c. of Mr. William Shakespear." In *The Works of William Shakespear*. London: Jacob Tonson, 1709.

Rowse, A. L. *William Shakespeare*. New York: Macmillan, 1963.

Schoenbaum, Samuel. *Shakespeare, the Globe and the World*. Oxford, UK: Oxford University Press, 1979.

———. *Shakespeare's Lives*. New ed. New York: Oxford University Press, 1991.

———. *William Shakespeare: A Documentary Life*. New York: Oxford University Press, in association with Scholar Press, 1975.

Wood, Michael. *In Search of Shakespeare*. London: BBC, 2003.

THE WORLD OF SHAKESPEARE

Barton, Anne. *The Shakespearean Forest*. Cambridge: Cambridge University Press, 2017.

Bate, Jonathan, and Dora Thornton. *Shakespeare: Staging the World*. Oxford, UK: Oxford University Press, 2012.

Bindoff, S. T. *Tudor England*. Harmondsworth, UK: Penguin, 1965.

Black, Jeremy. *Mapping Shakespeare's World: An Exploration of Shakespeare's World through Maps*. London: Conway, 2018.

Briggs, Julia. *This Stage-Play World: English Literature and Its Background, 1580–1625*. New York: Oxford University Press, 1997.

Byrne, Muriel St. Clare. *Elizabethan Life in Town and Country*. London: Methuen, 1961.

Camden, William. *Britain*. Trans. Philémon Holland. London: George Bishop and John Norton, 1610.

Frye, R. M. *Shakespeare's Life and Times: A Pictorial Record*. Princeton, NJ: Princeton University Press, 1967.

Greaves, Robert L. *Society and Religion in Elizabethan England*. Minneapolis: University of Minnesota Press, 1981.

Halliday, F. E. *Shakespeare in His Age*. New York: T. Yoseloff, 1956.

Harrison, G. B. *England in Shakespeare's Day*. 2nd ed. London: Methuen, 1949.

Kermode, Frank. *The Age of Shakespeare*. New York: Modern Library, 2003.

Knights, L. C. *Drama and Society in the Age of Jonson*. London: Chatto and Windus, 1937.

Lathrop, Elise. *Where Shakespeare Set His Stage*. New York: J. Pott, 1906.

Lee, Sidney, and C. T. Onions. *Shakespeare's England*. 2 vols. Oxford, UK: Clarendon Press, 1916.

Moryson, Fynes. *An Itinerary: Containing His Ten Years Travel through the Twelve Dominions of Germany, Bohemia, Switzerland, Netherland, Denmark, Poland, Italy, Turkey, France, England, Scotland and Ireland*. London: John Beale, 1617.

Picard, Liza. *Elizabethan London: Everyday Life in Elizabethan London*. London: Weidenfeld and Nicolson, 2003.

Rowse, A. L. *The England of Elizabeth: The Structure of Society*. New York: Macmillan, 1950.

Salkeld, Duncan. *Shakespeare and London*. Oxford, UK: Oxford University Press, 2018.

Schoenbaum, Samuel. *Shakespeare, the Globe and the World*. Oxford: Oxford University Press, 1979.

Singman, Jeffrey L. *Daily Life in Elizabethan England*. Westport, CT: Greenwood Press, 1995.

Speed, John. *The Theatre of the Empire of Great Britain*. London: Iohn Sudbury and Georg Humble, 1611.

Stow, John. *A Survey of London*. London: John Windet for Iohn Wolfe, printer to the honorable citie of London: And are to be sold at his shop within the Popes head Alley in Lombard street, 1599.

Sugden, Edward H. *A Topographical Dictionary to the Works of Shakespeare and His Fellow Dramatists*. Manchester, UK: Manchester University Press, 1925.

Thompson, Craig R. *Schools in Tudor England*. Washington, DC: Folger Shakespeare Library, 1958.

Tillyard, E. M. W. *The Elizabethan World Picture*. New York: Macmillan, 1944.

Whitfield, Peter. *Mapping Shakespeare's World*. Oxford, UK: Bodleian Library, 2015.

Wright, Louis B. *Middle-Class Culture in Elizabethan England*. Ithaca, NY: Cornell University Press, 1935.

ADDITIONAL RESOURCES CONSULTED

Adams, Joseph Quincy. *Shakespearean Playhouses: A History of English Theatres from the Beginning to the Restoration*. London: Constable, 1920.

Addis, John. "Was Macbeth the Third Murderer of Banquo?" *Notes and Queries* (October 2, 1869): 282–83.

Ascham, Roger. *The Schoolmaster*. London: John Daye, 1570.

Bennett, Gilbert. "The Third Murderer." *Anglo-Welsh Review* 15 (1965): 87–89.

Boitani, Piero. "Julio Romano." *Memoria di Shakespeare*, New Series 6 (2008): 145–51.

De Quincey, Thomas. "On the Knocking at the Gate in *Macbeth*." *London Magazine* 3 (October 1823): 353–56.

Fitzgerald, F. Scott. "The Crack-Up." *Esquire Magazine* (February 1936): 41+.

Fraser, Antonia. *The Wives of Henry VIII*. New York: Knopf, 1992.

Frye, Northrup. *Anatomy of Criticism*. Princeton, NJ: Princeton University Press, 1957.

Garber, Marjorie. *Dream in Shakespeare: From Metaphor to Metamorphosis*. New Haven, CT: Yale University Press, 1974.

G. E. P. A. "Sir Hugh Evans: A Gloucestershire Worthy." *Notes and Queries* 9, no. 3 (May 20, 1899): 381–82.

Greg, W. W. "Time, Place, and Politics in *King Lear*." *Modern Language Review* 35, no. 4 (1940): 431–46.

Hotson, Leslie. "Shakespeare and the Host of the Mermaid," *Atlantic Monthly* 151 (1933): 708–14.

Knight, L. C. *The Crown of Life*. London: Oxford University Press, 1947.

Martinet, Marie-Madeleine. "*The Winter's Tale* et Julio Romano." *Etudes Anglaises* 28 (1975): 257–68.

Rowse, A. L. *Shakespeare's Southampton: Patron of Virginia*. London: Macmillan, 1965.

Shapiro, I. A. "The Mermaid Club." *Modern Language Review* 45, no. 1 (January 1950): 6–17.

Studing, Richard. "'That Rare Italian Master'—Shakespeare's Julio Romano." *Humanities Association Review* 22, no. 3 (1971): 22–26.

Turner, Henry S. "*King Lear* Without: The Heath." *Renaissance Drama* 18 (1997): 161–93.

Williams, George Walton. "The Third Murderer in *Macbeth*." *Shakespeare Quarterly* 23, no. 3 (1972): 261.

Wills, Gary. *Rome and Rhetoric: Shakespeare's "Julius Caesar."* New Haven, CT: Yale University Press, 2011.

Wilson, Theodore Halbert. "The Third Murderer." *English Journal* 18, no. 5 (May 1929): 418.

Index

Page numbers in italics refer to figures.

About the Author

Joseph Rosenblum taught English at the University of North Carolina at Greensboro. He is the author or editor of several books, including *Chaucer Illustrated: The Canterbury Tales in Pictures over 500 Years* (2003) and *The Definitive Shakespeare Companion* (2017). His books have twice been recognized by *Library Journal* as Outstanding Reference works, and in 2006 he received the Roland H. Bainton Prize (Sixteenth Century Society) for *The Greenwood Companion to Shakespeare* (2005).

CPSIA information can be obtained
at www.ICGtesting.com
Printed in the USA
LVHW101122220120
644404LV00013BA/338